LAND TENURE AND PEASANT
IN SOUTH ASIA

Land Tenure and Peasant
in South Asia

Edited by
ROBERT ERIC FRYKENBERG

ORIENT LONGMAN

Published by
Orient Longman,
3/5 Asaf Ali Road, New Delhi 110 002
by arrangement with Land Tenure Center,
University of Wisconsin,
Madison, 53706,
Wisconsin.

Printed in India at
Indraprastha Press (C.B.T.),
Nehru House, New Delhi-110002

Contents

PART ONE: Landed Privilege in the Past

PART TWO: Dimensions of Landed Relations

PART THREE: Dimensions of Development and/or Reform

List of Contributors

MICHAEL P. ADAS
Associate Professor of History

Rutgers University
New Brunswick, New Jersey

JOSEPH W. ELDER
Professor of Sociology and South Asian Studies

University of Wisconsin
Madison, Wisconsin

ROBERT ERIC FRYKENBERG
Professor of History and South Asian Studies

University of Wisconsin
Madison, Wisconsin

CARL H. GOTSCH
Professor of Development Economics

Harvard University
Cambridge, Massachusetts

Program Officer, The Ford Foundation

Beirut, Lebanon

HENRY C. HART
Professor of Political Science and South Asian Studies

University of Wisconsin
Madison, Wisconsin

RONALD J. HERRING
Assistant Professor of Political Science

Northwestern University
Evanston, Illinois

PAUL G. HIEBERT
Professor of Anthropology and South Asian Studies

University of Washington
Seattle, Washington

F. TOMASSON JANNUZI
Associate Professor of Economics and South Asian Studies

University of Texas
Austin, Texas

Director, Center for South Asian Studies at Texas

JOHN R. McLANE
Professor of History

Northwestern University
Evanston, Illinois

BRIAN J. MURTON
Professor of Geography and South Asian Studies

University of Hawaii
Honolulu, Hawaii

BURTON STEIN
  Professor of History and South Asian Studies

University of Hawaii
Honolulu, Hawaii

ERIC STOKES
  *Professor of Commonwealth History and Fellow of
  St. Catherine's College*

Cambridge University
Cambridge, England

THIS volume is meant to serve many kinds of readers. Its conception grew out of a need to reach and challenge advanced undergraduate and graduate students at the University of Wisconsin. For years the Land Tenure Center at the University had been attracting students and training specialists; but despite a worldwide reputation, the Center was known mostly for its interest in the land tenure patterns of Latin America. Then, in 1970, the focus of the Center was widened so as to encompass agrarian problems throughout the non-Western World. It was at that time that Africanists and Asianists were brought into the Center. Courses on land tenure in countries of Africa, South Asia, Southeast Asia, East Asia, and the Middle East were introduced. The number of graduate students working on agrarian problems in these countries rapidly increased. It was within this context that the need for a volume such as this developed.

What we required was a volume of readings, an anthology which could approach questions of land tenure from the perspective of many disciplines —indeed, if anything, mainly from outside the traditional disciplines of agricultural economics and rural sociology. Our purpose was to show agrarian problems as sets of symbiotic relationships in which causes and consequences are conceptualized in holistic terms. That is to say, an agrarian order was to be understood best and solutions to its problems made most possible when the entire totality of its most complicated ecological and human formations and its most complex social institutions—within the whole framework of its interconnected relationships—was taken into account. Complete and self-contained systems of land tenure could not be dealt with effectively without reference to their entire past and present conditions.

Having once embarked upon this scheme, it was soon recognized that nothing could better serve its purpose than to bring together the latest work of research scholars from several disciplines. These scholars, all of them specialists on South (and Southeast) Asia, could provide in diachronic and synchronic analysis both a challenge to new research and a grounding within older intellectual disciplines. Moreover, their work could point to gaps and holes in current knowledge on the subject of land tenure and peasant in South Asia.

Of course once this scheme had been launched it was realized that perhaps with some more effort the same volume could serve a much wider readership. Both general readers with an interest in problems of worldwide hunger, poverty, and overpopulation, but without sophisticated skills, and

also specialist readers wanting to see what was being done by their colleagues
in other disciplines and in other parts of the world were seen to be among
those for whom this book could serve some purpose.

Such being the plan, its completion has proceeded all too slowly. Correspondence, together with a hazardous sending back and forth of manuscripts,
has had to circle the globe. The authors have shown remarkable patience.
Throughout many months of seemingly interminable delay they have all
had to wait for one another and to suffer through the editing process. This
work was done at the Center, and reviewed by me. The Center's staff—
Jane Knowles, Julia Schwenn, Teresa Anderson, Barbara Rhem, and
others—worked carefully and gave many hours to various details. To my
many colleagues at the Center, such scholars as Peter P. Dorner and Kenneth
H. Parsons, especially to Don Kanel, David J. King, and Bryant Kearl,
I owe a debt of gratitude. Their helpful counsel, criticism, and encourage-
ment provided a continual stimulus to learning. As I listened to their comments and discussions, I realized again how little I knew and how much
there was to know. Finally and perhaps most of all, I must give my personal
thanks to William C. Thiesenhusen, Director of the Center, from whom I
am constantly learning and without whose steady support and steadfast
confidence this enterprise would not only never have begun but would
certainly never have been completed.

R.E.F.

Madison, Wisconsin
April, 1975

LAND TENURE AND PEASANT
IN SOUTH ASIA

Introduction

ROBERT ERIC FRYKENBERG

MINDS in the West tend to boggle at the immensity and complexity of problems relating to land tenure and peasant in South Asia. Perhaps nowhere on earth are the intricate relationships between mankind and land so extremely complicated as in the subcontinental lands encompassed by the Indian Ocean Basin. And at the center of this complexity lies India, a country in which some 80 percent of nearly six hundred million people and more than three out of every four persons must work the land for a living. Most of what is grown on the land, some four-fifths, is food. Yet, generation after generation for centuries India has known famine and scarcity on a scale almost unknown anywhere else in the world. In fact no single problem has so persistently aggravated domestic tranquility, threatened international peace, frustrated efforts of governments, thwarted the work of administrators and development planners, and defied all attempts at solution—mocking all other human achievements—as poverty. And perhaps nowhere on earth are conditions of poverty seemingly so complex, so apparently irremediable and so tenaciously intractable, as in South Asia. So subhuman are conditions of existence for nearly half of India's population that many outsiders simply cannot comprehend, or, comprehending, cannot accept them. Hundreds of millions cling precariously at the very brink of extinction.

I

But what is the root, the basic cause of this problem? What has gone wrong to bring about this sorry state of affairs? What could have brought so much of mankind into this condition? And where does one look for answers to such questions, to say nothing about some solution to this consuming problem? Is the root cause primarily ecological and environmental? Is it a question of natural and human resources? —of insufficient land and water, of poor soil, or failing rains, or lack of labor? Or can one point to fundamental human failures? —to failures of humanity, or of society, or of political economy, or, simply, of justice? These are profound questions, perhaps even too far-reaching in their implications and too sweeping in their ramifications. The whole gamut of real or imagined difficulties, from fertilizer production and irrigation to marketing, distribution, and consumption patterns, have been much studied. Detailed data and sophisticated analyses have accumulated and continue to accumulate. But, when all is said and done, what have been the results? Is the central problem of appalling poverty and mass starvation solved? Is any solution even near at hand?

Of course, many specific obstacles to agricultural and economic development remain untackled. Development literature for South Asia is copious and informative. Broken down into various more manageable components, under different disciplines so as to be handled with greater facility, a deeper level of questions must then be faced. This pertains to procedures and priorities: which questions can be most easily discarded or at least postponed and which, because of urgency, deserve or require greater, more immediate attention? Questions of natural and human resources—quantas of arable land, of soil fertility or water sufficiency, and even of labor or technology—important as these may be, however, are no longer of central concern. Many of the solutions to production problems have already been discovered. Methods are already known. One can even plausibly surmise that, if the latest methods of intensive agriculture which have been utilized in Denmark, Holland, and Japan were applied to the Gangetic Plain, the surpluses produced would be more than sufficient to feed peoples of South Asia (if not half the world). Thus, it seems clear that the elimination of massive poverty can never be accomplished by surplus production alone. One can even go so far as to assume, perhaps arbitrarily but with justification, that South Asia's population-poverty problems do not arise just from lack of natural or human resources nor from want of technological potential necessary for the production of agricultural surpluses. In short, economic growth alone is not the answer to poverty.

Indeed, one may dare to suggest that perhaps all attempts to eradicate massive poverty in South Asia have been doomed to frustration, if not failure. This can be suggested, not because the efforts made and the questions tackled were unimportant. (Most emphatically, no one would deny the importance of what has been done.) But, at root, it might be that even more basic and central questions have been overlooked, evaded, or avoided outright. Thus, however much might be produced and whatever mechanisms for distribution might be developed, ultimately one must confront the necessity of coming to grips with those deepest questions of all. These are those matters of "spirit" from whence have come the cultural, social, and political legacies of South Asia. Those measures of conformity to commonly accepted norms, those concepts of man and of society which have been built into the very structures of corporate life, and those very institutions and symbols which have been recognized as legitimizing each established "constitution" (whether codified into written law or not and whether autarchic and autocratic or "democratic" or whatever): questions about such conditions must be answered. Attempts to abolish poverty by mere economic development, without dealing with questions at the deepest levels of "ideological" and institutional conflict, can only beg the question and must surely end in futility.

II

At this point, before plunging further into the deepest question, a cautionary note and disclaimer is necessary. Attention has already been drawn to the way Western minds boggle at the stark facts of poverty in South Asia and how they struggle within a miasma of incomprehensibility. Yet, whatever available information may tell us and whatever we learn about relative priorities and human values held by peoples in the West, as expressed in weekly domestic (family) budgets, the same information tells us something about the aggregate consequences of human feelings and values among those in South Asia who are in better economic circumstances and who are in a better position to know about stark poverty from first-hand experience, but whose senses fail to respond to the sights and sounds of abject hunger and of utter despair which day and night assault them.

For, when all is said and done, even the very best efforts to provide aid, of aliens and of those who live afar off are doomed. Only relative degrees of hopeless frustration, if not of complete breakdown and failure, can attend the best-intentioned and most carefully administered efforts of outsiders. While outsiders who render aid may see themselves merely as "fellow" humans, as only wishing to "lend a hand" to the fallen and destitute (some may even be so absurdly arrogant as to think that *only* they and their "know how" can "solve the problems" of poverty), to many if not most in South Asia such efforts can only be offensive. Such attempts "to help" stand as a rebuke to indigenous leadership, as an affront to their dignity and their proud civilization, and as so many more reminders of a most galling truth—the hard facts of indigenous failure. Such reminders may be necessary; but they surely can never evoke gratitude. By whatever name it is called and in whatever form it comes, whether as shiploads of grain (loaned or given), as "technical assistance," or as brilliant analytical studies by development experts, such aid may be intrusive and disturbing. More than that, it is *foreign*. It is not welcome.

Foreign aid can be unwelcome for many reasons. It disturbs existing circumstances and conditions. It undermines established arrangements. It pretends greater knowledge and presumes to possess better answers. It is even seen as threatening the very fabric of society and the very constitution of prevailing power relationships, those elements of government, politics, and law which time and tradition may have hallowed. Most of all, it stands as a mute condemnation of indigenous achievements as enshrined in local culture. And thereby it calls into question the grounds for indigenous self-confidence, dignity, and pride. All in all, as a testimony to local failure its impact can be magnified in proportion to the lofty standing and authority of the most privileged classes of society.

Foreign aid assaults existing privileges and power in proportion to their magnitude. If the hungry are to be fed and their "holdings" (or "tenures") on the good things of life are to be increased—even when overall productivity (GNP, etc.) is vastly increased—this can only be done at some cost to the power of those who hold more. (Iran and Saudi Arabia and Libya, with their enormous resources in oil might well attest to that iron, authoritarian hold which remains unshaken. This hold, free of foreign assistance, and bought and paid for by the rulers themselves for their own purposes has brought little redistribution of wealth or power.) For what the affluent and elite of a country hold is their superiority—their culture, their learning and literacy, their power and privilege, their rank and respect, their status and style. Custom and law, that consensus accumulated through ages and defined as the "weal of the people" if not even of "a people" such as those who are "united in . . . a common sense of right and a community of interest"[1] (as distinct from those who only make up a faceless mass or an impersonal mob), defines what exists. They produce and are the product of such views of life, of man, and of social structure and authority as they have been able to articulate and institutionalize.

And what exists at least to an important degree, in South Asia, therefore, are the aggregate statements of many peoples (and traditions) as to what is "the good" and "the best." Insofar as what is "good" and "best" have already been achieved and structured in existing relationships between individuals and between groups, by a process which took countless generations, and eras, even millenia, these are what we find represented in the institutions of South Asia today. Insofar as what exists is not good or could be made better, this is generally to be perceived as the concern of insiders, not the problem nor the responsibility of outsiders. Acts of foreigners, consequently, whether real or imagined ("non-actions" also constitute "actions" for purposes of this argument), are rarely appreciated, certainly not for long; moreover, they often serve as convenient focal points for animosity or blame. Such being the case, established indigenous elite groups tend to perceive aid as dangerous —as an intrusion to be blunted, corrupted, subverted, or destroyed, if not appropriated outright.

In political terms, therefore, the ultimate objectives and purposes of foreign assistance tend to be diametrically, fundamentally, even intrinsically opposed to "interests" of a recipient country. This is so, because what is ultimately required of the recipient is "reform"; and any but the most superficial and "technological" of reforms call for profound changes in the sociopolitical structure of the recipient country. For how else is income redistributed (or power reallocated)? Put in different terms, foreign economic assistance to meet domestic problems cannot help but be a device for fundamental constitutional change, an instrument for political revolution. If subverted or expropriated (diverted to other purposes), on the other hand, it becomes a pillar supporting the status quo. Likewise, the analysis or comment or observations of outsiders can receive the same treatment; and, by its very failure to represent an "inside view," such analysis carries dangers which may not have been foreseen.

Thus, one cannot avoid the root issue which underlies any attempt to study the infinite complexities of land tenures or of "peasants" as they exist in South Asia. At root, what is at issue is justice. However inexact or limited perceptions of justice may be within a given society, those imprecisions and limitations of perception are reflected within existing social institutions. "Remove justice, and what are [states] but gangs of robbers on a large scale? And what are robber gangs but petty [states]? A gang is a group of men under the command of a leader, bound by a compact of association, in which the plunder is divided according to an agreed convention. If this villainy wins so many recruits from the ranks of the demoralized that it acquires territory, establishes a base, captures cities and subdues peoples, it then openly arrogates to itself the title [state], which is conferred on it in the eyes of the world, not by the renouncing of aggression, but by the attainment of impunity." So wrote Augustine over 1500 years ago. Moreover, he would add that men, even when pushed to such extremes that they find it necessary to resort to some sort of banditry or subversion, sedition or outright rebellion, cannot achieve what they wish unless they maintain some semblance of peace, at least with their colleagues in conspiracy. Even "robbers" (or "rulers"), while outside the "law" or at odds with the rest of mankind—whether perceived as a family, a locality, a landholding group, a feudal patrimony, a bureaucratic department, a kingdom, an empire, or a nation-state—deeply desire and must have some sort of peace among themselves. In the final extremity of utter desolation, the solitary outlaw must at least have some minimal peace within his own home; or, failing even that, he will seek some semihuman solitude in a cave where no dread of another creature's violence need disturb his repose.

In no way can what exists in society, be it poverty or something worse, be disturbed without arousing some new sense of injustice and without provoking some forms of resistance. Hypothetically, for example, if one man were absolute master and sole owner of all land and all other men were his slaves and if the system of justice, peace, security, and tranquility which he had established were such that it brought satisfaction to most of his people, abolition of his establishment would conceivably be seen (at least by him) as an advent of great injustice and might be resisted strenuously on that ground. Farfetched as this may seem, the conditioning, perhaps even the controlling factors which hedge each man and each social or political or cultural institution are consensus on matters of justice and injustice. Surely neither justice, nor government, nor domestic tranquillity, nor landholding can exist unless there are some internal, institutional balances and controls on (social, economic, and political) appetite and will. The less internal control (or self-control) is imposed upon ambition and greed and fear, the more inescapable is the inevitability of such controls being imposed from outside. This is true no matter what the size or character of the object(s) being held—a family plot, a patrimony, a large estate, a rich cultural heritage, an empire, or simply a man's emotions and muscles. Tenure of land and relative status within an agrarian society such as that

of "peasant," are surely conditioned by aggregate perceptions of justice
and the forces generated by such consensus.

III

It is only when viewed in this light that the problems posed by the
different authors of this volume can acquire meaning and relevance for
application to problems in South Asia today. Each of the papers presented
herein is the work of a specialist preoccupied with some of the complexities
and difficulties of relating lord and land and labor in their intricate combinations and kaleidoscopic permutations. Indeed, the very extremeness of
these complexities can itself become an object of intense intellectual fascination. This fascination can be multiplied by problems of language. Terminology for various concepts and elements is compounded by interlacing
through a host of different languages, dialects, and usages. It is further
complicated not only by the arbitrary ways in which Western concepts were
introduced into local agrarian, bureaucratic, and legal institutions but also
by the gradual assimilation and *"prakritization"* of English in a process
which took nearly three centuries. When to this are added the bemusing
combinations of current American and English usage, including latest
fashions of slang and disciplinary jargon, with more archaic Indo-British
("Indish"?) survivals from the eighteenth century, the fine interplays of
connotation and denotation can scarcely be imagined; precise "scientific"
understanding is another matter. Then, there is the seemingly infinite complexity of social structures. For India alone, in classical and contemporary
forms, these are fantastically intricate and ornate—over two thousand
distinct communities will neither intermarry nor interdine (for fear of pollution) and each clings to distinct internal ("sacred and secret") rituals, styles
of life, and value systems (to say nothing of common hereditary occupations and traditions). No one can delve very deeply into problems of land
tenure and peasant without realizing the need to understand castes and
"classes" of castes (i.e., categories or *varnas*) and to see how these are structured in relation to one another.

Some extra words of guidance may be helpful to students, nonspecialists
and to general readers. First, some knowledge of the civilization and history
of peoples in South Asia is not only useful, but in some instances may be
requisite for the proper understanding of some of the papers found in this
volume. (For recommended readings for general background, one should
consult List of References.) Second, approaches to the subject matter of
land tenure and peasant in South Asia come from a wide range of disciplines, each of which serves not only as a sample of what can be learned by
looking at problems from the perspective of its peculiar methodological
prism, but, to change the metaphor, each of which also serves as a piece
fitting into a much larger puzzle. Put in other words, each study is a sample
of some cutting edge of new research in the field; but even all of the papers
taken together fill but a small part of a much larger mosaic, some of it

already fitted together and much of it requiring much more work. Third, both in diachronic and in synchronic terms, despite the narrow specificity of each piece of research (discrete within its own discipline), a wide-angle lens has been turned upon problems of land tenure and peasant in South Asia. Some papers, particularly those falling near the beginning of the volume, are avowedly historical. Others are works of anthropology, geography, economics, political science, or sociology. Moreover, in terms of area coverage, South Asia has been expanded so as to cover not only all of the Subcontinent but also at least one of those parts of Southeast Asia where British rule extended. Fourth, a note of caution is required in the use and application of all concepts, but especially of Western concepts to the phenomena of South Asia.[2]

Of particular concern here, for example, is the term "peasant," whether perceived as a category of degradation and landless serfdom or as some category of landholding or landlordship. As applied in South Asia, it has been used to cover everything from the most menial of outcaste (untouchable) laborers, often in conditions of virtually hereditary debt bondage or slavery, to the highcaste "peasant elites" or "peasant proprietors" or "peasant landlords" who ruled over the destinies of agrarian villages, whether individually or corporately. The history of the connotations and usages of this term in the West have been confusing enough; but when it is applied to Indian phenomena, extreme caution is called for.

IV

At the same time, it is necessary for readers to have some acquaintance with the three basic general categories of landholding which evolved during the history of the Indian Empire, forms which devolved from Mughal times (but which seem primordial) and which are still current (even persistent, despite reforms). These forms of landholding were called "settlements." They came from the Persian: *"jamabandi"*; literally meaning a "collecting" or "gathering-roll." They were the administrative and bureaucratic term applied to the "agreements" or "contracts" which were made between landholders and Government, whether made each year or made "permanently" (and meant to be immutable). The three categories were: (1) the Zamindari Settlement; (2) the Gramawari (or Mahalwari) Settlement; and (3) the Ryotwari Settlement.

The first, which began in Bengal in 1793—sometimes known as the Bengal Settlement or, more commonly, as the Permanent Settlement—and later spread to other parts of India, generally pertained to large holdings (or "estates"). A zamindar or "landholder" (zamin="land"; and dar= "holder"; dari="holding") usually held more than one village. Most zamindaris worthy of the title held scores and even hundreds of villages (600—800 village zamindaris were not uncommon in South India). Such being the case, their holding of "land" was not simply of land, not of a geographic area of physical soil or turf or fields and forests. Rather, what was held was tantamount to a grant of authority, in some cases dominion over hundreds of thousands, even millions of people. A zamindar was not the "owner" of these lands-cum-people as such. Indeed, the common law notion of property ownership was and is an alien concept, altogether inappropriate when applied to India and to zamindari landholding. A zamindar's "tenure" was, therefore, a form of political and socioeconomic authority or control; moreover, his "tenants" and "subtenants" and "sub-subtenants" all held similar kinds of power and privilege, each based upon a similar kind of "settlement" or agreement. What is further confusing to many outside observers is the fact that many a great zamindar in British India held more authority and power, and ruled over greater territories, than many of the princes of non-British (Princely) India. In fact, some princes were hardly more than village lords and the holdings of a few of them were so tiny that they controlled no more than a single well or field. (The largest princes, on the other hand, ruled domains the size of European countries, e.g., England or Ireland.) When seen in such terms, therefore, within ranges of sizes and conditions of tenure of great variety, the zamindari form of land tenure was enormously complex. Yet, for purposes of general communication, the term is usually applied to the holding of the largest "landed estates" (including, in early days, even power over police and armed retinues).

The second level of landholding pertained mainly to the revenue or "rent" village as a corporate entity. While zamindars themselves could and did "settle" with villages in this way, the term generally applies to a direct contract (i.e., "settlement") between each village community and officers of the Government. The "village community" was not, of course, the whole village population. Rather, it was that segment of elders, leaders, and notables of high caste who, in their joint capacity, governed the affairs of a village and faced the demands made by superior forces, backed by higher authority, in the outside world. Whether these demands came in the form of a "ransom" paid sporadically to marauder bands (e.g., *dacoits* or *pindaris*); of "tribute" paid annually to a predatory prince; of "rent" paid to rackrenting "renter" or "leaseholder"; or of regular revenue or taxes paid to officer of the Raj (under circumstances or conditions of variable integrity or corruptibility); an ancient and strong village community did what it could to preserve if not to enhance the holdings of its village lands. Meeting in their *"panchayat"* (literally: a "council of five" but commonly any family, caste, or village conclave), leaders were often remarkably astute in playing off outside forces and in retaining the integrity of their joint-holdings. Many names have been used to designate such tenures—such as "joint-rent," "joint-lease," "brotherhood," or "house holding" or "tract (*mahal*)-holding," and "village-folk" (*grama-wari*). All in all, this form is best thought of as the Village Settlement (or "Joint-Village" Settlement).

The third level was the lowest or smallest. It was the Ryotwari Settlement. Reaching past the corporate defenses of village power and tradition, it implied or was intended to deal with each *"raiyat"* or "cultivator" as an individual. At least at the beginning, in the initial stages of British administration, the *ryot* was one of the leading villagers. A ryot was a *"raya"* or local leader (chief) or notable whose cultivating of the soil was done through the authority of his status and his control over the forces of manual labor at his disposal. As perceived by British officers of the late eighteenth and early nineteenth centuries, an age when great reverence was given to ideals of vigorous free speech and unlimited free debate within the select circles of British aristocratic and landed gentry, local power in India should remain with "natural" leaders. (Parliament, it should be remembered, was then less a democratic forum than an exclusive gentlemen's club for Tory and Whig nobles who, for all their rivalry on policy, did not really differ much on ideological matters.) In South India and Western India, especially, "natural" leaders were seen as being best represented by the lords of the villages. Sir Thomas Munro, the great champion of this settlement, saw the *"ryot"* and the *"raya"* (*rayatu* and *rayalu*, in Telugu) as being essentially the same person. Those who saw to the cultivation of the village lands were the natural lords whose power and prestige brought deference from all other communities.

However, the policy of direct contact between the Government and each village lord contained two profoundly important ramifications. First, it implied or (later) recognized that the Raj (State) was penultimate holder of all lands, cultivated or uncultivated. By the later nineteenth century, as the concept of "ownership" from English common law was increasingly mingled with earlier local custom (*"mamool"*) and with the laws and precedents of Hindu and Islamic traditional institutions, the State was more and more seen as the ultimate "owner" of all land. (Paradoxically, complexity and simplicity increased simultaneously: English law, added to existing conventions, compounded confusion; but administrative and bureaucratic codification increased procedural uniformity.) Secondly, if the State was the ultimate controller, whether as ultimate "holder" or as ultimate "owner" of agrarian relationships, then an enormous administrative structure with a vast bureaucratic agency was required. In order for the State to deal directly and efficiently with each and every cultivator within each and every village—concluding a "settlement" contract (*patta*) with each person— meant that there had to be enough officials to carry out this enormous task. The subcontinent contained hundreds of thousands of discrete and separate revenue villages—India alone is considered to have over 550,000 such entities today. The number of ryots whose names were inscribed upon the "rent" or "tax-roll" (jamabandi) for any given year can easily be imagined. During the mid-nineteenth century, the number of Native Indian district officers and government functionaries came to over 36,000 in one Presidency alone. They were arranged in an elaborate triple hierarchy (revenue, police, and judicial) above the villages, but below the 200 to 250

European members of the Indian Civil Service (over half of whom held positions in the central headquarters of the Government of Madras at Fort Saint George). The members of this "nongazetted" native civil bureaucracy were becoming increasingly better qualified. Their admission was depending more and more upon rigorous entrance examinations in specialized fields, rather than upon personal patronage (and caste status per se). The numbers of this highly literate, specially trained, English-speaking bureaucratic elite doubled again by the twentieth century.

As this occurred, the very internal logic of a growing Leviathan brought about an enormous expansion of State power. Therewith, moreover, a gradual change brought redefinition to the ryotwari system itself. Whereas Munro had meant for the State to deal directly only with village lords as individuals, bypassing village leaders in their traditional roles as corporate entities, later Ryotwari Settlements bypassed all "natural" leaders of the villages to deal with any and all of the more common villagers (but still tending to exclude the landless laborers who made up nearly half of each village population).

Many lords and laborers were compressed into a common mold as "cultivators" or "ryots." As the definition of what was meant by "culti-vator" expanded, the pressure of modern state machinery upon villages increased. In theory, if not in practice, the ryotwari system implied State control over all economic enterprise. In essence, the most extreme forms of Statism were possible. The State as ultimate "owner" could incorporate the entire population into one vast bureaucratic structure in which every man could be considered as nothing more than an "official," a "worker," or a "landless" laborer. Only want of application, efficiency, and desire prevented the Ryotwari system from becoming a truly totalitarian machine. The logic of its totalitarian potential was certainly there. (For this reason, it is quite possible for the State today to espouse a "Socialist Pattern of Society" without changing much more than labels and names of the old system. State control of all productive enterprise has very deep roots in Indian tradition. Nor are the traditions of other countries in South Asia all that different.)

V

Finally, it is not unreasonable to ask some questions about the research found in this volume and about its significance. How much do we learn from its contributors about land tenure and peasant in the sub-continent which was not known before? What general trends, if any, can be discerned? Are conditions improving or are they becoming worse? Was tenancy more repressive before Independence—under the Raj, or under the Mughals—than it is now? Does the structure of landholding seem so immutable, so deeply ingrained in village traditions that nothing, neither government policy nor lack thereof, can make any difference? And what do these studies hold in common which might justify their being published together in one volume?

First of all, aside from the newness of data and the fresh insights contained in each piece, it is noteworthy that all of the research in this volume draws heavily upon intensive local and/or regional concentration. It is perhaps symptomatic of our day that academic disciplines increasingly, borrow from one another and that all of them concentrate upon discrete local, social, and economic phenomena. Thus, in this volume, attention has been focused upon land, tenure, and peasant from several disciplinary perspectives. Subjects (and questions) have been given an extra intensity, as it were, by being simultaneously illuminated within the circle of an interdisciplinary "crosslight" (or "crossfire"). Moreover, despite wide variations in approach, style, and phenomena under scrutiny, a cross-over benefit can be communicated from one study to another and from one to all.

Also, along with a multiplicity of intellectual disciplines, this volume contains a strong emphasis upon local studies. Local specificity, a "case-study" approach requiring deep and thorough mastery of local lore, is combined with comparative analysis of (or between) local studies. Included are studies ranging across the whole subcontinent and even across the Bay of Bengal. Indeed, it is for just such purposes of comparative analysis, both interdisciplinary and inter-regional, that a paper on Southeast Asia is included. Focusing upon "Indic" cultures in Burma, this study throws light across the basin of the Indian Ocean; and this, in turn, reflects back upon the subcontinent itself. No two studies, or descriptive treatments, are directly analogous; and certainly none are identical. But cross-correspondence along a graded continuum which extends Indic civilization into peripheral areas or regions—sometimes dubbed historically as "empty lands" or "frontier zones" (albeit some with nodes of high population density, as in Kerala)—enables examination and comparison between immediately contiguous regions and between more distant and different localities.

Next, what do we now know which was not known before? This is not a simple question. If one grants that no land tenure system on the earth has been or still remains so complex, this is hardly surprising. Attempts to gain new understanding and to come to grips with problems of landholding and of redistributing wealth are as old as our historical records. Just the list of legislation during the past two centuries is formidable.[3] Yet, both in terms of specific information and in terms of improved perspectives and understandings, this volume serves to illustrate what is now being accomplished. To pretend, however, that any simple conclusion or single and comprehensive generalization as to the nature and the strength of changes in landed relationships which have occurred or now are occurring is possible, is absurd. South Asia, even the federal Republic of India, encompasses a continent. Arbitrarily but loosely labelled a "subcontinent," its many conditions of existence and of cultural relationship do not readily admit to facile or glib generalizations.

Having said this, however, some cautious generalizations can still be made. Or, perhaps more pointedly, we can call into question some of the conventional wisdom, the easy answers, and the pat generalizations which have resulted in so much misdirected, unnecessary, and wasteful expenditure of energy. And among such, undoubtedly the most obvious example would relate to commonly held assumptions of development agencies and of aid-giving countries, together with many of their policy-makers, administrators, and technical experts who manage agricultural relief programs. The common view that, with a little more money and a little more fertilizer and technical know-how (too often directly transferred by agricultural economists from American experience in rural extension services), problems of land tenure and of redistributive wealth could be easily or quickly solved has by now hopefully been laid to rest. If not, papers in this volume should serve further to illustrate the ineffectiveness and limitations of many well-intentioned efforts in socio-economic engineering.

VI

But further observations can be made. Especially with respect to relationships between change and social structure, and therein with reference to relationships among landholding, landholders, land-labor, and land-laborers (including the "landless"), at least two sets of generalizations seem to emerge from studies in this volume. One concerns the relative strengths of vertical and horizontal linkages within the highly segmented social systems of South Asia; and another concerns the relative isolation of "have" and "have-not" elements and strata of people from each other.

Despite a continuous flow of literature—whether rhetorical, scholarly, journalistic, or ideological—concerning "the classes" and "the masses," in which, for example, "elites" are distinguished from "working classes" and these in turn from other vast "masses" of people, the very existence of such entities as self-conscious groups (or strata, whether in economic, in political, or in social terms) seems highly debatable. So dominant have been vertical (or "traditional") linkages of the social structure in any locality that, except among people at the highest levels of power and privilege, consciousness of any kind of horizontal linkage or identity have been very tenuous, when and where and if they have existed at all. Thus, for instance, strongest and most persistent links, have been between: patron and client; father and son; *guru* and *chela* (or *sishya*); lord (master) and servant (slave); landlord and tenant (and/or "landless laborer"); ruler (king) and subject; and between divinity and devotee. Feelings of intrinsic inequality in descending, straightline, or authoritarian relationships have been dominant over identifications of a more egalitarian nature.

Reasons for this seem scarcely surprising. Those very basic elements of social organization—family, caste, and village—have traditionally resisted centralization. Such resistance has been mainly silent and secret, rather than open or violent. Pollution and ritual distance, even between elite communities in each locality, as well as between groups in lower ranks of servility, have stood as barriers to social integration. Ethnic communities, within their subcultural holdings of power, rank, and status, have generally refused to intermarry and inter-dine, or even to drink water from the same well. (Exceptions within royal households have only served to confirm this rule.) Such behavior has tended to prevent even the very formation of a "society" or of any larger "social consciousness"—that is, in any Western sense of this concept.[4] Moreover, the lower down in status, rank, and power or the more local and parochial a given group has been, the less likelihood has there been of the formation of anything resembling feelings of "class" or of an identifiable "social consciousness" as such. "The very complexity of a highly textured, structured, and pluralistic web of *mamool*—of things "done according to custom"—has become self-enforcing and self-reinforcing to such a degree that each social segment in each locality has become more or less bound into its own place within an elaborately stylized, symbolized, and compartmentalized structure."[5] But, as a consequence, such self-enforcing local "apartheit" has not only hindered social mobility, virtually stopping it altogether in some instances, but also has prevented a horizontal (or lateral) spread of socio-political self-consciousness among all but the very highest ruling groups. Until very recent times, therefore, such localized mamool has served to forestall the formation of "classes" as self-conscious entities which might be readily identifiable, at least in a Western sense. In fact, such class consciousness as did exist can be seen as having existed in direct proportion to a consciousness of status in privilege and rulership and in inverse proportion to social degradation. "Classes" or "varnas" ("colors") served as categories of classification; and, as such, dating from classical times, they remained as part of the intellectual tradition of India. But 'varnas' as actually self-conscious social institutions, with some sense of shared identity and common felt needs, were something else. Horizontal linkages, transcending the ties of locality and caste and kinship and founded upon limited perceptions of shared status and common interest, have been strongest when rooted in contractual obligations and in personal bonds. Such linkages have been symbolized by shared "salt" (*"namak"*). Even in modern times, such linkages have not extended very far into the agrarian countryside. In other words, where there is an All-India sense of a common society and of nationhood, this exists mainly among the privileged, the ruling classes of India. Except perhaps in Kerala (and, possibly, in Bengal), other classes do not count, largely because they do not exist. (They are categories of analysis rather than self-conscious social groups.)

A second observation along this line is perhaps as risky to make, but it may be equally necessary. It is that the have-not peoples of South Asia seem to be "disappearing." By this I mean that, except for their place as part of the demographic and economic statistical data used by bureaucrats and scholars, that hundred million or so who hang on the very brink of extinction seems to appear more and more fading and ghostly. They are there and yet they are not there. One sees them on the sidewalks of Calcutta and one hears their faint cries in squalid hovels of mud and grass. But their existence has been so taken for granted—albeit "nasty, brutish, and short" —and their condition is assumed to be so irredeemable and permanent that the bustling and prospering modern world rushes on. For almost all intents and purposes, the better-off seem oblivious to those who lie in the dust. This obliviousness is not so much a deliberate and studied matter, as perceived in the actions of individuals, groups, or governments, as it is a kind of subconscious repression of facts and a sense of futility. Years ago Barbara Ward began to describe, in vivid terms, the widening gulf between the have and the have-not nations of the world.[6] In vivid terms, so also did Kusum Nair and Gunnar Myrdal, to name but two others.[7] Such observers have also alluded to the widening gulf between the have and have-not categories of people within those same nations, and with special reference to India. It is this second gulf, between "overdeveloped" and "underdeveloped" sectors within the same country—between those peoples who are "emerging" and those who are "disappearing"—which is especially profound.

Exactly what the implications of this second gulf are, and what ramifications may flow from them, are far from clear. Yet, if anything is fathomable, it would seem to be as follows: (a) that the gulf between conspicuous (and, at times, trivializing and wasteful) affluence and equally conspicuous (even abject) want is getting larger—with more and more millions becoming faceless, voiceless, useless, and redundant in their miserable isolation; (b) that this gulf can and probably will continue to exist into the indefinite future; (c) that the best efforts of the conscience-striken among the well-fed in the world outside South Asia can only be effective to the degree they are matched by greater efforts among the conscientious and compassionate within South Asia;[8] and (d) that not enough of the people who rank among the privileged (ruling groups) of the region, whatever their communal, ideological, or party affiliations, have cared enough to commit a sufficient amount of energy to the carrying out of such radical measures as may be required.

More importantly, no amount of aid, science, and/or technology, it would seem, can alter the direction of current processes without the occurrence of a more fundamental "awakening" or "conversion" among significantly larger numbers of people. Persuasion and propaganda and even some sort of "proselytizing" to this end must be carried on; and this, on a massive scale. Without such efforts inside South Asia, changes of sufficient magnitude to slow and stop and then reverse the process seem all but hopeless. Changes of a revolutionary character are required, changes which can only begin in the hearts and minds of individuals and which must then galvanize them in a common purpose. But historically many movements of such magnitude have tended to be totalitarian, or at least extremely authoritarian, in character. Indeed, the more highly organized and the more quickly accelerated such movements have been, the more violent and repressive have been the resulting changes. In the name of equality, liberty has been sacrificed—with ultimate loss of both dignity and freedom, in conscience, thought, and expression, for individuals. And then one master, the state (visualized by some as the corporate or collective embodiment of all people) has taken over the distribution of all benefits, bringing not only goods and services (or want thereof), but also a common slavery and thraldom to all. Yet, slower, more deliberate, and apparently nonviolent or peaceful changes have, for lack of social mobilization, tended to fall into the opposite ditch. The phrase "all deliberate speed" has become synonymous with "status quo." All too often the elements and essentials of a progressive movement have been co-opted by reactionary, backward-looking interests. Blind even to their own long-range safety and satisfaction, these interests have been too intent upon giving token appearance to change without allowing much, if any, of its real substance. And thereby, with culpable ineptitude and callous indifference to want (as well as to corruption), those in privilege seem to have courted their own destruction. Oblivious to the explosive frustrations and seething misery at their gates, such individuals have ultimately forfeited not only their own liberty (and lives), but have therewith wantonly destroyed the liberties of many others as well.

Thus, a tension exists. While the gulf in South Asia widens and more and more millions slide into a faceless twilight, paralysis grips leaders and halts or slows the pace of more essential social mobilization. Much more can be lost than mere economic privileges. A whole cultural heritage, hallowed from time immemorial, can be lost. But since only some of the privileged have, so far, become concerned and since only they can provide solutions to the dilemmas of change, especially those relating to its pace, those who care most seem caught between anxiety and fear. How to reach down and pull up the lowly and needy without falling into the same pit seems to freeze many of them into immobility. Conscientious leaders in South Asia are not unaware of the dangers and risks inherent in each alternative. Not the least of these risks would be an irreparable disintegration of power and a fissiparization of existing structures, with nothing to replace them. The secession of Bangladesh, followed by its further sinking into a morass of chaos and political disintegration, serves as a mute reminder of what could happen.

NOTES

1. Thomas Hobbes, *Leviathane* (New York: E.P. Dutton & Co., 1950): Part II, "Of Commonwealth," or Chapter XVII, "Of the Causes, Generation, and Definition of a Commonwealth," especially pp. 142-155. In my opinion, this is as fine a definition and description as has ever been written.

2. R.E. Frykenberg, ed., *Land Control and Social Structure in Indian History* (Madison, Wis., 1969), pp. xiii-xxi.

3. D.C. Wadhwa, *Agrarian Legislation in India,* 1793-1966: [*A Bibliography*] (Poona: Gokhale Institute of Politics and Economics, 1973).

4. R.E. Frykenberg, "The Inner Logic of Imperium in India" (Madison, Wis. 1974, unpublished draft soon to appear in the *Indo-British Review* and in a monograph), pp. 3-4.

5. Ibid.

6. Barbara Ward, *India and the West* (New York, 1961). Also see her *The Rich Nations and the Poor Nations* (New York, 1962).

7. Kusum Nair, *Blossoms in the Dust* (New York, 1962) and Gunnar Myrdal, *Asian Drama: An Inquiry Into the Poverty of Nations*, 3 vols. (New York, 1968). Also see: Daniel Thorner, *Agrarian Prospect in India* (New York, 1956).

8. Myrdal, *Asian Drama,* 1:14, deals with questions of motive and efficacy. Referring to "opportunistic" approaches to research and to assistance, he describes attempts to find "better based and politically appealing reasons for giving more aid to the under-developed nations"; but the same theme could be pursued further, especially with reference to aid-giving within such countries.

PART ONE
Landed Privilege in the Past

Revenue Farming and the Zamindari System in Eighteenth-Century Bengal

THIS essay has two basic purposes.[1] It seeks to demonstrate that the key to understanding the behavior of *zamindars* in Bengal after the Permanent (Cornwallis) Settlement of 1793 is to be found in developments before and just after the beginning of British rule in the 1760s. Second, it argues that among those developments, the spread of the practice of farming out the revenue collections through auction sales known as "the outcry," probably was decisive in bringing about a redistribution of power in rural Bengal. Decades before the Cornwallis Settlement, the farming of the revenue collections had become general. Farming of revenue collections decentralized zamindari management and shifted effective control over the land downward in the social hierarchy. The zamindars and their revenue collecting employees lost control, relatively, while intermediaries and village headmen became more independent. Viewed in this perspective, the effects of the Permanent Settlement were less a revolution than a failure to end a continuing revolution or turnover among the ranks of superior landholders. After the Permanent Settlement, when zamindars failed to pay their revenue and lost their lands through auctions, the sales were usually the culmination of a process of deteriorating control over the land rather than the cause itself. Much of the existing literature on Bengal's agrarian history focuses on the failure of zamindars to keep their lands under the harsh regulations of the 1793 Settlement. But by treating the Permanent Settlement as revolutionary in effect and by emphasizing again and again the destruction of major zamindari family fortunes, we tend to exaggerate the scope of change and to lose sight of the conservative, long-term effects of the Settlement. Most of Bengal's land did not change hands permanently in the two decades following the Cornwallis Settlement. And the evidence about both the surviving and the new zamindars suggests that the settlement worked to discourage social mobility and increases in agricultural productivity over the next century and a half.

Thus this essay seeks a clearer understanding of the Permanent Settlement in relation to other agrarian developments during the eighteenth century. It does this by concentrating on a single zamindari, the Burdwan zamindari. The Burdwan estate, northwest of Calcutta, is often cited as

the wealthiest in Bengal and as the premier example of successful zamindari
adaptation to the East India Company's shifting policies. The essay is also
intended to draw attention to the critical role of intermediaries in estate
management. The following discussion is preliminary and in places impressionistic, and it is based entirely upon printed sources.

Zamindars in pre-British Bengal were the collectors of land revenue
whose *sanads* (charter of appointment) were not inheritable but whose
right to succeed their fathers had generally been confirmed by the Mughal
emperor until the early eighteenth century. The emperor gave zamindars
a sanad following the payment of a succession fee or fine (*peshkash*) and the
execution of a security bond. Within their *pargannas*, zamindars behaved
in many respects as independent rulers, borrowing the nomenclature, forms,
and ceremonies of the Mughal court. Zamindars sat on a throne (*masnad*);
they held an annual *punya,* similar to the one conducted by the Mughal
governor at Murshidabad, which was a ceremony to which the chief subordinate revenue payers came to make commitments and their initial payments for the new revenue year; they collected their rents or revenue at a
"sadr katchari" or central revenue office, just as the Mughal government
was "sadr" in relation to the zamindars, and they referred to everything
outside their zamindari headquarters as the *"mofussil";* they collected
revenue through officers called *diwan* (chief revenue officer) and his *amils*
(agents), again using the same terms as the Mughal governor. In addition
to collecting the revenue for the Mughal state, zamindars were responsible
for maintaining internal order and for providing infantry and cavalry to
the state upon the order of the Mughal emperor. For these purposes each
zamindar was required to have at his disposal large bodies of men either
armed or ready to be armed. And because the level of specialization was
low, many zamindari *paiks* and *nagdis* (soldiers) also assisted in collecting,
escorting, and guarding the revenue as it was moved from the villages to the
zamindar's mofussil and sadr katcharis, and then to the Mughal katchari
at Murshidabad. Because of the overlap in functions performed by zamindari
troops, a change in the military function was likely to affect revenue
collection.

One of the most profound changes brought about by the East India
Company's rule was the demilitarization of the zamindars. It is also a
change the consequences of which are poorly understood. The three-
quarters of a century preceding Company rule were characterized by
frequent military action, often by troops under zamindari command. In
the first quarter of the eighteenth century, Murshid Quli Khan (1701–
1727) attempted to centralize the revenue system by resuming or transferring to Orissa the *jagirs* of the zamindars, by collecting a higher percentage
of the assessment, and by turning over the revenue collections to *khalsa
amils* or collectors under the direction of the central treasury. He also confirmed the annexation of small zamindaris by large ones, such as Burdwan,
and he dispossessed some of the more independent rajas, including Raja

Sitaram of Bhushna and Raja Udayanarayan of Rajshahi.[2] In this period of rearrangement, both the expanding and declining zamindars frequently put their own armies into the field. After Murshid Quli Khan, the repeated invasions of the Marathas in the middle of the century again required extensive mobilization of zamindari troops, at least in the western zamindaris.

The importance of military forces for the Burdwan zamindari in pre-Company days is suggested by comparing the Mughal land revenue demand (Rs. 31,00,390) with the sum required to maintain the nagdis or soldiers paid directly by the raja (over Rs. 3,00,000) just before Burdwan was ceded to the Company in 1760. In addition to nagdis, the raja relied upon *ghatwals* (frontier guards), *thanadars* (policemen), and village paiks (irregular watchmen), all of whom were paid through assignments of land or salaries.[3] The combined sum of the money paid directly and of the potential rents alienated to soldiers, ghatwals, thanadars, and paiks constituted a major expense, possibly amounting to as much as one-fifth of the revenue assessment.

The rajas of Burdwan, like other zamindars, had frequent need to use their military forces in the three-quarters of a century before Burdwan was ceded to the East India Company. In 1696, the Burdwan zamindar Krishna Ram Rai, lost his life while trying unsuccessfully to suppress the rebellion of Sobha Singh and other local rulers, including the Raja of Bishnupur. His surviving son, Jagat Ram Rai, took refuge with the Mughal Nawab of Bengal who restored him to Burdwan. In 1702 Jagat Ram Rai was murdered but the family's fortunes began to improve under his successor, Raja Kirti Chandra Rai. Raja Kirti Chandra defeated the neighboring rajas of Chandrakona, Barda, Balghara, Panchet, Birbhum, and Bishnupur and annexed part of their territory to his zamindari. In this way he added the lowland pargannas of Chitua, Bhursut, Barda, and Manoharshahi, which are in the modern districts of Hughli and Midnapore, as well as a large tract of hilly country to the west.[4] In 1741 the Maratha chief, Raghuji Bhonsle, invaded Bengal with 40,000 horsemen and drove Nawab Ali Vardi Khan's army northward through Burdwan district. Although Burdwan's forces were unable to keep out the Marathas on this occasion, in the following decade they repeatedly blunted the Maratha penetrations from the western hills. In consequence of Burdwan's defense of the western borderlands and the relatively regular remission of revenue, the Mughal government gave Tilak Chandra Rai the titles of Maharaj Adhiraj Bahadur and Panj Hazari (commander of 5,000 troops) in the mid 1750s. The Burdwan raj also added the distant pargannas of Mandalghat (in modern Howrah district), Arsha (Hughli district), and the remainder of Chandrakona (Midnapore).[5] By the time Burdwan was ceded to the East India Company in 1760, it contained the huge area of 5,174 square miles and extended to the vicinity of Calcutta.

It is significant that part of the Burdwan zamindari's rapid expansion occurred during the administrations of Murshid Quli Khan. What enabled the Burdwan raj to expand at the expense of neighboring zamindars during a period of Nawabi consolidation and centralization? Presumably the Burdwan raj's effective use of military force was a major factor. However the Murshidabad government could easily have defeated the Burdwan raj army, had the Nawab or Diwan of Bengal decided it was to his advantage to do so. Yet the Burdwan rajas were permitted to keep both their original small holding and the new pargannas they had seized. This was undoubtedly due to the efficiency of the Burdwan revenue collecting agency and the raj's loyalty to Murshidabad, in addition to its military strength.

Little information exists about the character of the early Burdwan raj family which would permit firm explanations of its remarkable ascendancy, although it may be relevant that the founder of the raj family, Sangam Rai, who settled near Burdwan town in the second quarter of the seventeenth century, was a Khatri Kapur trader and money-lender from Lahore. His grandson, Abu Rai, seemingly a trader also, won the favor of the Mughal *faujdar* (official with police and magisterial powers) of *chakla* Burdwan by supplying food to his troops in a time of special need and was rewarded by appointment to the administrative office of *chaudhuri* (head officer of a parganna) and *kotwal* (superintendent of markets/chief police officer) of Rekhabi bazaar in Burdwan town in 1657.[6] The literacy and computational skills of the Khatris must have eased the family's way into the Mughal administrative service and the accounting work of zamindari management.

That the Burdwan raj family was non-Bengali may also have helped in several ways. First, the rajas of Burdwan may have been more willing than most Bengali zamindars to cooperate with the non-Bengali rulers of the province in nearby Murshidabad, knowing that the family's good fortunes were intimately involved with that of the Mughals. And since the Burdwan rajas were up-country men and new to many of their paragannas, their subjects owed them less "natural" or instinctive allegiance. Possibly the rajas were correspondingly sensitive to the need for Mughal support. Second, because the Burdwan rajas relied heavily upon fellow up-country Khatris for marriages and high zamindari management personnel, and because these Khatris were outsiders, few in number, and dependent upon continued mutual aid for their welfare, it is reasonable to speculate that the Burdwan raj family and their fellow Khatris were relatively close-knit. In their early years as zamindars some members of the raj family also married into the ruling Sadgop families of Gopbhum, the zamindari west of Burdwan paraganna in the transitional zone between the lowlands and the western hills which Burdwan absorbed in the first half of the eighteenth century.[7] The Aguri caste claimed descent from these mixed marriages. The Aguris also claimed Kshatriya status (a claim made more plausible by their special relationship to the Burdwan raj family), many wore the sacred thread, and they were noted for their short temper and fighting ability.[8] In the nineteenth century they were one of the more prosperous of the cultivating castes, and they seem in the eighteenth century to have been another source of strength for the Burdwan raj in the army and in the eastern pargannas, where they appear in greatest numbers.

Burdwan was the most valuable of the three districts ceded to the East India Company in 1760 by Nawab Mir Kasim. However, the Company had already received a foretaste from Burdwan of the frustrations to be experienced in collecting its revenue. The previous Nawab, Mir Jafar, had assigned portions of the Burdwan revenues to the Company in 1758 to discharge debts but when Hugh Watts appeared in Burdwan to collect the assigned money, the raja interfered by arresting the zamindari officials who paid, by trying to seize the revenue en route to the katchari, and by killing fifty Company sepoys.[9] After the cession of Burdwan in 1760, the Company learned that the raja had collected ten to fifteen thousand men in preparation for a joint attack with the Birbhum raja on the Company's forces. The Company was able to break the Burdwan raja's military power by entering a fort, seizing his cannon, stationing marines at Burdwan town, disbanding many of the raja's troops,[10] and reducing the deduction allowed for payment to nagdis from Rs. 3 *lakhs* (a lakh equals 100,000) to Rs. 1 lakh.[11] Then the Company began its long series of experiments in collecting the revenue from the Burdwan zamindari, experiments which were hindered by the reluctance of the raja and his officials to surrender their military functions and the prestige, power, and patronage that were involved.

In pre-British days, the key to successful zamindari management, in both its military and revenue collecting aspects, had been control over men. The purpose of zamindari management was at least as much political as economic. Walter Neale has said the output of Indian land used to be measured in men rather than in economic profit.[12] Land was used by the superior holders to consolidate factions, to gain new supporters, and to build a political and military base, without which appointment to the office of major zamindar would be as unlikely as it would be fruitless. The political nature of zamindari management is suggested by the low prices for which zamindaris were sold in pre-British times. Sir William Hunter estimated that the selling price generally did not exceed one year's revenue demand or one year's arrears.[13] Philip Calkins has found examples of much higher prices. But on the many occasions in which prices were low, potential buyers apparently had little confidence in being able to assume control of the apex of a complicated social hierarchy and fulfill the conditions of the zamindari sanad. As a last resort, zamindars could send troops to force a recalcitrant village to pay its revenue. But this was often ineffectual or counterproductive. Villages were scattered, eighteenth-century roads and bridges were rarely worthy of the name and, because the harvest came in at roughly the same time throughout hundreds of villages within each zamindari, zamindari military action at best could only be selective and exemplary and could not be relied upon to secure a substantial portion of the harvest.

The literature on eighteenth-century Bengal contains so many references to cultivators who abandoned their land, thereby reducing the revenue roll, that heavy reliance upon troops must have been hazardous. Nevertheless, coercion or the threat to use it was a vital part of the eighteenth-century revenue system. Defaulting peasants and minor revenue officers were confined in zamindari katcharis where they were sometimes tortured. Salim Allah's *Tawarikh-i-Bangalah* (*Narrative of Transactions in Bengal,* 1763) gave details of the torture of defaulting zamindars by Murshid Quli Khan's officers. Nazir Ahmed "used to suspend the zamindars by the heals, and after rubbing the soles of their feet with a hard brick, bastinado them with a switch. In the winter he would order them to be stripped naked, and then sprinkled with water." He also had them flogged. Salim Allah wrote that in the middle of the century Sayyid Muhammad Reza Khan placed defaulting amils and zamindars in a pit filled with human excrement. "He also used to oblige them to wear leather longer drawers, filled with live cats. He would force them to drink buffaloe's milk, mixed with salt, till he brought them to death's door by a diarrhoea."[14] Although Salim Allah wrote this account years after the administrations of Murshid Quli Khan and Muhammad Reza Khan, and although he wrote it at the request of Governor Vansittart,[15] he did praise Murshid Quli Khan for making advances to the cultivators and for his "humane attention to the wants of individuals."[16] While Salim Allah's account may be colored, there is little doubt that confinement and torture of defaulters was common in eighteenth-century Bengal.

Ultimately though, effective zamindari management required that a zamindar have the allegiance of influential villagers who could be depended upon to see that their fellow villagers met their revenue obligations. This allegiance was conditioned by the special privileges awarded to village leaders, by the predictability and continuity of the village's obligations, and by the arrangements for adjudicating disagreements over the nature of each person's obligations. One of the little noticed features of zamindari management in pre-British days was the presence of a system of courts under the supervision of the zamindars. Harry Verelst, an astute observer, described nine types of courts in the Burdwan zamindari in 1765 and commented that a "like administration prevails in nearly all the provinces of Bengal." Some of the courts were for settling debts or trying persons accused of crimes. Three, however, were mainly concerned with revenue matters. Each of the three combined the executive function of revenue collection with the judicial task of settling disputes:

Sudder Cutcherry—In this court are received all the land-rents and revenues of the province, all accounts relative to them adjusted, all purchases and sales of land and property confirmed, all differences between landlord and tenant heard and determined, and from hence all orders respecting the rents and revenues are issued.

Ameen Dustore—Is, in a great measure, a court subordinated to the Sudder Cutcherry, as all complaints are first made to the former, and referred from thence to the latter. They relate entirely to the business of the revenue, and the conduct of those employed in the collections.

Karidge Dustore—The landholders' accounts, when settled, are sent to this Court for payment, and in such cases where the debtor is incapable of paying the amount, a power is lodged in this court to compromise the debt.[17]

There seems to be no way of determining whether revenue disputes were settled more commonly inside these courts than out, or by adjudication more commonly then by coercion. But the vividness of Salim Allah's description of torture should not lead us to assume that these courts and the less formal practice of *salishi* (arbitration) were not the usual vehicle for resolving revenue questions.

Further information about zamindari management was provided by the Amini Commission, which was appointed by the East India Company in 1776 to examine the traditional revenue system. After examining the equivalent of three rooms full of Persian and Bengali documents, the commissioners (Anderson, Croftes, and Bogle) described the organization of zamindari revenue collecting hierarchies.[18] Beneath the zamindar's diwan, generally there were three tiers of officials, corresponding to the units of zamindari administration. Zamindaris were divided into pargannas; pargannas each contained several *tarafs* or *dihs*, which in turn consisted of a number of villages. Zamindari management depended upon the relations between officials stationed at each of these divisions and upon the flow of information between them. The most stable element in the chain of zamindari management was the *mandal* or *mukaddam*, the chief *ryot* of each village. He was generally a respected villager who settled disputes within the village and who mediated between his fellow ryots and the subordinate revenue collectors. He held his position, according to the Commission, by virtue of "the good opinion of the ryots." The zamindar's major representative residing in a village was either the *karamchari* or *patwari*, or in large villages, both together, with the karamchari collecting the revenue and the patwari keeping the records. Mandals, mukaddams, karamcharis, and patwaris were not often changed.[19] They were compensated for their services to the zamindar by a share of the collections, by holding more land than was recorded, by holding land at a privileged rate of assessment, or by a combination of these.

The karamcharis and patwaris were indispensable to the zamindars because of their local knowledge. They alone, it seems, kept full revenue records for each village. Anderson, Croftes, and Bogle specified eighteen separate accounts maintained by the karamcharis and patwaris. They included records of each ryot's holding, rate of assessment, installments, payments, and arrears. The officers above them knew much less because a mere abstract of these accounts was sent to the officers in charge of the tarafs and pargannas who in turn sent a set of still less detailed abstracts on to the sadr katchari. The intermediate officer—the *ihtimamdar* or *shikdar*—

who managed a dih, taraf, or parganna, was not usually an hereditary officer, nor were his *gomastas* or agents.[20] If zamindars could not maintain continuity of management personnel and continuity of records in the sadr and mofussil katcharis, the village mandals, karamcharis, and patwaris had at least the potential power to rearrange and obfuscate the traditional revenue obligations of each village and of individuals within each village.

The continuity of zamindari management in many parts of Bengal seems to have been weakened in the first quarter of the eighteenth century by Murshid Quli Khan's resumption of jagirs, dispossession of certain major zamindars, and the expansion of others. When a zamindar tried to take possession of a new parganna, either from the previous zamindar or from one of Murshid Quli's khalsa amils, he faced the classical dilemma of zamindari management. Should he replace the existing, knowledgeable intermediaries and appoint his own men as ihtimamdars or shikdars and risk the almost certain noncooperation and falsification of accounts by subordinate revenue agents? Or should he continue the previous set of ihtimamdars and shikdars in office, knowing that while they were familiar with the real obligations of the parganna, many were also still loyal to the previous zamindar or to the pursuit of their own interests and therefore likely to fiddle the accounts?

Many early eighteenth-century zamindars tried to solve this dilemma by farming out the revenue collections to the highest bidders. This had the disadvantage that the zamindar surrendered the direct management of his estate and that if he should ever attempt in the future to reassert *khas* or direct management, he usually would be unable to verify the accuracy of local records. But farming of the revenue collections was so common by the mid-eighteenth century that zamindars, including the rajas of Burdwan, apparently regarded it as an effective arrangement. Many of the farmers were either the former khalsa amils or the ihtimamdars and shikdars who had collected when the zamindars directly managed the pargannas.

When the East India Company took over the 24-Pargannas (a district adjacent to and south of Calcutta) in 1757 and the Ceded Districts (Burdwan, Midnapore, and Chittagong) in 1760, it continued the Mughal practice of putting the collections up to public auction. The Court of Proprietors disapproved of revenue farming in 1766 and commented that "it appears to have been deemed by the natives an act of oppression and contrary to the customs of Indostan."[21] Revenue farming was, in fact, not new. It had been common in Bengal in Murshid Quli Khan's time, although Henry Colebrooke may have been right in saying that farming "did not become universal" until Nawab Mir Kasim Ali's administration (1760-63).[22] Gholam Hosein Khan, the son of a former Nazim of Bihar, believed that farming had been introduced in the time of Emperor Farukhsiyar (and of Murshid Quli Khan).[23] The British innovation was not farming per se but the shortness of the farmers' tenure as collectors and also, apparently, the openness of the auctions. It seems likely that under the Mughal governments of Bengal, most of the bidders were local men who were familiar with the real assets and obligations of the area, that the auctions were closed to all except prominent local persons, and that the auctions involved some amount of negotiation. British auctions, by contrast, were widely publicized in advance and were attended by persons from outside the zamindari. The British innovations may have significantly undercut the ability of zamindars and their officials to maintain control of their land.

In 1762, the Company's revenue collecting rights in the Ceded Districts were sold at public auctions for a term of three years. It was thought then, as it was in Warren Hastings' Quinquennial Settlement of 1772, that the economic laws of competition would demonstrate in the auction procedure what the real value of the land was. The Company made little effort to restrict the selling to local people. Bidders from outside the districts flocked to the auctions and forced the prices up beyond the level which either they or the former farmers could recover during their three years as collectors. Former farmers overbid in order to save their land, in many cases, and then either paid their commitments to the East India Company from their savings or defaulted. As a result of overbids at "the outcry" of 1762, the Burdwan *jummabundi* or rent roll was increased by one-sixth.[24] The farmers tried to recoup the increases from their tenants. Moreover, many new farmers refused to make advances to their tenants. Customarily revenue farmers and local mahajans had lent cultivators money to help with the cost of planting but now few would risk advances, knowing that they might be forced to surrender the land at the expiration of the three-year contract and that advances to cultivators as a rule were not completely repaid within three years. Among the new farmers were John Johnstone, William Bolts, and William Hay, the Company's Resident and Councillors at Burdwan, and the *banias* (commercial agents) of other "European gentlemen." In 1762 Tilak Chandra, the raja of Burdwan, played an insignificant role in the bidding, it seems. The raja's officers held in his name land paying a revenue of only Rs. 5.73 lakhs, or about one-eighth of the whole. When Harry Verelst arrived at Burdwan in 1765, he "found the Rajah, as he had before assured me, quite unacquainted with the transactions and affairs of his country, and without the respect due to his office...." Years of farming the collections out to the *muttaseddis,* or the principal inhabitants of the zamindari, had removed the raja from the practical affairs of revenue administration.[25] Many of the major muttaseddis had held their farms at beneath prevailing revenue rates, having taken advantage of the raja's ignorance to make collusive arrangements with the raja's officers during the auctions.

During the three years following the Company's 1762 "outcry," many farmers defaulted, but not before they milked their farms of all they could. At the next auction, following the expiration of the first three-year contracts, despite the publicity given to the auctions by beat of tom-toms, bids were received "for little more than two-fifths of the lands" in the Burdwan

zamindari.[26] Most of the remaining land was managed khas or directly
by East India Company officials. The defaults in both the farmed and khas
lands were again massive after the auction of 1765, amounting to over one-
fifth of the total demand in the first year. Many cultivators fled the land to
avoid attempts by both the old and the new revenue agents to collect rents
while a substantial number of the resident farmers dissipated their savings
and were ruined in their efforts not to lose their land.[27] Another problem
faced by revenue collectors in Rajshahi and other zamindaris still under
Mughal administration, and possibly in Burdwan also, was the activity of
East India Company's gomastas or agents. Company gomastas in the mid-
1760s were forcing ryots to sell them their produce at low prices; they
were intercepting ryots' land revenue payments on the pretence that the
ryots owed them money; and they were "pressing people into their service,"
according to zamindars' complaints which the Select Committee in Calcutta was inclined to believe.[28] Finally, in many farms and khas estates,
the former zamindars continued to collect rents from the peasants and to
throw other obstacles in the way of the farmers or government amils.

When Harry Verelst arrived in Burdwan in 1765, he recognized that
the Company's "outcry" system was a disaster both because revenues were
falling and land was being abandoned. He therefore reverted to a plan
akin to the late Mughal system. He engaged local farmers "of substance
and character" for terms of at least three years, "with a promise, that if
they exerted themselves in the improvement, they should never be dispossessed."[29] When the first five-year leases were made in Burdwan in 1771,
a year before Hastings' Settlement came into effect in other parts of Bengal,
they were in most cases made with the old farmers. Although Verelst's
reformed farming system had increased the Company's revenue from
Burdwan, the famine of 1770 disrupted the system. In 1771, as the Burdwan
farmers prepared to make their bids, the price of grain in Burdwan was
unusually high due to scarcities in other parts of Bengal, and many farmers
bid more than they were ultimately able to pay.[30]

The spread of the farming system coincided with a rapid rise in both
the government's revenue demand (*jama*) and revenue collections (*hasil*)
which was in marked contrast to the stability of earlier times. According to
F.D. Ascoli's calculations, from Akbar's settlement of 1582 until Murshid
Quli Khan's revision in 1722, the revenue demand in Bengal had risen by
a mere 0.2 percent per annum. Such stability must have produced an expectation of continued permanence. However, from 1722 to 1756, the increase in demand averaged 0.8 percent, and from 1756 to 1763, it reached
a rate of 6.0 percent per annum, according to Ascoli.

Revenue demand is not the same as revenue collections but the collections also rose markedly. Philip Calkins has shown that Murshid Quli
Khan brought the collections up to a level much closer to the demand,[31]
and the last Mughal governors and the Company raised the collections
even higher. The joint increase in the demand and collections probably

alarmed local revenue payers who may have felt fully justified in resorting to any subterfuge to avoid paying what must have seemed grossly unfair increments. Some peasants emigrated to escape the increases, and revenue farmers then assessed the remaining peasants for the deficiency. The revenue farmers also enticed deserters back to their villages with offers of *tuccavi* or advances and reduced rents. But at harvest time, revenue farmers reneged on their promises, thereby encouraging the secretiveness and resistance of villagers on which British officials so often commented. And according to Henry Thomas Colebrooke, this also was responsible for "that habitual breach of faith" found in the eighteenth-century revenue system. "The general disregard of usage and agreements rendered the offices of account and control useless and nugatory."[32]

After Warren Hastings' disastrous experiment with farming out the revenues between 1771 and 1777, the East India Company turned again to the zamindars. At first the zamindars were given short-term agreements; in 1789 they received decennial settlements; and in 1793 those settlements were declared permanent. Much of Cornwallis' Permanent Settlement was left unaltered until Zamindari Abolition in 1951. The 1793 Settlement meant the maharajas and smaller zamindars were vested with rights of private property in estates for which they were to pay a land tax that could not be increased, regardless of any eventual rise in population, rents, land values, and agricultural prices. As is well known, the Permanent Settlement had both an economic and a political aim. The government imagined that the zamindar would learn to pay his taxes promptly and to improve and manage his estate, understanding that future profits would go to himself and his tenants rather than to government. It was thought further that because their future was secure the zamindars would form a landed aristocracy giving the administration their loyalty and support.

Although Cornwallis intended to introduce stability into agrarian relationships, the immediate effect was to accelerate the turnover of persons responsible for paying the revenue. In the twenty-two years following Cornwallis' Settlement many zamindars failed to pay their revenue punctually and their land was attached and auctioned. Titles for more than one-third of the land changed hands in those years.[33] The standard explanation of this development has been that Cornwallis' Settlement was too high for the amount of land under cultivation at the time, that the zamindars were unbusinesslike in their methods, and that the "long-settled families" who lost land were, in Percival Spear's words, replaced by "Calcutta financiers."[34]

Actually, the notion that the traditional landed classes were ruined by the Permanent Settlement and lost one-third of their land due to overassessment and "compassionless punctuality" is misleading in several respects.

First, as we have seen, the traditional zamindari system had been shattered long before Cornwallis. The Permanent Settlement was an attempt to revive a system irreversibly altered. Second, many of the land transfers were made to relatives, dependents, and former employees of the old zamindars. The actual management and control of the land were only temporarily disturbed by many transfers after 1789. Third, there is little evidence that moneyed men from Calcutta were able to hold a major portion of the zamindaris sold at auctions except in the vicinity of Calcutta. Calcutta banias had farmed zamindaris in the mofussil in the 1770s but those who bought soon after the Permanent Settlement often were prevented by the local peasants and rent-receivers from keeping possession of their purchases.

Not only had more than half the land in Bengal been transferred from one zamindar to another in the eighteenth century prior to 1789,[35] but both old and new zamindars were often in reduced circumstances before the Permanent Settlement. Philip Francis, later a champion of a zamindari settlement, wrote in 1775 that the zamindars:

> have gradually sunk into a state of Sloth, Stupidity, Beggary and Contempt. Being almost universally overwhelmed with Debts, and few of them having any Knowledge of their Affairs, they of course have lost all Dignity and Consequence in the Eyes of the People. I am assured, and inclined to believe that the greatest Part of the younger Generation are likely to be Idiots.[36]

Other, more careful observers, including Sir John Shore in 1789 and Henry Thomas Colebrooke in 1794,[37] were no less impressed by the poverty of the zamindars. Shore said they were "almost universally poor," including the once great rajas of Birbhum, Bishnupur, Dinajpur, Nuddea, and Rajshahi. Their poverty was reflected in the crumbling walls of their forts, the decay of their palaces, in the decline in their authority and style of living, and in the smallness of their armed guards. Apart from the jungle rajas, by 1802 almost none of the zamindars of southwestern Bengal had armed retainers. When the rajas of Burdwan and Bishnupur left their palaces, they hired a small "retinue" of armed guards in an effort to appear still powerful.[39] This was very different from the early British period, before the Company had disbanded thousands of nagdis from the zamindari armies.

A second development had cut into the zamindar's powers and authority. Prior to Company rule, zamindars had supported many of their relations, agents, officers, favorites, followers, Brahmans, and gods with grants of revenue-free land. Possession of land conferred a prestige that cash did not. Cash salaries and gifts had been given, of course, but the judicious disposal of land was the major source of authority and good will. The rajas of both Burdwan and Bishnupur were quoted as saying that there should be no Brahman in their zamindaris without a land grant and both apparently tried to live up to this ideal. Many land grants made ostensibly to support religious specialists and activities were in fact made to ordinary supporters of the raja and his officials as a means of separating land from the revenue rolls. Mr. Johnstone's 1763-64 survey of revenue-free land in the Burdwan zamindari revealed that almost one-fifth of the arable land was *bazi-zamin* or revenue-exempt,[40] and this was presumably exclusive of *chakran* or service land which was also held revenue-free.[41] When the Company resumed many of these grants at the time of Johnstone's survey, it increased the Burdwan zamindari's assessment from Rs. 31.7 lakhs to Rs. 41.7 lakhs,[42] indicating that over one-third of the land revenue had been alienated. In Birbhum, adjoining Burdwan on the north, the Pathan rajas and the Mughal government had alienated even more land. An estimated two-thirds of the land in the Birbhum zamindari in 1760 was alienated for military purposes alone, and British resumption proceedings enabled the Company to more than double the land revenue assessment.[43] The survey and settlement operations in selected areas throughout Bengal in the late nineteenth and early twentieth centuries showed that considerable areas of land escaped the eighteenth-century resumption proceedings and that new alienations were made during the nineteenth century. But by removing a major part of this vast source of patronage in Burdwan and elsewhere, the Company was cutting at the roots of the zamindari system and forcing zamindars to seek new ways, often through the law courts, of forcing compliance with their rent demands.

A third factor contributing to the decline of most of the major zamindars before 1789 was the crippling effect of inter-family feuds. It is not certain that these feuds were more intense after Company rule began than before, but few families were spared from self destructive legal and military fights before 1789. In one of the best known cases, Raja Chaitanya Singh was driven from the Bishnupur zamindari by another branch of the family led by Raja Damodar Singh. In desperation, Raja Chaitanya fled to Calcutta with the image of the family god, Madan Mohan, and pawned it to a merchant in order to raise funds to pursue his claims to the Bishnupur zamindari through the courts. The degradation of this family was completed by the early nineteenth century when the rajas had lost all their land. From this time until after independence, the family lived in real poverty, in a small house among the ruins of the Bishnupur fort, clinging to memories of the days when they could feast thousands of Brahmans.

Whether or not zamindari families had been more unified in Mughal times, as seems likely, in the late eighteenth century certain families were being pulled apart by conflicting pressures and a loss of consensus about what constituted proper behavior. Before the mid-eighteenth century, rajas had commanded small armies, alienated land and handed out administrative and military offices to their supporters, and paid a relatively stable revenue demand. As rajas lost many of the older zamindari functions, many families quarrelled about how to reconcile traditional social obligations with the behavioral adjustments necessary for the preservation of their estates. Many had already lost practical control of zamindari management in any case. Therefore, to conclude about pre-Cornwallis developments, we may say that family feuds, the disbanding of zamindari armies, the resumption of revenue-free lands, and the discontinuity of zamindari management had substantially transformed the zamindari system. John Shore probably had not exaggerated in estimating that at least one-half of Bengal's land had been transferred from one revenue payer to another between 1700 and 1789 "on account of defalcations" alone.[44] Much land also changed hands through conquest, revenue farming, and other causes.

The zamindars of Bengal responded to the inflexibility and the high demand of the 1789 Settlement in varying and often ingenious ways. It is doubtful that most zamindars believed that the new Settlement would be permanent. Many previous settlements had fluctuated wildly. For example, Rangpur's had gone from Rs. 11 lakhs in 1762, to Rs. 5 lakhs in 1764, to Rs. 11 lakhs again in 1771, and to Rs. 7 lakhs in 1786. Moreover, under the new assessment there was little margin for bad harvests and inefficient management. Colebrooke reported that grain prices had changed by as much as 400 percent in a year without major scarcity. As the new settlement in theory left the zamindars with only a 10 percent profit from the collections, clearly they were vulnerable to bad seasons, inefficient collection staffs, and delinquent ryots. Operating with such a thin margin of safety, a zamindar had to be resourceful to survive.

The Burdwan raja, Tej Chandra, reverted to his ancestor's and the Company's earlier practice of farming out the revenue collections at public auction. He divided his estate into about one hundred lots and auctioned them to *sadr* farmers for terms of three, five, eight and nine years. Many of his chief zamindari agents (*amla*) took the choice lots. Each sadr farmer usually sub-let the collections to underfarmers (*kutkenadars*) who in turn settled with the chief ryots of the villages (gomastas or mandals). The chief ryots collected from the other village landholders who often engaged sharecroppers or landless laborers to do the actual ploughing, planting, and havesting.

The post-Permanent Settlement revenue farmers faced a situation similar to their midcentury predecessors. When the farmer was experienced with zamindari management and accounting, when he was familiar with the villages, and when he had the support of village elites within his lot, then he had a chance of collecting the rents and fulfilling the conditions of his lease. However, an outsider, and even the zamindar himself, often found upon taking over a farm that the previous farmer had made collusive arrangements with the sub-farmers and the ryots. The previous farmer at the expiration of his lease would sell fake leases, receipts, and even revenue-free grants to the sub-farmers and ryots. The new farmer would not have the means to distinguish with confidence between fraudulent and genuine documents. There were seldom reliable rent rolls against which the documents could be checked. The revenue farmers and the zamindar soon found themselves in arrears and their land was attached and sold at the public auctions.[45]

The attaching officers and the new purchasers met the same difficulties that the zamindar and the revenue farmers had. The government was no more able to provide the purchaser with accurate accounts of the lot's assets than the zamindar could guide his farmers. Land management was decentralized to such a degree that usually neither the government nor the zamindar had access to information about rent obligations at the village level. The government in 1793 had no officers stationed in the 92 farms in Burdwan and the zamindar had his men in the farms only when the farmer happened also to be one of his own amla. In the 1780s, only one-fourth of the Burdwan ryots held *pattas* (written leases) and these had been issued by the revenue farmers and their gomastas, not by the zamindar's officers.[46] Many of the ryots with pattas had them in order to mislead new rent collectors about the extent of their holdings or the rate at which they were assessed. With or without pattas, rents fluctuated as new *abwabs* (cesses) were added to the basic rental, as old abwabs went uncollected, and as new sets of rent collectors made fresh arrangements with powerful villagers. The rents and abwabs were seldom accurately recorded except in the minds of the head ryots. A new rent collector therefore had no option but to ingratiate himself with local head ryots by granting them preferential leases —leases with lower rental rates than those taken from other ryots. The ideology of caste provided justification for preferential arrangements of this type but the evolution of the revenue system made them a practical necessity.

Thus when a man obtained title of ownership or rentcollecting rights for a piece of land, he faced an intricate and shifting set of secret grain-sharing, work-reciprocating, credit-giving, and rent-paying relationships. Unless the holder or his agent could establish an understanding with the chief ryots of each village, the title to the land was without value. This was the painful lesson learned by zamindars, sub-renters, and buyers at auctions after the Permanent Settlement. The large estates were divided and sub-divided, and pieces sold and re-sold. The Burdwan raj was exceptionally successful in preserving a large and lucrative estate. But instead of consisting of one zamindari, by 1870 Burdwan district was divided into 4,860 zamindaris. Of these, only 48 paid revenue of £10 or more, which suggests that the 1789 Settlement gave decisive advantages to villagers rather than to the major intermediaries and that these villagers managed to separate their land from the parent estate.

The Burdwan Raj saved some of its most valuable land by devices used by zamindars in other districts. The Raja and his amla learned to utilize the attachment and auction procedure to their own advantage by a sort of juggling. They deliberately allowed over-assessed lots to be attached and sold while exerting themselves to pay the revenue on underassessed lots. They withheld the revenue on certain lots, and after the government had attached the land, written off the arrears, and sometimes reduced the assessment, the amla repurchased them under fictitious names. Perhaps Tej Chandra's most ingenious maneuvre was to plead that his zamindari was overassessed and to ask permission to sell it to his mother, Rani Bishnukumari, with whom he had poisonous relations. After handing over the zamindari papers to his mother, Tej Chandra withdrew to the part of the

Bishnupur zamindari which he had purchased at auction but he left his amla in Burdwan. When the Rani's amla tried to collect her rents, they found Tej Chandra had already received them. The Rani soon fell Rs. 6.8 lakhs in arrears and her estate narrowly escaped attachment by the government.[47]

After Tej Chandra legally regained possession of his zamindari following the death of his mother, he stopped farming out the rent collections and began instead to make permanent settlements with the intermediate rent collectors. He found that he could command a premium for his perpetual leases (*patnis*) which helped him to pay off his arears. And he persuaded the Government in 1819 to recognize the leases and to provide legal machinery for attaching and selling the collecting rights in the event of nonpayment. In other words, the zamindar shifted legal responsibility for rent collection to the intermediaries. In many cases, these leaseholders made similar arrangements with their under-renters. This process of subleasing is called sub-infeudation in the revenue literature. In west Bengal it generally did not extend down the rent collecting ladder more than two or three places. Burdwan in the 1870s, for instance, had 4,860 zamindari estates, 2,246 patnis, and 827 *dar-patnis* or sub-leases. But in eastern Bengal the collecting rights on a single peasant's plot sometimes consisted of a hierarchy of more than a dozen leases.

The patni or perpetual lease system was characteristically Bengali. It was not so much an innovation as a legal recognition and solidification of the rent collecting hierarchy. It was a product of both the looseness of the rent collecting structure and the failure of the zamindar to understand and control village-level elites and food-producing relationships. The zamindar had become isolated from village life. He no longer performed most of the major functions once associated with his office such as digging tanks (reservoirs), repairing the *bunds* which protected the paddy fields from floods, or supplying soldiers to the government. Yet the Burdwan rajas continued to exercise a major ceremonial role which helped to mask the real character of the change in rural life. For example, each year the raja celebrated the punya or first rental payment in the courtyard of his Burdwan palace. *Patnidars* from this estate attended to pay over their rents at dawn. The raja also maintained a mausoleum near the Bhagirathi River (regarded locally as the Ganga) at Khulna in which a bone of the previous Maharaja was displayed in old Khatri fashion. A nineteenth-century account described the bone display:

> It is regarded as if the Maharaja was living himself and is placed on a velvet state-cushion, with silver salvers, tumblers, hookahs, rose water and atar holders just as the late Maharaja used to sit with all the paraphernalia of state about him.[48]

And following ancient Hindu and Muslim tradition, in 1831 the raja built a road to Katwa to the most sacred bathing place in the district, where according to legend King Vikramaditya had come daily from Ujjain to bathe. Each eight miles along the road were bungaloes, stables, and tanks.[49] But throughout most of Bengal and the four thousand square miles (in 1910) of the Burdwan raj estate, effective control of the land had passed to village mandals and intermediaries.

It is to the head ryots and intermediaries that considerable scholarly effort should be devoted in the future. The zamindars, no doubt, are an easier and flashier subject of inquiry because of their numbers, visibility, human frailties, and misadventures. Nevertheless in most parts of Bengal, land management was under the control of others. Study of village elites and intermediaries will undoubtedly yield a richer understanding of the organization and practice of agriculture, "the structure of privilege," and social development as a whole. This study will require painstaking work in quantification and local history but the rewards should be high.

NOTES

1. I wish to thank Philip Calkins, Richard Fox, and Zillur Khan for their helpful comments on this essay.

2. Charles Stewart, *The History of Bengal from the First Mohammedan Invasion Until the Virtual Conquest of that Country by the English. A.D. 1757* (Calcutta, 1903), p. 420: also Philip B. Calkins, "Revenue Administration and the Formation of a Regionally Orientated Ruling Group in Bengal, 1700-1740" (Ph. D. diss., Univ. of Chicago, 1972).

3. K.A.L. Hill, *Final Report on the Survey and Settlement Operations in the District of Burdwan, 1927-1934* (Calcutta, 1940), p. 22.

4. J.C.K. Peterson, *Bengal District Gazetteers: Burdwan* (Calcutta, 1910), p. 28.

5. Ibid., p. 31.

6. Ibid., p. 27. Also, D.K. Mukerji, "The Annals of the Burdwan Raj," *The Calcutta Review* 130 (Jan. 1910).

7. W.B. Oldham, *Some Historical and Ethnical Aspects of the Burdwan District* (Calcutta, 1894), p. 18.

8. Peterson, *Burdwan*, pp. 64-65. The Kshatriya or warrior varna was the second of the four Varnas into which Hindu society was theoretically divided. Normally the sacred thread was worn only by the three highest varna and was denied to the fourth (Sudra) and the untouchables, who constituted the majority of Hindus.

9. Walter Kelly Firminger, "Introduction," *The Fifth Report from the Select Committee of the House of Commons on the Affairs of the East India Company. Dated 28th July, 1812* (Calcutta, 1917), p. cxxxii.

10. William Wilson Hunter, *Bengal MS Records,* 4 vols. (London, 1894), 1: 99-100.

11. Firminger, "Introduction," *The Fifth Report,* p. cxli.

12. Walter C. Neale, "Land Is to Rule," in *Land Control and Social Structure in Indian History,* ed. Robert Eric Frykenberg (Madison, Wis., 1963), p. 13.

13. Hunter, *Bengal MS Records,* 1: 42.

14. Quoted in John Herbert Harrington, *An Elementary Analysis of the Laws and Regulations Enacted by the Governor General in Council at Fort William in Bengal,* 3 vols. (Calcutta, 1814-15), 2:352-54.

15. Abdul Karim, *Murshid Quli Khan and His Times* (Dacca, 1963), pp. 88-89, doubts these stories on the grounds that they are unverified and that Salim Allah is inaccurate about other matters.

16. Harrington, *An Elementary Analysis,* 3:272.

17. Quoted in Firminger, "Introduction," *The Fifth Report,* pp. cxlvii-viii.

18. The Amini Commission's report was published in R.B. Ramsbotham, *Studies in the Land Revenue History of Bengal, 1769-1787* (London, 1926).

19. Ibid., pp 108-9. This is not an exhaustive list of village officials. Both the nomenclature and functions of revenue officials varied over time and from place to place.

20. Ibid., pp. 111-15.

21. *India Record Series: Fort William-India House Correspondence,* vol. 4 (1764-66) ed. C.S. Srinivasachari (Delhi, 1962), p. 185.

22. Henry Thomas Colebrook, *Remarks on the Husbandry and Internal Commerce of Bengal* (Calcutta, 1884 reprint of 1804 ed.) p. 53.

23. Harrington, *An Elementary Analysis,* 3:322.

24. Harry Verelst, *A View of the Rise, Progress, and Present State of the English Government in Bengal* (London 1772), p. 214.

25. Ibid., pp. 217-18.

26. Ibid., p. 71.

27. Ibid., p. 215.

28. Extract from "Fort William Select Committee Proceedings," 19 February 1766, ibid., pp 181-84.

29. Firminger, "Introduction," *The Fifth Report,* 1:cxlv, clxxviii.

30. Ramsbotham, *Studies in Land Revenue History*, pp. 61, 71.

31. F.D. Ascoli, *Early Revenue History of Bengal and the Fifth Report, 1812* (Oxford, 1917), p. 28, and Calkins "Revenue Administration," pp. 103ff.

32. Colebrook, *Remarks on . . . Bengal*, pp. 53-54.

33. Hunter, *Bengal MS Records*, 1:101.

34. Vicent A Smith, *The Oxford History of India*, ed. Percival Spear (3rd ed., Oxford, 1958), p. 636.

35. Sir John Shore's Minute of 18 June 1789, para. 538, *The Fifth Report*, 2:115.

36. Ranajit Guha, *A Rule of Property for Bengal: An Essay on the Idea of Permanent Settlement* (Paris, 1963), p. 121.

37. Colebrooke, *Remarks on . . . Bengal*, pp. 58-59.

38. Shore's Minute of 18 June 1789, para. 129, *The Fifth Report*, 2:31.

39. Answers to interrogatories by E. Thompson, Judge and Magistrate, Burdwan, 9 March 1802, ibid., p. 627.

40. Peterson, *Burdwan*, p. 146.

41. The term "bazi-zamin" sometimes includes and at other times excludes chakran land.

42. Peterson, *Burdwan*, p. 32.

43. L.S.S. O'Malley, *Bengal District Gazetters: Birbhum* (Calcutta, 1919), pp. 83-84.

44. Shore's Minute of 18 June 1789, para. 538, *The Fifth Report* 2-:115.

45. The discussion of the Burdwan zamindari in the 1790s is based on *West-Bengal District Records, New Series: Burdwan Letters Issued, 1788-1800*, eds. Ranajit Guha and A. Mitra (Calcutta, 1957), pp. 42ff.

46. Shore's Minute of 18 June 1789, para 416, *The Fifth Report*. 2:89.

47. *Burdwan Letters Issued*, pp. 98ff.

48. W.W. Hunter, *A Statistical Account of Bengal*, 20 vols. (London, 1876), 4:60.

49. The Mughals followed the same tradition and built mosques every eight miles on their road from Rajmahal through Burdwan district to Cuttack. Oldham, *Some . . . Aspects*, p. 20.

The Silent Settlement in South India, 1793-1853: An Analysis of the Role of Inams in the Rise of the Indian Imperial System

ROBERT ERIC FRYKENBERG

THE central thesis of this essay is an attempt to argue that the rise of Company Raj in South India, if not in all of the subcontinent, cannot be properly understood without an appreciation of British actions with respect to what were called *"ina'ām"* lands,"[1] and, indeed, that substantial bases of power beneath the authority of the new imperial system were formed by an accommodation to hereditary "landed privilege" with important tax-free concessions to those individuals and institutions having highest claims to social and ritual status and influence.[2] Among various components of Company authority and administration in the Carnatic (i.e., that part of South India technically under the authority of the Nawab of the Carnatic, nominal deputy of the Nizam of Hyderabad and of the Mughal Emperor at Delhi), no single ingredient so enabled the Company to cement and harden support for the foundations of its political structure from among disparate segments of local leadership—elites of village or caste, temple or business—as its dealings with inams. The "Inam" or "Silent Settlement" was like a linchpin holding a many spoked wheel onto the axle of Company power.

Put in different words, the English Company came to its position of supreme authority by using local, traditional, and indigenously acceptable implements and ingredients and by adapting to the internal customs and socio-political conditions necessary for the accumulation of power. Eventually and ultimately, such working within the structures of power required a coming to grips with various forms of inam holdings. Various piecemeal encounters with such institutions, without adequate or thorough knowledge of the profound intricacies and ramifications of the cultural context from whence they sprang, might conceivably have produced hopeless blundering and failure. Yet, by strange but partly explainable coincidences—accidents and incidents of circumstance—a cautious and pragmatic approach to each specific local problem brought about an accumulation of decisions which, in turn, became the very fabric of more general policies, such as those on inam lands. Such approaches to customs and institutions of great antiquity and complexity, even though the accumulated knowledge and experience of successive generations of British rulers was so often lost that the "collective memory" of the Company often flickered dimly, served to prevent extravagant measures or attempts at extreme and sweeping change.[3] At the same time, a pragmatic respect for time-hallowed precedent and for indigenous law, however customary, sprang from British political traditions and, as such, served to reinforce decisions arrived at by Englishmen a half century earlier.[4] The Company itself, after all, was grounded upon constitutional, and thus essentially conservative practices, precedents, and procedures which, when convenient, were elevated into ritual status as inspired doctrines. (In this regard, as in some of its style, it reflected the country of its origin.)[5]

Such certainly was the approach of Sir Thomas Munro. After a forty-five-year career in India and with a perception that years would pass before the Raj would possess more certain knowledge for the good government of India—despite a growing tendency of newer generations to act as if they knew everything—he wrote (in 1824):

> We must not be led away by fanciful theories founded on European models, which will inevitably end in disappointment. We must not too hastily declare any rights permanent lest we give to one class what belongs to another. We must proceed patiently and as our knowledge of the manners and customs of the people and the nature and resources of the country increases, frame gradually from existing institutions such a system as to advance... the country and be satisfactory to the people.[6]

That knowledge most necessary, he believed, was of the land, the landed, and those whose interests attached to the land.

Seen in such light, the term "silent" is not without significance. Much as the word "inam" was crossed and circled and continually present in local land settlement records of the Company, a formal and thorough investigation of the subject was never made—at least not before 1862, after the Company had ceased to exist. The adjective "silent" is used here, therefore, because there never was a formal "Inam Settlement" as such. (One must bear in mind, of course, that even no settlement or a "non-settlement" *was* a settlement. A non-policy is, after all, a policy.) Inam remained largely silent and secret, one can argue, either out of deliberate stealth on the part of those most involved, out of inadvertent ambivalence, or out of incompetence if not outright ignorance. While questions of motive still remain open and, indeed, may never be answered, one may surmise at possibilities. The silence may have been at least partly accidental and a combination of all the above factors. Many people, both British and Indian, may have been involved in a quiet and gradual development of local decisions at one time or another; but no single officer or person of influence ever became publicly identified with a clear-cut inam policy. No single action ever brought the inam question *fully* before the probing eyes of Board and Council Members, Company Directors or Parliamentary Ministers. In fact, very few Governors or even Members of Council and of the Revenue Board really understood its full possible implications. Even now, in attempting to break the silence and mystery which has surrounded this subject, deference to its extreme complexity prompts extreme caution. Secrets such as this are not easily broken.

I

Roughly defined, without a lengthy exposition on its origin and nature, an *"ina'ām"* was a gift or benefaction conferred by a superior to an inferior person or institution (or a recognition of privilege perhaps pre-existent in an inferior).

In India, and especially in the south . . . the term was especially applied to grants of land held rent-free, on hereditary and perpetual occupation: the tenure came in time to be qualified by the reservation of a portion of the assessable revenue, or by the exaction of all proceeds exceeding the intended value of the original assignment; the term was also vaguely applied to grants of rent-free land, without reference to perpetuity or any specified conditions. The grants are also distinguishable by their origin from the ruling authorities, or from the village communities, and are again distinguishable by peculiar reservations, or by their being applicable to different objects . . . .[7]

Grants by rulers were called *sanadi-inams.* Grants coming out of village resources, often on claims of ancient tradition, if not primordial origin, were called *grammu-inam* or simply *manyam* (with several sub-categories). Classified functionally and communally, hosts of inams were often known by distinct names. Muslim inams (such as *waqf* and *mu'afi*) were far fewer and generally easier to distinguish than Hindu inams (such as *agraharams, shrotiyams,* and *yatra-che-kathis*). *Devasthana-inams* (for the maintenance of temples, shrines, and such) were quite distinct from *dharmadaya-inams* (for eleemosynary institutions, especially those alms and charities administered by religious persons). *Devadasi-inams, devadaya-inams,* and *dehangi-inams* (for dancing girls, musicians, and other temple servants; for rituals; and for artisans, etc.) were very different from *watandari-* and *kattubadi-inams* (for village officers and "peons" or watchmen).[8]

So encrusted were inams with residues and segmental legacies from bygone ages that, for purposes of historical legitimization, questions about the validity of inam privileges and of the limits to such privilege were crucial to the nature and survival of any political system. Did such holdings spring from primordial local power, arising out of ancient patrimonial, communal, or village prerogatives later exercised and recognized by regional and imperial rulers, both Hindu and Muslim? Or did such holdings begin as regal or imperial alienations of land and of land revenue, either for the support of religious and charitable institutions, for special court favorites (family members, servants, concubines, dancing girls, etc.), or for administrative and military servants in lieu of salary remunerations (in a hierarchical structure of inams reaching all the way down to village *gramma-manyamulu*)?

The answers to such questions, on available evidence, seemed to be affirmative on both sides. Therein lay the dilemma for early Company authorities. Therein also lay a fantastic confusion of claims and counter-claims. Faced with such claims, concessions had been made by each successive dynastic power, whether Hindu or Muslim and whether grandly imperial or locally petty. Each such power, recognizing the hard realities of local influence and seeking to gain local support in order to stabilize or legitimize its own particular authority, had been prone to recognize existing realities and, indeed, to augment the number of grants by making more of the same. Grants from a ruler had been an important form of patronage and a means by which a ruler sought to gain and to keep social and political support.[9]

Records are filled with serious disputes over inam holdings, not just over the great and hoary "estates" of temples, nor over those of mosques and *dargahs* (shrines for various Sufi saints), nor necessarily even over the holdings of Brahmans and Kazis—some of which were enormous and others very tiny.[10] Serious disputes also revolved around what one might call the "political" inams, such as those for princely estates (*altamgha-inams*), or around petty "police" (kattubadi-inams), or around "private" privileges (*bhatti-vritti* and *khairati-inams*).[11] The oldest and largest inams were virtually inalienable. They may be described as representing the accumulated status, power, privilege, and "charity" of the country from most remote times and to have been successively legitimized by chiefs and sovereigns beyond number and almost without interruption. The newest or smallest inam might simply have been a life-time pension given by a recent Company servant (European or Native) to his favorite dancing girl. Heads of villages, heads of castes, heads of cults, and heads of almost anything else, could hold inams and could be considered as holding status sufficient to rank among the "leisured" and the "privileged" of the country. Servants of any status whose service could properly be appreciated and rewarded, whether of villages or of rulers, of mercantile or of military institutions, or of many other sorts could hold inams. In short, inams in one form or another were both the symbols of status and the substance of entrenched privilege and power for every important institution or elite group of the country. When serious attempts to lift the veils of mystery were finally possible in the mid-nineteenth century, "A Descriptive List of the Inam Tenures of the Madras Presidency," submitted to the Government on 30th October 1869, contained some 452 separate categories.[12] Most of these were then defined or described as land holdings either wholly or almost wholly free from taxation.

A. Socio-Religious Holdings:

Dating from very remote antiquity, gifts of land were extolled by Hindu laws (*shastras*) as being the most benevolent and meritorious of deeds.[13] Every king was ambitious, therefore, to show the greatness of his reign by the amount of lands granted to the religious lights of the realm. Such grants were made with much ceremony and impressive solemnity, with their details engraved upon copper plates or slabs of stone which generally declared them to be irrevocable "for as long as the sun and moon shine" and which, while invoking heavy curses and dire consequences upon anyone who would dare to tamper with them, promised great blessing and prosperity upon those who maintained and confirmed the holdings of olden times.[14] The oldest inscriptions of this sort, made by reigning Pandiya and Chola houses from their dynastic seats in Madurai and Tanjore, lesser princes of Kanchipuram or domains in Mysore, by Reddi and Gajapati chiefs along more northerly jungled hills or coastal plains, by the later monarchs of Vijayanagara, and by still later Maratha and Muslim conquerors—indeed, our oldest historical records—were of a religious nature.[15] Upon closer examination, these can be seen to fall into two categories: gifts to large religious institutions and gifts to individuals of peculiar religious merit (and their descendants). All these holdings, but especially the larger, institutional inams, can be considered to have fit into a general class called *"Devadayam"* which literally meant "Gift to God."[16]

1. *Endowments to Institutions:* Large tracts and estates—often whole villages but sometimes scattered among isolated villages, bits of villages, or even fields—comprised roughly a quarter of all tax-free holdings. (By the late nineteenth century, when information had become more complete and accurate, 1.458 million acres, having a hypothetical tax potential of Rs. 24,22,467 would come within this category.)[17] Hardly a village of any importance did not have its two main temples, one Vaishnavite and one Shaivite; in addition, it would have a shrine or temple for its tutelary deity, usually the local Village Goddess known by one of a variety of different names. While the value of each such village inam was not great, their aggregate values were substantial indeed. Far fewer really large temples stood in the northern (coastal), central, and western (inland) districts, exceptions being Jagannath, Hampi, or Sundur. For these there were extensive inams within the Madras Presidency. By far the greatest proportion of vast temple inams existed in the central south and extreme south. Attached to such great temples as those at Tirupati, Kanchipuram, Srirangam, Annamalai, Chidambaram, Rameswaram, Madurai, and Tanjore (Tanjavuru), there were land holdings of enormous size, value, and importance.[18]

Valuable endowments in land belonged to each of the different *maths* (and/or *matthams*), the establishments and headships of the three leading sectarian schools of Brahmans (Smartha, Sri-Vaishnava, and Madhava) for which branch holdings existed in nearly every district. Similar holdings belonged to leaders of every religious or sectarian organization, Hindu and non-Hindu. Among Hindu institutions not presided over by Brahmans were holdings for *jangams,* priests of the Lingayat community; *pandarams,* ascetic mendicants of lower caste; *bairagis* (*vairagis*), also wandering mendicants; and others. Landed endowments for Islamic institutions, such as waqf and

mu'afi estates, were fewer and comparatively much less complicated. By
and large, they consisted of lands attached to mosques (*masjids*) or places
of public worship—interestingly, some of these were located at walking
intervals along important roads so as to be reached in time for each of the
five times of prayer in each day; *takiyas* or "pillows" for the seats or spots
where fakirs sat or resided; and *dargahs*.[19] Endowments in land connected
to Christian churches were relatively few. These existed mostly in Tinnevelly
and Tanjore and Travancore or further up along the Malabar Coast where,
also, even fewer Jewish synagogues existed.

2. *Endowments to Individuals:* More than half of all the inams in the
Madras Presidency were held by persons of socio-religious (and political)
merit. These remained as the possessions of individual families and of their
descendants. Most of them were held by Brahmans and many were of great
antiquity. Such holdings were called *agraharams, brahmandayas,* or
shrotriyams. In later times they were also known as *bhatta-vritti-inams* (*bhatta-
vartulu* in Telugu; *bhattvartti* in Tamil). At the same time, those held by
Muslims were known as *khairati-inams.* Without further elaboration, one
may generalize by indicating that such personal inams represented the
accumulated propitiatory gifts made by the powerful of the country from
exceedingly remote times. Whether they were small plots, large fields, whole
villages, or larger stipendiary "livings" and "estates," this single form of
inam had grown and multiplied over centuries until it had become the
largest in aggregate land area and represented the biggest number of separate
holdings and the greatest aggregate value of all inams.[20] (By the 1869
accounting, it would be possible to identify 254,473 separate titles to land
covering an area of 3,694,394 acres and having an aggregate tax potential
of Rs. 54,89,928.)[21]

B. Socio-Political Holdings:

During the mounting political turbulence of the seventeenth and eighteenth
centuries, which led in turn to the progressive disintegration of larger into
smaller, ever more local Hindu regimes, and which continued after the
Muslim and Maratha conquests and the attempts at establishing Mughal
rule, the number of inams seems to have multiplied considerably. Powers
and purposes for granting inams were assumed by petty chiefs, aspiring
rajas, administrative officers, and any other would-be rulers. These often
made pretentions to authority which were more wishful than real. Many
minor inams of questionable origins or validity were granted, and held, by
zamindars, by faujdars, and even by aspiring villagers. *Polaiyagars* were
especially active and "open-handed," with each successor to local power
making numbers of fresh grants to immediate relatives, political adherents,
government servants, army officers, religious leaders, and even to potential
enemies—all so as to forestall antipathy and possible rebellion.

Of this character were the *dorasthanams* (and *bissois*) of jungled hills in
the Northern Circars, the *samasthanams* and *mukhasas* of the Carnatic, the

amarams and *umligas* of the interior, and the *jivithanams* of the deep south. Inams held by families of poliyagars, especially in Rayalasima and Baramahal, compared with the hereditary holdings of families which had served as *kanungos, despandiyas,* and *deshmukhs,* administrative officers of earlier regimes. Local registrars, revenue accountants, tax collectors, and executive chiefs had often, under a bewildering variety of titles, held positions and powers which compared roughly to those held by zamindars and/or poliyagars.[22]

At a lower level were kattubadi-inams. These had been the grants made as hereditary reimbursements to armed village warriors (the "peons," "pawns" or foot-soldiers) in return for the revenue-collecting, police, and military duties which they performed. Called into being by the needs of poliyagars and nayaks under successive regimes, village warriors had held their inams for generation after generation. Nor had rulers dared to tamper much with kattubadi lands since doing so was like trying to touch the hives of the dreaded black bees in the jungle. Thus, indeed, when called upon for active duty, "kattubadi-peons" had been paid extra allowances (*batta*) for their trouble.[23]

Also at the village level were inams for every form of village need, service, or function and for every kind of administrative duty performed for the benefit of higher levels of political authority. Manifold as these had been, the most important of them can conveniently be lumped together and called *grama-maniyams*. These lands also served as forms of hereditary pay and pension benefits given in lieu of cash salaries. Special inams to village headmen (*maniyakarans* or *"monigars,"* *desais,* deshmukhs, *nattars,* etc.), to leaders of castes (e.g., Periya Vellalars, Mudaliyars, Pillais; or Pedda Velamas, Kammas, Naidus, Kapus, Reddis, etc.—who were often the same as the village headmen), and to many other kinds of governing officers and functionaries (e.g., grants of *tambalas* or *jirars* to those who provided floral decorations for the ceremonies of village goddesses; of *matapatis* to those who cooked food for Reddis and other Sat-Sudras when they had to leave the village on business; and of *anakalas* to those kattubadi-peons whose duty it was to carry supplies and equipment for higher government officials): such had been but a few of the many perquisites which had accompanied each village status and function. In each village there were inams for the heads or leaders of every caste, most certainly of every important caste. There were inams for village artisans, musicians, and all functionaries who had traditionally contributed to the life of the village community as a whole. Lower level functionaries had been especially prone to cling tenaciously to whatever shreds of personal distinction, perquisite, or privilege had fallen to their places. Indeed, as evidenced from records of left- and right-hand caste conflicts, fights over successions to such crumbs had had a potential for special nastiness.[24]

Complete information and accounting for all of the bewildering variety and numbers of "political" inams has not, as yet, come to light. Because of

the lumping together of all "inams held for personal benefit" by the first
Inam Commissioner of Madras, figures of 1869 are not satisfactory. Nevertheless, if religious and political types are assumed to be lumped together
under "personal" grants and if these are then ignored and only Village
Police (kattubadi, etc.) and Service (Maniyam, etc.) Inams are counted,
the sum of separate holdings came to 21,220, amounting to 643,057 acres
and having a hypothetical tax of Rs. 7,29,859.[25]

C. "Social Service" Holdings:

As used here, the term "social service" can only have a very special and
limited meaning. Within the context of high social segmentation, social
exclusion, and social (ritual) pollution, "social services" were severely restricted, being reserved only for the "clean" and often only for the Brahman
elements of the population. While there was no "public" nor any "society"
in the modern, Western sense, there were many societies or many communities
structurally and spatially separated by varying degrees of social distance.
For a multi-faceted "plural society," service and charity had to be restricted
to what was provided by each community for its own members. But political
recognition of the economic (or agrarian) means for providing service was
essential to the preservation of privileged status. In general terms, therefore,
inams granted and maintained for the support of eleemosynary institutions
(as pertaining to "mercy," to "alms"; hence "grace and favor," "charitable"
and/or "social service" institutions) were also known by their older,
Sanskritic name as *"Dharmadayam"* holdings. But the connotations attaching
to older Hindu institutions carried a very different meaning from the comparatively more simple Arabic term *"ina'ām."*

The numbers and names of inams coming under this general description
were indeed many. But for simple convenience, this confusing variety can
be broken down into several sub-categories, as follows: (1) *Chattrams*
(*"Choultries"* or *Chavadi*)—rest or guest houses or traveler's bungalows
(i.e., caravanserais) placed at suitable intervals along roads, providing
halting places for the accommodation of pilgrims and travelers; (2) *Nirrlu-
Pandals*—giving water for the hot and thirsty; (3) *Topes*—groves of trees
giving shade and refreshment to wayfarers; (4) *Nandavanams*—flower
gardens for local village and temple festivities; (5) Wells, ponds, tanks, and
canals for giving water to the weary; and (6) *Patashalas* (usually *Veda
Pata shalas*)—schools for teaching the Vedas to village lads of clean caste.
While references in records are spotty, inams for hospitals (called *lungar-
khanas*) have also been found. (Altogether, along with other miscellaneous
inams, the number of Dharmadayam holdings listed in 1869 came to about
5,600. These covered at least 156,949 acres and were capable of producing
a hypothetical revenue of Rs. 3,07,912.)[26] When compared, not surprisingly, almost all such grants may be seen to have a common purpose—
namely, to provide rest and refreshment to weary strangers. In a severe
tropical climate where sun and heat have always been dangerous to the

health of travelers (or to anyone too long exposed), the giving of water and shade could be considered as acts of simple mercy and kindness. Such meritorious acts could serve to fulfil the requirements of righteous duty (dharmadayam).[27]

D. Socio-Economic Holdings:

Economic development being ever in the interests of an efficient, revenue-hungry political system, especially in a relatively static traditional agrarian economy—where water supply was crucial—it should not seem strange that inams were established for the specific purpose of developing and maintaining irrigation systems. The history of such establishments and of irrigation technology in South India is very old; and some knowledge about it is fairly common (if not yet thorough nor too accurate). We do know that in many places, from times unknown, responsibilities for irrigation had been borne by many villages themselves; but, in others, kings and princes had of necessity been obliged to step in so that regularity or expansion of productive capacity could be assured. Regular revenues called for regular water supplies. Regular water supplies called for regular expenditures for development and maintenance. Expenditures subtracted from revenues, especially if institutionalized permanently through hereditary grants of land, were a convenient way of removing burdens of administration from a central government and throwing them upon local government. In many areas, but especially in Rayalasima and Baramahal, inam grants of this nature were called "dasbhandams."

Dasbhandams were an institutionalized form of incentive or of hereditary remuneration to local leaders for the maintenance of water works. Thereby, village leaders were responsible: for making tanks and tank bunds (earthen and/or stone dams or wires were thrown across shallow streams or field-excavated catchment basins so as to form man-made lakes and reservoirs which could serve for storage of monsoon rainwater); for digging wells from which, by utilizing many forms of technology for the harnessing of animal and human power, water could be raised; for building aquaducts, channels, and canals so as to sustain a regular flow of water into the fields and topes; and for constructing *anicuts*, some small and simple and others very large and elaborate, across rivers in order to save, utilize, and regulate waterflow into networks of irrigation canals. Theoretically at least, no water from earth or sky was to be wasted.

Depending upon the extent and value of capital invested and upon the expected returns in revenue, irrigation inams were of two kinds: (1) "*Khanda Dasabhandams*" were grants given to specific localities for specific purposes; and (2) "*Shamilat Dasabhandams*" were deductible allowances, usually calculated as a proportion cut out of the fruits of each year's production to cover the costs of irrigation works and water supplies but actually also realized as a grant of inam land. The latter variety, not always registered nor easily identifiable by locality, may very well have been in existence prior to the rise of larger political systems. Indeed, the oldest may well have originated with the very genesis of settled agriculture (in the Kaveri River Delta and Valley), at the very dawn of Dravidian Civilization. Whatever the case, however, before the Company came to power, ordinary *dasabhandars* (by whatever name) had long been obliged to maintain their respective works of irrigation.[28] Lack of enforcement and supervision or lapses of hegemony had often meant, however, that such holdings as these inams had simply reverted into forms of hereditary local privilege, enhanced or depressed by the efficiency and skill of the local village culture and its leaders. (By the time accurate information for the whole Madras Presidency was compiled and reported in 1869, in which registration still may not have been complete, there were 6,938 separate inams for irrigation works. These took up 24,824 acres of land and had a hypothetical revenue potential of Rs. 1,40,715.)[29]

Connected to irrigation works was another equally large if not larger category known as *maramat*. In time this evolved and became synonymous with "Public Works" and, as such, covered responsibility for the engineering and technology of constructing and maintaining all government buildings, bridges, roads, culverts, dams, and the like. Revenues and expenditures under this heading are a complicated subject; moreover, the history of this subject is a separate study, too large to be touched upon here. It seems clear, however, that maramat and irrigation questions were so closely intertwined at the local level that there may well have been some *maramat-inams*. Indeed, district records of the late eighteenth and early nineteenth centuries reveal as much. Be that as it may, this aspect of inam holdings must remain in darkness until further studies have been completed.

II

Having defined the term *"ina'ām,"* described its usage and application within the records of the East India Company in South India, and differentiated some of the main categories in which it was functioning at the time when British officers of the Company found themselves coming increasingly into the political control and administration of local districts within the Carnatic, we can return to the central question—namely, of the historical significance of inams. Why was the "Inam Settlement" so important to the establishment of Company authority in the Carnatic? A careful examination of local records for each district and of documents left by those most closely connected to the "settlements" or contractual agreements made with leadership in each locality reveals a persistent and nagging preoccupation with inam questions.[30] Such collections of private papers as have been found—admittedly there are not many—seem to corroborate this concern. The Munro Papers, for example, are loaded with long listings and careful accountings of village inams, page after page, written in Munro's own hand.[31] Lists for the Baramahal; lists for Canara; lists for the Rayalasima (Ceded Districts); lists for Coimbatore; lists for the South-western Deccan, dispatched along with helpful suggestions to Mountstuart Elphinstone, the newly appointed Governor of Bombay charged with establishing British administration over the recently acquired territories of the Marathas—Munro spent a lifetime under canvas carefully record-ing the results of his conversations with local leaders. Why was there this constant preoccupation with inams? And why, when thorough and complete information in the form of detailed registers were repeatedly requested by the Madras Board of Revenue, were thorough inam reports never sub-mitted to the Madras authorities?

One possible answer to this question might suggest a combination of local evasion (by village leaders) with local ignorance (by European officers). Evidence of local evasion and local ignorance is certainly overwhelming. But this answer, for all the evidence in its favor, seems far too simple. Not all local leaders and Native servants of the Company were evasive; nor were all Europeans ignorant. Sir Thomas Munro and many men of his coterie certainly were not ignorant. Again, one must perceive that deliberate "non-policy" is indeed "policy," whether or not this arises from ignorance, neglect, incompetence, or non-interference with the status quo. In other words, a "non-settlement," for purposes of this study, can be seen as a "settlement," as a deliberate and tacit agreement to keep Company hands off inams and, by and large, to leave inams alone.

Thus, when in 1800, after establishing Company rule in Canara, he was put in charge of the newly acquired territories of the Ceded Districts (of Rayalasima)—Company claims based on sanads concluded with Hyderabad and Poona and on conquests and negotiations after the final Mysore War —Munro accomplished the seemingly impossible. He was able to arrange a political settlement with each of the important leaders and lords of the villages, the *gramma-doralu* (or *rayalu:* "potails" and "kadeem rayats" he wrote of them and most of them were Reddis and other Sat-Sudras). He could turn his forces against poliyagars and petty rajas who resisted the Company. Poliyagars, much like *pindaris* a dozen years later or like *dacoits* still later, had by their predatory and plundering habits become a bane to many villagers. Munro was able to form alliances with village leaders of Rayalasima; moreover he was able to codify these into more permanent political arrangements after the fighting was over. All too grate-ful to see peace established where it had not been known in living memory, the Madras Government wasted little time in accepting his "settlements." Munro's contribution was gratefully acknowledged.[32] It was not the first nor would it be the last time he received such public recognition; indeed, his great reputation and fame dates from this time.

But what was this settlement, these agreements with each village? Here-tofore, scholars and administrators have emphasized the three major "land settlements" or, more properly, systems of settlement:[33] (1) the Zamindari Settlement (also called the "Permanent" or "Cornwallis" Settlement, although Wellesley and Clive introduced its variant form in Madras Presidency;[34] (2) the Gramawari Settlement (known also as the "Village People," "Village Lease," or "Joint-Contract"; and as "Mahalwari" in the north);[35] and (3) the Ryotwari Settlement (occasionally called *"Kulwari"* and other names).[36]

The Ryotwari Settlement eventually became known as the Munro System.[37] Sir Thomas Munro had become convinced of its superiority when he had worked with Colonel Alexander Read in the establishment of Company authority and administration in the Baramahal (later known Coimbatore and Salem Districts).[38] Experiments at that time had convinced him of the political wisdom of ryotwari. On the basis of such experience he introduced the ryotwari system into Cuddapah and the other Ceded Districts.[39] Despite strenuous efforts by the Madras Board of Revenue to impose the Village (Gramawari) System in its place, Munro's arguments ultimately prevailed in London and his system was ratified.[40] When Munro was made Governor of Madras in 1820, he was able to see his system re-established virtually throughout the Presidency or, that is, wherever Zamindari Settlements were not already in force.

But was ryotwari the whole settlement? The central argument of this study is that it was not. On the basis of available documents one can at least infer a hypothesis that the Ryotwari Settlement was only half of the settlement with leaders and elite groups in each of the villages of South India. Implicit if not very explicit in the contents of the records is a faint if unmistakable shadow, a lurking suspicion that Munro reached separate, quiet agreements with village leaders. One or two at a time, he seems to have met them and concluded very personal political pacts. If village leaders would join him, he would support them. If village lords would work with him, the Madras Government would honor his word and would work directly with them. On such a pledge he would stand surety. If those who held privileged positions and inam lands, derived from ancient "right," would remain faithful to the Circari Company's salt, hereditary privileges would be guaranteed and preserved in perpetuity. But let a poliyagar or a village *dora* turn against Munro and, thereby, against the Company; and then there surely would be no mercy. Hereditary privileges and inams, however old they might be or however noble or valid the strength of their authority, would then be forfeited and lost forever. Inferences drawn from contents of special local regulations and from Munro's private papers, however hazardously one might draw them, seem to show that Munro made a personal *"inamdari settlement"* with the leaders of each village; that he confirmed them in their land holdings and positions of power; and that, thereby, he recognized inams as the perquisites of hereditary privilege. In short, his inamdari settlements became the obverse, silent, or dark side of the Ryotwari Settlement; and hence, they became part and parcel of the overall constitutional structure of the political system. This system was based upon contracts with each village leader. It rested upon the cultural and political consensus of the village community. Hereditary privilege, hallowed by tradition, was enthroned among agrarian warriors of clean caste. Henceforth and for a century or more, families of such elite groups would enjoy tax-free tenures to lands of great value. Their descendants would hold wholly or partially tax-exempt properties and powers over landless laboring classes of low caste; and they would hold these privileges in perpetuity.

What then was the significance of the "Silent Settlement?" One can contend that it was an important foundation stone if not the secret spring of Company power in South India. Through the Inam Settlement, the British secured the allegiances and loyalties of so many local elite groups that thereafter only pockets of resistance and rebellion or occasional disturbances from small groups or from transient or superficial forces ever ruffled the peace in South India; moreover, each localized instance of unrest could be carefully isolated and its causes studied and then effectively remedied.

One way to measure the significance of inams is to see how extensive they were and how large was their proportion to the whole of State revenues. It is difficult to find exact figures for all of the Company's southern domains in the early years of its paramountcy. Rough calculations taken from Munro's accounts for the Ceded Districts seem to indicate that inam lands constituted one-sixth of the total area under cultivation and that such lands were worth somewhere between one-fourth and one-third of estimated total revenue resources for those districts (11,85,195-29-09 *pagodas* out of 39,54,417-23-70 pagodas.)[41] Not until after the Company had been abolished and the Madras Inam Commission was finally established (16th November 1858) did a really sustained and systematic attempt to get accurate information for the whole Presidency begin. After many delays and difficulties, the Commission's Report did not emerge until the 30th October 1869. How accurately this report reflected the realities of inam holdings in its own day, much less threw light upon the realities of 1800, and how much change might have occurred, whether in further alienation and encroachment upon taxable lands, has not and perhaps cannot be ascertained.

Whatever the case, the importance of inam holdings became clear. This can be seen from summary figures contained in the Chart taken from the Commission's report. In 1869, inam holdings amounted to over six million acres of the richest, most cultivable, best watered lands in the Presidency. The assessed value of these holdings—their hypothetical loss of revenues to the State—came to nearly a crore, four-fifths of which was actually alienated from revenue rolls or entirely free of taxation. There were 367,427 separate holdings; and 346,473 of these were in "private" hands of individual families.[42] (If ever a case could be made for the existence of true "private property" in India this was it.) In proportion to the whole of State revenues, one can estimate that inams amounted roughly to one-tenth, more in some districts and less in others. Preservation of such perquisities for the privileged elites of the South can perhaps show or explain in some measure how Company authority became so firmly established. So much satisfaction enjoyed in perpetuity by so many leaders could argue very strongly and silently for maintaining security and status quo. (Not surprisingly, one can understand why sparks from the Great Rebellion of 1857 had little effect in the South.)

Another hint of the significance of inams is found in the Report of the Inam Commissioner. He wrote that the arrangements which had been in operation for over sixty years were perhaps too delicate to touch. "The subject was so fraught with important social and political consequences that...it was considered unsafe..." to probe into it too deeply. "The prescriptive right of the people in a vast mass of valuable property [had been], scrupulously respected and confirmed in perpetuity."[43] Lessons from the Cuddapah Rebellion in 1846 showed what might result from tampering with inams.[44] Such events reinforced the inam system, buttressed conservative attitudes, and strengthened resistance to change. After the Cuddapah Rebellion had been suppressed and its leader, Narasimha Reddy, had been executed, Company policy on inams was succinctly summarized in views expressed by the Honorable Court of Directors and dispatched from London in 1849:

that long undisturbed possession not only affords evidence of the existence of the right, but moreover, with respect especially to landed property, and to tenures affecting whole classes of persons, it creates, on considerations equally of policy and of justice, a powerful motive with Government for not wishing the possession to be disturbed.[45]

Clearly, the "Silent Settlement" was an important component in the constitution of the British Raj in South India—a constitution depending heavily upon a silent consensus between the government and the governed.

NOTES

1. Materials for this study were gathered while the author was engaged in research under grants from the John Simon Guggenheim Foundation from the American Philosophical Society, and from the Graduate School of the University of Wisconsin. Grateful acknowledgement is due to these institutions and to many individual colleagues.

The main theme of this essay, however, comes out of nearly two decades of reflection on the subject. The essay itself is a "spin-off" from a paper presented at the Duke University Symposium on Realm and Region in Pre-Industrial India, April 13-15, 1973, organized by Richard G. Fox (and soon to be published in a volume edited by him). A preliminary draft, moreover, was read at the International Congress of Orientalists in Paris, 15-22 July 1973.

2. A full treatment of this process in its development over centuries as seen from the perspective of a local village lord can be found in the *Memoir on the Internal Revenue System of Madras,* submitted by Bundla Ramasawmy Naidoo on 1st January 1820 and published in the *Selections from the Records of the South Arcot District,* vol. 2 (Madras, 1908). This rare document is found in the India Office Records (London) [cited hereafter as IOR].

3. Two works in particular serve to document and exemplify this process of "discovery" and adaptation, especially as it developed in the oldest Company holdings along the Coromandel: J. Talboys Wheeler, *Madras in Olden Times, 1639-1727* (Madras, 1861-62), in three volumes of details extracted from Fort St. George Records; and Henry D. Love, *Vestiges*

of Old Madras (London, 1913), in four volumes of the same. Numerous diaries of such long-time residents as Streynsham Master and Niccolo Mannuchi, when carefully sifted, reinforce this generalization.

4. Elaboration on this development is well set forth in two recent works. J. Duncan M. Derrett, *Religion, Law and the State in India* (London, 1968), provides a trove of analysis and reference. Especially useful, for our purposes, are Chapter 8, "The British as Patrons of the Sastra" (pp. 225-73); Chapter 9, "The Administration of Hindu Law By the British" (pp. 274-320); and Chapter 10, "The Codification of Hindu Law" (pp. 321-51). B.N. Pandey, *The Introduction of English Law into India* (London, 1967) focuses upon some pivotal episodes in the eighteenth century.

5. The best, most useful work on developing precedent which I have found is Sir Courtenay Ilbert's, *The Government of India: A Historical Survey* (Oxford, 1922), with its companion volume of charters, sanads, and statute law. More difficult to use is the classic work by Arthur Berriedale Keith, *A Constitutional History of India: 1600-1935* (London, 1936).

6. A.J. Arbuthnot, ed., *Sir Thomas Munro: Selections from His Minutes and Other Official Writings*, 2 vols. (London, 1881), 1:237, "On the State of the Country and the Condition of the People".

7. H.H. Wilson, *A Glossary of Judicial and Revenue Terms, and of Useful Words in Official Documents, Relating to the Administration of British India* . . . (London, 1855), pp. 217-18.

8. H.H. Wilson, ibid., is the standard reference for all such terms; but other manuals and gazetteers, especially those locally compiled, are of great value. Another standard reference, Henry Yule and A.C. Burnell, *Hobson-Jobson: A Glossary of Colloquial Anglo-Indian Words and Phrases and of Kindred Terms, Etymological, Historical, Geographical and Discursive* (London, 1886; 1968), is also very useful.

9. Recent research by Richard Eaton, "The Sufis of Bijapur: A Study in the Social History of Muslim Saints in Medieval South India" (Ph. D. diss., Univ. of Wis. 1972), contains a chapter on inams. Also see his, "The Court and the Dargah in the Seventeenth Century Deccan," *Indian Economic and Social History Review* (March 1973). Also see John F. Richards, "Mughal Rule in Golconda: 1687-1724" (Ph.D. diss., Univ. of Calif. 1970), pages on inam policies of Emperor Aurangzeb.

10. Some samples: "Memorial from the Dhurmakurtas of a Pagoda at Conjeveram, praying for the restoration of an allowance formerly enjoyed by them," enclosed with Madras Board of Revenue [Cited hereafter as MBOR] Letter, 10 Nov. (No. 53) 1846, "Board's Collections" 106.850, in IOR, 36 pp.; "Memorial from the Tengala Community of the Sreerungum Pagoda complaining of the infringement of certain privileges enjoyed by them in that Pagoda by people of the Vadagala Sect.," in MBOR, 8 July (46) 1848, "Board's Collections" no. 115.486, 187 pp.; "Reports from charitable grants by former Governments and the extent of the endowments derived therefrom," in MBOR, 24 Sept. (46) 1842, "Board's Collections" no. 90.134, 47 pp., IOR; "Disposal of Pagoda Endowments under the Management of the Officers of Government," Madras Public Dept., Despatch of 12 May (26) 1858, Madras Despatches, no. 500, IOR; "The continuance of the original allowance of Rupees 7 per mensam for teaching the Koran at Ongole," Board's Collections no. 90.136, IOR. C.D. Maclean, *Manual of the Administration of the Madras Presidency*, 3 vols. (Madras, 1886) 2: 61-62: "Public Endowments." From the Inam Records of the Madras Record Office (Tamilnadu Archives), I have collected several dozen documents, some for each district, giving the number, character, and value of inams within that district. By 1857, reports on inam enquiries began to appear in *Parliamentary Papers*, House of Commons Paper no. 143 (Sess. I., Returns, etc., 1859.) vol. 18, p. 1 ff.

11. Arbuthnot, ed., *Sir Thomas Munro*, 1:136-63: "Altamgha inams," which means "Red Seal" for a royal (Mughal or princely) inam. District records show disputes over inams occurring almost every year. Attempts to control inams were not successful. Cf. R.E. Frykenberg, *Guntur District, 1788-1848: A History of Local Influence on Central Authority* (Oxford-1965), pp. 37-38, 49, 57-58, 60-62, 215-16. By the 1840s, the Government began to push on the "inam question." MBOR, 21 August (34) 1843, "Board's Collections" no. 93.761), IOR, contains proceedings with respect to investigation into the validity of inam tenures of the Ceded Districts. MBOR, "Board's Collections" nos. 92, 225, and 123.405, IOR, put forward further measures for inam control and control of inam disputes.

12. *Inam Commission Report* [Cited hereafter as INR]. W.T. Blair (Officiating Inam Commissioner) to R.A. Dalyell (Acting Secretary to Government, Revenue Department, Fort Saint George), Madras, 30th October 1869, Appendix B., pp. 29-41.

13. S. Sundararaja Iyengar, *Land Tenures in the Madras Presidency, Student's Edition* (Madras, 1933), p. 111; *INR*, p. 1, para 3; C.D. Maclean, *Manual of the Administration of the Madras Presidency, In Illustration of the Records of Government*, 3 vols. (Madras,

1885-93), 2:166, note on the "Origin of Inams."

15. Robert Sewell, *Archaeological Survey of Southern India: List of the Antiquarian Remains in the Presidency of Madras*, 2 vols. (Madras, 1882-1884), Scores of sample inscriptions can be found on any page. Also see: Robert Sewell and S.K. Aiyangar, *The Historical Inscriptions of Southern India* (Madras 1932).

16. P.R. Ganapathi Iyer, *The Law Relating to Hindu and Mahomedan Religious Endowments* . . . (Madras, 1905), pp. xv-xx, indicates that such grants were never temporary, but perpetual and irresumable, that their great antiquity is attested on copper plates, and that religious penalties attached to any act of resumption. "In short the diety of the temple is considered in Hindu Law as a sacred entity or an ideal personality possessing proprietary rights," or "The idol is a juridical person capable to of holding property... ."

17. Maclean, *Manual*, 2:168. Also see *INR*, p. 12, para 42.

18. *Ibid.* Also: Sundararaja Iyenger, *Land Tenure in the Madras Presidency*, pp. 111-26; P.R. Ganapathi Iyer, *Law Relating to . . . Religious Endowments*, pp. xci-cxiii, Chapter VIII: "Examples of Hindu Religious Endowments—Temples and Mutts." This accords with a general description of the 18th century, as found in Abbe Du Bois, *Manners, Customs and Ceremonies* . . . (3rd ed., Oxford, 1968), pp. 577-88. Detailed studies of large temple institutions may be seen in Burton Stein's incisive "Economic Functions of a Medieval South Indian Temple," *Journal of Asian Studies* 9 (1960), and "The State, the Temple and Agricultural Development in Medieval South India," *Economic Weekly Annual* (1961). These articles are drawn from research on the Tirupati Temple, as embodied in Stein's Ph.D. Dissertation (Chicago, 1958).

19. Ganapathi Iyer, *Law Relating to . . . Religious Endowments*, xci-xliii: Chapter VIII: "Examples of Hindu Religious Endowments: Temples & Mutts"; Chapter IX: "Examples of Mahomedan Religious Endowments:—Durgas, Khankas, Mosques, etc."; Chapters X & XI: Special References to the Law of Waqfs.

Sir S. Subrahmanya Ayyar, "Application of the Surplus Funds of Public Religious Endowments Towards the Promotion of National Education," (Madras, A Tract dated April 1918), pp. 1-11, 13, gives a clear explanation of the historical role of these institutions.

20. Sundararaja Iyengar, *Land Tenures in the Madras Presidency*, Chapter VI: "Personal Grants," pp. 127-37.

21. *INR*, p. 13, para 49, and appended table of inam tenures. Also, Maclean, *Manual* 2:168-69.

22. Sundararaja Iyengar, *Land Tenure in the Madras Presidency*, Chapter VII: "Service Grants," pp. 139-61, gives us a good general description of these tenures. The records are so loaded with these intricate positions and functions that it is pointless to cite evidence. However, two printed selections from the records serve as excellent samples: Bundla Ramasawmy Naidoo, *Memoir on the Internal Revenue System of Madras, 1820* (Madras, 1908); and "Report on the Triuvendipuram Farm, 1775, from Charles Hyde, Collector for South Arcot, Cuddalore, 30 June 1775," IOR.

23. Sundararaja Iyengar, *Land Tenure in the Madras Presidency*, pp. 140-41.

24. Ibid., pp. 144-55. See: *INR*, "Descriptive List of the Inam Tenures of the Madras Presidency," Appendix B. This is alphabetical.

25. Ibid., pp. 14-17, paras, 51-65, and table on pp. 18-19.

26. Ibid., table on pp. 18-19.

27. All of the sources given elaborate on some aspect of these grants, but the best comprehensive description of various categories is found in the "Descriptive List of the Inam Tenures of Madras Presidency," in Appendix B of INR.

28. Sundararaja Iyengar, *Land Tenure in the Madras Presidency*, pp. 143-44; *INR*, p. 13, para 47.

29. Ibid.

30. The author has personally investigated the manuscript records for most of the districts of the Presidency, especially those of Arcot, Baramahal, Coimbatore, Dindigul, Ganjam, Guntur, Masulipatam, Nellore, Tinnevelly (Tirunelveli), and Tanjore (Tanjavur), to name just a few, for the period from the 1780s to 1860 in particular. See Frykenberg, *Guntur District*, pp. 37-38, 57-58, 215.

31. Munro Collection, IOL, Uncatalogued Eur. MSS.: "Statement of Enam Land in the Ceded Districts Showing the quantity in acres and the assessment by survey," undated, in 157 columns, 22 foolscap sheets of handwritten accounts, serves as the most fulsome example of his work.

32. Arbuthnot, ed., *Sir Thomas Munro*, 1:ixxxix-cxx, "Memoir" on the Life of Sir Thomas Munro, especially Lord William Bentinck's letter of 30 July 1807. This Memoir was also separately published. See also: Glieg, *The Life and Death of Major-General Sir Thomas Munro*, 3 vols. (London, 1830-31), 2:237-50.

33. B.H. Baden-Powell, *Manual of Land Revenue Systems and Land Tenures of British India*, 3 vols. (Calcutta & Oxford, 1882, 1894), is the classic, along with John Kaye, *Administration of the East India Company* (London, 1853). *Selection of Papers from the*

Records at the East-India House Relating to the Revenue Police and Civil and Criminal Justice under the Company's Government in India, 4 vols (London, 1820-26). A remarkably complete collection of documents arguing the relative merits of each settlement-system is found in the Parliamentary investigations connected to the Company's Charter renewal for 1833. House of Commons, *Minutes of Evidence taken befor the Select Committee on the Affairs of the East India Company and also on Appendix and Index.* III. Revenue, Parliamentary Papers, vol 12, pp. 1-436 Cf. pp. 358 ff., especially Appendix No. 98., pp. 411-36.

34. For Zamindari Settlement, see: S. Gopal, *The Permanent Settlement of Bengal and its Results* (London, 1949); Ranjit Guha, *A, Rule of Property for Bengal: An Essay on the Idea of Permanent Settlement* (Paris, 1963); F.D. Ascoli, *Early Revenue History of Bengal and the Fifth Report, 1812* (Oxford, 1917), B.S. Baliga, "Home Government and the end of the policy of permanent Settlement in Madras, 1802-1818," *Indian Historical Records Commission Proceedings 19* (1942) and his unpublished Ph. D. thesis on the same, "The Influence of the Home Government on Land Revenue and Judicial Administration in the Presidency of Fort William in Bengal from 1097 to 1822" (Univ. of London, 1933); H.R.C. Wright, "Some Aspects of the Permanent Settlement in Bengal," *Economic History Review,* 7, ser. 2 (1954).

35. For the Gramawari or Village Settlement, see: B.S. Baliga, "Village Settlement of Land Revenue in Madras, 1807-22,' *Indian Historical Reeords Commission Proceedings* 21 (1944); and to some degree Johan Matthai, *Village Government in British India* (London, 1915).

36. For the Ryotwari Settlement. see: Nilmani Mukherjee, *The Ryotwari System in Madras 1792-1827* (Calcutta; 1962); T.H. Beaglehold, *Thomas Munro and the Development of Administrative Policy in Madras: 1792-1818: The Origins of "The Munro System"* (Chambrige, 1966); K.N. Vankataubba Sastri, *The Munro System of British Statesmanship in India* (Mysore, (1939); and an unpublished D. Phil. thesis on the same by K.K. Pillai, "Local self-Government in the Madras Presidency, 1850-1910" (Oxford, 1946).

37. *Ibid.*, especially works of T.H. Beaglehold, N. Mukherjee, and K.N,V. Sastri.

38. *Ibid. Baramahal Records 1792-1799,* 13 vols (Madras, 1913); Arbuthnot., ed., *Sir Thomas Munro* 1: 1-54; "The Revenue Settlement of Salem District." James Ballantine Dykes, *Salem: an Indian Collectorate* (London, 1853).

39. *Ibid.* Arbuthnot. ed. *Sir Thomas Munro,* 1: 92-116, "On the Relative Advantages of the Ryotwari and Zamindari Systems, and other reports.

40. Minutes of the Board of Revenue, 5th January 1818: House of Commons, *Minutes of Evidence, Parliamentry Papers,* 1831-32 (735-III), vol. 12, pp. 405-436, and 387 ff.: "Translation of Answers... dated 2nd August 1814, by B. Sancarraya, late Sheristadar to the Collector of Madras, this is an adjunct to testimony by F.W, Ellis on "Meerassy Right." See also pp. 414 (para 17) 422 ff. 429-33, 435-36. The Madras Board of Revenue used contrary arguments to show that village leaders and perquisites were undermined by ryotwari.

41. "Statement of Enam Land...," in Munro Collection, IOL, Uncatalogued Eur. MSS., compared with "Abstract Statement of the Measurement and Assessment of the Land of the Ceded District," A pagoda is a small gold coin with the device of a temple on its face. The star pagoda of Madras was equal to roughly Rs. 3.5 silver or Rs. 5. gold.

42. INR, pp. 18-19. Broken down in Appendix C.

43. Ibid., p. 21, para. 72 & 73.

44. Catherine Margaret Sandin, "The Cuddapah Rebellion of 1846" (M.A. thesis, Univ. of Wis. 1973), has made a thorough investigation of the question of its cosequences.

45. Court of Directors to Government of Madras, 13 October 1847, *Madras Despatches,* IOL, IOR. Also see: "Fourth Report; Enams. On The Laws that Govern Exempted Lands, Grants, Pensions, in the Madras Presidency" dated 17th December 1855, by H. Stokes, *INR*, Appendix, p. 83, para 20.

Privileged Land Tenure in
Village India in the
Early Nineteenth Century

ERIC STOKES

THIS paper poses two questions. Why was revenue-free or revenue-privileged tenure in the form of inam or *lakhiraj* land apparently far less extensive in northern than in other parts of India? What role did such tenure play at the village level?

Straight political and historical considerations doubtless supply part of the answer to the first question. The North felt the full weight of Muslim imperial power over a protracted period and so was precluded from the massive alienation of revenue-bearing land to Hindu temples that occurred in the far South. Even so, religious and charitable inam in the Madras Presidency, when at last brought to book in the 1860s, proved to be only a quarter or so of total inam, the great bulk of which—that is, some three-fifths—was by this time classified as personal inam.[1] But allowing the historical argument its fullest scope, it may still be urged that the survival of extensive revenue-free or favorably rated land into the mid-nineteenth century is to be explained by the particular form of the initial colonial impact rather than by endemic differences in the pre-colonial period. While settling at first with a heterogeneous mass of revenue-engagers (*malguzars*), the British in the North, in the Ceded and Conquered Provinces, recognized in effect only two superior tenures—the temporary revenue farm and the proprietary zamindari right (of which the *taluqdari* was merely a later refinement).[2] Privileged superior tenures like jagirs, *jaedads, mukararis, istimraris,* and he like, were bundled roughly into one of these two forms, and hence rapidly disappeared. Practice was different in other Presidencies. Despite the éclat of the ryotwari system, a considerable proportion of the Deccan territories of the Bombay Presidency was left as jagir and so was classified as inam. In the Madras Presidency a substantial amount of intermediary privileged tenures—such as jagirs belonging to relatives and dependents of great zamindars and poliyagars—were left untouched, although the greater part of the superior tenures were subsumed under straight zamindari tenure.

Allowing for the better survival of the upper privileged tenures in the West and South of India—by 1900 almost half the 7.75 million acres of inam at Madras consisted of whole villages[3]—it would still appear that at the village level inam played a much more important role in the Bombay and Madras territories than in the North. Why was this? Why should village inam have been a minor feature in the North and a common occurrence elsewhere? How far were differences of basic tenure a decisive influence? Baden-Powell has rightly taught us to draw a sharp distinction between the "joint landlord" village of the North and the ryotwar form prevailing elsewhere. The characteristic of the one was the existence of a dominant body of kinsmen, exercising the political and revenue management, claiming proprietary dominion of the culturable waste, and enjoying an economic superiority over other ryots by the levy of rental payments from them in a quasi-landlord role. These rental payments might be enjoyed in common or in severalty, or both, the joint character of the tenure arising not from joint ownership but from joint management and joint responsibility for the revenue demand. The characteristic of the ryotwar village, in contrast, was the existence of a number of dominant office-holding families, one of which traditionally exercised political and revenue control as village head, subject to recognition by the ruling power. Government levied the revenue demand in detail on the individual ryots without the interposition of any joint landlord body and controlled the renting out of the waste. The village elite clustered not around landlord profits but around office and its perquisites. The key offices were those of headman (*patel, reddi, kapu, naidu*) and accountant (*karnam, kulkarni*); their perquisites were partly dues in cash and kind (*haqs*) and partly in revenue-exempt or revenue-privileged land (manyam, wattandar inam). In short, village service inam was integral to the ryotwar village. Baden-Powell had to admit at once that his models were too tightly drawn, that joint-landlord tenures in the form of *mirasi* right were widespread throughout western and southern India, and that conversely in the North the Mughal revenue system was constantly striving to get behind the landlord body and become ryotwar.[4] Allowing for some measure of geographical intermixture, how far were the two types mutually exclusive?

At first glance some forms of mirasi tenure in western and southern India look remarkably analogous to the joint tenures of the North. This is particularly true of the Tamil country where "office mirasi," the property in village office and its perquisites, gave way to "landed mirasi," that is, direct proprietary dominion over the land. Here there was a right not merely to engage for the Government revenue but also to appropriate a landlord's share of the produce (*tunduvaram*) from the subordinate ryots. Such mirasdars claimed joint ownership or control of the village, including the arable waste, and accepted joint responsibility for revenue payment. Landed mirasi could vary, as in northern India, between joint undivided tenure and complete severalty, the latter tending to prevail in mirasi villages south of the Coleroon River. Moreover, where landed mirasi was to be found, the system of village officers supported by office mirasi seems to have been weakest. In Tanjore, where a landlord's rent of a quarter of the produce was reported in 1818, *karnika* mirasi (the village accountant's proprietary haqs and inams) was nonexistent, as indeed was the office of headman itself. At the same time, the Madras Board of Revenue stated that in "Tondai Mandalam [Chingleput and N. and S. Arcot] or anywhere east of the Payenghaut" the patel and his office were generally absent.[5] Apparently the internal structures of the ryotwar and the joint-landlord village could not co-exist together.

Would it then be true to say that village inam appeared on a significant scale only where landed mirasi did not occur, or where it had been so reduced by overassessment as to be nugatory? There is a good deal to support this argument and its presupposition that inam was an escape mechanism for a village elite denied landlord profits or wilting under an excessive revenue demand. The existence of substantial landed mirasi in a region like Tanjore, which also had a fairly high amount of inam, does not confute this. For there is every reason to believe that landlord rights, which were here of a muted kind, were not characteristic of areas in which there was substantial inam. Landed mirasi in southern India conferred a much more limited landlord right than the joint tenure of northern India, and even in Tanjore was largely confined to the area under wet cultivation. Here the ruling power had always maintained a close involvement in the village through its provision of irrigation works and its collection of land revenue in kind. It also never surrendered its rights to interfere in the disposal of the waste. While personal inam was found on a moderately extensive scale in Tanjore, it is noticeable that two-thirds of such inam rested on sanad grants from the raja, that such grants consisted for the most part of entire villages, and that two-thirds of such villages were situated in the dry highland taluk of Pattukkotai, often paying a heavy jodi or quit-rent and clearly owing their origin to the raja's efforts to open up the waste.[6] In this sense they simply followed the pattern of other mirasi villages, not reckoned as inam, which had originated as *agraharams* for Brahman or Vellalar colonists. Inam was, therefore, largely separate from the ordinary village structure; it was a device for encouraging colonization rather than one to escape the revenue demand.

North of Tanjore, however, matters were different. Here the mirasi right, whether landed or office mirasi, was unsaleable and practically worthless, so Munro claimed, the weight of the revenue demand having left the mirasdar paying higher rates than the temporary cultivator. Yet it is a curious and undoubtedly significant feature that where mirasi had least value and the revenue demand bore down at its heaviest, there privileged tenure in the shape of inam or favorably rated land was often at its most extensive. This was particularly true of the Ceded Districts of Bellary and Cuddapah. Here according to A.D. Campbell, writing in 1831, alienations were so extensive that the lands liable to the payment of the Government revenue were little more than half "or as 19 to 16 to those of which the entire Revenue has been alienated, in very small lots, by the Native Governments, chiefly to Brahmins or other individuals, on hereditary tenure denominated Enam."[7] It is true that a considerable portion of these alienations were taken up by grants made by poliyagars to *kuttabadis* or military and police peons in the hilly tracts. But village service inams were twice as large again.[8] The *Bellary Gazetteer* states that this formed the largest class of inam, amounting in 1862 to some 635,000 acres, or about one-sixth of the cultivated area. The conditions under which it was acquired were described by William Thackeray in 1807 in colorful terms. In the anarchy and plundering that prevailed from 1788 to 1799 "the Potail or the Kurnum acted like a little prince in his own village....In most parts of the Ceded Districts the Potail or head Rayet, and the Kurnum, so peaceable in our other provinces, had become captains of banditti garrisoning independent castles."[9] In these conditions one man's gain was another man's loss, and although inam functioned to preserve a village elite, that elite was doubtless subject to much internal revolution.

There was no doubt as to the function that inam was intended to play at the village level. "The possession of enam on such favourable terms," wrote Campbell in 1831, "enables the ryot more easily to pay the revenue of the fields he holds which are subject to public assessment." Munro had noted earlier: "The land held by bramins under the denomination of dhirmadey is chiefly cultivated by ryots who seldom pay the enaumdar more than a fourth or a fifth of the rent. In many villages these enaums are divided among the ryots, who allow the enaumdar only a small quit-rent, and regard the rest as their own from long possession."[10]

The historical conditions under which village inam appeared are clearly important. It could swell to the monstrous size it assumed in the Ceded Districts only when the authority of the ruling power to control revenue alienations had largely slipped away and the poliyagars felt strong enough to exercise such authority themselves. With the prospect of tight bureaucratic rule ahead there was every reason to secure and extend these encroachments in the confused conditions following the British takeover in the late eighteenth and early nineteenth century. They were far from confined to the Ceded Districts. In North Arcot and areas of the Northern Circars like Rajahmundry such encroachments are well attested. In 1857 the Madras Government estimated service inam to comprise some 40 percent of total revenue alienated, although much of this was later to be classified as personal inam.[11]

There were contrasts and parallels in the Bombay territories. Elphinstone found that more than half the revenue of the new Deccan conquests acquired from the Peshwa was alienated in jagir (some 65 out of 115 lakhs) and much of this he felt bound to confirm. In 1835 Col. W.H. Sykes wrote that in the Deccan the inam tenure was very extensive, pointing to 231 wholly alienated villages in the Poona collectorate and 581 partly alienated or *domala* villages in Ahmadnagar.[12] H.D. Robertson, the first collector of Poona, put the figure higher in 1821, finding almost a quarter of the 1,200-odd villages held in inam and accounting for some one-third of the total revenue. Henry Pottinger in Ahmadnagar district found the same proportion of alienation. Yet curiously the Bombay Government reported in 1823 that there was but little alienated land in the Deccan and that investigation into the validity of titles was not likely to be attended with much advantage.[13] What appears to have been implied was that the vast bulk of inam, even when in the shape of *umuls* or a fixed percentage of the revenue in Government villages, was held as a form of jagir by superior tenure holders, but otherwise, apart from the wholly alienated villages, inam did not figure significantly. In Poona district Robertson estimated that the 317-1/2 wholly alienated villages carried an assessment (*tunkha*) of Rs. 3,13,776 while the assessment of the extraneous inam and mokassa and jagir umuls came to no more than Rs. 38,258.[14] It is possible that village service inam was not included in this figure, but it is unlikely that encroachments had swelled this unduly. As Gooddine argued, the fate of the village patels must have varied enormously under the pressures they encountered in the later Maratha period, but political conditions were not such as to make possible substantial enlargement of village inam even for those most favorably placed. Poona was too close. Where the patel was not depressed but extended his sway, he appears to have enlarged his financial perquisites by selling vacant miras land (*gatkul* miras) and inflating village expenses. Gooddine's celebrated study of 33 villages of the Patoda taluk of Ahmadnagar district was undertaken in the mid-nineteenth century when admittedly circumstances had greatly changed and when for a lengthy period the patel's pickings had doubtless been pared right back. Gooddine's findings showed that in 1253 F.S. (1845-46 A.D.) the whole body of village officers, including the village servants, enjoyed fees and perquisites equivalent in value to 90 percent of the land revenue collections. Of the total income of the village officers some 11 percent came from commission on the revenue collections, some 43 percent from revenue remissions on inam land, and some 46 percent from haqs or traditional dues. Of this total sum the patel families received something over 10 percent, but since there were some 284 patel families in the 33 villages, the share of each amounted to no more than Rs. 14-13-0 per annum.[15]

Inam was greatest at the extremities of the Peshwa's dominions both to north and south. When Goldsmid took over as superintendent of the revenue survey in the Southern Mahratta Country he was startled at the enormous proportion of land held in alienation in the Dharwar and Belgam collectorates. Besides whole clusters (*mahals*) of alienations, comprising 12 to 25 villages each, he found about 700 entire villages in the government portion claimed as inam. In the remaining 2,452 villages left to Government, there were minor alienations comprising some 60,000 estates, "the share left for Government even in these its own villages, not averaging one half thereof."[16] Conditions at the time of British accession resembled those in the nearby Ceded Districts, but it is not clear how far village service inam was significant. In some areas, like Badami in Dharwar, excessively high quit-rents on village service lands suggest Maratha revenue farming may have depressed the chief village officers, or in other places the local petty notables (desais and despandiyas) had made good at their expense. But inam and privileged tenure clearly played an important part in the internal economy of the village.

As in the Ceded Districts, these were devices to help meet the demand on the overassessed *chali* or land under permanent cultivation (in the Ceded Districts, *upanum*); and similarly the ryot was compelled to cultivate parcels of both the highly and the lowly assessed soils.

At the other geographical extremity, in Gujarat, the extent of alienated land was again enormous. In Kaira district, Elphinstone estimated that some 10-1/2 lakhs of revenue had been alienated, which must have represented something like 40–50 percent of the total revenue assets. In Broach, Monier Williams reported in 1821 that nearly one-third of the cultivated area was exempt. There were many outward similarities with the Southern Mahratta Country. Much of the alienated area was composed of entire villages under the control of former warrior chieftains or turbulent groups (*grassias* and *kolis*), who also held partial rights in many of the Government villages. Because of the excessive alienation of land even in the Government villages, the full revenue-bearing or *talpad* lands (or at least the most fertile soils in continuous cultivation, known as *vaita*) carried a revenue rate that could go as high as Rs. 90 per bigah. So that again the ryot was compelled to hold a parcel of differently rated lands, among which the revenue-privileged inam land played a vital function in keeping him solvent. Yet the resemblance to conditions in the far south ceases at this point. For in much of Gujarat the patel was in the saddle. Securing the revenue farm he had largely succeeded in turning it into a form of *pattidari* property. Although there is some evidence that the patel families had extended their service inam (*pasaita*), as in the Nadiad parganna of Kaira district, they could look to more lucrative sources than inam or dipping their hand into the village expense account. Not only did they practice the illicit leasing out on mortgage of portions of the talpad, but their dominance was such that grassias and others had tamely to submit to the later reimposition of the full assessment on these lands, effectively cancelling out the mortgage interest. But of far greater significance was the development of the patel's office into a joint-landlord village structure in which the office-holding system characteristic of the ryotwar village withered away. In Broach, it is noticeable that the patel was the mere representative, or one of many muqaddam patel representatives, of the *bhagdars,* and according to Monier Williams he derived no profit and held no land as a reward for office.[17] In similar fashion the Kaira pattidars resisted the British attempt to foist village accountants upon them. Here are all the characteristics of coparcenary communities shedding their ryotwar integument. Why the village heads should have won out against the local baronage is to ask a question in political history, but that they should have managed to get so far in the development of joint-landlord villages can be more readily answered. Kaira moved even the dry-as-dust Alexander Rogers to write lyrically that "there is no richer country in the Bombay Presidency, or proabbly in all Hindustan."[18] Only in such regions of secure agriculture, with a high population-land ratio, could the joint-landlord form of tenure flourish and support the village elite with a landlord rent. Indeed, so far from being a recent innovation as Baden-Powell contended,[19] these semi-coparcenary communities encountered by the British in Gujarat may have represented the original tenure, according to Rogers. In other parts like the Deccan it had been deranged by revenue-farming arrangements and oppression and so had been transformed into ryotwari.[20]

This lengthy prolegomenon should serve to offer suggestions as to why formal privileged tenures at the village level were comparatively rare in the North. Not that there was no inam problem. Hastings, the Governor-General in 1815, noted that rent-free grants in the Ceded and Conquered Provinces amounted to 44,95,177 bighas, "an extent exceeding the recorded area of the cultivated land in the largest of our Zillahs."[21] Much of this was reckoned to be fraudulent. When the British took over the Mathura (Muttra) district from Sindhia the greater portion of the *huzur* parganna was not assessed to revenue, having been alienated to the temples and religious institutions of this region sacred to Krishna and the gopis. Even in 1879, 9 percent of the district was *muafi*, the proportion rising in the huzur parganna to nearly a third. Much more provocative of official ire and cupidity were the muafi grants of the upper Doab and Rohilkhand region. In 1839 Edward Thornton could report that he had raised the revenue of the Saharanpur district by 1-1/4 lakhs in a single year through the resumption of muafi. Here the character of the muafidars was quite different:

> Mafee parcels given by the Zemindars are rare; those that have been resumed were professedly the gift of Government, the Mafeedars were chiefly Mahomedans, and not of an agricultural class, and they resided chiefly in the Qusbahs or head Towns of the Pergunahs. Of the parcels that lay in the Villages the agricultural management was exercised by the Zemindars, and the Mafeedar held nothing more than the Government right. Of these the settlement has been made with the Zemindars. In the Qusbahs the Mafeedars held the agricultural management . . . . The ex-Mafeedars were admitted to the settlement of the resumed land, and the Sudder Malgoozars were some from their party and some from the Zemindars of the old Khalsahs.[22]

The *milki* men, as the muafidars were known in Rohilkhand, fared no better, being castigated as late as 1874 by the settlement officer of Bijnaur as "lazy, useless profligates, habitues of the bazaars of the larger towns." By 1840 some 281,241 acres of muafi had been resumed in Rohilkhand, but in 1870 there still remained some 660,276 acres of rent-free land, only a small portion of which had been granted for Mutiny services.[23] Resumption was part of moral uplift.

> Either the milki men . . . will have to reform their ways—lay aside their thin muslins, leave their couches, and discharge their favourites; gird up their loins, and exert themselves in the management of their plots, or they will have to make way for honester men. It is a strange collateral result . . . that the making these men pay their fair share of the Government land revenue will very sensibly reduce public prostitution of all sorts in the larger towns, notably in Nugeena.[24]

Muafi of this type could hardly be said to be an integral part of the village economy.

In the North it would seem that we are brought back to Baden-Powell's joint-landlord village as the basic model—a community composed essentially of a proprietary body of kinsmen whose representatives engaged for the Government revenue but who bore no taint of Government appointment as patels enjoying service inam and official haqs. But the vicissitudes to which this structure was subject should warn us against the notion of any fixed type. Indeed the distinction between landlord and ryotwari village could be worn thin to the point of obliteration. Given prolonged political turbulence, a large area of cultivable waste, and an oppressive revenue demand, the landlord village in the North could crumple almost beyond recognition. In much of the upper Doab and Rohilkhand in the early decades of the nineteenth century there was almost nothing in the shape of landlord rent to be derived from land control. The aim of the village elite consisted in securing more preferential revenue rates than outside or temporary cultivators. Failure in this aim under unremitting pressure could result in all ryots being forced down into an undifferentiated mass, except perhaps for the revenue managers who could become separated out as an office-holding elite, more the appointees of outside authority than the spokesmen of a common proprietary body.

As with the Deccan patel, so with his equivalent in the North, the muqaddam, the perquisites of office now became important. In the North such perquisites comprised exemption from assessment of the muqaddam's garden land, a percentage commission (varying from 2 to 5 percent) on the revenue collections, and the quiet embezzlement of village expenses. Vestiges of the old zamindari right might remain in the form of a zamindari allowance (*russoom*) of some 5 percent, but this could become confounded with the muqaddami allowance if the muqaddams were drawn from among the ranks of the old village zamindars. Where the former proprietary body had been set aside by a superior revenue farmer, jagirdar, or taluqdar, it might be given some compensation in the form of a small grant of *nankar* or revenue-free land, as was done in the Sukrawah paraganna of Farrukhabad after the jagirdar had dispossessed the Brahman zamindars of the villages of "Suddurpoor and Beebeepoor."[25]   In such cases the taluqdar or *mukararidar* (holder of a privileged permanent revenue farm) might put in a muqaddam of his own choosing, emphasizing the increasingly appointive nature of the office. In the village of "Ummerpore" in the Meerut district the Gujar mukararidar, Raja Nain Singh, put in a Gujar cultivator as muqaddam over the heads of the old Tyagi proprietors. He was given "the general management of the village, with authority to allot lands for cultivation, and to settle ryots. He received as mocuddumee two rupees per cent on the jummabundee, and two biswahs [rent-free] per bigah of zubtee [cash-crop] land, paying also less rent than other cultivators for the land he tilled."[26]

In these circumstances, with a continuously high pitch of assessment, the only land of any value would be muafi. In 1832 in the Bareilly district in Rohilkhand, while the revenue engagement (malguzari) was selling for no more than one year's revenue, muafi fetched ten years' purchase. Boulderson, the settlement officer, thought that to talk of proprietary right for any but revenue-free land was a mockery:

> The whole allowance of 25% on the gross rental is not a fraction more than will cover the ordinary village expenses and the chances of season. In point of fact there is no proprietor's rent throughout the country, where an estate is settled up to the Regulation mark, and the rent-roll is well ascertained. Government is indubitably the proprietor in the English sense of the word, and it is a mere farce to talk, up here at least, of proprietors in any other sense than that of Government officers for the collection of the revenue with a small remuneration for the trouble of collection.[27]

Yet where a village and its headmen were not crushed by external pressures, the situation could encourage polarization within the village community. Cavendish observed in Muzaffarnagar district in the early 1820s that "in many villages...the headmen have made themselves farmers, that is, levying the full Government share of the produce, and setting aside the right of their parceners to have a proportionate distribution of the assessed jumma, they have taken to themselves all the profit and loss on the engagement. This has also occurred in Delhi, where the mocuddums have been supported by powerful men."[28] Thomas Fortescue, in his celebrated report of 1820 on the Delhi Territory, confirmed that the muqaddams were persons of much consequence in pre-British times, and that contention for the office was still eager.[29] John Lawrence found the same among the dry, thinly peopled tracts of the Rewari district, as did M.R. Gubbins in Rohtak in the late 1830s.[30] But here the principle of tribal union was so strong among the Jats and other communities that the ruling power had never managed to break into the village structure. Despite the region being one of precarious agriculture and more scarce in men and capital than land, so inhibiting the growth of joint landlord forms, there was nothing comparable to the chain of state-dependent village officers that prevailed in much of western and southern India. The *bhaiachara* structure of the Jat villages was ryotwar except for the sense of tribal union which kept the ruling power at bay. The latter lay alongside the "village republics," able to grant portions of its own revenue in superior privileged tenures but powerless to secure for them proprietary dominion. The settlement officer in Rohtak noted perceptively that the Nawabs of Jhajjar, Bahadurgarh, and (even the home of Indian cricket) Pataudi were not lords of the soil except in villages reclaimed from the waste and founded by themselves. Their tenures were in effect service jagirs of an unusual extent.[31] Inam at the village level had no role here.

In the eastern districts of what is now Uttar Pradesh, conditions offered a complete contrast. Here population pressed on resources, and the fertile soil was excellent for producing landlord-type villages and complex mahals.

Privileged tenure was everything since only in those comparatively few instances in which the village landlord body was small and noncultivating did the rental collections exceed the Government revenue demand, so yielding a true landlord rent. For the most part where the proprietary body cultivated part of the land themselves as home farms (*sir*), the object was rather to lower the rate on which the revenue fell on their own proprietary cultivation by shifting the burden on to the nonproprietary ryots. But if the proprietary body had proliferated so that the entire village lands were partitioned into sir, and sub-letting of the sir had fallen to a minimum, then the old ryotwari structure reemerged. At this point the heads of the *pattis,* or lineage sub-divisions, could readily constitute themselves as a new elite of managing proprietors. Thomason observed in the Sithwul taluqa of Azamgarh in the mid-1830s how the *lambardar* of each patti was rewarded with an allowance of Rs.25 charged to village expenses, although he said such instances were rare "because the other unauthorized advantages possessed by the [managing] proprietor have generally caused the office to be much an object of desire."[32] With all the cultivating ryots being members of the proprietary body and paying an equal *bach* or revenue rate, the perquisites of office had once again become important. Privileged tenure by virtue of proprietary right having disappeared, privileged tenure by virtue of office takes its place for a new elite. At this juncture the state authorities might step in, and according to their disposition and power either put in their own officials and collect directly (*kham*) from each ryot, or support the managing proprietors with appointive village office, or indeed go so far as to vest the sole proprietary right in them. The latent power of tribal union among swollen and feud-ridden Rajput proprietary communities would usually deter the ruling power from the first course, although in order to collect a heavy demand it was the practice adopted among the turbulent thakurs of Mehrabad in the Shahjahanpur district of Rohilkhand.[33] The British followed one of the two latter courses. But either way, so long as the revenue demand ate deeply into agricultural profits, privileged tenure was fundamental to the land tenure system of the north.

SUMMARY AND CONCLUSION

Indian agriculture was characterized by a peasant *petite culture* in which the cultivating holding was often on an average no more than six acres, the amount of land that could be farmed directly by a family using its own or tied labor.[34] This meant that even at the village level the major source of additional income for a village landholder of any substance was tributary or quasi-rental receipts from his nondemesne or "tenant" lands, rather than ordinary agricultural profits won from direct farming of a large holding.[35] Since the external revenue demand was tending constantly to absorb these rental receipts, privileged tenure was of importance in assisting the village elite to maintain its economic superiority. Where the ryotwari type of village prevailed, such privileged tenure was formally separated out as inam, and appears to have been most extensive where not only the revenue pressure was severe but also where conditions made possible the enlargement of inam through private grants such as the transparent fiction of transfers to Brahmans. At its greatest extent village inam appears to have been partnered by much more substantial alienations of revenue rights in jagir (and other revenue-free or favored tenures) to superior landholders above the village level. This usually occurred in regions distant from the centers of imperial or state authority.[36]

By the beginning of the nineteenth century a long period of disturbed political conditions and unstable central authority had swelled inam to an unnatural extent. Even so, it provided no permanent defense against a rapacious revenue demand since this merely pitched up the rates on revenue-bearing land to extraordinary levels which could only be met through the simultaneous exploitation of specially low-rated land like inam. In such circumstances inam might no longer provide a secure buttress of privilege for the village elite. The other perquisites of office, particularly traditional dues and the collection and management of the revenue demand, might attain much greater significance. The transformation of the patel into a petty revenue farmer could work an internal revolution among the old elite, especially where office had for long been a hereditary property whose rewards were fragmented among a host of co-shareres. The elevation of one man or family could occur amid the general depression of the old elite. Yet only where secure agriculture and pressure of population of land prevailed was there a possibility of landlord rents. Only there could there be a willingness to accept permanent responsibility for the revenue of the entire village lands. Only there could office mirasi be supplemented and overtaken by landed mirasi. Hence only there did village service inam cease to be of formal importance.

In the bulk of the ryotwari areas at the time of the British accession to power, the possession of office remained the key to economic superiority in the village. But whether this superiority was secured primarily through the possession of inam land or primarily through the direct financial gains of office and revenue management appears to have varied greatly and depended on the internal political configuration of the village elite and the distance of the area from central authority. In the Ahmadnagar and Poona districts, close to the centers of Maratha power, village inam appears to have been relatively unimportant. In contrast, in parts of the Madras Ceded Districts, like Bellary, it was at least one-sixth of the cultivated area. Yet even in the joint-landlord villages of northern India, where formal village service inam was confined to minor officials like village police and detectives (goraits), privileged tenure remained of key importance. In a swollen proprietary body the compensatory advantages for bearing the revenue responsibility for the entire village lands were limited to social prestige and the enjoyment of reduced revenue rates on the proprietary sir or demesne land. Where the proprietary body encompassed almost the whole cultivating community as a result of lineage proliferation, as among some of the Rajput village committees of eastern Uttar Pradesh, or where by virtue of the special structure of bhaiachara communities, as in insecure tracts like much of the Delhi region, almost the entire village lands were regarded as sir, there many of the features of ryotwar village could be reproduced, particularly the importance of office and its perquisites.[37] As Baden-Powell was constrained to acknowledge, the practical difference between the joint-landlord and the ryotwari village could be worn to a shadow.[38] Hence the functional role of village service inam has to be assessed as simply one in the complex of variables that determined the distribution of economic power within the Indian village.

NOTES

1. *Selections from the Records of the Madras Government. New (Revenue) Series no. 1. A Collection of Papers relating to the Inam Settlement of the Madras Presidency* (Madras, 1906, p. 17 [cited hereafter as *Papers re the Inam Settlement*].

2. Zamindari was not a superior, revenue-collecting tenure in this region as in Bengal, but designated actual and immediate proprietary dominion.

3. *Imperial Gazetteer of India: Madras* (Calcutta, 1908), 1-101.

4. B.H. Baden-Powell, *The Indian Village Community* (London, 1896), pp. 424ff.

5. Minute of Board of Revenue, 5 Jan. 1818, para 89, *Parliamentary Papers 1831-32*, vol. 11, Appendix, p. 425 [cited hereafter as *P.P.*].

6. *Papers re the Inam Settlement*, p. 244.

7. *P.P. 1831-32*, vol. 11, Appendix, p. 45.

8. *Papers re the Inam Settlement*, p. 176.

9. *The Bellary Gazatteer* (Madras, 1904), 1:154.

10. A.D. Campbell, Paper on the Land Revenue of India, *P.P. 1831-32*, vol. 11, Appendix, p. 45; Thomas Munro, Report on the Ceded Districts, 26 July 1807, ibid. *1812*, vol. 7, p. 787.

11. *Papers re the Inam Settlement*, pp. 17ff.

12. W.H. Sykes, "On the Land Tenures of the Deccan," *Journal of the Royal Asiatic Society* 2 (1835):218-19.

13. H.D. Robertson to Wm. Chaplin, 10 Oct. 1821, *Selection of Papers from the Records of the East India House relating to the revenue, police, and criminal justice under the Company's government*, 4 vols. (London, 1820-26), 4:425 [cited hereafter as *Papers at East India House*]; Rev. Letter from Bombay, 5 Nov. 1823, para. 436, *P.P. 1831-32*, vol. 11, Appendix, p. 655.

14. *Papers at East India House*, 4:525.

15. R.N. Gooddine, "Report on Deccan Village Communities," *Selections from the Records of the Bombay Government*, no. 4 (Bombay, 1852).

16. "Narrative of Bombay Inam Commission," ibid., no. 132 New Series (Bombay, 1879).

17. *P.P. 1831-32*, vol. 11, Appendix, p. 584.

18. A. Rogers, *The Land Revenue of Bombay*, 2 vols. (London, 1892), 1:103.

19. Baden-Powell, *The Indian Village Community*, pp. 387ff.

20. Rogers, *Land Revenue of Bombay*, 2:9.

21. *Selections from the Revenue Records of the N.W. Provinces, 1818-20* (Calcutta, 1866), p. 348.

22. "Saharanpur Settlement Report 1839," para. 46, in *Reports of the Revenue Settlement of the North Western Provinces of the Bengal Presidency under Regulation IX, 1833* (Benares, 1862), 1:112.

23. L. Brennan, "Agrarian Policy and its Effects on Landholders in Rohilkhand 1833-70," *University Studies in History* 5 (1970):10.

24. *Bijnaur Settlement Report 1874* (Allahabad, 1874), p. 77.

25. "Settlement of Pergunnah Sukrawah, Zillah Furruckabad," *Selections from the Records of Government North Western Provinces*, no. 22 (1848), pp. 256.

26. Holt Mackenzie, Memo, 1826, *P.P. 1831-32*, vol. 11, Appendix, p. 254.

27. *Bareilly Settlement Report 1874* (Allahabad, 1874), p. 126.

28. *P.P. 1831-32*, vol. 11, Appendix, p. 244.

29. *Papers at East India House*, 3:401ff.

30. *Selections from Reports of the Revision of the Settlement Under Regulation IX, 1833 in the Delhi Territory*, no. 1 (Agra, 1846).

31. *Rohtak Settlement Report 1873-79* (Lahore, 1880), p. 109.

32. Azamgarh Settlement Report 1839, in *Reports of the Revenue Settlement of the North Western Provinces under Regulation IX, 1833* (Benares, 1862), 1:31.

33. Ibid., 2:7.

34. Cf. *Aligarh Settlement Report 1882* (Allahabad, 1882), p. 50; and *Mainpuri Settlement Report 1875* (Allahabad, 1875), p. 88.

35. Cf. Dharma Kumar, *Land and Caste in South India* (Cambridge, Eng., 1965), pp. 20-23, 29.

36. Cf. K. Haraksingh, "The Revenue Administration of Sylhet District" (Ph.D. diss., Univ. of London, 1973), p. 31, where Lindsay formed the impression in 1779 that "not even one eighth of the district was revenue paying, the rest being either jaghire, burmutre [brahmottra], muddut muash, etc." On the amount of revenue-free land in Bengal, cf. A.M. Waheeduzzaman, "Land Resumption in Bengal 1819-1946" (Ph. D. diss., Univ. of London, 1969), p. 171.

37. For swollen Rajput communities in the Benares region, cf. *Jaunpur Settlement Report 1877-86* (Allahabad, 1886), p. 107 passim; *Ghazipur Settlement Report 1880-85* (Allahabad, 1886), p. 89 passim; *Ballia Settlement Report 1882-85* (Allahabad, 1886), passim. Also B.S. Cohn, "Structural Change in Indian Rural Society," in Robert E. Frykenberg, ed., *Land Control and Social Structure in Indian History* (Madison, 1969); Richard G. Fox, *Kin, Clan, Raja & Rule* (Berkeley, 1971); Eric Stokes, "Agrarian Society and the Pax Britannica in Northern India in the Early Nineteenth Century," *Modern Asian Studies* 9 (1975).

38. Baden-Powell, *The Indian Village Community*, pp. 425-26, 429.

"PRIVILEGED LANDHOLDING":
The Concept Stretched to Cover the Case

BURTON STEIN

THE concepts "privileged landholding" and "landed privilege" have been proposed by Robert Frykenberg as means for deepening our understanding of one of the crucial elements of East India Company power in South India. Appropriately, these concepts are seen to have provided the foundation for that collection of special tenurial types comprising the category of inams in Madras as well as in Bombay.

"Privilege" in landholding as in other social arrangements pertains to advantages (rights and immunities) enjoyed by some, usually a minority; it originates from a grant from those in authority in a political community. Recent writing on the subject of social stratification perceived as "inequality"[1] reminds us that it is scarcely possible to imagine any social arrangements, including, and perhaps most especially, landholding which do not confer or recognize advantages for certain individuals and groups. Thus, while it is appropriate to consider the category of inams as a necessary step in an improved understanding of "privileged landholding" in South India, as Frykenberg has,[2] it is also simultaneously necessary to broaden the address of the matter. We must ask: what is meant by "nonprivileged landholding" if inams are construed as "privileged landholding"? Do inam tenures exhaust the extent of privileged landholding? Must we not also examine the entire system of landholding in nineteenth-century Madras to ascertain the variety of advantages held by individuals and groups of whom those designated as "inamdars" may have been a small part?

Determination of nonprivileged landholding in nineteenth-century Madras might be presumed a straightforward task. Cultivable land in the Presidency was apportioned between two broad tenurial types: about one-third of the taxable acreage was under zamindari tenure, the rest under ryotwari. Hence, to determine the proportion of nonprivileged landholding, assuming that inam holdings represented privileged landholding, it would appear to be adequate to deduct inam from total landholdings.

The Inam Commission of Madras enumerated 426 inam tenures covering twenty-seven lakh acres (2.7 million acres) of ryotwari lands, the total of which in 1855 was 17.5 million acres.[3] On this acreage basis, one would conclude that privileged tenure holders—those totally exempt from land revenue or subject to a fixed quit-rent (jodi)—comprised about 15 percent of total ryotwari holdings. However, this procedure yields a deceptive answer. According to other data regularly collected only after 1886,[4] half of the cultivated acres of Madras Presidency were exempted from the full rate of revenue and therefore must be reckoned as privileged landholding. By 1886, total ryotwari acreage in the Presidency was reported as 59 million acres, of which 30 million was reported as either not fully assessed under ryotwari regulations or as estates taxed at "privileged rates."[5] The proportion of ryotwari holdings exempt from full assessment in Bombay at the same time was almost the same: 21 million acres out of a total of 43.6 million acres.[6] If then we seek to understand the nature of privileged landholding in Madras during the nineteenth century, it is necessary to recognize at the outset that on the basis of available evidence, we are dealing with one-half of the cultivated acreage under ryotwari tenure. If Madras zamindari tenures are included—approximately 31 million acres in Madras, of which 7 million acres were not fully assessed[7]—the Presidency proportion of privileged landholdings falls to about one-third, still a substantial part of the whole.

The second point of the argument is that the entire system of landholding was based on privilege. The *structure of privilege* in nineteenth-century Madras landholding may be considered to have four facets. There were *groups of privilege,* including Europeans and landlords, the latter often designated *mirasidars;* there were *zones of privilege,* portions of districts and entire districts which were treated with special advantage as compared to other districts or parts of districts on their being *nunja* or wet-crop tracts; there were *privileges of administration* deriving from the nature of the ryotwari system of land settlement in Madras; and there were *privileges of social class* derived from the encompassing nature of British colonial rule in this part of India. Each of these facets can be examined only briefly in this paper; its limited focus does not permit the complete consideration of these various facets of privilege. It is recognized that in using the concept of "class" there are important ancillary questions raised relating to stratified groupings in pre-British India (i.e., did the British "create" social classes?) and relating to the special context for class analysis posed by "colonial society." To these questions only the most brief references are possible in this discussion.

Under the first category, there were groups which benefitted (e.g., landlords), those which suffered (e.g., resident cultivating groups), and those whose fortunes were not fundamentally affected by the land system of nineteenth-century Madras and other parts of British India (e.g., many merchants and artisan groups). Whether the benefitting and suffering groups that can be identified were created by British land policies or whether that system largely recognized and fixed land arrangements that preceded British control remain unsettled questions worthy of serious attention. However, that there were such groups enjoying special privilege seems indisputable.

Two groups of privilege were the indigenous landlords of the Presidency and Europeans. In contrast to northern India, the lexicon of revenue in

Madras, and to some extent Bombay, excluded the term "landlord" until the twentieth century. This was in part a legacy of Munro whose absurdly egalitarian phrases continued to permeate revenue reports and, in part an aspect of the ideological component of the ryotwari revenue system which spoke of yeomen ryots and village republics. But landlords there were. There were district lists of great holders, such as that of Tanjore for 1851, in which twenty-one landholders paying an annual revenue (*kist*) of between Rs. 5,000 and Rs. 15,000 were enumerated.[8] Alternately, there were Presidency statistics such as one widely circulated for 1848–49 of ryotwari title (*putta*) holders in which 82 percent of the million or so puttadars paid an annual average revenue of only Rs. 8.75,[9] or somewhat later, in 1886–87, in which the average annual revenue paid by putta-holders with kists in excess of Rs. 100 was Rs. 195 and those paying kists of less than Rs. 100 paid an average of Rs. 10.[10]

Landlord power can be seen to have operated in three spheres during the nineteenth century. In relation to the Presidency government in Madras city, landlords combined in associations, the most impressive of which were widely discussed in and out of official circles.[11] Suits in Presidency courts by landlords was another way in which their influence was made felt; some of these reached the Privy Council and had a profound effect upon administrative measures under existing land law as well as influencing new legislation. In relation to local government, the power of landlords was easily and constantly translated into privilege. Revenue scandals in the Presidency during the nineteenth century were consistently rooted in the landlords' collusion with Indian revenue officials, and while extortion and oppression of large landholders by revenue officials was not unheard of, the usual victims of this oppression were those more vulnerable landed groups who were alike exploited by officials and larger landholders.[12] Again, in terms of local influence, it was the large landholders of any locality who controlled such village officials as headmen, accountants, policemen, in contrast to the regular revenue servants who operated under the supervision of *tahsildars*. The privileges derived from being astride the linkage points in the most vital element of the British administrative structure, that of revenue, resulted in easy control of tenants, agricultural workers, and small landholders; it facilitated revenue frauds.

Even before the mid-century interest of the Madras government in developing the plantation sector of agriculture in coffee and tea, Europeans were in privileged positions with respect to landholding arrangements as tax farmers in more prosperous districts such as Tanjore. In the latter place Europeans were mentioned among those who had contracted to purchase grain owing to the government in kind under the *amani* tenure of Tanjore. The arrears of Europeans constituted 32 percent of the total balances for the year of 1830.[13] But, it was primarily as holders of great upland acreages, suitable for plantation cultivation, that Europeans constituted a privileged class. Until the promulgation of the Waste Land Rules in 1862, much of the land devoted to coffee and tea cultivation was held under doubtful title, very often because the land was purchased from headmen possessing neither title nor right to alienate such lands. Still, the lands so purchased were generally safe not only for planting, but for speculation, and once ensconced upon such lands, even with defective title, Europeans had little trouble fending off the operation of formal regulations connected with survey and assessment. As Bourdillon, one of the most respected revenue officials of the Madras establishment, wrote of the Wynaad planters, "the majority... are notoriously a rough set, and I believe the Surveyors employed to ascertain every year the extent of newly opened land will have much difficulty."[14]

Zonal privilege is a striking feature of the Madras revenue system of the nineteenth century. From the earliest records of the century, invidious distinctions were regularly made between those tracts favored by reliable water availability and those in which agriculture was based upon hazardous rainfall. The ryotwari system of "fixed field assessment" based upon "accurate survey" was originated in the dominantly dry-crop Baramahal under Read and applied by the system's greatest spokesman, propagandist, and patron-saint, Munro, in the Ceded Districts, also a dry-crop region. Coimbatore, another dry-crop area, was viewed by most ryotwari proponents, including Munro, as the Madras district in which the system had had its earliest, most full and fair trial and where it was found a successful mode of revenue management under its influential Principal Collector, John Sullivan. It is thus interesting and ironic to note that throughout the century, cultivators in dry-crop (*punja*) tracts were consistently disadvantaged relative to those in districts which were cultivated under reliable irrigation conditions (*nunja*). The general features of ryotwari tenure—its theory and its regulatory procedures as well as its actual operations—are well known to students of Indian revenue history.[15] Less well recognized than other oppressive aspects of the system are the special advantages enjoyed by those in control of wet (nunja) lands as compared with those of dry (punja) areas.

Tanjore district was the great nunja area of the Presidency, and it was probably never under anything approximating a ryotwari settlement, but remained a tract of village revenue settlement under extremely favorable revenue terms.[16] Tanjore also enjoyed the most assiduous governmental investment in productivity of any Madras district including irrigation and drainage works, roads, and bridges.[17] That Tanjore produced a very substantial and reliable proportion of total government receipts of the Presidency would appear to justify this favorable investment regime. However, some members of the Madras Board of Revenue and critics of ryotwari often pointed to the adverse effects of high revenue demand and investment neglect in dry-crop areas; they suggested that with fewer disadvantages, these dry districts could prosper and ultimately contribute a larger share of revenue proceeds to the Government. In the early part of the nineteenth century, it was pointed out that rates on wet lands in Tanjore were 50 to 100 percent

lower than on wet lands in Coimbatore, the Arcots, Chittoor, and Tiruchira-
palli districts.[18] In Tanjore district itself, some dry-crop lands were assessed
at 150 percent higher than some wet lands in 1850.[19] Moreover, the operation
of ryotwari rules which made all fields theoretically subject to full assessment (in fact this was not followed) systematically penalized dry-crop
cultivators by charging a full assessment on fallow lands. Short-term fallows
were essential for dry-cropping, whereas in Tanjore and in other wet areas
fallows were rarely necessary and wet fields under full assessment always
yielded some produce. In fact, this failure of British revenue regulations in
Madras to recognize the pattern of short-term fallows in dry-crop cultivation
may be one of the most discriminatory and short-sighted aspects of the
ryotwari system.[20] The full consequences of this persistent, adverse discrimination between wet and dry tracts are unclear. Among the consequences
which may be mentioned, however, is that there was a higher rate of agricultural insolvency and revenue arrearages in dry-crop districts.[21]

The ryotwari system can easily be seen as an administrative nightmare.
Even its advocates occasionally conceded this. What was never conceded,
nor apparently seriously recognized, was that the system could and did
fulfill dreams of privilege never before available to many Indians. This
does not distinguish ryotwari from any of the other major revenue systems
of British India except that, again, the rhetoric of ryotwari obscured the
extent to which this system, like the other revenue systems of British India,
was intended to achieve a set of relatively unprepossessing objectives. These
included the careerist ambitions of the British Indian Civil Service and the
maintenance of sufficient order to realize the level of revenue necessary for
support of an imperial structure not only in the sub-continent, but in Asia
as a whole. The complexity and irresponsibility of the administrative system
conferred upon minor, local officials the means of distributing maximum
advantage to those relatively few within the social order whose wealth and
influence were the mainstay of the entire imperial system.

One easily grasps the fundamental confusion of which the Madras
system was capable by simply examining its structure. In the middle years
of the nineteenth century, the twenty-two districts of the Presidency contained about 22 million people. Each of the districts was under a European
officer (collector) assisted by two or three English sub-collectors under whom
were fourteen to sixteen subordinate Indian revenue officials, tahsildars,
each of whom had responsibility for 200 to 500 villages. Each village contained from 500 to 2,000 fields to survey, assess, and ultimately to make
collections from. The number of Indian revenue servants under a collector
might thus range from 1,500 to 2,500 and this did not include village officials
(headsmen, accountants, police).[22] These tens of thousands of subordinate
revenue officials, working with an elaborate system of land classification
(Read's settlement in the Baramahal involved sixty-one different rates of
dry-crop assessment and fifty-one rates for wet crops)[23] were evaluated and
rewarded solely on the basis of the consistency with which they met their

revenue quotas. The scope for advantage as well as local, arbitrary action by Indian revenue officials becomes entirely predictable.

As in other provinces of British India, advantage derived from the fact that minor revenue servants were strategically placed to possess land at privileged rates—whether legally or illegally—and also to benefit others to whom they were linked in a variety of ways. While this advantageous position was demonstrated throughout the nineteenth century by the "revenue scandals," and while many stern warnings were issued and a few stern actions taken by the British, Madras revenue records continue to provide hundreds of examples of land acquired directly by revenue servants or through family agents as well as examples of preferential rates being levied upon such lands.[24]

Nor was the matter much different with respect to coercion. The ultimate irresponsibility and the high inflexible monetary demands of the Madras revenue system provided an obvious setting for the use of force. Torture and other forms of coercion were exposed without being eliminated in the middle years of the century.[25]

Discussion of these matters of special advantage and even of coercion occurred in the British Parliament, in the British and Indian press, as well as within the government of Madras; they were fully known to all. Here there was neither ignorance nor incompetence, but rather the tacit understanding of the relationship between class privilege and the maintenance of colonial society and the imperial system of British India.

To speak of the privilege of class is to be redundant, of course: class means privilege. However, it is remarkable how seldom and how tentative have been analyses based upon social class in nineteenth-century Madras, except in urban studies. While it is true that urban life in India as elsewhere has lent itself more readily to class analysis, still it is clear that the concept of class has a place more dominant in rural India than it has received in studies even though such an approach would create anguish among scholars who see caste society or peasant society in India as preventing useful class analysis.

If we are to view social classes as sections of a social order defined by social and economic influence supported by the prevailing political, administrative, and judicial structure, then it would appear that strata defined by these criteria did exist in nineteenth-century Madras. Among cultivating groups there were great and small landlords; there were lower cultivators, often denominated "pauperized ryots" by some revenue officials and by all critics of Madras revenue arrangements; and there were landless laborers constituting a vast rural proletariat. Both the extent to which these categories of rural society were transformed into social classes proper by British power and methods—whatever British intentions might have been—and the extent to which such categories were continuous with pre-British rural society are unclear and, for purposes of the discussion here, irrelevant. These categories appear to have existed during the nineteenth century and may be looked upon as an important fact of the structure of privileged landholding.

The great landlords of the Presidency included zamindars of the permanently settled portions of the province, but the category went beyond zamindars established by the first comprehensive land statutes of the Madras Presidency of 1802. Among landlords were men who were, in the odd, levelling parlance of the ryotwari system, called "ryots," but often further identified in revenue documents as "substantial," "respectable," or "leading" ryots. These euphemistic adjectives designated landholders with very great control over human and natural resources in ryotwari districts. In addition to possessing ryotwari titles (puttas) on lands both consolidated and scattered (at times over several *taluks*), they possessed animals for work as well as food; they possessed regular surpluses of food and seed that contributed to their stock of wealth at any time, especially at times of scarcity, and provided them with a substantial trade good to either hold or sell with advantage, in contrast to smaller producers.[26]

Landlords were principal tax payers in every district, but, because they were also the major source of recruitment of local revenue officials or were allied with such locally influential persons, and also because they chose and paid for village officers, they had opportunities for shifting many of their tax liabilities to others. Such shifts were achieved by numerous means deriving from the central fiction of the ryotwari system—supposed fixed field assessments. The actual revenue demand upon the hundreds of thousands of cultivable fields in ryotwari tracts was set on a district basis by the Board of Revenue. Revenue was then further set on a taluk and finally on a village basis by the joint decisions (indeed, they were negotiations) of "substantial" ryots and local revenue officials. Under this system, few landholders paid full revenue on the fields for which they held puttas.[27] This could be avoided in many other ways such as, for example, through the instrumentality of "revenue *kauls*," that is, negotiated engagements to pay an increasing part of the regular assessment for several years until the full assessment was reached, by which time new land was taken up by the landlord and the old land dropped. Another method for minimizing the tax liability of a landlord household or family was that of sharing ryotwari titles ("joint puttas") thus exempting most persons of landed wealth from house tax.[28]

Within the landlord class, a useful distinction can be made between those of agrarian regions with more well-developed irrigation facilities and those with less. This corresponds to the nunja-punja zonal distinction drawn above. Smaller landlords were to be found in both wet and dry tracts and agricultural strategies were different in each kind of tract just as their relationship to the British government of Madras differed. These differences were perhaps most striking in the case of "substantial" ryots of the dry districts. The mode of land management for many dry-area landlords was based not on the quality of land and water which they held, as was true for landlords in the wet zones, but upon the cultivation skills and agricultural resources of a landlord which alone could make dry-crop cultivation profitable. Many of the dry-area landlords were mobile cultivators of substantial means who, particularly in the dry uplands of Salem and Coimbatore, were willing to move considerable distances within a district or even across district lines to where there were more favorable revenue arrangements. This appears to have continued an earlier, pre-British, pattern of peasant mobility, an enterprise that has been little noticed among historians, and it was precisely by such groups that many of the crop innovations of the middle of the nineteenth century were made, especially in cotton cultivation.

Beneath this landlord class of privilege was a stratum of cultivators possessing small means and often serving as tenants under large and small landlords. When a season looked promising, they might take up land on their own accounts with the slim hope of advancing their socio-economic positions. Because revenue officials were under constant pressure to meet and even increase their revenue quotas and also because the Board of Revenue of Madras continued to insist that more putta holders were somehow a mark of greater prosperity, such small agricultural speculators on rainfall were encouraged to take puttas on kaul arrangements of diminished demand for several years. When kauls were granted to substantial cultivators—and this was done as a way of fraudulently diminishing their revenue liability—this must be seen as a privilege or special advantage. This was not true for cultivators of marginal means for whom failure was far more predictable than success, and modest resources, painfully saved over years as a tenant, were easily wiped out by the high revenue demands of an even partial "rent." Revenue officials reported quite ingenious forms of cooperation among these pauperized cultivators, but the rate of insolvency was nevertheless very high. When it is considered that most of these cultivators were persons whose long-standing tenancy rights had been progressively eroded by British revenue policies favoring landlords and that Madras tenancy legislation was as biased in favor of landlord interests as that in any other Indian province, this stratum of vulnerable cultivators must be counted a deprived class by any measure.[29]

In dry districts, the category of "pauperized" ryots was not easily distinguished from landless laborers, for here, in contrast to wet districts and tracts, social and economic statuses were distributed in a gradual gradient. In wet zones—Tanjore's Kaveri basin, Malabar, and part of the Kistna-Godavari delta and Chingleput—the gradients of status and wealth were much steeper. Legal and social means have been capable until recently of preventing much movement from this lowest stratum. Moreover, the diminution of customary patron obligations of landlords—abetted by the class bias of revenue officials and the judicial system—made of the lowest segment of the rural population a proletariat. It was incapable by its resources and the framework of the social and political system of improving its claims upon total wealth and welfare. The utterly obfuscating discussion of "slavery" in respect to landless laborers by British officials throughout the century served to prevent any serious consideration of altering the structure of agrarian relations involving landless workers. It conveniently placed off limits any changes in the system of class privilege through administrative usage and law by alleging that to ameliorate the condition of these "slaves" and "serfs," as they were variously called, would violate the customary rights and cultural traditions of the people![30] This was indeed sensibility for the "ancient rights" of Indians.

In a discussion of this brevity it has been impossible to qualify all propositions to the measure necessary or to present detailed evidence in their support. It should therefore be reiterated that this paper has intended an exploratory extension of the idea of "privileged landholding" in order to frame the consideration of inam tenures more adequately. To state the conclusions of the paper most judiciously, they may be taken as hypotheses for further research, or at least further discussion. These are linked hypotheses stated, rather starkly, in the following way.

A. Beneficiaries of inam tenures in Madras were part of a larger set of beneficiaries of the land system generally and most generally of the class system of colonized, nineteenth-century Madras.

B. The hundreds of inam tenures of Madras do not exhaust privileged landholding. Rather, these legal forms point strongly to the persistent policy of the nineteenth-century Madras government to favor landlord interests for the same exigent political reasons as existed in other British-Indian provinces. However, this policy has been less clearly seen by scholars owing to the rhetoric of the ryotwari revenue system.

C. The notion of "privilege" or special advantage applied to certain sectors, such as "landholding," of this colonial society (and probably most others in the nineteenth and twentieth centuries) has questionable analytical value since all the procedures, regulations, and laws were predicated upon all-pervasive privilege.

To these concluding propositions can be added a final one dealing with the working of the Inam Commission in Madras, but not dealt with in the main body of this paper. That is, the various steps taken by the Madras government from the 1840s to the 1860s to alter the terms of inam tenure, particularly through the Inam Commission, were not an attack upon "privileged landholding" or "fraud" within the land and revenue systems of the Presidency. Rather, they demonstrated the recognition by senior British officials that the class system of landholding had become strong enough and the bureaucratic structure elaborate enough to dispense with some of the earlier forms of inam without fundamentally weakening the class character of landed privilege.

NOTES

1. Lloyd A. Fallers, *Inequality* (Chicago, 1973), and Andre Beteille, ed., *Social Inequality: Selected Readings* (Baltimore, 1969).
2. This paper was originally prepared for a symposium panel entitled "Privileged Landholding in India," XXXIVth International Congress of Orientalists, Paris, 16-22 July 1973, chaired by the editor of this volume, where these and other similar questions were raised.

3. *Selections from the Records of the Madras Government, A Collection of Papers Relating to the Inam Settlement in the Madras Presidency*, New (Revenue) Series, no. 1 (Madras, 1906), Appendix B, "A Descriptive List of the Inam Tenures of the Madras Presidency," pp. 320-32. This list contains a duplicate word arising from linguistic differences within the Presidency. Also, see ibid. p. 17, for a Government of Madras Order of 19 January 1857 providing the estimate of inam holding. Also: *Selections, Papers Relating to the General Revenue Survey of the Madras Presidency*, 2nd Series (Madras, 1858), p. 19. Within the district of Tanjore in 1865, it was stated that 1490 of the 6332 villages of the district were under inam tenure; thus, on a village basis, the extent of privileged inam tenure may be reckoned at 23 percent. "Settlement Report of Tanjore, Fasli 1275 (1865-66)," in *Reports of Land Revenue of Madras, 1865-66-67*, dated 8 September 1856, India Office Library [cited hereafter as IOL], L/5/II, 1865-67.

4. "Statistical Abstract Relating to British India, 1886-87," *United Kingdom, Parliamentary Papers and Accounts*, 1888, vol. CIV (C. 5534), table entitled: "Surveyed and Assessed Area, 1886-87". The first listing for "agriculture" in this series began in the 1888 volume when six tables were included for 1886-87. Subsequently, the proportion under ryotwari tenure remained about the same: 1899-1900, 61 percent; 1909-10, 59 percent; 1919-20, 54 percent; 1928-29, 47 per cent; ibid. 1902, Vol. CXII; 1912-13, Vol. CIII; 1922 Session II, IV; 1931-32, Vol. XXV.

5. Ibid., 1888.

6. Ibid., 1888.

7. Ibid., 1888. According to Baden-Powell, inam tenures for entire villages was reported under this zamindari heading which, in the case of Tanjore, nominally a "ryotwari" area, resulted in undercounting inams; *Land Systems of British India*, 3 vols. (Oxford, 1892), 3:79.

8. Tanjore Collector, J.T. Bishop to the Secretary of the Board of Revenue [cited hereafter as BOR]; W.H. Bayley, 8, May 1851, *Madras Board of Revenue Proceedings* [cited hereafter as MBORP], 1851, IOL, P/309/52, 6281-6302. The Tanjore landlords privileges were widely and sometimes bitterly recognized, as we find in the comments of an Indian writer from Coimbatore who wrote in 1906; "It is the Tanjorean's boast that he has scarcely anything to do except move the field bund aside and let in water to raise a bumper crop of paddy": Madras, The Central Agricultural Committee, *Some Suggestions for Madras Ryots (by a Special Correspondent of the "Madras Mail")*, Bulletin no. 3 (Madras, 1906) IOL. P/V 2148, p. 5.

9. Baden-Powell, *Land Systems of British India*, 3: 142; and J.B. Norton, *A Letter to Robert Lowe Esq., Joint Secretary of the Board of Control from John Bruce Norton on the Conditions and Requirements of the Presidency of Madras*, IOL Tracts, no. 539 (Madras, 1854), p. 21, apparently citing J.D. Bourdillon.

10. Baden-Powell, *Land Systems of British India*, 3: 142.

11. For example, Norton, *Letter to Robert Lowe* . . . .

12. See R.E. Frykenberg, *Guntur District, 1788-1848: A History of Local Influence and Central Authority in South India* (Oxford, 1965).

13. From Tanjore Collector, W. Kindersely, to BOR, 10 February 1831, *MBORP*, 1831, IOL P/298/5, 2035-46.

14. "Proceedings of the Madras Government," 22 June 1859, no. 822, "Wynaad" *Selections, Papers Relating to the General Revenue Survey of the Madras Presidency* (Madras, 1863), p. 384.

15. See the essay by N. Mukherjee nd R.E. Frykenberg, in *Land Control and Social Structure*, ed. R.E. Frykenberg (Madison, Wis., 1969).

16. There is massive evidence on this point; it can only be indicated by the following selected citations from *MBORP*: 28 February 1818, IOL P/292/59, pp. 2794-2812; 5 December 1831, IOL, P/298/27, pp. 12505-22; 2 September 1841, IOL, (P 303/16, pp. 10770-ff; 8 August 1865, IOL P/315/15, pp. 4343-50. Also see: "Minute by Mr. John Hodgson, President of Revenue Board, Madras, 1819," in: "Cumming's Papers," IOL, *Home Miscellaneous Series*, vol. 528, 22 p. and passim.

17. *Selections from the Records of Madras Presidency*, 2nd series, no. 29, *Replies to the Collective Memorandum on Public Works in the Madras Presidency*, 1856, referring to a letter from the Tanjore collector, H. Forbes, to the Madras Government, dated 9 November 1855, para. 14.

18. From Tanjore Collector, J.T. Bishop, to Secretary BOR, MBORP, 1851, 8 May 1851, IOL P/309/52, 6297.

19. *Revenue Letters from Madras*, 6 March 1807, para, 61, IOL, L/E/3/232.

20. "Extract of the Revenue Letter from Fort St. George," 2 June 1822, *Revenue Selections*, vol. 3 of *Selection of Papers from East-India House*, 4 vols. (London, 1820-26), p. 502.

21. See, C.M. Ramachandra Chettiar, "The Geographical Distribution of Crime and Civil Litigation in South India," *Journal of the Madras Geographical Association*, 12 (1937): 70.

22. Norton, *Letter to Robert Lowe* . . . , p. 127, citing J.D. Bourdillon, Secretary of the Board of Revenue, 1843-45.

23. "Minutes of the Madras Board of Revenue, 5 January 1818, "On the Subject of the General Introduction of the New Ryotwar Settlement," MBORP, P/292/53, p. 193. (Reprinted in *Parliamentary Papers,* vol. 24 [1828]).

24. *Report of the Commissioners for the Investigation of Alleged Cases of Torture in the Madras Presidency, Submitted to the Right Honourable the Governor in Council of Fort St. George on the 16th April 1855* (Madras, 1855), IOL, V/4977. Press comment on the Report: *The Athenaeum* (Madras) for June, 1855; *Bombay Gazette* for 2 July 1855; *The Times* (London) for 8 July to 20 September, especially, 31 August 1855, p.5; *Hansard's Parliamentary Debates,* 3rd Series, vol. 135, 11 July 1854, "India: Tenure of Land in Madras," col. 43. Also see Patrick B. Smollett, *Madras: Its Civil Administration; Being Rough Notes from Personal Observation Written in 1855 and 1856.* London, 1858), IOL Tracts 5111, pp. 1-34. From the records see: "Report from the Commissioners of Coimbatore," 26 February 1816, *Revenue Selections,* 1:712-54, regarding the notorious Casi Chetty case; on the same issue "Mr. [John] Sullivan's Observations on the Report of the Coimbatore Commissioners," MBORP, 2 March 1819, P/293/12, pp. 791-810.

25. On one of the early revenue scandals in Tanjore, 1803-4, see *An Historical Account of the Administration of the Land Revenue in the Territories under the Presidency of Fort St. George,* in "Cumming's Papers," IOL, *Home Misc. Series,* vol. 528, pp. 4828-5. Also: *Revenue Dispatches to Madras,* 2 January 1822, IOL L/E/3/365, para, 22 ff.; From Tanjore Collector, Bishop, to the Secretary of BOR, 24 January 1848, MBORP, P/307/49 and 50, pp. 929-46 and 1049-69; From Coimbatore Collector, E.B. Thomas, to Secretary BOR, 25 August 1851, MBORP, P/309/62, pp. 11327-33.

26. Descriptions of the structure of grain trade operations are remarkably difficult to find even at times of crises, such as famines. Among discussions which refer to trade operations of grain producers, see: *Report of the Famine in the Madras Presidency 1896 and 1897,* vol. 1, *General Report and Govt.* [sic] *Order,* (Madras, 1898), IOL, W838, pp. 48-9 and Government of India, *Agricultural Marketing in India; Report on the Marketing of Rice in India and Burma,* Marketing Series, no. 27 (Delhi, 1941), pp. 248-69.

27. Two very authoritative statements on these matters from among the most respected revenue officials of the Presidency are: "Minute of the Madras Board of Revenue, 5 January 1818, on the Subject of the New Ryotwar Settlement," MBORP, P/292/53, pp. 197-8; and J.D. Bourdillon, *Remarks on the Ryotwar System of Revenue as it Exists in the Presidency of Madras* (Madras, 1853), IOL, Tracts 567, pp. 22-3.

28. From Coimbatore Collector, E.B. Thomas, to Secretary BOR, 25 August 1851, MBORP, P/309/62, pp. 11327-33.

29. Smollett, *Madras,* p. 7; *Selection of Papers of East-India House,* III, "Extract of the Revenue Letter from Madras," 19 February 1822, *Revenue Selections,* 3:596-97; Minute of Hodgson in "Cumming's Papers," IOL, *Home Miscellaneous Series,* vol. 528, pp. 62-3.

30. The work of Dharma Kumar is important on this point, see *Land and Caste in South India* (Cambridge, Eng. 1965). Also see: *The Indian Law Commission: Report on Slavery in India, 1st February 1839,* 2 vols. (N.P., 1842), 1: 182-256, 2:423-24.

PART TWO
Dimensions of Landed Relations

Land and Class: Cultural, Social and Biophysical Integration in Interior Tamilnadu in the Late Eighteenth Century

BRIAN J. MURTON

SCHOLARS from different disciplines have long discussed and debated the nature of the agrarian system in India. During the past decade or so, a number of works have appeared which seek to throw more light upon the complex interrelationships of social structures and land control from Mughal times to the present.[1] All of these works are in marked contrast to studies of policy at the highest levels because they draw upon fresh materials from manuscript records and writings and have attempted to organize and analyze this data in such a way as to bring about a clearer understanding of agrarian processes in India.[2] Given the interests of the scholars involved in this enterprise—mainly historians, and anthropologists, with a leavening of economists—it is not surprising that research has focused primarily upon socially structured land control relationships. What has emerged from the various enquiries has been, first of all, a realization that there is a need for better terms and concepts which more accurately approximate the phenomena and conditions being described. The second point to emerge is that there is a need to develop new methodological tools and analytical models, particularly ones containing ideas about process as well as structure, and of dynamic relationships of social entities moving within a defined structural whole.

The concept of agrarian system has become known through the works of a number of scholars working on Indian historical data.[3] Yet, as Stein has pointed out, most of these writings do not claim comprehensive treatment of the relationship between people, groups of people, and the land as a systemic unity.[4] Thorner and Habib do view relationships between persons and land as part of a whole, but pursuant to the specific problems of their respective works they fall short of comprehensive analysis.[5] Likewise, Stein, while emphasizing the need for an agrarian system concept embodying a whole and developing complex of relationships among groups of people and the basic resource, land, focuses upon control of land: "Utilization of the concept demands recognition of the manifest dependence of power, livelihood, and status upon control of land; and any adequate analysis of dominantly agrestic societies must indicate the way in which political, economic, and social institutions are related to and integrated with control of land."[6]

Thus far geographers have not been involved in this dialogue, but they have employed the concept of system in their general work.[7] The usage which most closely approximates that of the agrarian system of the historians falls within the ecological framework in geography.[8] In this research it has been found that, rather than considering the whole ecological system, or ecosystem, it is more profitable to focus initially on descriptions of agricultural systems or agro-ecosystems.[9] This discriminating selection of a critical aspect of human behavior for intensive analysis is similar to Steward's notion of "culture core" in ecological anthropology.[10] More recently it has been stated by Waddell that cultural geographers should direct their attention to technology with reference to resources as the substantive core in their study of the man-environment interface.[11] In similar fashion we find those historians of India who employ an agrarian systems framework for their research focusing upon a "core," normally an aspect of land control or land holding.

An appropriate focus then for a geographer is upon the structure and functioning of the agro-ecosystem component of the agrarian system. A plethora of studies of agriculture and agricultural change on a subcontinent and regional level are in existence,[12] and there are innumerable micro-scale studies on the same topics.[13] These tell us something about changing patterns of agricultural organization, output, productivity, and the developing and shifting pattern of regional crop specialization, but, with the exception of one of the most recent works,[14] this research basically emphasizes structure. In other words, it is not fundamentally concerned with what is, or was, going on in the system at any particular time.

QUESTION AND PROBLEM

In this paper a cultural ecological perspective is employed as a framework to raise a question about the structure and operation of the agro-ecosystem in part of interior Tamilnadu in the late eighteenth century: how were land use categories conceptualized and utilized in relationship to the operational habitat,[15] demographic factors, and social groups? That is, attention is focused upon the identification and interrelationships of the key land use categories of the agro-ecosystem, and of the keys groups involved in utilizing the land. I thus direct my attention initially to resource, or land use, categories, and then come to grips with what was going on in the system, by relating these categories to habitat, population, and the groups involved in utilizing the land. By examining these aspects of the agrarian system certain I argue that questions raised by the historians about land holders, tenants, and laborers, and the ways in which these groups relate to local ecological and demographic conditions in a particular part of Tamilnadu are answered, at least in part. Specifically, the existence of rural structure in the late eighteenth century can be documented and interpreted only within local ecological and demographic contexts. These contexts can provide us with the settings in which the impact of the British assumption of territorial control can be assessed. Fundamentally, when East India Company officials took over "they had to choose between several claimants to rights in tenure systems largely unknown to them and described in a multiplicity of terms in Tamil, Telugu, Malayalam, and Canarese. Added to these were Arabic and Persian terms...which often were only substitutes for local words. And the British added their own elements of confusion in their natural tendency to look at everything from an English law or 'Lord-of-the-Manor' point of view."[16] As Frykenberg points out, all sorts of error and misinterpretation was possible,[17] despite an overt policy of building upon what was, and interfering as little as possible in rural life.

The British misinterpretation which emerges from the approach used in this paper was probably inadvertent, but it nonetheless created conditions which led to major changes in the structure and functioning of the agrarian system in the nineteenth century. The error I speak of was the total misunderstanding by the British of the concept, nature, and role of "waste" in the agro-ecosystem of interior Tamilnadu in the eighteenth century.

Study Area

The study area, Salem District, lies in the interior of Tamilnadu (Figure 1). As constituted in the 1790s it consisted of approximately 3,000 square miles of plains and hill ranges. When the British assumed control in 1792 they frequently referred to the area as the Talaghat portion of Salem and the Baramahal. Under the previous ruler, Tipu Sultan, the area formed the *Subadari* of Sankagirithurkam, and prior to that had been part of a larger Subadari, administered from Srirangapatnam, which included Coimbatore District. The area, significantly, was one of the earliest areas in Tamilnadu to come under British control, and it was the area in which many of the principles that later became involved in the ryotwari system of revenue management were initially investigated and put into practice. It is thus an unusually appropriate area in which to investigate an issue such as the possibility of a British misinterpretation of "waste."

In Tamil regional terms, most of the study area belongs to *Kongu Nadu,* one of the five macro-regions within Tamilnadu that had emerged by the late eighteenth century.[18] Nadu or *Mandalam,* as they are more often called, are territories, each of which contains a different mixture of the complex of common elements that make up the Tamil agrarian systems. I emphasize this point because the bulk of what follows can only be supported for the particular ecological, demographic, and sociological context that is Salem.

Land Use Categories

In this section I endeavor to identify the categories that Tamils in Salem used to conceptualize their resource base at the end of the eighteenth century. This approach is used for two basic reasons. First, although most of the source materials are in English they can be fully utilized only if it is realized that they are based upon Tamil, and more generally South Indian, categories

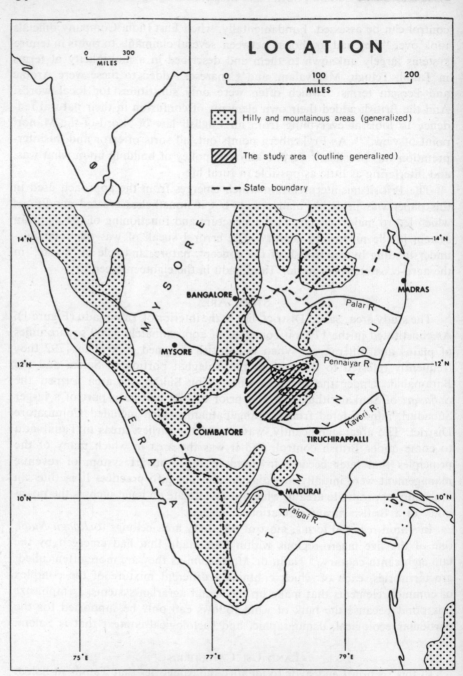

FIGURE 1: LOCATION OF THE STUDY AREA

The study area, Salem, consists of the southern part of the territory known to the British as Salem and the Baramahal. The Baramahal is that area enclosed within the broken line.

for resources. Attempts to reorder and impose alien categories on the data can prove to be most unrewarding and frustrating.[19] The second reason involves the contention that cultural ecology can most advantageously be carried out when it is derived from description ordered according to the principles by which the group under investigation interpret their environment and make behavioral decisions.[20] This does not mean, of course, replacing the analytical methods of Western science, a task considerably beyond my powers. Rather, I approach the matter through the question of culturally relevant categories in relationship to the agro-ecosystem. Such an approach recalls Sauer's exhortation to historical geographers to develop "the ability to see the land with the eye of its former inhabitants, from the standpoint of their needs and capacities."[21] It attempts to develop some sense of the "world view" of the group under investigation, the spatial organization it mentally and physically imposes on the landscape, its understanding of perceived environmental processes and patterns, its repertoire of categories and techniques of resource management, and its rationale for applying techniques to different portions of the environment.

At the end of the eighteenth century in Salem there were a number of categories of land utilized for agricultural or pastoral purposes, of waste lands, and of lands incapable of cultivation, or set aside for public or communal purposes. These categories reflect the profile of environmental types in the area at the time, and are indicators of Tamilian exploitation of local ecological conditions. Agro-ecosystems can be viewed simply as consisting of one or a combination of distinctive types of man-made ecosystems or ecotypes, defined as sets of food transfers and of devices used to harness organic sources of energy to the productive process, making up a system of energy transfers from the environment of man.[22] Each Tamil category of land was an ecotype and the agro-ecosystem of Tamilnadu in the late eighteenth century was made up of the integration of these ecotypes into a functioning whole.

A problem in dealing with ecotypes in Salem in the late eighteenth century is the multiplicity of terms used by the British to refer to the same type. However, throughout much of South India, regardless of exact terminology, a threefold system of classifying cultivated land into wet, dry, and groves and orchards is universal and quite ancient.[23] An elaborate system of land classification existed by at least the eleventh century, when numerous inscriptions distinguish between the three types of land.[24] The inscriptions also mention other categories of land: wastes for grazing cattle, forest lands, barren lands, brackish lands, tanks, and tank catchments.

In his final report on Salem and the Baramahal, Colonel Read, the first Collector, states that "the natives distinguish as Sutwa or productive and poonjay as barren."[25] More commonly, however, cultivated land was referred to as *zirat zamin*,[26] and this particular usage of the term "poonjay," or punja, is the only one in the early British records referring to the study area. A more common usage, and that followed by the British, of the term punja,

is in reference to land incapable of irrigated rice cultivation and suitable
only for millets and pulses. In the early records this type of land is referred
to as *kadarambam,* or "land which was dry or chiefly watered by
rains."[27]

The second major category of cultivated land was *niranambam,* or "wet,
requiring an abundance of water, which is necessarily collected in reservoirs
for cultivation purposes."[28] This type of land also was known as nunja
in the British records dealing with the study area.[29] In some of the early
reports garden land was referred to by its Marathi or Kannada term,
baghayat.[30] At this time a distinction was made between kadarambam
baghayat, or gardens "watered by raising water from deep tanks or wells"
and *niranambam* baghayat which was "plentifully supplied by talabs or large
reservoirs, or by running streams."[31] However, by the late 1790s in the study
area the term garden, now more appropriately called by the Tamil term
tottam, or *tottakkal,* came to refer to lands irrigated by raising water either
by hand or by bullocks. Such lands were said to be "much more valuable
than punjai in every situation and rather less valuable than nanjai in most
situations on account of the labour required to raise the water."[32]

But regardless of variations in terminology, and in the slightly different
ways in which garden land was defined, there is little question that all cultivated land was assigned to one of the three categories of nanja, punja, and
tottam. Certainly the British, with their policy that innovation would cause
extensive disruption to agriculture and hence revenue, immediately adopted
the threefold system, and subsequently all available information on land
use in the 1790s is given in these categories.[33]

A further category of land, in parts of the study area at least, was that
which is called "pasture" in the early British records. Publications in the
nineteenth century indicate that "grass farming" was a feature of most of
Coimbatore, the parts of Salem adjacent to Coimbatore, and in Palni Taluk
in Madurai District: that is, in Kongu Nadu.[34] Certainly, considerable areas
of "grass" or "pasture" existed in Salem in the late eighteenth century.
Munro, in commenting upon his superior, Read's, ideas on assessment
rates, put it this way: "In many of the populous and well cultivated villages
in the Southern Districts the Rayets are obliged to send their cattle several
miles to graze. The more substantial of them however who have a number
of fields generally leave one or two of them fallow for the use of their cattle
which they change every second or third year in succession, and as they are
all enclosed and yield abundant crops of grass they are as profitable in this
way as they were sown with grains."[35] This was particularly true in Tiruchengodu "where both the grass and the enclosures are in the greatest perfec-
tion."[36] A later entry indicates that such pasture lands generally belonged
to Vellalas (probably Kongu Vellalas), and that they had been assessed at
one-third the usual dry land rate "from time immemorial."[37] Significantly,
these lands were located only in Namakkal, Paramathi, Sankagirithurkam,
Rasipuram, and Tiruchengodu Taluks, the part of Salem truly lying in

Kongu Nadu. In 1826, in areas under direct government control (in distinction to zamindari estates) the following acreages of pasture were found: Namakkal, 838 acres; Paramathi, 4877 acres; Sankagirithurkam, 543 acres; Rasipuram, 1701 acres; and Tiruchengodu, 3085 acres.[38] During the 1820s the government began to raise assessment rates on these lands, to get them under cultivation.[39]

Another important category of land recognized by Tamils was "waste," *tarisu,* but more commonly called *banjar* in the British records of the late eighteenth century. "Waste" has always been a troublesome category to interpret from the records.[40] Apart from that land called *puramboku,* or land incapable of cultivation or set apart for public or communal purposes, and thus unassessed,[41] all land in a *gramam,* or village, was classified as either cultivated or waste. But there were many kinds of waste, and "fallow" also was included in this category at times. In fact, at the end of the eighteenth century, at least three types of banjar existed: land which had been uncultivated for five years, or for ten years, and land that had never been cultivated.[42] That large areas were in one or other of these categories emerges from the cultivation statistics (Table 1). Forty-four percent of the total acreage contained within surveyed village lands was under fallow and waste, and in some taluks (Attur, Viraganur, Sendamangalam, Namakkal, and Nangavalli) over 50 percent was in this category. In the first four of the above taluks evidence from the nineteenth century tells us that it was customary practice to fallow lands lying at the bottom of the hills every alternate year.[43] The cultivators gave the delightful, if somewhat dubious, explanation that such lands were so moist that they required brushwood to be burnt to dry them out.

In addition, it was usual in some taluks, such as Attur, to leave lands fallow every second year "particularly when the first year crop had been Codroo which is said to exhaust the soil more than any other grain. By leaving it fallow then a full crop of Ragi or Cholam may be expected in the third."[44] The British records thus tell us that "a good proportion of the lands which appear in the accounts as Bunjar (or waste) are simply fallow in order to increase the lands productive powers."[45]

With regard to five- and ten-year waste, a constant theme in the records is the fact that "small portions of waste in every District are annually brought into cultivation and again after two or three years forsaken for fresh lands."[46] That this was a well-established practice, and one which had been taken into account in the pre-British revenue collection system, is evidenced in statements such as: "Waste lands are given the first year for a third or a fourth (or even less) of the annual rents of arable lands. They seldom rise to one half the second year and it is never before the third and often not till several years later that they are assessed equal or nearly equal to the neighboring cultivated lands."[47]

There is little doubt, however, that much of the permanent waste was forest of long standing. I am not suggesting that this forest was in any way

Table 1
CULTIVATED, FALLOW, AND WASTE LANDS IN THE LATE EIGHTEENTH CENTURY

Taluk 1796	Cultivated		Fallow and Waste contained with village boundaries		Total Cutlivable Acres
	Wet Acres	Dry Acres	Acres	% Total	
Salem	3,234	36,163	10,914	22	50,311
Chennagiri	2,169	23,042	5,759	19	30,970
Bellur	3,711	41,555	42,506	48	87,772
Attur	2,275	27,184	43,317	59	72,776
Viraganur	2,732	27,933	36,292	54	66,957
Sendamanagalam	3,122	58,548	67,830	52	129,500
Rasipuram	1,606	15,895	16,073	48	33,574
Namakkal	3,995	51,137	72,128	57	127,260
Paramathi	2,586	43,555	27,117	37	73,258
Tiruchengodu	925	55,205	26,730	32	82,860
Sankagirithurkam	3,304	75,957	49,442	38	128,703
Edapadi	1,401	44,444	29,278	39	75,123
Omalur	3,236	63,477	33,576	33	100,289
Nangavalli	97	31,495	35,494	53	67,086
Total	34,393	595,590	496,456	44	1,126,439

SOURCE: "The State of the Lands," *The Records of Salem and the Baramahal*, volume 2: *Geography*, Madras Records Office.

in its "natural state," because man has been interfering with the vegetation in Salem for perhaps 5000 years.[48] At the best in the late eighteenth century on the plains, such forest consisted of much modified scrub-woodland, consisting of a few trees, and a thick and continuous shrubby layer. Considerable areas of this type of woodland, or "dense thorn forest" were located in the western part of the study area. The hill ranges, plus most of the isolated hills, and the lands around their bases were still clothed with what appears to have been substantial forest of a dry deciduous type. These areas were much "berun with Jungle" in which some "teak of small size" were found.[49] The forest land on the plains were called "gidagauvel,"[50] "gedigauvel,"[51] or "goodagavel,"[52] terms which are derived from *gidagawal,* a Telugu word for taxes levied on forest.[53] In Salem they were "distinct pieces of jungle where a small tax on firewood was formerly collected."[54] In 1806–1807, to encourage cultivation, special low assessments were placed on such "jungly tracts," with the result that by 1830 they had been "extensively reclaimed."[55] The low assessments were made permanent in this year because of the "trouble in clearing and breaking up such lands, and because of their general light and sterile quality."[56]

The final important category of land mentioned in the late eighteenth century records was that called *puramboku*. Such lands consisted "of roads, sites of towns, houses and forts, beds of tanks,"[57] which commonly did not yield any revenue, although it was liable to revenue if the government so chose.[58]

NATURE AND ROLE OF WASTE IN THE SALEM AGRO-ECOSYSTEM

The fact that there was so much uncultivated land bothered the British in the late eighteenth century, and continued to do so in the nineteenth.[59] In particular, it concerned them that this unused land paid little or no revenue, and thus efforts were made to extend the cultivated area through continuing the system of lower assessment rates for a number of years on waste land taken under cultivation. Initially, it was thought that because of the wars the area had been depopulated. For example, it was estimated in 1793 that Namakkal, Paramathi, and Sendamangalam taluks contained but one-fifth of their normal population.[60] Population decrease does seem to have occurred in some places, but it is more likely that the British misinterpreted the nature and role of waste in the agro-ecosystem in late-eighteenth-century Salem: much of the five- and ten-year waste has to be considered as land under a form of "short-fallow cultivation."[61] In short-fallow cultivation systems nothing but wild grasses invade the fallow, and hence there is some justification for labelling the system "grass fallow." Indeed, in those parts of Salem where the "pasture" category occurred, this usage appears appropriate. Livestock, grazed on both "pasture" and "waste," must therefore be regarded as an integral and important part of the agro-ecosystem in such areas. Short-fallow cultivation can be regarded as intermediary between forest- and bush-fallow (swidden) and annual cropping. Dry land, wet land, and garden land fall into the annual cropping system, where land is left uncultivated for several months between the harvest of one crop and the planting of the next. Some wet land, and most garden land, was certainly under a multi-cropping system, where the same plot bore two or more successive crops each year.

While the proportion of land under "waste" and "pasture" must have varied widely regionally throughout Tamilnadu, they formed extremely important components in the agro-ecosystems of areas such as Salem where rainfall was low and variable, and which, in the late eighteenth century, were relatively sparsely populated. I thus argue that the nature of "waste," and the role that it played in the agro-ecosystem in late-eighteenth-century

Salem is the key to understanding the operation of the overall agrarian system, including aspects of social structure. The key role of "waste" in the system is now discussed in relationship to habitat, population, and the groups involved in utilizing land.

Habitat: The Drought Factor

Tamils inhabit an uncertain environment, the productivity of which varies enormously, not only from place to place, but over time as well. The agro-ecosystem in Salem in the late eighteenth century was adapted not only to a certain amount of rainfall, but also to acute seasonal variation. However, even these seasonal rhythms had been repetitive enough for Tamils in Salem to learn to cope with them. It was the irregular and uncertain fluctuations in rainfall that hit the system hardest in Salem, and the amount and timing of the rains in any given year was one of the determinants of the acreage under the annual cultivation of rainfed crops, in addition to being a key factor in the area under short-fallow cultivation.

That seasonal uncertainty existed in the late eighteenth century was recognized by the British when they investigated reasons for the non-payment of land revenue: "There are probably more causes of insolvency among farmers than among men of any other vocation owing to their being subject to misfortunes from which others are exempt."[62] Six major causes of "defalcation" were listed: those arising from the seasons, those from casualties among the ryots, those from sundry personal factors, those from patels and karnams, and those from tahsildars and collectors. The principal cause, however, was "the want of rain," the certain effect of which was "lands being left in fallow."[63]

To help them assess the situation, the British collected descriptive data on the behavior of the monsoon and its impact on crops in Salem back to 1770. Between this year and 1790 "full crops" were obtained only five times three-quarter crops seven times, half crops five times, three-eighth crops twice, and a quarter crop once.[64] The worst years were 1778–1798, 1785–1786, and 1790–1791. Low rainfall was also a problem in the 1790s and the acreage cultivated in 1792–1793 was acknowledged as the "worst for many years."[65] British reports usually concluded with a statement such as:

> It was well known that the rains are extremely precarious and that when they do fall, they are either partial or scanty, or if plentiful, that the season has passed and the only purpose they serve as at present is from their violence to destroy half the tanks in the country. How often has the farmer, deceived by a passing shower, imprudently committed his seed to the ground and how often have his hopes of a return been blasted by a succeeding drought, equally fatal to his crops, as to his cattle.[66]

At the end of the eighteenth century there was a range of ecotypes in this drought-prone area but annual cultivation of rainfed crops, and short-fallow cultivation dominated. The latter type of cultivation was a flexible and viable method of using land in a hazardous environment. It could respond very rapidly to an absence of rain through acreage reduction. At those times when there was plenty of moisture large areas could be taken up on a temporary basis. However, this integration of ecotypes, and the importance of the short-fallow type, was only possible because of the relatively low population in the late eighteenth century.

Population

I have argued that the study area was not totally occupied by various types of annual cropping in the late eighteenth century. In addition I assert that the area was not so depopulated by the wars of the late eighteenth century as the British records indicate. To be sure, some areas had been affected by the marching armies, the predatory *palaiyakars,* and the rapacious commissaries. In many places irrigation facilities, especially tanks, had fallen into disrepair. But few people seen to have been killed and those who fled soon returned after peace was established. Certainly, by the time the first estimate of population was made in 1795, there had been five years of British rule and order. At this time it was estimated that there were about 282,000 people in the study area, although the Collector considered that the estimate was low by about 10 percent.[67] Ultimately the population was set as 313,598 (Table 2). That this estimate was approximately correct was borne out by later estimates by slightly different methods in the early years of the nineteenth century, when the population fluctuated between 320,000 and 340,000. It was only after about 1810 that population began to increase, reaching just over one-half-a-million in 1828.[68]

People were found everywhere in the study area in the late eighteenth century, but perhaps of more fundamental importance for my argument, is that in many parts of Salem population densities were not great (Table 2). The average rate of density per square mile for the plains portion of the study area was 131. Four taluks—Belur, Attur, Viraganur, and Nammakkal—had densities below 100 per square mile, and three—Rasipuram, Salem and Paramathi—densities of over 150. Only in Rasipuram (238) did density per square mile get over 200, and there is nothing in the British records that indicates that there was any sense of overpopulation in any part of the area. Today, for example, although the population has increased enormously, Salem ranks eleventh out of the thirteen districts of Tamilnadu in population density, with a figure of 529 per square mile.[69] There is little reason to assume that Salem ranked other than at the lower end of the population density scale for Tamil districts in 1800. This makes the abundance of fallow, waste, and forest land, and the way in which it was used, of great potential significance when comparing the study area with other more densely inhabited parts of Tamilnadu. I tentatively suggest that in areas of higher and denser population there was much less land under the short fallow system of cultivation.

In summary, in the late eighteenth century Salem was one of the most

Table 2

ESTIMATED POPULATION IN THE LATE EIGHTEENTH CENTURY

Taluk	Population Numbers	Population Density (p.p.s.m.)
Salem	28,105	182
Chennagiri	12,884	142
Bellur	25,164	96
Attur	17,343	93
Viraganur	14,717	67
Sendamangalam	28,652	104
Rasipuram	19,282	238
Nammakkal	22,228	86
Paramathi	23,506	171
Tiruchengodu	21,245	122
Sankagirithurkam	23,551	125
Edapadi	22,884	140
Omalur	27,117	127
Nangavalli	17,920	124
Total	313,598	

SOURCE: *The Baramahal Records.* Inhabitants, volume 3, (Madras, 1907), p. IV. The figures are estimates based upon the application of a ratio of persons per house.

sparsely settled areas of Tamilnadu. Large areas of fallow, waste, and forest land existed as a normal condition in this area of low population numbers and densities, where local habitat conditions, particularly rainfall, created uncertainty. These conditions in turn created a profile of ecotypes which was very different from coastal Tamilnadu where population densities were greater and rainfall higher and more reliable.

Resource Regulators

Any agro-ecosystem cannot meaningfully be considered apart from its social context,[70] because there are causal links between the "network of relationships between man and his physical environment" and the "network of relationships among men."[71] Further, these links are reflexive in the sense that the social system is a mechanism which can be exploited in certain ways or modified in the interests of more efficient utilization of a resource complex. But the same system can also impose considerable restrictions on both the mode of utilization and actual composition of that complex. A cultural ecological approach to the study of agro-ecosystems must, consequently, be placed in some context of human behavior.

The particular social context significant to this study is that of rural class structure in relationship to land categories, especially the utilization of land types by different groups. By examining these relationships I hope to demonstrate the functional interdependence among social (class structure), cultural (land types), and biophysical (habitat and population) systems in the late eighteenth century.

Analysis of social classes in Tamilnadu has not received much attention from the historians, perhaps because of the overwhelming dominance of caste analysis. But as Stein has suggested: "If we are to view social classes as sections of a general social order defined by social and economic influence supported by the prevailing political, administrative, and judicial structure, then it would appear that strata defined by these criteria did exist in nineteenth century Madras."[72]

By extension such groups would have existed in earlier times as well. In Salem in the late eighteenth century, where agriculture was the primary economic activity, cultivating groups formed the basis of class differentiation. Unfortunately, although considerable research has been done on land tenure in South India in the late eighteenth and early nineteenth centuries,[73] little attention has been paid to the identification of social classes.[74] But there is little doubt that basic to any identification of such groups is the fact that in the pre-British era the prevailing system of land control focussed on territorial divisions rather than on individual cultivators.[75] Mukherjee and Frykenberg make the point generally for South India that, while it is not entirely correct to assert that the ryotwari system originated with the British, it is quite certain that immediately prior to the introduction of Company rule the prevailing mode of land control was the gramawari, or village, system.[76] This was the case in Salem, where, as I have demonstrated elsewhere, there can be little doubt that a gramawari system can be dated to at least the late seventeenth century.[77]

Furthermore, at the end of the eighteenth century, the gramam or *mauza* consisting of either one large settlement site or, more commonly, one main settlement and several smaller ones,[78] were under the control of people who can only be described as "superior" landholders.[79] Research by Sarada Raju and Kumar has demonstrated that "superior" landholders or mirasidars, throughout Tamilnadu either cultivated their lands by means of laborers, or leased them to tenants.[80] Two types of tenants can be distinguished: *parakudi,* or tenant from outside of the village; and *ulkudi,* or resident of the village. Parakudi tenants were tenants-at-will who cultivated some of the superior landholders' lands for a year or longer, according to arrangement. At the expiration of their lease they were liable to eviction and rent enhancement, but they could leave the gramam for another. Under this system the landlord frequently bore all the expenses involved in the preliminary stages of cultivation and the responsibility of the parakudi began with the ploughing and ended just before the harvest. Harvest expenses were met from the gross crop before the division between landlord and tenant. Parakudis often were paid during the harvest like other hired laborers and then the crop divided according to the agreed shares.

The second type of tenant was called ulkudi. Such a person was a permanent resident in the gramam in which he cultivated land. An ulkudi could never acquire absolute rights to land but in cases where the same family held lands for several generations they acquired quasi-proprietary right to the fields they occupied and could not be dispossessed as long as they rendered the customary dues. Ulkudi lands were passed on from father to son, and the holding only reverted to the mirasidar in the absence of heirs, or in the case of desertion. However, ulkudis could not sell their lands, although Sarada Raju cites evidence which indicates that they could mortgage their holdings.[81]

Lands not leased were cultivated for mirasidars by laborers. Such laborers were known as *pannaiyal* (men who worked the *pannai,* or home farm), *padital* (men who were paid by the measure), *muladulu,* and *adami.*[82] Sarada Raju calls such laborers "serfs" or "slaves" and states that they were provided with a house and yard, and were given gifts of money, grain, and cloth at festival time, besides their regular remuneration.[83]

These types of arrangements were also found in Salem and the Baramahal. In agraharams, for example; the land was cultivated largely by tenants,[84] although some Brahmans apparently did use laborers,[85] in a manner similar to the *pannaiyal* system. The cultivation of lands entirely by the use of laborers is also mentioned by Read in referring to "different other castes" whose occupations were other than agriculture.[86] But apart from this no other direct evidence exists to document the cultivation of land by laborers. However, other evidence which indicates that patels managed to avoid paying rents on their own land, suggests that most of the superior landholders did cultivate pannai, in addition to renting out land.

But most of their holdings were cultivated by tenants. While the terms parakudi and ulkudi are not found in *The Baramahal Records,* and in his official statements Read makes no distinction among farmers of the *kudi* class,[87] other evidence definitely indicates that both types of cultivator were common. "Inferior ryots, or husbandmen" who were "by much the greater number"[88] cultivated "lands under the *patels* and principal farmers for a certain share of the crop."[89] According to Graham, the "inferior ryots" were divided into two groups: those attached to the village, and "those who belonging to another have been in the practice of giving a part of their labor to it."[90] This is a direct reference to ulkudi and parakudi tenants. There is also indirect evidence to document the existence of these types of tenure. Many of the sources describe migrations from one village to another.[91] There is much discussion of cultivators moving in the immediate pre-monsoon period, "especially during the months of March and April, the period at which the *ryots* from motives of caprice, superstition, or other causes migrate from one district to another, and that at which they receive their cowle for the year from the renters...."[92] Such people were most certainly parakudi tenants and, from the sources, it appears that some of them did move considerable distances: from gramam to gramam, from taluk to taluk, and even between districts.

A final but important question relates to the manner in which "superior" landholders actually held land. I have suggested elsewhere that the most common method of holding land in the late eighteenth century in Salem was either a decaying form of *karaiyedu* tenure, where the gramam lands were jointly held by co-sharers, but temporarily assigned in shares for cultivation, the shares being redistributed by lot a certain times according to custom,[93] or *arudikarai* tenure, where cultivated lands were permanently distributed, but where waste was held in common.[94] Such villages were divided into *pangu* (shares), each made up of lands which in theory yielded an equal amount of produce and each including a proprietary share of all the benefits of common property, such as waste land. A certain number of pangu comprised a *karai*, the basic division of such a village. The division into shares was supposed to have been made when the village was originally settled and the number of shares corresponded to the number of settlers who first occupied the village. The common feature in all of these types of villages was that waste was jointly held, and this raises some potentially interesting questions about the mechanisms of utilizing short fallow land before the 1790s, which will not be answered here.

In summary, "superior" landholders and their permanent (ulkudi) tenants cultivated permanent fields under either annual or multi-cropping systems of management. At propitious times these groups would have used short fallow lands as well, but this latter land was cultivated, in distinction to being used for livestock grazing, mainly by parakudi tenants. The mobility of this group bothered the British, who in their records, give the impression that it was of considerable size. But given population and habitat conditions in Salem in the late eighteenth century, parakudi tenants played an important and well-defined role in the agrarian system. In fact, the size of the group and the way in which short fallow was utilized, in relationship to the more sedentary social groups and permanent field agriculture, is the key to understanding the functioning of the agrarian system in the area at the time.

DISCUSSION AND CONCLUSIONS

At the end of the eighteenth century multi-cropping, annual cropping, short-fallow cropping, and, on the hill ranges, swidden, coexisted in Salem. But more striking is the fact that the first three systems of land use coexisted in the same village territories, each of them occupying land relatively well suited to that particular degree of intensity. The coexistence of these ecotypes reflects the profile of both habitat and population conditions in Salem. In this analysis attention was focussed initially upon one aspect of the agro-ecosystem, ecotypes as defined by the people under investigation. In doing this a cultural-ecological framework, where the system was described according to the principles by which Tamils interpreted their environment, was employed.

This approach enabled a number of objectives to be achieved. First, the interdependence of these culturally defined ecotypes with habitat conditions, especially low and irregular rainfall, with population numbers and density, and with local class structure was demonstrated. In other words linkages were made between the networks of relationships among men and those between man and his biophysical environment. Second, a major British misinterpretation of the nature and role of waste and the significance of a mobile section of the cultivating population was identified. Third, the class system in Tamilnadu emerged as a dynamic entity: it was obviously flexible enough to be modified to exploit areas of ecological and demographic difference, at least within the pre-British agrarian context. Questions remain to be answered on whether or not it imposed restrictions on the mode of utilizing the resource complex in Salem when new forces, including British misinterpretations, began to operate in the nineteenth century.

In conclusion, these research findings have the following importance: first, they relate to wider questions concerning land control and social structure in South India; second, they enable us to "locate" a key ecotype, the nature and role of which was misinterpreted by the British leading to problems in the agrarian system in the nineteenth century; third, they provide baseline information for understanding this problem, and identify some critical variables which should make the interpretation of change in the nineteenth century an easier task; fourth, they enable us to relate the groups utilizing land to ecotypes; and fifth, they enable us to conclude that the cultivating population of Salem was organized in a socially distinct way, reflective of the local integration of ecotypes, so that elsewhere in Tamilnadu social organization would be different.

NOTES

1. Robert Eric Frykenberg, ed., *Land Control and Social Structure in Indian History* (Madison, Wis., 1969): S.C. Gupta, *Agrarian Relations and Early British Rule in India* (Bombay, 1963); Irfan Habib, *The Agrarian System of Mughal India: 1556-1702* (Bombay, 1963); Dharma Kumar, *Land and Caste in South India* (Cambridge, Eng., 1965); Nilmani Mukherjee, *The Ryotwari System in Madras: 1792-1827* (Calcutta, 1962); Walter C. Neale, *Economic Change in Rural India: 1800-1955* (New Haven, 1962); Daniel Thorner, *The Agrarian Prospects in India* (Delhi, 1956).
2. Frykenberg, *Land Control*, p. xvii.
3. B.H. Baden-Powell, *The Land Systems of British India*, 3 vols. (Oxford, 1892); W.H. Moreland, *The Agrarian Systems of Moslem India* (Cambridge, Eng., 1929); K.M. Gupta, *The Land System of South India Between c. 800 A.D. and 1200 A.D.* (Lahore, 1933); M.N. Gupta, *Land System of Bengal* (Calcutta, 1940).
4. Burton Stein, "Integration of the Agrarian System of South India," in Frykenberg, *Land Control*, pp. 175-76.
5. Thorner, *Agrarian Prospects;* Habib, *Agrarian System.*
6. Stein, "Integration of the Agrarian System," p. 176.
7. John Langton, "Potentialities and Problems of Adapting a Systems Approach to

the Study of Change in Human Geography," *Progress in Geography* 4 (1972); pp 125-80.

8. D.R. Stoddard, "Organism and Ecosystem as Geographical Models," in R.J. Chorley and P. Haggett, ed., *Models in Geography* (London, 1967), pp. 511-48.

9. J.M. Blaut, "The Ecology of Tropical Farming Systems, in *Plantation Systems of the New World* (Washington, 1959), pp. 83-103; H.C. Brookfield, "Questions on the Human Frontiers of Geography," *Economic Geography* 40 (1964): 283-303; H.C. Brookfield, "New Directions in the Study of Agricultural Systems in Tropical Areas," in E.T. Drake, ed., *Evolution and Environment* (New Haven, 1968), pp. 413-39.

10. Julian Steward, *Theory of Culture Change* (Urbana, 1955), pp. 30-42.

11. Eric Waddell, "Methodology and Explanation in Cultural Geography, or the Quest for an Interface in Man-Mileu Relationships," Paper Presented at Meetings of Association of American Geographers, San Francisco, 1970.

12. See George Blyn, *Agricultural Trends in India, 1891-1947: Output, Availability, and Productivity* (Philadelphia, 1966); D.H. Buchanan, *Development of Capitalist Enterprise in India* (New York, 1934); R. Ratman, *Agricultural Development in Madras State Prior to 1900* (Madras, 1967); A. Sarada Raju, *Economic Conditions in Madras Presidency, 1800-50* (Madras, 1941); Elizabeth Whitcombe, *Agrarian Conditions in Northern India* vol. 1: *The United Provinces Under British Rule, 1860-1900* (Berkeley, 1972).

13. For example, Harold Mann, *Land and Labor in a Deccan Village* (Bombay, 1917); Albert Mayer *et al, Pilot Project India: The Story of Rural Development at Etawah. Uttar Pradesh* (Berkeley, 1958); Scarlett Epstein, *Economic Development and Social Change in South India* (London, 1962).

14. Whitcombe, *Agrarian Conditions in Northern India.*

15. The term habitat is used here to refer to the biophysical environment. Operational habitat is that aspect of the biophysical environment most pertinent to the people and/or problem under investigation.

16. Kumar, *Land and Caste*. p. 9.

17. Frykenberg, *Land Control*, p. xv.

18. Burton Stein, "Historical and Cultural Geography of Tamil Country: A View from the Peasantry," Paper Presented at Meetings of Association for Asian Studies, New York, 1972; Brenda F. Beck, *Peasant Society in Konku. A Study of Right and Left Subcastes in South India* (Vancouver, 1972).

19. I attempted to reorder agricultural data for my Ph.D. dissertation, "Man, Mind, and Land. A Peasant Production System in Late Eighteenth Century South India" (Univ. of Minn. 1970) with singularly unrewarding results.

20. Charles O. Frake, "Cultural Ecology and Ethnography," *American Anthropologist* 64 (1962): 53-59.

21. Carl O. Sauer, "Foreword to Historical Geography," *Annals of the Association of American Geographers* 31 (1941): 1-24.

22. Eric Wolf, *Peasants* (Englewood Cliffs, New Jersey, 1966), p. 69; Brian J. Murton, "Folk Classification of Cultivated Land and Ecology in Southern India," *Proceedings of the Association of American Geographers* 5 (1973): 199-202.

23. William A. Noble, "Agricultural Classification: Extreme Southern India," *The Professional Geographer* 19 (1967): 247.

24. A. Appadorai, *Economic Conditions in Southern India* (Madras, 1936), p. 85.

25. "Report of Colonel Alexander Read, Late Superintendent of Baramahal and Salem, 4 April 1800," *The Records of Salem and Baramahal* (Manuscript) Read's Reports, 1800. Madras Records Office.

26. "Read's Fifth Report, June 1793," *Records of Fort St. George: The Baramahal Records, Land Rent* Section 6 (Madras, 1918), p. 27.

27. Ibid., p. 25.

28. Ibid.

29. See "Sketch of Revenue Management in the Countries North of the Caveri under the Gentu, the Moorish, and the Honble Company's Government," ibid., Section 1 (Madras, 1907); "Read's Fifth Report."

30. Ibid., p. 25; H.H. Wilson, *Glossary of Judicial and Revenue Terms* (London, 1855), p. 262.

31. "Read's Fifth Report," p. 25.

32. Macleod to Read, 29 April 1798, *Records of Fort St. George: The Baramahal Records, Land Rent,* Section 6, p. 144.

33. Of course there were a large number of further divisions, particularly with reference to soil type and crop capability, for each of the major ecotypes.

34. E.H. Hazelton and C. Benson, "The Supply of Cattle in the Madras Presidency," *Bulletin,* Department of Land Records and Agriculture, Madras 8 (1890): 51-57; "Grass-Farming in Coimbatore," ibid. 27 (1893): 249-57.

35. Thomas Munro, "Notes on Captain Read's Observations on Objections to Making the Settlement of 1204 Permanent Till Superseded by the Lease," *Selections from Old Records. The Baramahal Records. Salem District,* 157: "Agrahars 1793-1798" (Salem,

1902), p. 12.
   36. Ibid., p. 13.
   37. Madras. Proceedings of the Board of Revenue, 5 September 1821. Madras Records Office.
   38. Madras. Proceedings of the Board of Revenue, 18 September 1826. Madras Records Office.
   39. Ibid., 5 September 1826.
   40. See B.H. Farmer, *Agricultural Colonization in South and South East Asia* (Hull, 1969).
   41. S. Sundararaja Iyengar, *Land Tenures in the Madras Presidency. Student's Edition* (Madras, 1933), p. 38.
   42. "Read's Fifth Report," p. 27.
   43. Proceedings of the Board of Revenue, 21 May 1840. Madras Records Office.
   44. Proceedings of the Board of Revenue, 18 September 1826. Madras Records Office.
   45. Ibid.
   46. Munro to Read, 31 July 1796, "Agrahars, 1793–1798," p. 8.
   47. Ibid.
   48. Brian J. Murton, "Man-Induced Vegetation Change in Interior Tamilnadu," in J.G. Nelson and R.C. Space, eds., *Impact of Technology on Environment: Some Global Examples,* Studies in Land Use History and Landscape Change, no. 6 (London, Ont., 1974), pp. 175–200.
   49. Mather to Read, 9 March 1798, *Records of Fort St. George: The Baramahal Records, Miscellany,* Section 21 (Madras, 1925), p. 153.
   50. Proceedings of the Board of Revenue, 4 June 1813; 5 November 1813. Madras Records Office.
   51. Ibid., 9 August 1820.
   52. Ibid., 20 December 1830.
   53. Wilson, *Glossary,* p. 178.
   54. Proceedings of the Board of Revenue, 4 June 1813. Madras Records Office.
   55. Ibid., 20 December 1830.
   56. Ibid.
   57. Ibid., 5 September 1821.
   58. Sundararaja Iyengar, *Land Tenures,* p. 38.
   59. See H. Le Fanu, *A Manual of the Salem District in the Presidency of Madras,* 2 vols. (Madras, 1883), 1: 240–476.
   60. Macleod to Read, 29 June 1793, *The Records of Salem and the Baramahal.* Manuscript, Section VII. Land Rent, Vol. 1, June–Sept. 1793. Madras Records Office.
   61. Ester Boserup, *The Conditions of Agricultural Growth. The Economics of Agrarian Change Under Population Pressure* (Chicago, 1965), p. 16.
   62. Read to Saunders, 6 May 1796, *Records of Fort St. George: The Baramahal Records, Balances,* Section 15 (Madras, 1922), p. 2.
   63. Ibid., p. 27.
   64. "Comparative View of the Crops in 20 Years to Show Their Relative Proportions, The Prices of the Grain and the Circumstances of the Ryots During that Period," ibid., Section 6, p. 163.
   65. Read to Haliburton, 29 January 1793, ibid., Section 21, p. 74.
   66. Graham to Read, 24 August 1797, ibid., Section 22 (Madras, 1933), p. 192.
   67. "Introduction," ibid., Section 3 (Madras, 1907), p. iii.
   68. Proceedings of the Board of Revenue, 31 December 1828. Madras Records Office.
   69. Population data, 1800–1901 in Kumar, *Land and Caste,* pp. 120–21, demonstrate that population growth in Salem has been little different than that in other Tamil Districts. Map 17, "Intercensal Changes in Population, 1901-1961," in the *Atlas of Madras State, Census of India,* vol. IX, part IX (Madras, 1964), further demonstrates that growth in the twentieth century has not been too different from other districts, especially North Arcot, Coimbatore, Madurai, and Tinnevelly.
   70. Eric Waddell, *The Mound Builders. Agricultural Practices, Environment and Society in the Central Highlands of New Guinea* (Seattle, 1972), p. 183.
   71. Frake, "Cultural Ecology," p. 54.
   72. Burton Stein, "Privileged Landholding: The Concept Stretched to Cover the Case," infra., p. 67.
   73. Sarada Raju, *Economic Conditions,* pp. 28–41; Kumar, *Land and Caste,* pp. 6–48; Mukherjee, *The Ryotwari System,* pp. 292–303; N. Mukherjee and Robert Eric Frykenberg, "The Ryotwari System and Social Organization in the Madras Presidency," in Frykenberg, *Land Control,* pp. 217–28.
   74. Brian J. Murton, "Key People in the Countryside: Decision Makers in Interior Tamilnadu in the Late Eighteenth Century," *The Indian Economic and Social History Review* 10 (1973): 157–80.
   75. Sarada Raju, *Economic Conditions,* p. 28; Mukherjee and Frykenberg, "The

Ryotwari System and Social Organization," pp. 218–19.
    76. Ibid., p. 219.
    77. Murton, "Key People in the Countryside," pp. 164–65.
    78. Ibid., p. 165; Brian J. Murton, "Culturally Relevant Categories for the Inter-
pretation of the Evolution of the Settlement Pattern in Salem District, Tamilnadu," Paper
Presented at the Conference on Settlement Geography, Dayanand College, Ajmer,
Rajasthan, 1973; Murton, "Territorial and Resource Structure of Tamil Villages in 1800:
Implications for Settlement Evolution," Paper to be Presented at International Geographical Union Regional Conference, Palmerston North, New Zealand, December 1974.
    79. Murton, "Key People in the Countryside," pp. 166–74.
    80. Sarada Raju, *Economic Conditions,* pp. 30–34; Kumar, *Land and Caste,* p. 22.
    81. Sarada Raju, *Economic Conditions,* p. 34.
    82. Ibid., p. 39.
    83. Ibid.
    84. Macleod to Read, 23 May 1794, *Records of Fort St. George: The Baramahal Re-
cords, Property,* Section 5 (Madras, 1915), p. 33.
    85. Agraharam villages are a type of inam or manyam, words which are generic terms
applicable to all grants or gifts from government. Gifts of this sort can be classified into
several hundred categories, but their underlying purpose may be broadly described under
four heads. Some of them were intended for the maintenance of the families of rulers and
other notables. Others were set aside for the support of such public utilities as schools,
bridges, and irrigation works. A third group went in payment for past or current service
by officials and specialist workers. Lastly, they were granted to temples, mosques, Brahmans, and the like, or to persons carrying out various offices in places of worship.

The Ryotwari in Lower Burma: The Establishment and Decline of a Peasant Proprietor System

MICHAEL ADAS

DURING the past decade there have been a number of significant changes in the methodology of historians who are concerned with questions relating to Asian land tenure and land use.[1] Underlying these changes has been a decided shift away from studies focusing on government policy formation[2] toward an emphasis on the actual impact of land tenure policies and the ways in which abstract theory and official intentions are altered by the social and economic context into which they are introduced.[3] This emphasis on the actual workings of tenure systems has been expressed in two approaches which have dominated recent work on land tenure and land use. The first approach is characterized by detailed analysis of the workings of tenure systems at the local or micro-level. The historian's growing awareness of the importance of the use of anthropological data and techniques in the study of peasant societies has greatly influenced this shift to emphasis on the micro-level. The resulting fusion of anthropological methodology and historical perspective is perhaps best exemplified by Gananath Obeyesekere's pioneering study of *Land Tenure in Village Ceylon*.[4] A second approach to land tenure which has been increasingly adopted in recent years involves the rigorous examination of general social, economic, and demographic factors which have traditionally been considered important determinants of cropping patterns and systems of land rights. Ester Boserup's provocative essay on *The Conditions of Agricultural Growth,* which focuses on the relationships between population change and agricultural practices, is a superb example of this approach.[5]

Both of these approaches to land tenure systems and the factors which shape them have contributed much that is of great value to the social scientist. Micro-studies have yielded empirical data which can be used to test the assumptions of earlier historians who focused on economic theory or official decision-making. Local studies have also drawn attention to the influence of local conditions and institutions, such as kinship networks and village social hierarchies, which were much neglected in earlier works. Studies dealing with general determinants of tenure patterns have provided well-supported challenges to some of the most basic premises which shape our thinking on the workings of agrarian societies, such as that levelled by

Boserup in her assault on the Malthusian view that technological change and resultant agrarian growth determine population increases.[6] Both approaches have produced new insights and theories to be tested and new models to be applied in future studies. They have also reaffirmed Dennis FitzGerald's observation that land tenure involves more than land rights; it also includes factors such as rents, taxation policies, and rural credit facilities,[7] and one could add land use and income.

Despite the important contributions made by scholars employing these two approaches, both manifest a tendency to obscure the broader configurations of physical, technological, institutional, and ideological variables which shape systems of land control and use. Obeyesekere, for example, scarcely mentions the broader "factors of change" (such as government ordinances and taxation policies and population trends) which influenced landholding patterns in Ceylon until after he has discussed in elaborate detail the traditional tenure system with reference to village structure and kinship connections. He introduces pieces of the broader configuration to explain changes in landholding at a specific point in time, rather than establishing the configuration as the context in which his local analysis is set and examining its complex impact throughout all of the stages he identifies.[8] Boserup stresses the impact of demographic trends to the near exclusion of the influence of market factors on changes in land use and property rights, despite the fact that the market has played a critical role in most areas in the modern era.[9] Rawski's study of agricultural change in South China reverses Boserup's stress by focusing on marketing and transportation factors and neglecting the impact of demographic variables.[10]

As these examples illustrate, many recent studies represent an unfortunate movement away from the approach of historians like Marc Bloch and Irfan Habib who have analyzed land tenure and land use as parts of broader configurations in the context of which they can best be treated. Bloch and Habib clearly demonstrate that the complex webs of land rights and claims to produce and services which characterized the feudal system in Medieval Europe or the jagirdari system in Mughal India cannot be fully understood unless they are related to the political and military needs, the ecological and technological givens, the social and economic conditions, and the historical precedents which gave rise to them.[11] The broader configuration of variables not only determines the actual arrangement and functioning of a land tenure system; it also shapes ideas relating to the meaning of land itself, which as Walter Neale, Paul Bohannan and others have pointed out may vary widely from one culture to another.[12] In addition, it is important to note that the impact of a particular tenure system on social, economic, or political development results not from the tenure system in and of itself, but from the tenure system as it relates to the broader configuration of variables.

The task of the social scientist who attempts to analyze the nature and impact of land tenure in the Afro-Asian world is further complicated by the fact that he is almost invariably dealing with a composite system. He shares with the European historian the need to take into account influences and remnants of past configurations indigenous to his area of concern. Unlike the European historian, however, he must come to terms with changes and hybrid forms that have resulted from the imposition of elements and influences of an alien, western European configuration upon the configuration indigenous to his area of interest. Although European influence in different areas has varied widely, a number of common concepts and institutions relating to land tenure have generally been introduced into Afro-Asian cultures as a result of European commercial and political penetration. These commonalities, which are largely a product of the commercial-industrial revolutions in western Europe,[13] include: the concepts of land as private property and a market commodity, emphasis on land rather than population control, impersonal contractual relationships, and political and legal systems oriented to regulating and preserving these forms.

The degree to which these concepts and practices have affected tenure arrangements indigenous to Africa or Asia has varied in part according to the extent of European political control or influence, the nature and intent of European economic activity, and the degree to which European ideas, institutions, and technology have resulted in the general transformation of the society and culture of the peoples encountered. The nature of the changes in landholding patterns which have resulted from the imposition of European colonial rule in non-Western areas has also been determined by the revenue needs of the European overlords, the availability of trained manpower for the colonial bureaucracy,[14] and the cost of irrigation systems or other improvements which have been essential prerequisites to agrarian development in many areas.[15] The impact of the introduction of elements of the European configuration has also, and perhaps more importantly, been determined by the strength and/or adaptability of the indigenous African or Asian configuration. In this connection, the actual, as opposed to the intended, impact of the introduction of European land tenure concepts and practices has often been proportional to the depth of the Europeans' understanding of the workings of the society they were attempting to influence.[16]

One could plot a continuum of the hybrids that have resulted from the mixture of European and Afro-Asian configurations. At one pole would stand the densely populated core areas which prior to the coming of the Europeans possessed ancient and deeply rooted religious and legal codes and customs, and complex socio-political arrangements relating to land tenure. In these areas elements of the European configuration have normally been substantially altered as a result of the strength and resilience of indigenous givens.[17] At the other end of the continuum would lie the sparsely inhabited, shifting cultivation zones of Afro-Asia where the Europeans established plantations which, in terms of the tenure patterns they displayed, were fundamentally products of European commercial expansion and little affected by the indigenous setting.[18]

The case examined in this essay, the development of the Irrawaddy Delta[19] region of Lower Burma during the period of British colonial rule, falls much closer to the plantation than to the core area pole of the continuum. For this reason, the changes resulting from the introduction of elements of the European configuration were extensive and profound. Lower Burma provides one of the best documented examples available of the rapid transformation of a subsistence-oriented, self-sufficient, natural economy into one that was market- and export-oriented and highly monetarized. This study will focus on the role of land tenure in that transformation, but considerable attention will also be given to the broader configurations which shaped tenure patterns in different periods. I will also deal in general terms with changes in social structure that resulted from configurational and tenurial transformations. Although for the purposes of analysis I will proceed from configuration to tenure patterns and then to social change, this should not be regarded as a causal sequence. The interplay between tenure and the broader configuration is complex and reciprocal with elements of the configuration determining tenure patterns and these in turn affecting broader economic, social, or political changes.[20]

As the result of the Burman victories in the Burman-Mon wars of the mid-eighteenth century, the Delta heartland of the Mon people was reduced to the status of a frontier area on the periphery of the slowly expanding Burman, wet-rice core located in the Dry Zone of Upper Burma. Although there was more development and less devastation in Lower Burma in the Konbaung period than historians have generally assumed, the region was sparsely populated and its great potential little exploited prior to its annexation by the British to their Indian Empire in 1852.[21] Among the central factors contributing to the area's low level of development were the Konbaung regime's ban on the export of rice, and its policy of using surplus rice to regulate and stabilize domestic grain prices. The low price paid for rice sold on the domestic market as a result of these policies, in combination with the elaborate sumptuary laws and restrictions on consumer imports enforced by the Konbaung regime, meant that there was little incentive for cultivators in the Delta to produce rice beyond that needed for subsistence, seed (*wunsa*), and taxes. This low level of incentive, coupled with the serious obstacles (such as malaria, flooding, wild animals, and insect crop pests) which faced cultivators who sought to bring virgin areas into production, greatly limited migration into and new settlement on the Delta frontier in the pre-British period.

In settled areas, which were concentrated along the Irrawaddy River, the peasant family was virtually a self-sufficient economic unit, which occasionally bartered surplus rice for salt or implements that it could not produce itself. If extra labor was required for planting or harvest, it was normally obtained on a mutual-assistance basis. Little capital was available, and it was almost exclusively invested in domestic trade.

Given the low ratio of population to land and the poor returns received for surplus agricultural production, land tenure arrangements in the pre-British Delta were extremely loose.[22] There were no concepts of private property or proprietary rights in the western European sense. Land rights were determined by personal relationships rather than by impersonal contracts. In Konbaung times, most of the Delta's inhabitants lived in small hamlets which were comprised of nuclear households often linked by kinship or ethnic ties. The land in the vicinity of the hamlet was held in common. Individual usufructuary rights (termed *dama-u-gya*) over a particular piece of land were established by the act of clearing and cultivating it. These rights were retained by the clearing household as long as the plot was cultivated.[23] If the land was abandoned or left fallow, it reverted to the common pool held by the hamlet unit. If another household chose to cultivate the land, it could do so with or without the permission of the original occupant, depending on local custom. Given the great abundance of cultivable land, elaborate formal mechanisms for land distribution proved unnecessary. Holdings were small, averaging less than ten acres. Competition for land was virtually nonexistent, and land sales were rare. Even in exceptional cases where sales transactions took place, the vendor had the right to repurchase the land should he decide to do so within ten years.[24] The buyer could not ordinarily resell the land without the original owner's permission.

In Lower Burma, as in many traditional societies where the population-to-land ratio was low, emphasis was placed on manpower control rather than the control of land. That portion of the Delta's population which was effectively regulated by the Konbaung administration was divided into regiments or orders called *athin*. Membership in a particular athin was normally determined by occupational, kinship, or ethnic ties, rather than by territorial considerations. Each athin unit of Delta society was linked to the elite hierarchy by officials known as *thugyis,* who were chosen from the ranks and considered the representatives of local athin groups. Officials above the thugyi level were appointed by the central government and normally recruited in the Dry Zone of Upper Burma. Given a low population density, the athin arrangement produced a society in which there was considerable geographical, but little vertical, mobility. Shifting, rather than wet-rice, cultivation was practiced over much of the lower Delta, and there are references to the migration of households and whole hamlets from areas where the exactions of Konbaung officials proved too burdensome.

Following the annexation of the Delta to the Indian Empire in 1852, the British colonial regime acted quickly to remove the impediments to growth which had existed under Konbaung rule and to promote economic development.[25] The ban on rice exports was lifted, and Burman sumptuary laws were no longer enforced. The British introduced legal and political institutions geared to a capitalistic economy, along with transportation improvements, embankments, and other public works. Private British investors built processing plants for rice, which was to become the Delta's predominant export, and European and Indian merchants furnished links with overseas market outlets. British and Indian merchants also imported consumer goods that were to prove an important stimulus to surplus production for export on the part of Burmese agriculturists.

These measures to promote economic development brought rapid and dramatic returns, for the British were acting upon a rich, but little developed frontier region. Most of Lower Burma was made up of a vast and fertile alluvial plain which had been formed, and was watered and nourished, by the Irrawaddy and Sittang rivers. In addition, abundant and reliable rainfall was provided annually by the Southwest monsoon. Prior to its annexation in 1852, numerous British merchants and diplomats had noted the favorable climate and fertility of the region and speculated about its potential as a source of a wide variety of export crops. After 1852, however, international market demands and the preference of the Burmese cultivator determined that the Delta would develop a monocrop economy dominated by rice for export. In the decades after 1852 there was a rising world demand, first centered in Europe and later India, for Burma's rice. This demand supported a steady rise in the price of rice on the Burma market which persisted into the first decades of the twentieth century.

Steadily rising prices in combination with an abundance of fertile unoccupied land, the spread of rural credit agencies, and the development of rural retail networks, which made available cheap consumer goods, provided both the means and incentives for Burmese agriculturists to bring the Delta wilderness under cultivation and engage in surplus production for the market. Many of the settlers on the Lower Burma frontier were migrants drawn from the Dry Zone or other regions within Burma. Some were Indians, though the Indian migrant stream tended to flow primarily to Rangoon and other urban centers. The ready response of the Burmese agriculturist to new market incentives was also facilitated by the British abrogation of many traditional restrictions and the very low level of risk involved in innovation, which consisted chiefly of the surplus production of their staple crop for the market.[26] For the Burmese cultivator the added labor input required to grow this surplus brought more than satisfactory returns. Consequently, the great majority of cultivators in Lower Burma made the shift from subsistence-oriented, self-sufficient peasants to full-time, market producers in a matter of decades. Their efforts made possible the Delta's rapid transformation into the world's premier rice-exporting region in the last decades of the nineteenth century.

The land tenure system which was introduced after 1852 was shaped by the needs and nature of the new political and economic framework which the British were working to establish in Lower Burma. The tenure system represented a blend of Indian precedents, contemporary British social and economic theory, and indigenous Burmese patterns.

In the years before the Indian Mutiny of 1857-58, the influence of the English Utilitarian philosophers on Indian revenue systems reached its height. Writers like James Mill strongly opposed the Whig-oriented settlements through which the British had created a true landed aristocracy in Bengal and other areas in the late eighteenth and early nineteenth centuries. Mill and other Utilitarian thinkers argued that profits which accrued from agricultural production in the form of rents should go to the state and not landed intermediaries like the taluqdars of Oudh or the zamindars of Bengal. Their works deeply influenced Indian administrators like Holt Mackenzie and George Wingate, who worked for the introduction of land systems under which the revenue was collected directly from the cultivator or the communal village.[27] One such system, the ryotwari, had been established in the first decades of the nineteenth century through large portions of the Bombay and Madras Presidencies. After 1852, in keeping with the government's declared policy of protecting and promoting the interests of the smallholder, the ryotwari system was introduced into Lower Burma.

Although Thomas Munro had not been the first to apply the ryotwari system, he became its chief proponent in the first decades of the nineteenth century. He was mainly responsible for the fact that it had become the dominant land revenue arrangement in the Madras Presidency. Munro believed that the ryotwari system would best promote the interests of the small landholder and, in doing so, further the interests of the state. He contended that the peasant proprietor was more likely to improve his holdings than the large landholder. Munro reasoned that since the peasant proprietor personally supervised the cultivation of his land, he would strive for maximum crop output, and thus in the long term prove the greatest source of revenue for the state.[28] Munro also advocated the ryotwari system because he believed that in furthering the interests of the bulk of agriculturists, rather than a landed elite, the system would best promote the general social welfare and social stability.[29] In addition, Munro believed that by granting agriculturists proprietary rights over particular holdings, the ryotwari system would render the cultivating classes more stationary. This aspect of the system was particularly relevant to the British and Indian officials who were struggling to establish order in the Delta after the second Anglo-Burman war in 1852. Wartime dislocations combined with the shifting cultivation which had traditionally been practiced over much of the region made it difficult for colonial bureaucrats to count their new subjects accurately, much less to tax and administer them effectively.[30] Munro's arguments for the ryotwari system, especially those relating to the incentives it would instill in the cultivator to innovate and produce more, have been borne out by modern research. There is a general agreement in the literature on agrarian development that tenure systems based on smallholder proprietorship are far more likely than landlord-based systems to generate "dynamic responses to opportunities for commercial farming."[31]

Lower Burma seemed to provide ideal conditions for the successful functioning of a tenure system based on the peasant proprietor. In fact, the case of Lower Burma demonstrates the importance of focusing on local conditions not only to discover the actual impact of tenure policies, but also in order to understand factors that play an important role in the formation of those policies. Relative to the heavy government expenditure on canals, irrigation, and related public works required to bring other frontier areas, like those in the United Provinces in India or in Cochin China,[32] into agricultural production, the sums which the British invested in Lower Burma were low. Bunds for water control and railway lines linking limited areas were the only major public works necessary. Thus, the new regime was not burdened with great debts which might have caused it to favor estate agriculture which in the short term would yield greater revenue returns than a small-landholder-based system. In addition, the abundance of cultivable land on the Delta frontier in the late nineteenth century meant that agriculturists could claim holdings of a size sufficient for them to produce a substantial surplus for the market and at the same time maintain a high level of home consumption. The presence of an open land frontier also permitted successful cultivators to increase the scale of their operation, and thus contribute to the further growth of the Delta's export economy.

Although Konbaung nobles and administrators had exercised prebendal domain[33] over certain Delta areas in the pre-British period, there was no true landlord class prior to 1852. Local leaders, like the thugyis or *ywa-oks* (local hamlet leaders), possessed none of the rights or means of control over the cultivating classes that were exercised by groups like the zamindars in pre-British India. The tenuous and indirect control of Konbaung officials and nobles was broken by the British conquest when most fled into Upper Burma (which was not brought under British control until 1886) or perished in futile resistance to the British advance. The absence of caste in Burmese society meant that there was no danger that high caste groups could frustrate the intent of the ryotwari system by acting as intermediaries between the government and the mass of the cultivators. In India high caste groups, like the mirasidars of the Bombay and Madras Presidencies, had gained considerable advantage from the ryotwari arrangement through collusion with indigenous revenue officials and by exercising their traditional control over lower caste cultivators and laborers.[34]

Buddhist inheritance laws were initially the only element in the indigenous society which posed a serious threat to the success of the ryotwari system in Lower Burma. According to Theravada Buddhist law as it was observed in Burma, all of the property of a deceased household head must be divided equally between his widow and both male and female children. If it had been strictly observed, this injunction would have rapidly resulted in the fragmentation of Delta holdings and undermined the cultivator's ability to produce for the market and ultimately to adequately support his own household. In some cases holdings were divided, and this process often led to quarrels among the heirs that were fought out in financially ruinous court suits and countersuits.[35] In most instances, however, Buddhist legal injunctions were not strictly applied or were circumvented. Since nuclear and neo-local households were prevalent in Lower Burma, a cultivator's children had normally married and moved away from their parental household long before the death of their parents. The abundance of open land on the frontier also meant that they were frequently well established on their own holdings before it came time to divide their parents' estate. Thus, the original family property could either be turned over to unmarried children who still lived in the parental home or to the least successful of the heirs. In either case, cash compensation was paid to the other heirs. Division of the parental estate was also obviated by a verbal agreement which stipulated that the heirs would work the holding on an annual rotation basis with a fixed portion of the harvest alloted to the noncultivating heirs for their support. More commonly, one heir would purchase the shares of the others, who would thereby gain the capital needed to go into trade or moneylending, or to move to another area on the Delta frontier and claim their own holdings.[36] In this way, Buddhist inheritance laws, at least in the early phase of development, resulted in most cases in a further extension of cultivation, rather than the financial ruin of the parties involved.

Through regulation of the means by which tenurial rights were acquired, the colonial regime sought to insure that a smallholder, rather than a large landlord, class would develop in the Delta. Several forms of land grants were experimented with, but two types proved dominant.[37] The government favored the patta system under which government officials allotted and to persons who could prove they were bonafide agriculturists an average of from fifteen to twenty acres of unoccupied land. The Burmese cultivator, however, preferred the "squatter" system, which closely resembled the pre-British dama-u-gya pattern of settlement. A cultivator established his claim to a particular holding by clearing and cultivating it. After 1876, his tenurial rights were recognized once he had occupied and paid revenue on the holding for twelve years. In that period he was prohibited from selling or mortgaging the land. At the end of the twelve years, the settler held a permanent and heritable title to the occupied land, which he could sell, mortgage, or transfer to another.

During the last decades of the nineteenth century the government sought to encourage Burmese cultivators to settle unoccupied lands or add to their existing holdings by granting revenue remissions during the first years of cultivation and temporary exemptions from the capitation tax, which was a carryover from the Konbaung period. Compared to the revenue rates established in the ryotwari areas in India in the first half of the nineteenth century, those charged in Lower Burma were low. The government normally took about 10 percent of the gross output, depending on the quality of the land assessed.[38] The moderate rates prevailing in Lower Burma were in part a product of the many errors and persistent overassessments which had characterized ryotwari settlements in both Bombay and Madras where the government had not infrequently taken 50 percent or more of the cultivator's net income.[39] In addition, in the years after 1852 the Government of Burma felt little need to raise large amounts of revenue from land taxes, a need which Dharma Kumar has argued led to assessments by the East India Company at "high, almost penal, rates" during the decades of the ryotwari's introduction into Madras.[40] By contrast, administrators in Burma were anxious to encourage the surplus production of rice for the export market, and peasant consumption of cheap manufactured goods imported from Great Britain and India. These ends could best be achieved by leaving the bulk of the cultivator's surplus in his own hands.[41]

Set in the context of a capitalist, export-oriented configuration, the introduction of the ryotwari system resulted in a radical transformation in the relationship between the Burmese agriculturist and the land. Rights to land use once regulated by the communal village gave way to proprietary rights vested in the individual. Traditional agreements regarding land control based on age-old customs, personal relationships, and informal verbal understandings were codified and impersonalized through legal contracts and property laws. Loosely demarcated boundaries were replaced with those carefully measured, marked, and registered at the local settlement office. Holdings once used to provide the mixed-crop, subsistence requirements of largely self-sufficient households were transformed into monocrop production units feeding a seemingly insatiable foreign demand for Burma's rice. Formerly a "free gift of nature," land became a market commodity and an object of competition to be sold, mortgaged, and inherited.[42] Birth and/or bureaucratic connections that had traditionally been the prime determinants of wealth, social status, and political power diminished in importance as land acquisition and Western education emerged as the chief means of achieving these ends. The sum of these transformations produced a profound change in the Burmese agriculturist's attitude toward the land he worked. This new attitude was succinctly summed up in the following passage by a British revenue official:

> The Burman in Lower Burma at least sits loosely on his holding, he has no sentimental attachment to it, he regards the land simply as the material with the aid of which paddy is produced, and therefore one field or holding is as good as another in his eyes if each yields the same amount of grain. In fact, the Burman prefers paddy to the land which yields it and if he could get paddy from the air or water alone, he would forsake the land altogether.[43]

The combination of extensive political and economic change and the new tenure arrangements introduced by the British resulted in a restructuring of rural Delta society. The vertical, highly stratified social system of the Konbaung period gave way to a more fluid, horizontally arranged social order in which four main strata can be distinguished for the purposes of analysis: landlords, cultivator-owners, tenants, and landless laborers. These groups were defined largely in terms of their relationship to the land. In the last half of the nineteenth century there was a high degree of mobility among the different strata, and the boundaries of the strata themselves were vague and highly mutable. It was possible for a cultivator who began as a landless laborer to work his way upward until he attained the status of a large landholder. The number of persons who began as laborers and rose to become landlords was small, but large numbers of agriculturists moved one or two notches up or down on the social scale. Although some owners became heavily indebted and fell to the status of tenants or laborers, movement was largely upward. Tenants and landless laborers generally regarded their positions as temporary, a phase in which they would acquire the means to clear and cultivate their own holdings.[44] There was also considerable differentiation within each social stratum. Some tenants, for example, owned small plots of land which they hoped to enlarge and thereby move up to full landonwer status. Other tenants worked part-time as wage laborers. Considerable numbers of tenants worked the same landlord's holdings for season after season, while many others moved about the Delta in search of more favorable rent rates or leasing conditions. With the population-to-land ratio on the Delta frontier running heavily in favor of the laboring classes and agriculturists at all levels retaining a substantial share of their production, the condition of the rural population was generally solvent, and in many cases prosperous until the first decades of the twentieth century.

The basic configuration, which had developed in Lower Burma in the decades after 1852 as the result of a blend of British and Indian innovations and indigenous givens, persisted throughout the British colonial period. In the last decades of the nineteenth century, however, there were major changes within this configuration, and, after 1910, new trends on the international rice market which gradually undermined the dominant position of the small landholder and the solvency of the great majority of Delta agriculturists. Although detailed examination of the factors which led to the deterioration of the Delta economy lies beyond the scope of this essay, some of the key factors can be indicated.[45] Perhaps the most critical development was the closing of the rice frontier, which greatly restricted the agriculturist's avenues of opportunity and in combination with rapid population growth turned the population-to-land ratio against the tenant and laboring classes. The growing scarcity of cultivable, unoccupied land was felt in some areas of Lower Burma as early as the 1890s, and prevailed throughout most of the Delta by the time of World War I. This shortage greatly impaired the ability of tenants and landless laborers to gain their own holdings or of cultivators, who had lost their original holdings through debt, to start again in a new area. It also resulted in a great increase in the sale price of land which made it difficult for the average cultivator to extend his holdings. Because there had been no in-depth transformation of agricultural techniques or technology in the late nineteenth century, the unavailability of additional inputs of land, which had been the basis of the early expansion of rice production, meant that the average cultivator's output stagnated and in some areas declined due to soil depletion.

These checks on the cultivator's capacity to increase his production came at a time when the claims of nonagricultural groups on his crop were growing, and when the market value of his surplus was fluctuating and often falling. As a consequence of his shift from self-sufficience and subsistence production to full-time production for the market, the Delta agriculturist became increasingly dependent on credit advances from professional money-lenders, rice brokers, local merchants, landlords, and other middlemen. These groups took ever greater shares of his harvest for payment on the interest and/or principal on loans. In addition, the great proliferation of marketing middlemen and the formation of marketing pools on the part of the milling interests meant that the cultivator received less for the surplus he was able to market. By the first decade of the twentieth century it was necessary for most cultivators to sell to brokers or rice merchants on the threshing floor at the peak of the harvest season when prices were the lowest. Recurring market slumps in the early twentieth century, which had severe effects on the Delta monocrop economy, further reduced the worth of the cultivator's surplus. His plight was compounded by a rather high rate of inflation in this period and was further exacerbated by the fact that in shifting to full-time market production, most Delta agriculturists had given up their self-sufficient base.

Worsening economic conditions exposed a number of serious weaknesses in the seemingly ideal land tenure system which the British had introduced into Lower Burma. The most critical of these was the fact that under the ryotwari arrangement the cultivator-owner was permitted to offer mortgage liability for loans obtained from moneylenders, rice merchants, and other sources. From the earliest decades of the Delta's development, a high percentage of loans to agriculturists had been secured by mortgages on their holdings. As long as the majority of cultivators cleared sizable profits and were able to repay the interest and principal on their loans, mortgage security did not present a danger to the maintenance of a peasant-proprietor-dominated economy. However, when the average small landholder found it increasingly difficult to meet his own expenses and repay his creditors, chronic indebtedness, widespread defaulting and foreclosures, and land alienation began to undermine the very foundations of the land tenure system which the British had originally established.

These problems and land alienation were, of course, not entirely new. Profligate landholders had lost their lands to moneylenders, merchants, urban speculators, and their more frugal neighbors in the early decades after 1852. Landgrabbers, both urban and rural based, had also found numerous ways of circumventing government safeguards and acquiring large estates long before land alienation became a serious problem in the last decades of the nineteenth century. For example, the government regulation which prohibited cultivators from mortgaging newly settled holdings until after twelve years of occupation was quite frequently violated through the use of "veiled" mortgages. These mortgages, which were almost certainly in use before the early 1900s when they are first mentioned in revenue reports, involved loans granted to settlers who offered their newly cleared holdings as security, but did not report the transaction to the government authorities. There was a clear understanding, however, between cultivator and creditor that should the former fail to meet his payments, his land would become the property of the latter. If a cultivator defaulted, his land would be "sold" to his creditor at the end of the twelve-year period. The lender-speculator, who was normally a Burmese merchant, moneylender, or landlord with considerable local influence (and often with a gang of client-ruffians on hand), felt little need to rely on the government to insure returns on his investment.[46]

As in many other agrarian societies, land speculators also relied on collusion with subordinate revenue officials to acquire large holdings. At times, they would direct their clients and retainers, who were often deeply in debt to them, to settle unoccupied tracts and register them in the client's name. The local revenue officer would, of course, be well paid for failing to discover and report these transactions. In other instances, the collusion between local officials and speculators was more direct. For a suitable bribe or a share of the profits, local revenue officials would register unoccupied tracts or the holdings of bonafide cultivators in the name of the land speculator. A popular tactic was for the revenue officer to under-report the output of his landlord partners' holdings, or to wipe sizeable portions of their estates off the revenue map with the comment that the area had relapsed into jungle.[47] In more remote areas of the Delta frontier, the land grabber did not bother with these costly and time-consuming subterfuges. He merely directed his retainers to harass and intimidate a cultivator who had just finished clearing a fertile holding. Violence was used if necessary to convince the settler to give up his hard-earned plot, after which one of the speculator's toughs became the new squatter in residence.

Although a number of large estates comprised mainly of noncontiguous holdings were pieced together through foreclosures and illegal tactics in the early decades of the Delta's development, land alienation was not a serious problem in most areas. As late as 1905, for example, only 18 percent of the occupied land in Lower Burma was controlled by nonagriculturists and of this amount 40 percent was held by resident owners who lived within three miles of their holdings.[48] Widespread alienation was also limited by the general solvency of the cultivating classes combined with the fact that most moneylenders, especially the South Indian Chettiars who had dominated rural credit provision since the 1880s, did not want the cultivator's land. Most lenders were content to collect the interest on their loans to cultivator-owners for season after season and leave the principal unpaid. As the general economic situation worsened, however, credit became more restricted and cultivators fell more and more deeply into debt. By the 1920s, many moneylenders, including some Chettiars, were increasingly forced to foreclose on mortgages due to defaulting on the part of their clients and/or pressures for repayment of the working capital which the lenders had origi- nally borrowed from rich merchants, banks, and other agencies. By 1930, 31 percent of the occupied land in Lower Burma was owned by nonagri- culturists, of whom nearly 75 percent were nonresidents.[49]

As early as the 1880s government revenue officials in Lower Burma began to voice concern regarding rising indebtedness and the spread of land alienation and tenancy.[50] No measures were taken, however, until the 1890s when a small group of British officials mounted a campaign to enact agrarian relief measures. Tenancy and land alienation bills were submitted for approval to the Government of India in 1896. Both bills were accompanied by detailed opinions written by revenue and judicial officers, the memorials of special interest groups like the Chettiars' and landlords' associations, and surveys which had been conducted by the Government of Burma to test the attitudes of landlords, cultivator-owners, moneylenders, and tenants with regard to the measures. As this great mass of evidence demonstrated, the main support for the relief measures came almost exclusively from the small, but articulate, group of British revenue officials who had instigated the legislative campaign. These officials were opposed by a powerful coalition of Burmese and Indian landlord and moneylender associations, the Chambers of Commerce of all of the main ethnic groups resident in Burma, Burmese rice brokers, Indian and Chinese merchant groups, and the British and Indian export-import and milling interests. Well attended public meetings were held in Rangoon and other urban centers to protest against the proposed bills, and special petitions were addressed to the Governor-General of India.

Most disheartening for the sponsors of the bills was the fact that a majority of the cultivators surveyed opposed the measures. A minority of agriculturists favored the legislation with a vehemence that was best expressed by a heavily indebted smallholder in the Hanthawaddy District who declared that should the bills be passed he would "bend [his] head to the Government three times a day."[51] However, most agriculturists, both large and smallholders, opposed the measures, primarily because they feared that the provisions for restricting mortgage liability would greatly impair their ability to obtain credit from Chettiar, Burmese, and Chinese money- lenders. In the absence of large-scale or effective government credit agencies, these private sources were essential to agricultural production in the Delta.

The Government of India refused to approve the bills drafted in the 1890s on the grounds that firmer statistical data were required regarding tenant conditions and the extent of land alienation. The accelerating spread of chronic indebtedness and land alienation and the worsening position of the agrarian classes, however, generated renewed efforts to enact relief measures in the first decade of the twentieth century. These efforts were spearheaded by the then governor of Burma, Sir Herbert Thirkell White. Once again, a small group of British officials waged a lonely campaign against the forces which had opposed the earlier bills. Despite White's fervent advocacy and his close association with the Governor-General of India, Lord Minto, the campaign again ended in defeat. In a revealing letter from Colonel Dunlap-Smith, the Secretary to the Governor-General, to White in December of 1907, Minto apologized to his friend for the embarassment caused by the Government of India's rejection of the proposed legislation. He argued that "hard figures" on the question were still lacking, but stressed the complications that the bills would have in view of circumstances in India. After explaining that there had been "serious objections" to similar legislation already enacted in the Panjab, Minto went on to explain that: *"Even if an Alienation Act is required in Burma,* its introduction would cause a certain amount of uneasiness in other provinces, where similar legislation has been threatened, and it is advisable to avoid anything of this sort at present."[52] White's successor as governor of Burma, Sir Harvey Adamson, shelved the legislation indefinitely in 1911. The campaign would not be renewed until the late 1930s when tenancy and land alienation bills were enacted only after the Great Depression, a major agrarian rebellion, and a series of bloody communal riots had made a shambles of the Delta economy and society.

In view of the government's failure to intervene to ameliorate the conditions that were steadily undermining the peasant-proprietor-based tenure system in the Delta, potential for effective adjustments rested mainly with the cultivating classes themselves. With rare exceptions, however, agriculturists in Lower Burma made few changes in their cultivating techniques or consumption patterns which would have allowed them to remain solvent in the face of less favorable economic circumstances and population growth. The revenue records and settlement reports for the early decades of the twentieth century indicate that there was very little intensification of cultivation, introduction of new crops, or adoption of new tools. New rice strains were used on only a small percentage of Delta holdings, and fertilizers continued to be used for nurseries and not on the main fields in most tracts. Broadcasting continued to be favored over transplanting in most of the lower Delta, despite the higher yields obtained by transplanting. The use of familial labor, as opposed to hired wage workers, actually declined as the landless laboring class grew steadily, fed by an increased influx of Indian migrant laborers. Multiple cropping remained confined to a limited area. Most agriculturists eschewed the introduction of alternate crops, and persisted in the monocrop production of rice despite adverse trends in the internal and international market. In the absence of these changes, the productivity of holdings in most areas of Lower Burma declined, in part due to the spread of embankments which prevented nutrients carried by the Delta's rivers from reaching the soil. There is also little evidence that cultivators in Lower Burma cut back on their consumption, at least not until the 1930s. Purchase of cheap consumer goods remained at high levels, and perhaps expanded as bicycles, watches and other tempting items became available. Expenditure on traditional pastimes, such as initiation ceremonies, monastery festivals, bullock racing, and gambling also showed few signs of tapering off.

The failure of the Delta agriculturist to alter significantly his cultivation and consumption patterns was determined by a complex combination of economic and social variables. In view of adjustments made by cultivators in other areas, the most important of these variables should be indicated. Unlike his counterparts in India or China, the Burmese agriculturist had traditionally functioned in a setting where Malthusian pressures rooted in high population density were low. Although there were occasional droughts and food shortages in the Dry Zone, these were not so severe as elsewhere in Asia and they were virtually unknown in the Delta region.[53] Even in the depression period of the early 1930s, when the crisis of the Delta economy was the most severe, few, if any, cultivators starved, though some may have been forced to cut back on food consumption. In addition, in the last half of the nineteenth century the cultivator in Lower Burma had come to expect steady rises in the market demand and the price paid for rice. Price slumps had for the most part been mild and temporary until World War I. Thus, the cultivator understandably calculated his production costs and possibilities for consumption on the assumption that rice prices would rise, or at least remain roughly equal, in the coming season. Decades of living at a high level of income, relative to peasants in most other areas, had also ingrained spending habits and a strong preference for the use of hired labor that most cultivators were reluctant to give up.

The spread of credit agencies in Lower Burma, which accelerated after the entry of the Chettiars into rural moneylending on a large scale after 1880, made it possible for the average cultivator-owner to maintain his high standard of living. Possessing little understanding of the intricacies of moneylending or mortgage liability, the cultivator freely offered his land for credit. The ease with which large amounts of cash could be obtained from moneylenders by landowning cultivators encouraged both small and large owners to run up sizable debts. Much of the money so easily obtained was squandered on village celebrations and consumer goods. The tendency to become deeply indebted was reinforced by the Burmese and Chettiar moneylenders' policy of leaving the principal on loans outstanding as long as the interest was paid.

Chronic indebtedness, widespread defaulting, and land alienation which eroded the smallholder base of the Delta economy also limited the capacity of Burmese agriculturists to innovate in response to changing conditions. Most landlords in Lower Burma closely resembled those whom Gunnar Myrdal has seen as typical in South Asia. They "managed to enjoy the prerogatives of a capitalist landlord without giving up the privileges of a feudal chief," while simultaneously avoiding "nearly all the obligations of both." With rare exceptions, they did not improve their holdings, nor did they encourage their tenants or laborers to do so.[54] Tenants had little incentive or spare capital to improve holdings they worked on a temporary basis. Increased productivity merely meant higher rents, and often jeopardized the tenant's position because the landlord would be tempted to evict him and find a replacement at higher rental rates.[55] As more and more Delta land was alienated to nonagriculturists and worked by tenants, the potential for creative responses to new economic pressures diminished steadily.

Agrarian indebtedness, land alienation, rising rent rates, and declining real wages became the dominant themes of the Delta economy in the first decades of the twentieth century. The depression of the 1930s merely accelerated and intensified these well-established trends. By the mid-1930s over half of the cultivated land in Lower Burma was claimed outright by nonagriculturists, a sizable percentage of whom were absentee owners. In addition, a large percentage of the land that still remained in the hands of smallholders was heavily mortgaged to moneylenders, local shopkeepers, landlords, and urban speculators. The lines dividing the different social strata increasingly rigidified, and the upward mobility that had characterized rural Delta society in the early period of growth was largely a thing of the past. For all but members of the large landlord class, movement was largely downward from cultivator-owner to tenant or landless laborer. In the first decades of the twentieth century living conditions for all but the landlord class deteriorated markedly. In combination with the breakdown of the institutions of traditional Burman society, the erosion of the social and economic position of the agrarian classes in the Delta had important consequences in the last decades of British rule when agrarian unrest and urban strife attested to the manifold failures of the colonial system that had begun with such promise.

The decline of the smallholder, export economy of Lower Burma clearly demonstrates the need for ongoing government regulation of land tenure systems set in the unstable context of export-oriented, capitalistic configurations. When, beginning in the 1890s, the favorable market conditions and low population-to-land ratio that had made possible the successful application of the ryotwari system changed, the government failed to introduce countermeasures to control lending practices and marketing agencies and to protect the smallholder's ownership rights. The government's poorly financed and half-hearted attempts to provide agricultural loans, develop cooperative societies, or stimulate change in agricultural technology fell far short of the measures required to preserve the smallholder economy that remained its professed ideal. The repeated attempts of a number of British officials in the 1890s and early 1900s to enact legislation which would check land alienation and regulate tenancy conditions ended in failure. As a result, the Delta agriculturists who had responded with great alacrity to the incentives provided by an alien system, which they never fully understood, were forced to cope with that system when factors which for the most part they could not control had radically altered it to their disadvantage. Without extensive government assistance, most cultivators proved unable to adjust successfully to changing conditions. By the 1930s the smallholder economy of the late nineteenth century had largely given way to a system of extraction dominated by large landlords, moneylenders, millers, and wholesale merchants.

The failure of the ryotwari in Burma also calls into question the notion that full ownership rights vested in individual small landholders represent *ipso facto* the ideal form of land tenure. In the early stages of the introduction of a market-oriented, cash-nexus economy into societies that have traditionally been natural- and subsistence-oriented, certain governmental checks on the rights of cultivator-owners to alienate their land through sale or mortgage would seem necessary.[56] As the resistance of many cultivator-owners in Lower Burma to land alienation legislation in the 1890s and early 1900s indicates, however, the government must at the same time provide sufficient sources of agricultural credit at reasonable rates, and make available at a low cost tools, fertilizers, and seeds. Most critically, land tenure arrangements must be geared to the configuration into which they are introduced, and altered to meet changes within that configuration.

NOTES

1. A preliminary draft of this essay was read for a panel on land tenure and social change at the Association of Asian Studies Convention in Chicago, March 1973. I would like to thank Edgar Wickberg, Clark E. Cunningham, Karl Pelzer, Traian Stoianovich, and Karl von Loewe for their comments on and criticisms of the original draft, though I am solely responsible for the content of this subsequent essay.

2. B.H. Baden-Powell's multi-volumed study of *The Land Systems of British India* (London, 1892) provides a classic example of the policy approach. The fact that studies of this nature are not currently in vogue does not mean, of course, that they are without value. In fact, Eric Stokes' *English Utilitarians in India* (Oxford, 1959), which deals with land tenure questions mainly at the level of political and economic theory and policy-making, is one of the finest studies to date on the British period in India.

3. For examples see Dharma Kumar, *Land and Caste in South India* (Cambridge, 1965); Ravinder Kumar, *Western India in the Nineteenth Century* (London, 1968); or the chapters by Bernard Cohn, Thomas Metcalf, Tapan Raychaudhuri, Burton Stein, and Nilmani Mukherjee and Robert Frykenberg, in Robert Eric Frykenberg, ed., *Land Control and Social Structure in Indian History* (Madison, Wis., 1969).

4. Cambridge, 1967. See also W.T. Chambliss, *Chiaraijima Village: Land Tenure, Taxation, and Local Trade, 1818-1884* (Tuscon, Ariz., 1965). The influence of anthropology on the historiography of agrarian Asia has been paralleled by a growing tendency for anthropologists to give serious attention to the historical dimensions of the social and cultural systems under analysis. See, for examples, L.M. Hanks, *Rice and Man: Agricultural Ecology in Southeast Asia* (Chicago, 1972), and H.T. Lewis, *Ilocano Rice Farmers: A Comparative Study of Two Philippine Barrios* (Honolulu, 1971).

5. Chicago, 1965. For other examples of this approach with reference to specific geographical areas see Evelyn Sakakida Rawski, *Agricultural Change and the Peasant Economy of South China* (Cambridge, Mass., 1972), or Clifford Geertz, *Agricultural Involution* (Berkeley, 1966).

6. See *Conditions of Growth*, especially pp. 11–14, 116–18.

7. As cited by K.H. Parsons in "Land Reform and Agricultural Development," in Parsons, et al., eds., *Land Tenure* (Madison, Wis., 1956), p. 44.

8. *Tenure in Village Ceylon*, esp. pp. 98–143.

9. *Conditions of Growth*, passim. She deals briefly with market factors in Chapter 7.

10. This approach is somewhat puzzling in view of her admission at the outset that population trends are of "obvious importance" to changes in the agrarian sector. See *Change and the Peasant Economy of South China*, p. 9.

11. Bloch, *Feudal Society*, 2 vols (Chicago, 1964); and Habib, *The Agrarian System of Mughal India, 1556-1707* (Bombay, 1963).

12. Neale, "Land is to Rule," in Frykenberg, ed., *Land Control in Indian History*, pp. 3–15; and Bohannan, " 'Land,' 'Tenure' and Land Tenure," in Daniel Biebuyck, ed., *African Agrarian Systems* (Oxford, 1963), pp. 101–115.

13. Although their ideological and institutional origins may in part be traced back to ancient Greece, see Richard Schlatter, *Private Property* (London, 1951).

14. The importance of adequate manpower is strikingly demonstrated by Thomas Beaglehole's observation that Cornwallis' decision to make a permanent settlement with the zamindars in Bengal was in part determined by the limited numbers of able administrators at his disposal. See *Thomas Munro and the Development of Administrative Policy in Madras 1792-1818* (Cambridge, Eng., 1966), p. 5.

15. As Ammar Siamwalla has argued, the great costs involved in canal building and the desalinization of the soil in the Transbassac area of Cochin China were important causes of the rise of a large-landlord-based tenure system in the area. The small-scale cultivator could not raise the capital or afford the considerable delay in returns on investment required to make the land cultivable. See "Land, Labour and Capital in Three Rice-Growing Deltas of Southeast Asia 1800-1940." Yale University, Discussion Paper no. 150 of the Economic Growth Center, Mimeo, p. 39.

16. As Boserup has pointed out, European errors with regard to tenure matters were often also due to the inconsistencies and imprecise nature of European tenure concepts themselves. *Conditions of Growth,* p. 87.

17. For examples see the fine case studies in Frykenberg, *Land Control,* or Geertz's *Agricultural Involution,* especially chapters 2-4. In some cases, the process of colonization led to the virtual elimination of long-standing land tenure arrangements in conjuction with the general collapse of the institutional framework of the indigenous society. See, for example, Andre Nouschi, *Enquete sur le niveau de vie des populations rurales Constantinoises de la conquete jusqu'en 1919 : Essai d'histoire, economic et sociale* (Paris, 1961).

18. Although in some cases there was considerable adaptation to local givens. For an extreme example, see Karl Peltzer, "Western Impact on East Sumatra and North Tapanuli: The Roles of the Planter and Missionary," *Journal of Southeast Asian History* 2 (July 1961): 66–71.

19. For the purposes of this essay, the Delta or Lower Burma comprises the thirteen principal rice-growing districts of British Burma: Prome, Tharrawaddy, Henzada, Bassein, Myaungmya, Pyapon, Maubin, Hanthawaddy, Insein, Pegu, Toungoo, Thaton, and Amherst. With the exception of the portions of Amherst which lie east of the Salween River, all of this region was annexed by the British to the Indian Empire in 1852.

20. The importance of stressing the reciprocity and interrelatedness of economic, social, and political change was suggested by the writings of Hans-Ulrich Wehler who deals with these factors in industrializing societies. See *Bismarck und der Imperialismus* (Koln, 1969), pp. 19–20 et passim.

21. For a detailed discussion of social and economic conditions in Lower Burma prior to 1852, see Michael Adas, *The Burma Delta: Economic Development and Social Change on an Asian Rice Frontier* (Madison, Wis., 1974), Chapter 1, pt. 1.

22. There is considerable disagreement both in the primary and secondary sources as to the nature of these arrangements. The following discussion is based largely upon the information provided by government reports which related the findings of special inquiries conducted in the first decade of British rule. Some of this material is cited by J.S. Furnivall in his early article on "Land as a Free Gift of Nature," *Economic Journal* (Dec. 1909), pp. 552–62.

23. As V. Liversage has shown, tenure rights of this nature were quite common in traditional societies. See *Land Tenure in the Colonies* (Cambridge, Eng., 1945), pp. 4–5 et passim.

24. This pattern of redeemable purchase was also quite common in traditional African and Asian societies. See ibid., p. 15 et passim.

25. On early British measures to develop the Delta and early economic growth in the region see Adas, *Burma Delta,* Chapter 1, pt. 2, and Chapters 2 and 3.

26. For a fine discussion of the risk factor in agricultural change, see C.M. Elliot, "Agriculture and Economic Development in Africa: Theory and Experience, 1880–1914," in E.L. Jones and S.J. Woolf, eds., *Agrarian Change and Economic Development: The Historical Problems* (London, 1969), pp. 123–50.

27. Stokes, *Utilitarians in India,* pp. 76–78, 87–99, 104–9, 122–28.

28. Beaglehole, *Thomas Munro,* pp. 8, 18, 28–29, 80–81; and D. Kumar, *Land and Caste,* pp. 81–82.

29. Beaglehole, *Thomas Munro,* pp. 28–29, 80.

30. Ibid., p. 81; and Government of India, *Foreign Proceedings (Revenue),* Range 205, vol. 31 (November, 1862), nos. 7, 10, 11.

31. Gunnar Myrdal, *Asian Drama: An Inquiry into the Poverty of Nations,* 3 vols. (New York, 1968), 1:442. See also John W. Mellor, *The Economics of Agricultural Development* (Ithaca, N.Y., 1966), p. 249.

32. For detailed discussions of the magnitude of government expenditure in these areas and some of their implications see Elizabeth Whitcombe, *Agrarian Conditions in Northern India* (Berkeley, 1972), especially pp. 61–119; and Charles Robequain; *L'evolution economique de l'Indochine Francaise* (Paris, 1939), pp. 122–27, 243–47. The fact that large government investment on public works need not necessarily lead to the rise of large

landlord or estate agriculture is demonstrated by the case of the canal colonies in the Panjab. See Malcolm Darling, *The Panjab Peasant in Prosperity and Debt* (Bombay, 1947, 4th ed.), pp. 111–31.

33. As the term is defined by Eric Wolf as noninheritable rights to command services and collect a share of the cultivator's produce granted by the ruler to compensate government officials. See *Peasants* (Englewood Cliffs, N.J., 1966), pp. 50–53.

34. Nilmani Mukherjee and Robert Eric Frykenberg, "The Ryotwari System and Social Organization in the Madras Presidency," in Frykenberg, ed., *Land Control in Indian History*, pp. 217–26; R. Kumar, *Western India*, pp. 94, 101–11, 121–22 et passim.

35. Baden-Powell, *Land Systems*, 3:491–92; and O.H.K. Spate, "The Beginnings of Industrialization in Burma," *Economic Geography* 17 (1941): 90–91.

36. Ibid. In Burma, the frontier and a rapidly expanding economy provided the alternate means of support that Liversage has viewed as critical for the avoidance of fragmented holdings (see *Land Tenure*, p. 65). When the frontier closed and economic growth slowed after 1900, it is probable that fragmented estates became more common. This trend is impossible to trace statistically, however, due to the spread of land alienation and large estates in this period.

37. The best discussion of land grants in the printed literature may be found in Government of Burma, *Report of the Land and Agriculture Committee* (Rangoon, 1938), pt. 2, pp. 39–43.

38. Compare the sections on output and land revenue in the district settlement reports for this period; or see John Nisbet, *Burma under British Rule and Before*, 2 vols. (London, 1901), 2:342.

39. In this connection, it is important to note than in 1853–54, when settlement policy was being shaped in Lower Burma, there was a farreaching enquiry into the problem of overassessment in Madras. See D. Kumar, *Land and Caste*, pp. 77, 82–89, 95.

40. Ibid., p. 77.

41. As it functioned for roughly the first half century of British rule in Lower Burma, the ryotwari system not only left the cultivator with the bulk of his surplus produce, but also met all of the basic criteria which have been set forth by R.F. Carroll as a means of "Appraising the Adequacy of Land Tenure Systems for Agricultural Production" in Parsons, ed., *Land Tenure*, pp. 583–89.

42. Like many other colonial situations, the case of Lower Burma provides an important exception to Ester Boserup's generalization that "there is never a direct transition from a state where land is free to everybody to one of private property in land." See *Conditions of Growth*, p. 79.

43. Government of Burma, *Revenue and Agriculture Proceedings*, vol. 8633 (November 1911), p. 651.

44. This high degree of upward mobility indicates that frontier situations such as that found in Lower Burma in the late nineteenth century need to be included in Gunnar Myrdal's list of the limited circumstances under which tenants and landless laborers possess upward social mobility. See *Asian Drama*, 2:1060.

45. For a detailed analysis of these trends see Adas, *Burma Delta*, chapter 6.

46. Government of Burma, *Report on the Suspension of Grants in the Hanthawaddy District* (Rangoon, 1910), p. 13.

47. For examples, see C.H. Duffin, *Report of the Second Settlement...of the Bassein District, 1912-13* (Rangoon, 1914), p. 43, and U Tin Gyi, *Report of the Original Settlement Operation in the Labutta Township of the Myaungmya District, 1924-25* (Rangoon, 1926), p. 12.

48. Government of Burma, *Report on the Land Revenue Administration of Burma, 1905-6*, Tables on landholding in Lower Burma.

49. Ibid., *1929-30*.

50. The following discussion of the struggle to enact tenancy legislation from 1890 to 1911 is based on the special reports and enclosures in the Government of Burma *Revenue and Agriculture Proceedings, 1890-1911*.

51. Ibid., vol. 4886 (March 1896), p. 49.

52. India Office Archives, MSS European 254, The Herbert Thirkell White Collection, File 190. Emphasis added.

53. Mya Maung has stressed the absence of these pressures in shaping the Burmese outlook and Burmese responses to economic changes. See "Cultural Value and Economic Change in Burma," *Asian Survey* 4 (March 1964): 575–64.

54. *Asian Drama*, 2:1039.

55. For more detailed discussions of the factors which restrict the innovative capacity of tenants and sharecroppers see ibid., pp. 1065–67; Mellor, *Economics of Agricultural Development*, p. 254; and M.F. Millikan and David Hapgood, *No Easy Harvest: The Dilemma of Agriculture in Underdeveloped Countries* (Boston, 1967), pp. 91–92.

56. Liversage's arguments along these lines, which were made nearly three decades ago, have been largely neglected. See *Land Tenure*, pp. 123–34.

Land Tenure and Credit-Capital Tenure in Contemporary India

RONALD J. HERRING

The future of rural credit lies with those who being of the people, live among the people, and yet by their intelligence, prescience, and energy are above the people.

SIR FREDERICK NICHOLSON, 1895

The failure of cooperative credit is explicable in terms of the total impracticability of any attempt to combine the very weak in competition with the very strong . . . . Such forces can be generated not by co-operation alone but by co-operation in conjunction with the State.

ALL INDIA RURAL CREDIT SURVEY REPORT, 1954

THE purpose of this paper is to explore the changing significance of land tenure in India under conditions of technological change and the development of modern capitalist relations and institutions in agriculture. One specific manifestation of that changing significance is an evolving hierarchy of rights to credit and thus of access to agricultural capital under conditions which make position in that hierarchy increasingly important.

Several themes will be treated:

1) Agricultural capital (and its embryo form, credit) is an increasingly good functional equivalent of land, provided that one already holds a secure position in the land tenure system, since it means access to more produce, access to more productive opportunities, control of more employment opportunities (which are still a source of diffuse power in a labor-surplus economy), and more power to make decisions regarding the uses made of land and the terms on which others have access to it.

2) Land in the sense suggested above thus becomes a more crucial power resource in Parsonian terms[1] within the economic sphere at the same time that land as a medium of exchange in other arenas is being devalued. Rights in land become potentially transferable to rights in agricultural capital as the traditional transferability of rights in land to rights in political capital, authority, patron status, deference, and so forth is markedly diminishing.[2] Land is no longer "to rule" (in Walter Neale's memorable formulation), but to capitalize, and capital means a different kind of rule to the extent that it means any rule at all.[3]

3) The prevailing system of land tenure tends to be reproduced as a hierarchy of differential rights to institutional credit, often preserving the very distinctions which were the core of the "traditional" agrarian system. The latent (and sometimes manifest) function of modern institutions in perpetuating traditional structural and power relations raises important questions about the tradition-modernity dichotomy in a dynamic system.[4]

4) The working rules of various credit institutions in India tend to reinforce a cumulative dynamic toward increased disparities in wealth and security. Carl Gotsch refers to these cumulative properties as "positive feed-back loops," meaning that the system's overall direction is reinforced by the prevailing dynamics.[5] In concrete terms, the allocation criteria embedded in the concept of credit worthiness reinforce the circular positive feed-back path already inherent in a system of marked inequalities which is experiencing growth in production; this dynamic is itself reinforced by technological changes and the infrastructure created to accelerate and accommodate technological change.

5) The propositions suggested above should be viewed as the result of decisions or nondecisions by a political system which has taken responsibility for change in the agrarian system as a central concern.[6]

LAND TENURE

The concept of "land tenure" may be given a broad or narrow construction. The narrow sense is implied by the Latin root of tenure—the variable terms on which individuals "hold" the land, often differentiated in the Indian case by complex legal formulae defining classes of "tenure holders" and delineating those whose hold on the land is more tenuous. The narrow construction of land tenure is essentially that of the state, the idealized formal-legal system of land rights. Narrowly, who holds how much of what kind of land with what rights and restrictions in terms of the norms of a national judicial system?

The broader notion of a land tenure system is that of a system of society rather than of the state. This conceptualization is reflected in Daniel Thorner's accurate comment: "The rights of a tenant depend more on the size of his holding and his status in the village than on his status in law."[7] Because production relations relate to various combinations of land and labor, and these relations are "embedded" in social relations,[8] the broader construction is concerned with a range of social facts—ritual, social, political, economic, linguistic. For example, it may prove critical in the Indian context to know not merely that a given Jat holds twelve irrigated acres as a legal owner, but also that all of the village land is owned by Jats, that landless laborers in the village are of untouchable social status, and that the word for "tenant" also means "dependent," "criminal," and connotes "one who is exploitable."[9]

Obviously these idealized constructs are often inextricably fused. But as the state extends itself deeper into society, the position of an individual in the formal-legal tenure system, though clearly influenced by the local social-ritual-political system, becomes critical as new institutional forms with new rules appear; one example I will examine later is the land mortgage bank.

The meanings of land tenure given above correspond to a problematic distinction between state and society. Despite the obvious imprecision of this distinction, it is useful in explaining the dynamics in credit allocation arenas. The local credit cooperative often reflects "society" in a striking way—the head may well be the village *sarpanch* or leader of the dominant caste or faction; those excluded from the cooperative are typically those consistently excluded from the ritual, social, political, and economic life of the village. The land mortgage bank, though often dependent on evidence affected by the social system (e.g., kinship ties to the land record keepers), relies on formal-legal rules which may prove incompatible with usages of the local social system. For example, the legal conception of land as owned property in the capitalist sense often ignores the peculiarities of a given piece of soil in its social setting—the rich variety of customary land use rights, obligations, diffuse claims, and so on.

The distinction is important also because discrepancies may emerge when the state attempts to remake society; the result in India is a duality in both land tenure and credit tenure systems. The discrepancies between the systems sanctioned by the state and those sanctioned by society account for important dynamics in the evolving agrarian system.

The conceptualization of a hierarchical system of land tenurial strata accords well with both common terminology and the concrete conditions of Indian agriculture. British India recognized a variety of "inferior," "superior," "pucca," and other varieties of tenure holders. The notion of system implies that the aspects of social organization and production relations in agriculture are systematically related; superior position on any one dimension was likely to imply superior position on others as well. From the perspective of this investigation, the important dimensions of the land tenure hierarchy include: (a) the extent and quality of land controlled; (b) the security of control or access; (c) the terms of control or access. These distinctions become important when the state attempts to intervene in rural credit markets and must formulate rules for allocational priorities and security procedures. The notion of "credit tenure" suggests a reproduction of these dimensions. Classes of cultivators vary in terms of: (a) the amount and term of credit they can command; (b) the certainty, regularity, and facility of access; (c) the terms on which credit is available.

STATE INTERVENTION AND CUMULATIVE INEQUALITIES

It is precisely because rural credit interactions have historically resulted in serious distortions of the land tenure system (foreclosure, disinvestment, the creation of absentee rentiers, etc.), and because traditional rural credit relations tend to aggravate inequalities of income and wealth, that the state has intervened in the form of providing "institutional" credit. Independent India accepted the rationale, the models, and the mechanisms of intervention developed by the British. In the absence of intervention, it seems obvious that those with superior access to land and control of surplus from the land will be in a superior position to augment their land resources, whether by purchase, development of new land, or making land-augmenting capital improvements. The early credit studies in independent India confirmed that larger land-owners were far more active and successful in land markets and in capital formation.[10] This ability is of course reinforced when the state imposes no effective constraints and creates infrastructure which increases the value of land; for example, the virtual absence of a tax on agricultural income and the low incidence of all direct taxes on agriculture reinforce the translation of superior position in the traditional land tenure system to superior access to modern capital and technological change.[11]

It is possible to illustrate this phenomenon with data collected in the All India Rural Debt and Investment Survey of 1961-62. At that time only a small fraction of borrowing for capital investment was provided by institutional sources; the data thus essentially represent the situation without state intervention.

Table 1
Fixed Capital Formation in Farm Business

Asset Group (Rs)	Percentage of Cultivating Households	Percentage of Aggregate Value of Recorded Assets	Percentage Reporting Capital Formation	Percentage of Aggregate Capital Formation
Less than 500	6.5	0.3	10.1	0.7
500 - 1,000	9.7	1.1	13.1	1.2
1,000 - 2,500	24.8	6.3	16.9	5.1
2,500 - 5,000	23.3	12.5	22.2	9.2
5,000 - 10,000	18.6	19.5	27.5	17.6
10,000 - 20,000	10.7	22.2	33.3	21.4
20,000 and above	6.4	38.1	49.3	44.9
All Asset Groups	100.0	100.0	23.3	100.0

SOURCE: All India Rural Debt and Investment Survey, Tables I and XVII, Reserve Bank of India *Bulletin* (June 1975)

The concentration of assets and capital formation illustrated by Table I and the accompanying Lorenz curve (Fig. 1) is rather striking. The poorest three groups, those households reporting less than Rs. 2,500 each in assets,

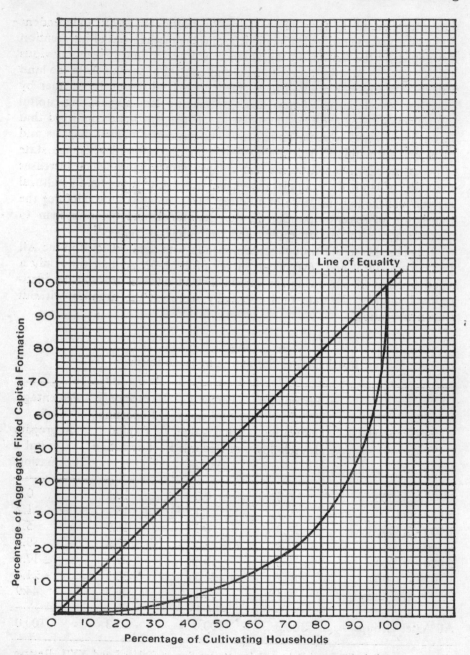

constituted 41 percent of the cultivating households, but controlled only 7.7 percent of recorded assets and reported 7.0 percent of fixed capital formation. The wealthiest group constituted only 6.4 percent of the culti-vating households, but owned 38.1 percent of all recorded assets and made 44.9 percent of the investment in fixed capital. As a rough comparison, the National Sample Survey reported that the top 6.81 percent of all cultivating households operated 36.32 percent of the cultivated area.[12] The data suggest that new capital formation is more concentrated than ownership of existing assets.

Capital formation may be financed from current income or borrowing. The income of households at the bottom of the land tenure pyramid is frequently inadequate, reflecting both the small area of land controlled per family and, for many, unfavorable tenurial terms. As a result, borrowing is frequently necessary simply to maintain the household. Table 2 illustrates this phenomenon. Larger farmers incur a higher percentage of total ex-penditures for capital expenses, a lower percentage for nonagricultural expenses, compared to small farmers. The weakness of small farmers in credit-investment interactions is likewise reflected in a higher rate of dis-investment and sale of assets or new borrowing simply to repay outstanding debts, resulting in a decreased ability to invest in productive ways.[13]

Table 2
Investment, Expenditure, and Borrowing Behavior

1. 1970–71

Size of Holding (has.)	PERCENTAGE OF TOTAL EXPENDITURES FOR:		PERCENTAGE OF BORROWING FARMERS WHO BORROWED FOR:		
	A. Nonagri-cultural Expenses	B. Fixed and Working Capital	A. Nonagri-cultural Expenses	B. Fixed Capital	C. Working Capital
More than 6	61.0	39.0	26.7	57.9	89.1
4–6	63.3	36.7	31.8	24.0	59.9
2–4	68.1	31.9	43.7	18.8	54.1
0–2	76.8	23.1	61.5	20.2	33.8

2. 1950–51

Size of Holding	PERCENTAGE OF TOTAL BORROWING FOR:		
	A. Family Expenditures	B. Fixed Capital	C. Working Capital
Big (top decile)	37.2	35.5	13.3
Large (top 3 deciles)	41.2	34.7	12.1
Medium (middle 4 deciles)	49.5	30.5	10.1
Small (bottom 3 deciles)	59.8	23.2	6.8

3.   1970–71

PERCENTAGE OF TOTAL BORROWING FOR:

Size of Holding (has.)	A. Family Expenditures	B. Fixed Capital	C. Working Capital
More than 6	31.5	33.4	35.2
4–6	38.5	34.8	26.7
2–4	36.4	27.4	36.2
0–2	56.0	27.7	16.3

SOURCE : 1 and 3 from *Credit Requirements for Agriculture,* National Council of Applied Economic Research. Calculations from Tables 20, 16, 12, 3, 21, 18, 14. Percentages for borrowing purposes may exceed 100 percent because some farmers borrowed for several purposes. 2 from *All India Rural Credit Survey,* Vol. 1, part 2, p. 382.

The nonstate credit arena exhibits cumulative tendencies in other ways as well. Superior position in the land tenure hierarchy is likely to mean access to resources of wealthy friends and relatives, a major source of "non-institutional" credit. Most of this credit is available without interest (though there are often concealed charges), so that larger farmers are advantaged in both the amount and cost of credit available through this channel. Table 3 presents illustrative data collected by the National Council of Applied Economic Research for the year 1970-71.[14]

Table 3
Friends and Relatives as a Credit Source*

Size of Holding (has.)	Average Amount Borrowed from Friends and Relatives (Rs)	Percentage of Total Borrowing Interest Free (%)	Average Rate of Interest on All Borrowing (%)
More than 6	3,675	44.1	9.0
4–6	687	2.5	14.9
2–4	465	5.1	14.3
0–2	402	10.6	16.0

*All credit supplied was reported to have been interest free.
SOURCE : *Credit Requirements for Agriculture,* Tables 37, 46, 47.

Likewise, we should not be surprised that this translation from superior land tenure to superior access to capital is made very directly by commercial credit institutions since market forces are allowed to operate. Banks prefer to allocate credit on the basis of owned, saleable resources—the greater the value of the security, the more the credit that is potentially available, manifesting the cumulative model. A succinct statement of credit allocation by commercial banks illustrates this point: "Agricultural credit, at present, is provided neither according to the needs nor based on the production potential of the farmer, but only in terms of material security."[15]

Thus the interesting part of our investigation stems from the fact that credit is a scarce resource and is subject to allocation by political as well as market mechanisms. The goals of the Indian state, as in Article 39 of the Constitution, and ruling party have been clearly stated in egalitarian terms—not merely the checking of cumulative tendencies but active intervention to reduce disparities in wealth and security based on the traditional system. The effort to disperse inequalities rather than providing mechanisms to accelerate cumulative tendencies based on differential ownership of the means of production I take to be the bare minimum meaning of a "socialist pattern of society." Given the "natural" dynamic of cumulative disparities created by an interaction between the prevailing distribution of resources and market mechanisms, what impact is likely from the response of the political system to this dynamic?

Fragmented and varied as the Indian institutional credit structure is, responses by the political system, conceived of analytically as a national system, have consequences for the allocation of access to agricultural capital. The responses may be decisions or, as significantly, nondecisions; a decision not to intervene to mitigate an on-going process affects the future distribution of power and privilege just as does a concrete action. By analyzing the working rules of institutional credit, we begin to see how the Indian political system is responding to and mitigating the challenge of technological change and capitalist development in the agrarian sector. As capital-intensive new technology spreads under present institutional arrangements and institutional sources supply an increasing proportion of rural credit, the working rules of credit allocation become more important in altering the distribution of power and privilege,[16] and presumably will become increasingly important objects of action by various units in the political system. (The enormously expanded role of the state in the commercial banking sector since 1969 is an important example.)

Credit, Capital, and Technological Change

The perspective of this paper, emphasizing the positive potentialities of agricultural credit, may seem incongruous with the warnings in numerous reports of historical importance and the common perception in rural areas of many countries concerning the negative potentialities of debt. Much of the treatment of rural credit on the sub-continent has been in the spirit of the French proverb: "credit supports the farmer as the hangman's rope supports the hanged." Historical example certainly justifies the fear, but it was precisely as a response to the disinvestment and foreclosure syndrome that institutional credit agencies were initiated by the state. Institutional credit is a boon to the cultivator for a number of reasons. Not only may it protect the farmer from the necessity of disinvestment or contact with usurious sources, but pressure to repay loans is often slight and debt remissions are frequent. Interest rates are far below those prevailing in the unorganized rural credit market and indeed at present rates of inflation are negative.

Credit is not a sufficient condition for realizing the potentialities of technological change, but it is often, especially for the small farmer, a necessary condition. The notion of debt as a weakness in the rural economy and the bane of the peasantry is applicable primarily to conditions of stagnant technology, uncertain yields, unproductive borrowing, and usurious sources. As agriculture increasingly becomes a rational capitalist enterprise, debt, particularly to institutional sources, is more likely to be a sign of strength than weakness in the farm economy.

Under conditions of technological change, the importance of credit lies in its provision of new productive opportunities through access to both fixed capital improvements and working capital in the form of new inputs. In one sense, credit or financial capital has always been a substitute for land. For example, provision of water may make possible doublecropping which effectively doubles the scale of production. Working capital allows the production of high value crops which entail much higher production costs, e.g., sugar cane or betel. And yields per acre have traditionally been subject to increase through such expense-incurring techniques as fertilizer application, more careful ground preparation, intensive weeding, etc. Thus cash resources or credit have always been capable of augmenting land resources, either through an increase in the scale of production or through an increase in yields or increased value of crops grown.

Recent changes in available technology intensify these effects in several crucial ways so that the change seems more qualitative than quantitative. These changes include the new high yielding varieties of seed (HYVs), which in the case of wheat may double or even triple output, and their necessary complements—assured, timely water; heavy doses of fertilizer; often herbicides and pesticides—and the more diffuse notion of modern management techniques which include careful cost accounting and rationality in decision-making spurred by the high cost of the enterprise and intensified government extension inputs of technique and information.

The new technology is capital-centered and dependent in a number of ways; outlay for working capital—seeds, fertilizers, water, pesticides, etc.—is dramatically greater than for traditional methods of cultivation. But the new technology is capital-centered and dependent, at least potentially, in several other ways. Since the high yields which make possible the increased expenditure on inputs are dependent on assured and timely application of water, capital improvements on the land often must be undertaken. Even in areas irrigated by canal, the unreliability of canal irrigation may force cultivators to seek private sources of water, such as a tubewell. Efficient water management often requires costly levelling and bunding. There may be costs involved in water-lifting equipment and in electricity installation for pumps. In the longer run, at a stage already reached in the Punjab, there may be capital costs to mechanize operations as costs of labor and animal power increase;[17] tractors also allow rapid preparation of the soil after harvesting a first crop to provide for more efficient multiple-cropping. Since the HYVs mature in a shorter time than traditional varieties, this potential for multiple-cropping (increasing the scale of production) is enhanced.[18]

Table 4 illustrates differences in capital and current farm expenditure and borrowing for growers of HYVs in 1970-71. These differences are not so dramatic as those often presented in the literature on the "green revolution" which frequently reports cost figures for the biologically optimal level of inputs. The data presented below are more representative in that the farmers classified as HYV growers were typically growing the new varieties on only a part of their land and were applying moderate levels of inputs. The comparison is among small farmers, for whom we would expect credit to be one constraint on higher levels of inputs. The figures apply to households but would not differ if expressed in per acre terms, as the average size of holding for the two groups is virtually the same.

Table 4
Expenditure and Borrowing of HYV Small Farmers*

	Expenditure for Current Farm Expenses (Rs/Household)	Expenditure for Fixed Capital	Borrowing for Current Farm Expenses	Borrowing for Fixed Capital
HYV	994	177	337	776
Non-HYV				
(a) Irrigated	685	158	215	739
(b) Unirrigated	378	41	182	457

*Less than 5 acres operated.

SOURCE : *Credit Requirements for Agriculture*, Tables 12, 14 16, 18.

The important point about recent changes in technology is that inadequate access to both long-term development credit and short-term production credit is a far more critical deprivation now than before. Access to capital increasingly determines the productive possibilities of the cultivator, potentially placing him in a new relation to the production process. Adequate access to agricultural capital is often the breaking point between continued subsistence cultivation and participation in broader alternatives that are creatures both of a modern scientific world community and of the conditions created by India's political system to render more viable those alternatives.

To underline the critical nature of this breaking point, I want to suggest several thresholds created by the pure technology. These thresholds exist because of several physical complementarities involved in growing the HYVs. First among these is the complementarity of inputs, which places a special demand for a quantum of working or production capital. To obtain the optimum yields which make investment in inputs profitable, the new varieties must have sufficient quantities of commercial fertilizer, water, and often pesticides and herbicides. Depending on a variety of factors, these physical inputs (often coupled with increased labor costs) significantly increase outlay per acre; insufficient quantities of any one input jeopardize investment in the others, since maximum yields may not be obtained.[19]

The centrality of water raises a second complementarity—that between production capital and fixed capital. Permanent improvements on the land may prove necessary to assure adequate water at proper intervals. Water control, often necessitating large investment, becomes a precondition for the yields which make investment in production capital profitable. Canal irrigation often proves too unreliable for secure cultivation of the new varieties, so that tubewells are sought even on irrigated land. Moreover, not only must the water supply be sufficient and dependable, but the field must be protected from receiving too much water at the wrong time, often necessitating improvement in bunding or drainage systems.

Finally, there is a technological complementarity among fixed assets.[20] Digging a well which allows use of new varieties or multiple cropping may require additional capital assets such as water-lifting equipment, an electricity connection, bunding and levelling to allow efficient water management, and so on.

The discussion of complementarities and high costs of new inputs suggests that access to credit should predict differences in levels of capital formation, particularly for poorer farmers. Although it is very difficult to assess the independent effect of credit availability on investment decisions, some recent data, presented below, indicate support for the view that access to credit is often critical. In Table 5, the expenditure of borrowing households is expressed as a percentage of nonborrowing households of the same size. The differences in expenditure on fixed farm capital are especially substantial, except for the category of large farmers, for whom borrowing is arguably less necessary.

Table 5

Expenditure by Borrowing Cultivators Expressed as a Percentage
of Expenditure of Nonborrowing Cultivators

Holding Size (has).	Fixed Capital Expenditure	Current Farm Expenditure	Non-agricultural Expenditure	Net Disposable Income
0–2	324	144	110	102
2–4	421	117	117	115
4–6	371	123	127	112
More than 6	132	122	133	99
All Sizes	189	129	120	108

SOURCE : *Credit Requirements for Agriculture,* Calculations from Tables 26, 28, 30, 31.

The short sketch of the green revolution presented here does not do justice to the diversity of Indian agro-economic situations and de-emphasizes the extent to which much traditional agriculture has remained untouched by the new technology. Nevertheless, some generalizations can be made; even in the traditionally less innovative areas, increased potential for agricultural profits is having an impact, particularly where production of wheat is possible. Thus many of the same dynamics operate in Purnea District, Bihar, as in Ludhiana District, Punjab.[21] But neither the obvious regional qualifications nor the other caveats to be raised later seem to detract from the central point: there is continuing and invigorated pressure towards modernization and capitalization of Indian agriculture, spurred both by a pure new technology and its institutional infrastructure. In the process of change access to capital determines much of the evolving form of the agrarian system. And in predicting differential access to capital, the land tenure system provides an effective tool.

PERSISTENCE OF SOCIETY—COOPERATIVE CREDIT

The tendency of elites to preserve and extend their power by utilizing traditional resource bases to co-opt new opportunities as external parameters of change is hardly a startling observation. The question of the dynamics of translating one power base into another—at what discount? through what mechanisms?—may prove interesting but the propensity and ability of traditional elites to do so should surprise no one. There is nothing startling about the observation that local landed elites have dominated local credit cooperatives in India, nor that they have used cooperative credit as an additional power resource. Daniel Thorner's study is classic, and insightful; and though somewhat impressionistic, his conclusions accord well with more rigorous studies.[22] As we explore the rules of institutional credit, it will become clear why Thorner's observations are more generally applicable.

Put most simply, Thorner found that the dominant elements in the cooperatives, and those who benefited most from their operations, were the "big people in the village." Though in the official ideology co-ops were to "rehabilitate the weaker sectors" and to "develop the social cohesion and unity of the village" so that all might "work together for the common good,"[23] Thorner notes that "the evidence suggests that the structure of village power has imposed, and will continue to impose, its own pattern on the cooperatives,"[24] and that "there is nothing in the record of cooperatives (or indeed any other organization in India) to suggest that it is the interest of the weak that will prevail" when interacting with the strong.[25]

The mechanisms whereby the advantaged monopolize new advantages provided during the process of modernization vary from case to case. Thorner found in his study of a cooperative in Saurashtra that only Khatedars (landowners) were members of the society, and the statutes prohibited nonmembers from obtaining credit. In this case the landless comprised more than 50 percent of the cultivators supposedly served by the co-op.[26] In India

as a whole, only 24 of every 100 cultivators were members of credit cooperatives in the mid-1960s and only 12 of these 24 received credit.[27]

A curious inversion of the exclusion of subordinate groups was found
by Thorner in an Uttar Pradesh (U.P.) cooperative. There large landowners boycotted the society altogether, leaving only low status Chamars
without resources as members, resulting in the failure of the society.

A second method of controlling cooperative credit opportunities was
evident in Thorner's case study in Baroda; membership was not restricted,
but "all elected members of the managing committee are landholders and all
are Patels." Not surprisingly, the society "prefers" to lend to owners of
land. Many primary societies lend to landless cultivators, but with predictable
results. Throner's example in Maharashtra extended total short-term credit
of Rs. 191, 677 the prior year, over half of which was loaned to 11 members,
while the other 142 members shared the remaining sum. Thorner noted
that the Mukhyestaru ("all-in-alls") of Mysore have typically used dual
tactics; at first they opposed the cooperatives as a threat to their moneylending interests but if the opposition failed they would enter the cooperatives and dominate them. In Kerala, "as in Madras and Mysore," most
members of the societies are holders of rights in land and the co-ops prefer
to loan against land as security.[28] In the U.P. case, Thorner found that
ex-zamindars obtained disproportionate shares of credit while the landless
workers and tenants were largely excluded.[29]

Thorner's examples could be multiplied endlessly, from his and other
studies, but some important generalizations are already suggested. First, the
flow of credit tends to follow the lines of power in the village in the case of
primary societies; power in the village typically is a mirror image of the land
tenure system.[30] If the dominant landed group is split into factions, for
example, the result is likely to be rival cooperatives to serve the rival factions
or no cooperative at all. Secondly, as will become clearer with the discussion
of credit limits and long-term development credit, even if those with inferior
position in the tenure system can obtain credit, they typically can obtain
very little credit. Thus the primary society's credit tenure system often reproduced two critical distinctions of the land tenure system: how the land
is held and how much land is held.

Though the evidence is too bulky to be presented fully, a number of
studies accord with Thorner's observation. In summary: 1) tenants are less
likely than owners to be members of cooperatives;[31] 2) small owners are less
likely than larger owners to be members;[32] 3) small holders in cooperatives
are less likely to receive loans and the cooperatives meet a smaller percentage of their total credit needs compared to large owners.[33]

Moreover, the exceptions to this general pattern often underline the
pattern's validity. Thorner found that in Vizagpatnam District of Andhra
"big people are not in control of the societies and are not exploiting them
for their own ends." But special structural circumstances explain the
situation; the local Maharaja had previously renounced his zamindari rights

and settled all tenants as ryots. Thus there were few extreme inequalities of wealth. These exceptional conditions made possible the equitable distribution of credit resources under conditions very similar to those prevailing in the promising Comilla project in Bangla Desh; there, too, the great zamindars no longer held rights in land and the resultant mix of small holders rendered less likely the emergence of a closed elite which could dominate credit allocation.[34] The State of Jammu and Kashmir, which for special historical reasons carried out a relatively thorough land reform, presently has by far the highest percentage of cooperative borrowers to total cultivators in India (38 percent).[35]

A summary of the distributive aspects of cooperative credit shortly after independence is presented in Table 6.

Table 6
Access to Cooperative Credit

Size of Holding	Amount Borrowed from Cooperatives (Rs/household)	Amount Borrowed from Cooperatives as % of Total Borrowed	Proportion of Families Borrowing from Cooperatives
Big (top decile)*	21.0	4.0	5.1
Large (top 3 deciles)	13.5	3.8	4.5
Medium (middle 4 deciles)	4.7	2.7	3.3
Small (bottom 3 deciles)	1.9	1.7	1.9

*"Big" is a subset of "Large."
SOURCE : *All India Rural Credit Survey*, Vol. 2 part 1, p. 234.

The first comprehensive study made of credit in independent India was the Rural Credit Survey of 1950-51 done by the Reserve Bank of India. A major conclusion of that report was that large sections of the agricultural population were excluded from membership in or benefit from the cooperatives.[36] For those who received credit the amount was seldom adequate; moneylenders and other private sources dominated the credit system.[37] Moreover, as Thorner suggests, though the rationale for primary credit societies argued that individuals could be evaluated by their peers in terms of "character and repayment capacity," as the Committee on Cooperative Credit reported in 1963, in practice "the finance provided by the cooperatives was mostly on mortgage security," tied to ownership of land.[38] A report by the Programme Evaluation Organization of the Planning Commission found in 1959 that "right in land remains the most important consideration taken into account" and "the discrimination in favor of landowners against tenants persists."[39] There is good evidence of the persistence of this pattern through the late 1960s.[40] Indeed, the *Fourth Five Year Plan* summarized in 1969:

> The bulk of loans issued by cooperatives is in small amounts of less than Rs. 500 each. Even so, farmers with relatively larger holdings are the main beneficiaries of cooperative credit. The traditional emphasis on linking of credit to security offered by a borrower in the form of land and other tangible assets, exclusion of small farmers from the membership of the cooperatives, domination of cooperatives by the more affluent and powerful section of the rural community, absence of tenancy records and prevalence of oral tenancies are among the major factors that have led to denial of adequate credit to small farmers (p. 220).

The Prime Minister, speaking to the Sixth Indian Co-operative Congress in 1971, feared that "cooperative" was becoming synonymous with vested interest and that the cooperatives were acting as little more than "conduits for the transfer of resources on concessional terms" to special interests.[41]

CREDIT LIMITS AND SECURITY—PRODUCTION CREDIT

Having seen from Thorner's analysis how the village society imposes its power structure on the credit system, we need to look to the formal-legal mechanisms which flow down from the state. As would be expected, there are impressive similarities, but also divergences which suggest that a more plural power structure, though still attuned to landed interests, has operated at the State level, and certainly at the Center.[42]

Primary credit societies are intended to handle the short-term production credit needs of cultivators as well as medium-term loans for such purposes as purchasing bullocks, etc. Long-term loans have historically been granted for redemption of old debts, consolidation of holdings through land purchases, and so on, but increasingly long-term credit is specified and used for capital improvements on the land.[43] This change in emphasis is reflected even in the change of the name of the major institutional source of long-term credit—from Land Mortgage Banks to Land Development Banks. But as the earlier name suggests, long-term credit for land improvement has been based on mortgage security, and thus restricted to cultivators with ownership rights in land.

The kind of security demanded for credit and the effective credit limit vary over India, but two generalizations can be made: first, as the term and amount of credit sought increase, so does the likelihood that ownership of land will be required as security; secondly, the more land one owns, regardless of the variations in credit criteria, the greater the credit that can be obtained.

Both of these principles are so natural to traditional modes of finance that their irony in the Indian context may be overlooked. First, both propositions imply that credit should be allocated in such a way that those specially advantaged by the old dispensation (the traditional system of land control) should be disproportionately benefited under the new dispensation, that development is a process that further develops the developed.

Clearly, under certain institutional conditions disparities become cumulative; in Gotsch's model, the feedback loops are positive. But for such a dynamic to operate in India's credit system is clearly a capitalist phenomenon—the criteria for obtaining access to increasing control of the means of production consistently operate to reward those who own the means of production. So the first significant point about the processes of the credit allocation system is that the dynamic created thereby moves away from, not toward, a "socialist pattern of society."

The second curious point is that mortgage requirements of clear title to ownership ignore the social reality of land control in the Indian context. Production credit is meant for producers and producers often have had negligible rights in land, and certainly may not be the owners of land. Land improvement credit is meant for the productive unit, which may not include the owner at all. If the goal is to increase productivity then both production and fixed capital must be in the hands of the decision-making producer, in adequate amounts. Thus two central systemic values are denied—the twin goals of increased productivity and enhanced equality.

A third irony in the land mortgage security system is that it is not at all secure. The idea behind land mortgage is to ensure repayment of loans. Yet institutional recovery rates have been abysmally low in India, despite the dependence on land mortgage, and defaults have often led to the collapse of cooperative credit institutions. Foreclosure on mortages by institutions has been extremely rare, partly because of the maze of laws preventing or impeding alienation of land from cultivators (originally enacted for protection from the money lender) and the hesitance of institutions to deal in land sales or management. Moreover, recovery pressure is light because the loan repayment is typically the responsibility of managing committees, whose members are often the biggest defaulters or lower government officials who lack the power, prestige, and incentive to confront powerful men in the village. The net result is frequently the obverse of a security system—large owners, with access to the greatest quantity of credit, are able to withstand pressures for repayment, whereas the supposedly less "credit worthy" small farmers, lacking bases of social power, can be forced to repay loans.[44]

Credit limits are set in a number of ways; one of the more frequent relates to the amount of land revenue paid, directly linking credit to the amount of land controlled. But the land revenue limits are sometimes subject to qualifications introduced by the land tenure system. For example, in the Punjab in the early 1960s, though no formal rule governed the limit,

in practice the maximum credit limit of an individual land-owning cultivator is fixed at 30 times the land revenue paid by him, plus $\frac{1}{4}$ of his miscellaneous income. For tenant cultivators or non-cultivating landlords, the limit is fixed at 15 times the land revenue plus $\frac{1}{4}$ of miscellaneous income.[45]

This distinction in the Punjab is interesting, for capitalist relations in agriculture are well advanced there; note that the landlord, who is a pre-capitalist form to the extent that he performs no economic function other than rent receiving—i.e., no productive function—is given inferior ranking in the credit tenure system just as is the tenant vis-á-vis the entrepreneurial owner. This provision is in contrast to the laws for long-term credit in Madhya Pradesh, for example, where explicit provision is made for the traditional absentee rentier in the credit tenure system.[46]

In Mandsaur district, the limit was set at fifteen times the land revenue for holders of less than fifteen acres and twenty times the land revenue for owners of more than fifteen acres.[47] In Hissar district, "loans could be advanced up to fifteen times the land revenue on land unowned and culti-vated by an occupancy tenant, up to twelve times on land cultivated under tenancy-at-will, and up to thirty times on owned and self-cultivated holdings."[48]

In U.P. the individual credit limit is fixed as 40 times the land revenue on *Bhumidari,* 10 times the rent paid on *Sirdari,* 4 times the rent paid as *Adivasi* and *Asami*[49] plus and minus various assets and liabilities. *Bhumidar* originally represented the new name for superior tenure holders after zamin-dari abolition—the talukdars and zamindars.[50] Other kinds of intermediaries as well as "rent-free grantees" likewise became Bhumidars upon passage of the Zamindari Abolition Act of 1949. Bhumidars had full rights to land, including the right to mortgage. *Sirdars* were former occupancy tenants, hereditary tenants, exproprietary tenants, and so on. Sirdars could not mortgage their rights in land; the rights are heritable but restricted in that, unlike Bhumidars, Sirdars could use land only for agricultural purposes and could be evicted for violating this restriction. Sirdars may acquire Bhumidari rights upon payment of a sum to the state. *Asami* tenancies are recognized only in special and limited cases, including working the land of a disabled or soldiering Bhumidar or Sirdar. *Adivasi* tenures were to be held by pre-abolition sub-tenants and were meant to be a transitional form of tenancy.[51]

The net effect of the U.P. land reforms was to simplify the multiplicity of pre-Independence tenures but to retain the crucial distinctions; these distinctions are then translated into the credit hierarchy: bhumidars have superior rights in land and can use these rights to gain superior access to credit; sirdars have fewer rights, and can be evicted for a number of reasons, but have the right to obtain bhumidari rights, most critically the right to mortgage land to gain access to credit. Asamis have no rights to mortgage land, and thus inferior access to credit. Various unrecognized sub-tenants and sharecroppers fall at the bottom of the credit and land tenure hierarchies while landless laborers may be considered virtually outside those systems.[52]

Mortgage security, essential for longer-term loans, is often a distinct advantage for production loans. For example, "in Assam it is stated that short term loans are given against personal security, but it is common for societies to obtain a mortgage even for a short term loan."[53] In West Bengal, all loans over Rs.125 had to be secured by mortgage of land.[54] In parts of Bihar, in the early 1960s loans over Rs.50 required ownership of land. Similar low limits are applied to personal security loans in Andhra and Madras, whereas some States required mortgage of land to advance any loan whatsoever. In Orissa the State government has stipulated that loans up to Rs. 250 need not be secured by land, but the cooperative banks continued to require land mortgage even for small loans.[55] The net effect of these working rules is to force the non-landed cultivator or small holder back to the very institutions the credit cooperative was meant to replace— the usurious moneylender or landlord.

Other criteria for setting credit limits are indirectly related to the distribution of land rights and provide positive feedback loops. For example, cooperative rules often take income into account, but for most cultivators the addition of an income consideration to a land consideration changes little. Income in the agrarian sector is obviously linked to control of land: a tenant who retains half or less of his harvest has far less income to augment his credit potential or generate savings for investment compared to an owner. As position in the land hierarchy declines, more of the crop is demanded of the least secure and socially powerless cultivators (such as the bargadars of Bengal) as less capital is supplied by the tenant. Sharecroppers who provide nothing more than labor are virtually equivalent—in both the land tenure and credit tenure systems—to landless labor.[56]

Likewise, credit limits are often set as multiples of share capital held by the cultivator; ability to purchase shares is obviously related to how much land of what kind one holds and on what terms. And ownership of land often mitigates the working rules; in Assam and Manipur the credit limit has been ten times the cultivator's paid-up share capital unless he has land to mortgage, in which case the limit is doubled.[57] In some areas the limit was set at five times the value of shares for landowners, but only three times for tenants, even when no mortgage was executed.[58] Other limits relate to the value of crops grown or cost of production. The precondition for growing high value crops, however, is usually a high level of working capital. But the land tenure system sometimes imposes restrictions on the seemingly rational method of allocating credit on the basis of cost of production; the scale of finance for tenants was in some cases set at a lower level than for land owners growing the same crop (whether or not the landlord supplied inputs).[59]

Most States also provide for sureties (co-signers) to increase the personal security credit limit of a borrower. Rules vary, and the option of requiring that sureties be landowners is frequently left to the panchayat of the society, but the Reserve Bank's Committee on Cooperative Credit noted that "usually the sureties are among owners of land."[60] In West Godavari district, surety loans, which do not require the mortgage of land, were nevertheless limited by the amount of land held by the borrower. Even then, the limit was different for owners and tenants, an owner being entitled to twice as much credit per acre operated.[61] In West Bengal, for example, the by-laws do not require that sureties be landowners but in practice they must be. The Committee's *Report* goes on to argue that:

> A tenant requiring a loan for a credit worthy purpose may be honest and industrious, but he is not able to obtain loans under existing practice if he does not own land or is not able to offer sureties who own land. This practice has an adverse effect on agricultural production.[62]

But the effects of the surety requirement may extend beyond the obvious impact on productivity. The mechanism could work to cumulate inequalities in the village and strengthen the dominance of patrons over clients. The production loan has traditionally been a bond between landed patrons and dependent client-tenants. As early English liberals realized, tenant clients are not socially or politically free agents. The original ideology of the co-operative movement stressed just this point, recognizing that the basis of an inegalitarian agrarian system lies in the superior access of certain groups to the fixed and working means of production—land and short-term capital—in a labor surplus economy. To the extent that client-tenants are forced to ask landed patrons to stand surety for production loans, the traditional structure of power is reinforced. Moreover, the provision for sureties facilitates the consolidation by landed communities of their position in the village by easing access to credit for less prosperous members.

The Rural Credit Follow-Up Survey of 1956–57 noted an interesting example of patron mediation in credit relations. In Coimbatore district, "a tenant cultivator was eligible for a loan provided he produced a certificate from his landlord to the effect that the landlord had no objection to the produce grown by him being sold through the marketing society to which the credit society was affiliated."[63] The translation here is direct. Just as the owner stands between the producer and control of the produce in the land tenure system, the modern institution places the owner between the producer and production capital in the system of credit tenure.

The final comment on short-term cooperative credit is that policy recommendations have been virtually unanimous since the early 1950s on one concept; especially short-term credit, but increasingly also longer-term credit, should be allocated more on criteria organized around a "production nexus" rather than an "asset nexus." The Second Five Year Plan, following the recommendations of the All India Rural Credit Survey Committee, officially proposed extension of the crop loan system begun in Maharashtra whereby cultivators receive credit in kind (as fertilizer, seed, etc.) on a scale related to cost of production on the expectation of a crop. The principle is that the viability of the productive unit, not the assets held, should determine credit allocation.[64]

This stance implies a minimal recognition that the prevailing concept of "credit-worthiness" is a contributing force in cumulating inequalities. Obviously the creditworthy may or may not be those who will use credit more efficiently; much cooperative credit is used by moneylenders and land-lords to replenish their stock of private financial capital for lending to those who are less creditworthy.[65] Productivity concerns are consistently slighted by an asset-oriented credit policy.[66]

But recommendation of the crop loan system from the top may have little effect on actual policy.[67] In 1950, the Bombay State Cooperative Bank officially adopted a policy of lending against crops rather than assets. In 1956 the Crop Loan Evaluation Committee termed the system a "dis-appointment." Specifically:

> The membership of primary societies is still small and exclusive, and generally excludes persons of lower status, other factions, castes, etc. Tenants are still not admitted in any large proportion, and even where they are admitted, they receive no credit at all, or lower credit limits are allowed them.

As a result, finance for "weaker sectors" is "inadequate" and the process "inevitably forces the cultivator into the arms of the moneylender."[68]

Nehru argued in 1958 that the small credit society closest to the village, and farthest from official interference, offered the greatest hope for co-operative development, for in the village community knowledge of potential borrowers was intimate.[69] But it is also in the village that social control mechanisms are most powerful; intimate knowledge of a potential borrower's skills cannot be separated from intimate knowledge of his caste, faction, propensity to resist the dominant group, and so on. The model which seems to have been operative is that of a true village community, an organic unit in which the "weaker sectors" could be continually "uplifted." Because of the myth of the cooperative, almost socialist, village, Nehru termed the interference of government in cooperative affairs the "embrace of death."[70]

But a laissez faire policy in a traditional society leaves control in the hands of traditional elites. The central question for democratic political development may indeed concern the way in which a political system protects oppressed groups from local elites and yet allows the people to control their own institutions. The dilemma is not one limited to poor nations, of course. Advocates of participatory democracy in the United States must contend with the consequences of local control for oppressed minorities to cite but one example. In the field of cooperatives, the evidence seems to indicate that unless the power base of the elites is broken (e.g., through effective redistribution of land), the modern form (cooperative credit) will become yet another source of power and control for the traditional landed elite. From this perspective it is naive to believe that locally controlled cooperatives will move very fast from land-based credit policies, since the power base of the cooperative elite is typically a superior position in the land tenure system.

STATE VS. SOCIETY—TACCAVI LOANS AND GOVERNMENTAL INTERVENTION

The perspective of political science directs attention to the responses of the political system to developmental challenges so as to direct the course of societal change in accordance with certain values. The decision to channel credit through local cooperatives has provided mechanisms for persistence of societal patterns counter to systemic goals of enhanced equality and higher productivity.[71] It is possible to view the decision to channel state credit increasingly through local cooperatives as conditioned by a number of factors: by low system capabilities (how *could* Delhi intervene effectively in thousands of credit-allocating decisions?), by fragmented federalism (State-level elites consistently mitigate central directives in conservative directions), by political responsiveness to landed interests (the patron vote-brokers), and by the amorphous myth-paradigm of the village community infused with quasi-Gandhian notions of development. But what are the consequences of the intervention of the state directly in the credit allocation system; is this impact more likely to reinforce or disperse the inequalities of the society's agrarian system?

Taccavi, or direct governmental, loans began with the Land Improvement Loans Act of 1883 which empowered local administrative units to issue loans "for the purpose of making any improvement on land, to any person having a right to make that improvement, or with the consent of that person to any other person."[72] This seemingly simple requirement presupposed that the instruments of the state can penetrate the societal web of customary rights and norms with reasonable ease and efficiency. That local elites were often able to dominate the flow of information regarding land rights seems axiomatic and illustrates an important constraint on actions by the state to change societal patterns.[73]

A second constraint on the state's efforts to interact with society in credit allocation is the gap between the culture and meaning systems of representatives of the state and most members of society. In Henry Hart's conceptualization, because the "field" is "hinged" rather than "linear," intermediaries or brokers are necessary to bridge the gap.[74] The gap did not disappear with the British, and Myron Weiner has documented the role of local elites in intervening with the contemporary bureaucracy both to do favors for clients and co-opt favors for themselves.[75] Taccavi loans constitute one such favor.

Taccavi loans in independent India became the mode of institutional credit preferred by cultivators. The reasons for this include liberal land evaluation practices, relative speed and ease of application and disbursement, very low interest rates, subsidies, grace periods, longer repayment periods, and absence of mandatory contribution to share capital, although the loans often incur corruption costs since officials have great leeway in awarding loans. Pressure to repay taccavi loans may be slight and the recovery rate is very low.[76] Ladejinsky reports that in Bihar in the late 1960s these loans were virtually gifts and were monopolized by large farmers.[77] A study in 1970 by the Reserve Bank noted that compared to those who received taccavi loans, those who did not were farmers "with small holdings and low incomes." Compared to receivers of loans, non-receivers made meager investments on their land.[78] This tendency has been documented repeatedly by the Rural Credit Survey reports.[79]

The causes of this phenomenon are not merely social and economic— wealthy cultivators have superior resources to pad applications when necessary and superior social and political resources at the local level as well as family and caste ties to administrative elites—but also formal-legal—the basis for granting taccavi loans has primarily been ownership of land.

The rules for setting loan limits illustrate the familiar translation of the land tenure hierarchy into differential credit rights. In U.P., limits were set at 60 times the land revenue for bhumidari tenure, 10 times for sirdari, twice the rent for adivasi, and equal to rent for asami.[80] Tenants without legal status, such as sajhis, are thus formally excluded from consideration. The rules also state that no loan can be sanctioned without two "solvent and substantial sureties."[81] Delineation of who is sufficiently solvent and substantial is left to the loan officer. What is suggested, then, is the familiar combination of both formal-legal and more informal rules (who is substantial in the village?) working in concert to strengthen positive feedback loops.

Official policy at the Center has evolved to the position that direct taccavi loans should be eliminated, except for emergency relief, and the credit channeled through cooperatives. Given the history of cooperatives, it is not at all certain that the credit would find its way to Thorner's "little people" in the villages, but whatever the consequences, the change, like so many of the Center's policies, has been resisted at the state level and, as of 1970, had not occurred. Remembering the increasingly crucial nature of credit as a resource, the concrete advantages to cultivators of taccavi loans and the political power of dominant agricultural communities, this is not surprising. Likewise, the potential that taccavi credit gives to bureaucrats for amassing a loyal, supportive clientele of powerful people suggests another core of resistance.

The point in discussing taccavi loans was to illustrate the similarity in consequences for allocation of credit of two seemingly different decisions by the political system—first to delegate authority and resources to a societal mechanism (the village) and secondly to use governmental administrative apparatus directly (taccavi). We can test the impact in a number of ways.

To compare the consequences in the early period of independence, we can use data from the Rural Credit Survey relating to 1950-51. The comparisons are in terms of average amounts obtained per household and the proportion of total borrowing provided by the institution for each size group. Table 7 shows that large farmers fared better on both measures from both agencies. At the aggregate level there is a remarkable similarity in outcomes.

However, there has been continuing pressure on all institutional agencies to realign allocation priorities, and the share of institutional credit in total borrowing has dramatically increased in the two decades since the Rural

TABLE 7
Cooperatives and Government Credit Allocation Priorities

Size of Holding	Borrowing (Rs/Household)		Percentage of Total Borrowing Provided by	
	A. Government	B. Coops	A. Government	B. Coops
Big	24	21	4.5	4.0
Large	14	14	3.8	3.8
Medium	6	5	3.2	2.7
Small	2	2	2.0	1.7

SOURCE: *All India Rural Credit Survey, 1950-51,* Vol. 1, part II, pp. 111, 234.

Credit Survey.[82] Have there been significant changes in the relative performance of mechanisms of the state and those of society?

A partial answer to this question is possible from analysis of data
collected by the National Council of Applied Economic Research (NCAER)
for 1970–71. To measure institutional priorities, we can use a ratio of percentage of loans received by a given tenurial class to the percentage of total
cultivators represented by that class in the sample. If an institution favored
no particular tenurial group, we would expect in aggregate terms that the
ratio be 1. For example, if small farmers constituted 40 percent of the sample
and received 40 percent of the loans granted, we would obtain a ratio of 1
and conclude that in aggregate terms the institution manifests no operational
priorities related to tenurial class in granting loans. A ratio greater than 1
suggests over-representation of a class; a ratio less than 1, under-representa-
tion. Table 8 presents the results for three kinds of loans, borrowing for farm
capital, current farm expenditure, and nonagricultural expenditure.

TABLE 8
Institutional Priorities—Ratio of Percentage of
Loans Received to Percentage of All Cultivators

Institution and Purpose	Size of Holding (Hectares)			
	0–2	2–4	4–6	>6
A. Capital Expenditure				
1. Government	0.59	0.03	0.71	3.16
2. Cooperatives	0.63	0.52	0.81	2.43
B. Current Farm Expenses				
1. Government	0.71	1.80	1.26	0.48
2. Cooperatives	0.76	1.29	1.16	1.58
C. Nonagricultural Expenses				
1. Government	0.11	0.78	0.76	3.20
2. Cooperatives	0.93	0.98	1.18	1.06

SOURCE: *Credit Requirements for Agriculture,* calculations from Tables
40, 42, 44.

The conclusions to be drawn from Table VIII would seem to be: (a) There is no evidence that government agencies have made consistently more or less progress in reallocating credit to small farmers. The smallest farmers, those operating less than 5 acres, about 65 percent of all farms in India, were not accorded institutional priority by either institution for any purpose. (b) Over-representation of the largest farmers is the rule for both agencies, especially for fixed capital credit. (c) Medium-size cultivators fared well in borrowing from both institutional sources for current farm expenditures. (d) As in other cases discussed in this essay, the concentration of credit for fixed capital is greater than for short-term working capital, reflecting the importance of the land mortgage security system in contributing to the concentration of capital formation on large farms.

As important as institutional priorities for cultivators near the bottom of the land tenure hierarchy is the question of institutional adequacy. Because of low farm income, it becomes more important that institutions supply a high percentage of the cultivator's total borrowing needs if he is to avoid high interest costs, disinvestment, chronic debt, and so on. Adequacy is a reflection of the working rules of the institution; once a farmer is granted a loan, the setting of credit limits in relation to need becomes important. We have seen how credit limits are directly related to tenurial status. Since these rules typically constrict the credit potential of small farmers, and small farmers consistently have much higher costs and credit requirements per acre because of the greater intensity of land use,[83] one would expect the adequacy percentage to be lower for smaller farmers. Table 9 presents the share of total borrowing provided to different classes of cultivators in the NCAER data.

TABLE 9
Institutional Adequacy—Percentage of Total Borrowing Supplied

| Institution and Purpose | Size of holding (Hectares) | | | | |
	0–2	2–4	4–6	>6	All
A. Capital Expenses					
1. Government	2.7	0.1	1.5	6.5	2.6
2. Cooperatives	22.1	7.8	13.6	38.0	20.3
B. Current Farm Expenses					
1. Government	15.6	16.5	14.8	4.6	12.7
2. Cooperatives	59.1	66.8	77.3	85.5	71.8
C. Nonagricultural Expenses					
1. Government	Neg.	0.2	0.2	0.4	0.2
2. Cooperatives	3.8	4.9	4.6	2.2	3.5

SOURCE: *Credit Requirements for Agriculture,* Tables 41, 43, 45.

On balance, there is no evidence that the state is more effective than are cooperatives in meeting the credit needs of small cultivators. In general, except for working capital, the percentage of credit needs supplied by these sources is very meager for all classes of cultivators. But one important fact should be considered in interpreting these results. For wealthy agriculturalists, institutional sources may not be the preferred source of credit for a number of reasons. Friends and relatives in the NCAER data supplied credit to large farmers on a very large scale, and without interest charges. The consequences of not receiving adequate institutional credit also vary by tenurial class; for large farmers, a high percentage of noninstitutional credit was obtained from friends and relatives, whereas small farmers were forced to rely more on moneylenders, traders, and so forth. The pattern is especially pronounced in borrowing for fixed capital expenses and nonagricultural expenditure (which represent a high percentage of small farmers' aggregate borrowing). Table 10 presents these differences.

TABLE 10

Percentage of Total Credit Supplied, by Purpose
and Source (Noninstitutional)

| Source and Purpose | Size of Holding (Hectares) | | | | |
	0–2	2–4	4–6	>6	All
A. Capital Expenses					
1. Moneylenders, etc.	57.9	88.4	52.2	24.2	57.9
2. Friends, Relatives	8.2	0.4	0.3	11.0	5.1
B. Nonagricultural Expenses					
1. Moneylenders, etc.	81.3	74.7	80.3	27.2	61.2
2. Friends, Relatives	14.1	12.9	4.8	69.9	32.2

SOURCE: *Credit Requirements for Agriculture,* Tables 43, 45.

One other test of the impact of state as distinct from society is in possible differences between "large-sized" and "small-sized" cooperative societies. As the names imply, the types differ by size, the small ones in one sample averaging 2 villages, 64 members, and very little share capital, the large ones covering 11 villages averaging 418 members.[84] The large-sized societies are characterized by greater official intervention—nomination of directors, intervention in managing, government contribution of share capital, provision of a full-time paid secretary, etc.

But the differences in credit allocation decisions between those societies which are clearly state-penetrated and those which are not are not great. In both cases rarely were more than one-fourth of the cultivators members. Small cultivators do poorly in both, even somewhat more poorly in the large cooperatives. Maximum credit limits are set by various criteria, but: "Right in land remains the most important consideration taken into account in setting the limits. The discrimination in favor of land-owners against tenants persists and the large society is not better than the small societies in this respect." Moreover, in both cases, the management of the societies tends to become semi-permanent.[85] The first Rural Credit Follow-Up Survey produced the same conclusion.[86]

In these cases in which governmental inputs in the credit allocation process seem to have very little countervailing effect, we see more clearly the operation of a dominant paradigm embedded in the notion of creditworthiness. As we move on to the larger medium- and long-term loans, the connection between land and credit becomes more pervasive and dominant, and as we have shown, it is this larger quantum of credit which often marks the threshold between subsistence and commercial agriculture.

LONG-TERM CREDIT AND LAND MORTGAGES

Rules for medium-term credit raise no special questions. Since the amounts are typically larger, the likelihood that land mortgages will be required is greater. In a number of States medium-term cooperative loans are allowed only to cultivators of a specified minimum extent of land—usually five or ten acres and typically larger than the median size of holding. Again, the mortgage requirement denies credit to tenants who have heritable but not alienable rights in land, as well as to other inferior classes of tenure; the *Report of the Committee on Cooperative Credit* argues that tenants with heritable but not alienable rights constitute "a substantial portion of the total number of cultivators."[87] The Rural Credit Survey reported that mortgage by "superior tenants" was allowed in Bihar, Bengal, Assam, Madhya Bharat, Rajasthan, and Hyderabad, "but the condition is generally imposed that it should be a usufructuary mortgage of defined minimum duration." Mortgage was permitted on the same terms to a "pucca tenant" in Madhya Bharat, though lower categories of tenants were denied the option.[88]

The possession of heritable but not alienable land rights introduces a crucial distinction with regard to credit and capital improvements on the land. Unlike holders of inferior tenures which are not heritable, or which are not even secure from year to year (tenants-at-will), the hereditary tenant has a clear incentive to improve the land's productivity with capital assets (assuming the rent cannot be raised to expropriate the gains in productivity). Denying the means for capitalization (long-term credit) to hereditary tenants adversely effects agricultural development; denying both the incentive and the means to various inferior categories of tenants has a more pronounced detrimental effect and points to consequences of failures in reforms of the land tenure system for the evolving credit tenure system.[89]

Given the ambiguous status of various tenures, mortgage of land based on the Western legal conception of "ownership" poses a special problem. The delineation of mortgageable rights in land preserves a crucial distinction in the traditional tenure system, but in a somewhat arbitrary way. Early in this century, the Central Provinces Banking Committee noted that tenants in Berar with occupancy rights which were alienable had access to credit denied to occupancy tenants in contiguous Nagpur District whose rights were not alienable. These somewhat arbitrary distinctions resulted from a series of Alienation Acts in British India which sought to protect tenants from moneylenders and landowners who were encroaching on their hereditary rights; thus in some areas, but not in others, certain tenancy rights were made inalienable. As these distinctions introduced by historical accident are inherited and translated into the new vocabulary of independent India, their origin becomes irrelevant but the distinctions themselves serve to differentiate classes of tenants with regard to long-term credit. And whereas some States are now making the rights of tenants alienable and mortgageable (Kerala, for example), others have made the land rights of cultivators belonging to the "scheduled tribes" inalienable and thus non-mortgageable (Bihar, Madhya Pradesh, etc.).[90]

LAND MORTGAGE (DEVELOPMENT) BANKS

The possession of rights to mortgage land becomes important because of the working rules of the primary institutional source of long-term credit —land mortgage (now "development") banks. As noted earlier, without adequate and controlled water, a cultivator typically cannot significantly increase the scale of production or obtain yields which characterize the green revolution. Control of water is in effect control of more land, i.e., control of more produce, more labor opportunities, more wealth, more access to credit. And control of water often requires extremely large outlays relative to current output. Likewise, long-term credit allows the kind of mechanization which is accelerating throughout India.[91] Access to capital in the form of labor-replacing machinery frees the cultivator from at least some of the constraints in dealing with increasingly organized and militant laborers. Control of this kind of capital is again a functional equivalent for control of land: it allows the owner to occupy a position of strength vis-à-vis labor; it grants the owner more power to determine how wealth will be distributed in the system. And, of course, under the present dispensation, long-term credit for land improvement makes the owner still more creditworthy by increasing the value of his land.

It was noted by the Agricultural Finance Sub-Committee in 1945 that "all long-term rural finance is based ultimately on mortgage security."[92] The Rural Credit Survey of 1954 concluded that not only were cultivators without ownership rights excluded from long-term credit, but that small farmers, relative to large, received little credit from Land Mortgage Banks just as they did from other levels of the cooperative system. There is no evidence that this picture had changed by as late as 1970.[93]

Though Land Development Banks (hereafter LDBs) are in theory cooperative, with managing structures varying in composition of elected, appointed, and official members, in fact, as a careful student of these banks has argued:

> It may be not very far from the truth to say that the formal structure of land mortgage banks is being utilized for distribution of official credit, coming from the Reserve Bank of India, and in nature is little different from the governmental investment-cum-outlay in aid of the private sector in other branches of the economy.[94]

The LDB thus represents a direct link in the process of translating landed elites into progressive capitalist elites with the aid of the state.

Although the formal criteria for determining the amount of an LDB loan are: 1) cost of the project; 2) profitability of the investment and repayment capacity of the borrower; and 3) value of the security offered, the working rules stress the last criterion, often to the exclusion of the other two.[95] The Ahmednagar LDB uses the following formula to fix loan limits: 330–500 times the land revenue plus one-half the cost of the improvement.[96] By adding only one-half the cost of the improvement, farmers with little land may receive loans insufficient for the project. Their options are then to fall back on a moneylender, damaging the chances of repaying the loan, or not completing the project, likewise damaging repayment capacity. One study found that LDB loans for wells to small farmers covered an average of only 55 percent of the cost of the project, whereas loans to large holders covered 110 percent of the project cost.[97]

Thus capital becomes more costly to small holders than to large; the latter category, because of over-financing, are often able to recycle cooperative credit at usurious rates. A second result is an increasing capital, and thus technological, gap between small and large holders of land: N.S. Jodha's study found that small holders are typically able to borrow only for traditional assets such as wells and bunding, whereas large holders borrow mainly for engines, electric pumpsets, tractors, etc.[98] In the Ahmednagar study it was noted that as a result of the land-based credit system, "a large part of the increase in the availability of irrigation facilities financed by the LDB's remains concentrated in relatively largesized (holding) groups and the rich peasantry."[99] As a result of this phenomenon, large farmers are able to take up innovations rapidly, thus reinforcing the "progressive farmer" myth-paradigm.[100]

The cumulative nature of creditworthiness as a principle seems to be illustrated in the Ahmednagar case study.[101] The report shows, as we would expect, that the average size of loans to large farmers was greater than that to small farmers. But what seems interesting, and was curiously omitted by the author, was the fact that although prices had risen by over 50 percent in the four years studied (1963–64 and 1967–68), the average loan to small farmers increased only marginally (Rs. 1830 to Rs. 1917), whereas the average loan to largest holders increased by over Rs. 1,000 per loan (from Rs. 2330 to 3333). Those who obtain the largest loans are potentially able to make more capital improvements and thus increase the value of their land so as to be eligible for larger loans. But since over a four-year period this long-term dynamic could hardly be expected to operate, I would guess that the increase in loans to large holders reflects the increased availability of new seeds and fertilizer over the period studied, which increased the need for capital improvement (especially irrigation) for all farmers; when demand on institutional credit rapidly increases, the priorities become most clearly manifest.[102]

The formal rules of LDBs for mortgage of land tend to force the capitalist form of production relations onto the owner if he wishes to obtain credit. The Madhya Pradesh statutes specify that the owner must show the land to be conclusively in his full "possession and enjoyment...no loan can be advanced to an applicant who may have title but is not in actual possession of the land."[103] The provision in the Gujarat and Maharashtra statutes is clearer and seems to have a similar effect: land with tenants may be a legal problem and hence is something the banks strongly discourage.[104] Tenants may possess subordinate use rights which make the property a less than clear-cut case of property in the Western legal sense; there are often difficulties in selling a piece of land complete with tenants who have variable rights and customary arrangements. "Possession," like "self-cultivation" in the land reform statutes, seems to imply management of wage labor in the capitalist sense.

However, the caveat concerning the evolution toward a fully capitalist rural system still applies: clearly there are remnants of the traditional system even where new relations take hold.

We noted that in the Punjab the non-cultivating landlord is penalized in the credit hierarchy vis-á-vis the fully capitalist, land-owning manager. But the Madhya Pradesh laws contain an explicit provision for providing capital to an absentee rentier class: "If an applicant is not in a position to offer as security land which is worth double the amount of the loan applied for, but if he owns a residential building in places like Jabalpur, Raipur, Indore, Bhopal, Gwalior, etc., the value of the buildings will be taken into account for making up the deficit."[105]

SOME THOUGHTS ON EXPLANATION

The final question to consider is that of causality: why, in the face of very good and plentiful evidence that inferior classes of cultivators are unable to obtain credit necessary to increase productivity (or advance egalitarian goals), does credit continue to follow lines of the traditional land tenure system?

No decisive answer will be attempted; the answer varies with level of analysis. We have seen how dominant landed elites typically have controlled primary societies and quite naturally have used these new resources to enhance their power base. Control of land in this situation is power in a modified Parsonian sense[106]—a medium of exchange which can be transferred from one institutional setting to another and retain its ability to command preferred outcomes. It may be useful as an index of societal transformation ("modernization"?) to ascertain the extent to which a traditional power resource such as land becomes a medium of exchange in fewer and fewer arenas, or must be used with increasing discounts in new arenas. Clearly land is no longer "to rule" in Walter Neale's sense, and in much of India land is an increasingly discounted resource (relative to earlier periods) in obtaining political power. New power contenders with new power resources (militant students, bureaucrats, numerically superior castes) force these discounts as does the process of economic development which offers alternative employment opportunities to those once subject to the power generated by land (as in the Punjab).

But while this devaluation of land as power currency has been taking place in some arenas, concomitant changes in others have produced counter forces. The new arena is capitalist agriculture, more secure and profitable because of state support of the necessary infrastructure, and access to capital is the translation of land as a power medium. And in this arena capital means enhanced control of the labor of others and the produce of the land, as well as access to more subsidized capital. For this reason, where land is scarce and the man-land ratio high, the power of landed elites to retain control of local institutions should come as no surprise, at least until vertical patron-client ties deteriorate and clients are organized politically.[107]

The same explanation in terms of the power of land controllers probably applies to the State-legislated rules of cooperatives and the actions of State officials in allocating credit.[108] The power of landed elites in State governments is well known, of course.[109] But we often find similar allocation criteria in effect in states such as Kerala where political power has devolved considerably toward the have-nots at the State level. It thus seems profitable to explore briefly some of the more diffuse but important reasons for the phenomenon I have described.

Perhaps the first point to be made is that the structure of roles in institutions may force decision-makers to act conservatively in seeking security in those roles. Nothing makes one who approves a loan look worse than to have the borrower default. Cultivators with insecure or inferior rights to very little land are especially vulnerable to natural disasters; their marginal income and lack of surplus often make them "poor risks" in a very tangible way. Moreover, the poor risk syndrome becomes a self-fulfilling prophecy and thus part of social reality; the poor risk is often supplied with inadequate credit so that he is unable to supply optimal levels of water, fertilizer, pesticides, etc., resulting in low yields and thus inability to repay the loan, confirming his status as a poor risk. Moreover, very low incomes necessitate borrowing for consumption, debt repayment, and other purposes which generate no new resources.

The important point here is that poor cultivators are often poor risks only because they lack capital, and are thus unable to benefit fully from the new technology, or because of the inflexible rules of the credit system, or because of their necessary connections with moneylenders whose usurious rates consume surplus income, or because of victimization by rack-renting, and so on *ad infinitum*. The institutional setting which creates such disadvantages is typically assumed to be static and immutable; this perception, while quite accurate both in the short run and for any single individual, reinforces the social-institutional inertia. We should not lose sight of Barrington Moore's point that social inertia serves concrete interests,[110] those of the powerful, and that conservative attitudes towards change are related functionally to the distribution of power in society, but I want to argue that such attitudes, perceptions, and myths have a logic of their own. Institutional conservatism often persists in the face of radical alterations in the distribution of power and this persistence may be attributed partly to perceptions which grow from concrete experiences of individuals seeking security, in their individual roles and partly to socially dominant myths (or in scientific incarnation, paradigms) which make operating in terms of alternative myths (paradigms) dysfunctional.[111]

The myth-paradigm confluence in India revolves around the notion of "progressive farmers" with an undertone of "sturdy peasant castes" and an overlay of an international paradigm of economic development which has stressed work with "progressive and responsive farmers" to generate growth which trickles down to the less responsive and less progressive.

For example, there is good evidence that caste stereotypes do exist and are consistent from high to low caste, with Harijans, for example, being seen as—and seeing themselves as—less competent, energetic, knowledgeable, etc.[112] That oppressed groups typically incorporate into their collective identity social myths propagated by dominant groups is indisputable, and that these self-perceptions increase the self-fulfilling prophecies on a societal level seems likely.[113] The point here is that the "substantial" Jats who dominate the primary cooperative may be acting in good faith in refusing a large loan for a risky innovation to a landed Chamar; the Department of Agriculture officer may be acting in terms of the same myth-paradigm in channeling taccavi loans to the large, progressive Jat farmers. The more secure the individual cultivator is in the village, both psychologically and institutionally, and the more credit he can command, the more progressive he can be, so that myths, too, have cumulative properties. In an important sense, policy thinking on the ground has not progressed beyond the colonial outlook of Sir Frederick Nicholson which introduces this essay.

And, finally, relating myths back to concrete consequences for role occupants, the Jat farmer is probably the safest option for any individual loan officer or bank; social institutions are interrelated and the farmer with a large amount of land with secure rights is also likely to call on a community of like farmers if help is needed, is likely to have the social connections necessary to obtain extra extension help, complementary credit, marketing connections, and so on. The exact opposite of these conditions is more likely to characterize the Harijan sharecropper. Social mythologies typically apply reasonably well within a given set of institutional parameters (with some distortions, of course) but neglect (or screen out) the changeable nature of those parameters.

The argument then is that causality in linking credit to land is cumulative and reflects a number of forces operating at different levels, each with an internal logic but all together producing a mutually reinforcing effect. The only caveat I wish to introduce is that the level of paradigm, being more subject to empirical confirmation, seems to change more easily than that of myth or political power and social influence. Thus while we have seen a long-term evolution in policy thinking at the Center, the conservatism of loan-dispensers, the myths of poor risks, and the dominant power position of landed interests have kept the links between land and credit strong and persistent at lower levels in the system. These propositions seem buttressed by more recent developments.

CREDIT REFORM

The credit system of India, plural and fragmented to begin with, seems to be in a state of flux at present. The dominant trends are pressures from above for liberalization of terms and movement toward productivity rather than asset-centered allocation criteria, and resistance from below. Conditions vary enormously and the recent redistribution of political power at State and national levels makes generalization difficult. But I would like to cite a few illustrative examples from Francine Frankel's recent book on technological change in India.[114] The special interest of her observations is that she studied five districts which vary greatly in most relevant characteristics, but which have been exposed to the most intensive developmental efforts of the political system.

One impression from Frankel's work, bolstered by other recent works,[115] is that the Center is able to obtain *pro forma* compliance but not much real change in credit policy. Of the original seven Intensive Agricultural Districts only three could be induced to institute crop loan systems.[116] One of these three was Thanjavur and even there Frankel found that despite official policy, primary credit societies would not recommend tenants for loans, so that tenants lacked the production credit to obtain maximum yields.[117]

Another recent source is the Report of the Intensive Agricultural District Programme. Much of the pattern outlined in this essay persisted in the intensive districts, where government developmental efforts were concentrated. Indeed, even in Raipur district, where special programs were instituted to help small farmers, it was reported that "it is precisely this group which remained neglected by the cooperatives."[118] As an over-all summary statement:

> The IADP promised the farmer that he would get production credit on the basis of his production capacity and not on that of his creditworthiness based on securities, land value, mortgages, and other standards. Although the Reserve Bank agreed to the issue of crop loans to facilitate

this, this promise was not generally fulfilled at the field level . . . . The cooperatives in many areas did not make any radical change in either policy or procedures . . . . Many of the personnel in the cooperative department especially at the field level showed lack of understanding of the development needs and revealed an unduly security and rules oriented approach.[119]

Frankel's study confirms several major propositions of this paper. First, official policy in Thanjavur raised the personal surety loan limit to Rs. 1,000, but for landowners that limit, linked not to mortgage of land, but to personal surety, was Rs. 5,000. The new limit was to apply to tenants with or without lease deeds. "In practice, however, primary agricultural credit societies will sanction loans only to cultivators who enjoy a customary, if not legal, right to till the same holding year after year."[120] Likewise, Frankel notes that the Reserve Bank succeeded in formally instituting a crop loan system in Burdwan District (Bengal), but in practice loans are sanctioned only against land.[121]

The Thorners remind us that the rights of a tenant depend more on the social situation within the village than on his status in law.[122] We have several times come across this social, as opposed to legal, mechanism of translating land tenure distinctions into credit tenure distinctions. Often the two mechanisms have worked in the same direction, but there is a widening divergence; those at the bottom of the land tenure system increasingly can neither be ignored nor mobilized through their patrons. That legal changes may be only *pro forma* goes without saying, but the presence of laws dissonant from social reality often initiates important dynamics. For example, Frankel notes that sharecroppers in Thanjavur are excluded from access to credit because they are shifted from plot to plot annually and thus represent no stable production unit (land plus labor) on which to extend credit. But this shifting of sharecroppers has been encouraged by land reform laws which give tenants rights in land vis-á-vis the landlord if the tenant can prove occupancy. This fear on the part of landlords is widespread in India, often with good reason, and reflects an impact of the idealized legal system of land tenure on the system of credit tenure.

This impact is strengthened by the importance of LDB rules which demand a clear title to extend long-term credit. A landowner whose land is tied up in the courts by recalcitrant tenants seeking realization of the formal/ idealized system of rights in land (an increasingly frequent occurrence) is prevented from obtaining capital. He may even find it difficult to sell or cultivate land tied up in litigation.[123] This is an added incentive for landlords who are evading the law to minimize the security of tenure of tenants and to prevent them from obtaining any formal recognition of land use rights (as a crop loan implies).

Thus changes in the legal structure seem on balance to be moving toward greater access to credit for those inferior in the tenure system, but the laws themselves may generate social forces at the top of the tenure-power spectrum which frustrate the intent of the law. These responses, and subsequent counter-responses, point to the inconclusiveness of any conclusions reached.

Political decisions (or non-decisions) evoke responses from groups which are affected. The analysis of this paper has been static, but clearly the dynamics created by change in the rural sector will generate pressures on the criteria for allocation of access to capital. As decisions affecting agriculture devolve to lower levels,[124] mobilization of new groups at the local level will almost certainly question the asset-oriented credit system. Likewise, the Reserve Bank of India, directly concerned with productivity, efficiency, and newly sanctioned models of equity, has powerful levers to influence lending policies of credit institutions from the top. With consolidation of Congress (R) strength at both the Center and in the States, pressure from the Center for a more progressive credit system will probably emerge.[125] Finally, the technological imperatives of extending the new varieties to more acreage will necessitate allocation of developmental and production credit to more and more small cultivators.

CONCLUSION

As a part of more general goals of changing the traditional distribution of power and privilege in rural areas and organizing agriculture along more productive lines, modern institutions have been promoted and subsidized by the Indian political system to dispense agricultural credit. Both the formal-legal regulations and the operational procedures of these modern institutions have typically preserved, even strengthened, the position of traditionally advantaged groups. There has been a tendency to translate, often very intricately, differential status in the existing land tenure system into differential status in an emerging hierarchy of access to and rights in agricultural credit and capital. Such a translation frustrates objectives of equity and productivity, yet persists. The reasons for persistence lie not only in the failure to redistribute the primary power resource of local elites—i.e., the failure of land reforms—but also in the influence of inherited and sanctioned paradigms such as that of "credit worthiness" buttressed by prevailing social mythologies and also in the internal dynamics of the development bureaucracies.

Policy implications seem clear but drearily familiar. Because credit in many respects represents an increasingly good functional equivalent of land, the potentialities of a credit reform are similar to those of a land reform in terms of improving efficiency of resource use, productivity, and income distribution. But precisely because the hierarchy of access to credit reproduces, in several critical respects, the hierarchy of land control, reform measures have not been operationalized. This is to say nothing more or less than that control of the policy-making apparatus and implementation machinery—the organs of the state—has not been sufficiently freed from control by or fundamental empathy for those classes which disproportionately command the agricultural means of production.

NOTES

1. Cf. e.g., Harold Gould's "Is the Tradition-Modernity Model All Bad?" in *Economic and Political Weekly* (Bombay) [cited hereafter as *EPW*], Special Number, July 1970, p. 1171.

2. Cf., Talcott Parsons, *Sociological Theory and Modern Society* (New York, 1967).

3. Documenting this proposition properly would be a massive task. For one summary of thoughts and sources, see T.K. Oomen, "Green Revolution and Agrarian Conflict," *EPW*, 26 June 1971, p. A–99.

4. See Walter Neale, "Land is to Rule," in Robert E. Frykenberg, ed., *Land Control and Social Structure in Indian History* (Madison, Wis., 1969).

5. Carl Gotsch, in a presentation to a Seminar at the University of Wisconsin, Spring 1972. See also "Technical Change and the Distribution of Income in Rural Areas," Economic Development Report, no. 205, Development Research Group, Harvard University, (1971).

6. The framework here is suggested by Bachrach and Barratz, "Two Faces of Power," *American Political Science Review* 56 (1962), and Bachrach and Barratz, "Decisions and Non-Decisions," ibid. 57 (1963).

7. Daniel and Alice Thorner, *Land and Labor in India* (Bombay, 1965), p. 149.

8. Karl Polanyi elaborates this important point in *The Great Transformation* (London, 1944).

9. I am referring here to "asami" and thank Professor Manindra Verma, Department of Indian Studies, University of Wisconsin, for clarifying this point.

10. *Rural Credit Follow-Up Survey, 1956–57*, Reserve Bank of India (Bombay, 1960), pp. 190,203, 227. *Rural Credit Follow-Up Survey, 1958–59*, Reserve Bank of India (Bombay, 1961), pp. 70, 80.

11. The sum of all direct taxes on agriculture is barely 1 percent of net domestic product in agriculture. *Report of the Committee on Agricultural Wealth and Income*, Ministry of Finance (Delhi, 1972).

12. National Sample Survey, 17th Round, 1961–62 (New Delhi, 1968).

13. *Rural Credit Follow-Up Survey, 1956–57*, pp. 142, 239; *Rural Credit Follow-Up Survey, 1958–59*, pp. 50, 59.

14. *Credit Requirements for Agriculture*, National Council of Applied Economic Research (New Delhi, 1974).

15. *Seminar on Financing of Agriculture by Commercial Banks*, Reserve Bank of India (Delhi, 1969), p. 247.

16. *The Fourth Five Year Plan* (Delhi, 1970) pp. 220ff, notes that the gap between availability and need for institutional credit is growing as the new technology spreads and is thus becoming an increasingly critical obstacle to participation in the green revolution (cf. also pp. 140ff).

17. C.H. Hanumantha Rao, "Farm Mechanization in a Labor Surplus Economy," *EPW* Annual Number, Feb. 1972, p. 393.

18. The burgeoning 'green revolution' literature is voluminous. A good general view is Lester Brown's *Seeds of Change* (Praeger, 1970). A study of Indian conditions in the Intensive Districts often mentioned in this essay is Francine Frankel's *India's Green Revolution* (Princeton, 1971). Articles of special interest will be cited throughout.

19. See Brown, *Seeds of Change*, and Frankel, *India's Green Revolution*. Articles on the microeconomics of particular crops under particular conditions are numerous. For an example, see Thomas Dobbs and Phillip Foster, "Incentives to Invest in New Agricultural Inputs in North India," *Economic Development and Cultural Changes* (1972): 101.

20. See M.L. Bhat, "Diversion of Long-Term Agricultural Finance," *EPW*, 9 Oct. 1971.

21. Compare the two articles by Ladejinsky: "Green Revolution in Bihar," ibid., 27 Sept. 1969, p. A–147; and "The Green Revolution in Punjab," ibid., 28 June 1969, p. A–73.

22. Daniel,Thorner, *Agricultural Cooperatives in India* (Bombay, 1963). Also, *Effectiveness of Cooperative Credit for Agricultural Production*, National Council of Applied Economic Research (Delhi, 1972), pp. 23, 134, 136, 89, et passim.

23. See *Report of the Committee on Cooperative Credit* (New Delhi, 1963), p. 62ff. [Cited hereafter as *RCCC*.]

24. Thorner, *Agricultural Cooperatives in India*, p. 32.

25. Ibid., p. 30.

26. Ibid., p. 44.

27. S.N. Ghosal, *Agricultural Financing in India* (Bombay, 1966), p. 31.

28. Thorner, *Agricultural Cooperatives in India*, p. 76.

29. Ibid., p. 98.

30. See David G. Mandelbaum, *Society in India* (Berkeley, 1970), p. 208–209, and passim.

31. *Rural Credit Follow-Up Survey, 1956–57*, p. 357; *Effectiveness of Cooperative Credit for Agricultural Production*, p. 42.

32. *Rural Credit Follow-Up Survey, 1956-57*, pp. 392, 571; *Rural Credit Follow-Up Survey, 1958-59*, pp. 126, 239, 240; *Effectiveness of Cooperative Credit for Agricultural Production*, p. 42.

33. *Rural Credit Follow-Up Survey, 1956-57*, p. 393 and calculations from data on p. 644; *Rural Credit Follow-Up Survey, 1958-59*, p. 47; *Effectiveness of Cooperative Credit for Agricultural Production*, pp. 21, 56. Data from the *All-India Rural Credit Survey* (Bombay, 1954), and the 1974 NCAER study support the three points in the text as well and will be treated separately.

34. Gotsch, "Technical Change and Distribution of Income."

35. Ghosal, *Agricultural Financing in India*, p. 27.

36. *All-India Rural Credit Survey*, esp. vol. 2, part 1, pp. 235–79. Also *RCCC*, p. 78.

37. Ibid. Just as the land tenure system differentiates holders by relative advantage in the terms of holding land, the credit tenure system consists of levels of advantage in holding credit. Since moneylender's rates are typically at least double those of cooperatives and government sources, those unable to obtain institutional credit pay far more for the use of money, just as powerless and socially inferior *bargadars* pay more for use of land than high-status and powerful tenants. See *Seminar on Problems of Small Farmers*, Indian Society of Agricultural Economics (Bombay, 1968), p. 116.

38. *RCCC*, p. 78.

39. *Report of the Committee on the Working of Large-Sized and Small-Sized Credit Cooperatives*, Program Evaluation Organization (New Delhi, 1959).

40. The section on agricultural credit (especially pp. 220ff.) in the *Fourth Five Year Plan* is one source. For other more recent data see the section on recent developments in this paper. Also see *Report on the Intensive Agricultural District Programme*, Expert Committee on Assessment and Evaluation (New Delhi, 1969) p. 25, and p. 68–91. Also R.C. Diwedi, *New Strategy of Agricultural Development in India* (New Delhi, 1972) p. 181.

41. *The Hindu* (Madras), 9 April 1971.

42. A parallel struggle is being waged at present; the Center is urging reforms in both land tenure and credit tenure systems and resistance is being offered by landed elites and their political spokesmen. For a general view, see Wolf Ladejinsky, "Land Ceiling and Land Reform," *EPW*, Annual Number, Feb. 1972. For one illustrative state study, see "Tussle over Ceilings (Punjab)," *EPW*, 8 April, 1972, p. 745.

43. Ghosal, *Agricultural Financing in India*, p. 51 and passim.

44. *Effectiveness of Cooperative Credit for Agricultural Production*, pp. 61, 100, 101, 155.

45. *RCCC*, p. 79.

46. To be discussed in the section on land mortgage banks, which follows.

47. *Rural Credit Follow-Up Survey, 1956-57*, Appendix VI.

48. *Rural Credit Follow-Up Survey, 1958-59*, p. 113.

49. *RCCC*.

50. See Walter Neale's chapter on Uttar Pradesh in *Land Reforms in India*, A.I.D. Spring Review of Land Reforms (Washington, D.C., 1970) p. 38.

51. See Frank Moore, *Land Reform Legislation in Uttar Pradesh* (Berkeley, 1955).

52. Estimating the total number of such tenants is terribly difficult because of the dubious legality of their positions; landholders obviously have good reason to conceal illegal sub-letting and tenants may accede for fear of eviction (given the scarcity and enhanced value of land). A study by the Ministry of Home Affairs in December 1969, estimates that 82 percent of all tenants in Andhra, Assam, Bihar, Punjab, Haryana, and West Bengal are either "tenants at will" or subject to eviction should the owner decide to "resume" the land. (P.C. Joshi, "A Review Article," *Seminar*, May 1970.) At the very bottom of the land tenure hierarchy it becomes analytically questionable to distinguish between "landed" and "landless," as sharecroppers who provide no capital are essentially paid as laborers on a piece-rate basis. The Allahabad High Court (U.P.) has ruled that a *sajhidar*, or sharecropper, is not legally a tenant at all but a laborer who "pools his agricultural skill and efficiency and labor with the superior resources and land of another." The land is legally treated as "under personal cultivation by owners." The Court notes that: "It is reported that a considerable area is cultivated by the owners through Sahjis." R.S. Singh and V.B. Verma, eds., *Cases on the Uttar Pradesh Zamindari Abolition and Land Reforms Act* (Allahabad, 1971) p. 561.

53. *RCCC*, p. 83.

54. Ibid.

55. *Evaluation Report on the Procedure of Obtaining Loans from Agricultural Credit Cooperatives in Orissa* (Government of Orissa, 1966).

56. Frankel in Chapter VI of *India's Green Revolution*, notes that sharecroppers who are indebted to owners may find themselves in a position actually inferior to that of free wage laborers in terms of income.

57. *RCCC*, p. 85.

58. *Rural Credit Follow-Up Survey, 1956-57*, Appendix VI.

156 Ronald J. Herring

59. Ibid., p. 327.
60. *RCCC*, p. 85.
61. *Rural Credit Follow-Up Survey, 1956–57*, p. 336.
62. *RCCC*, p. 85.
63. *Rural Credit Follow-Up Survey, 1956–57*, p. 334.
64. *RCCC*, Chapter V.
65. See M.L. Bhat, "Diversion of Long-Term Agricultural Finance," *EPW*, 9 Oct., 1971, and Thorner, *Agricultural Cooperatives in India*.
66. This is the conclusion of official investigations over the years. For a summary, see *RCCC*, Chapter V; also N.S. Jodha, "Land-Based Credit Policies and Investment Prospects for Small Farmers," *EPW*, 25 Sept., 1971.
67. *Rural Credit Follow-Up Survey, 1956–57*, p. 334. More recent evidence is discussed in the section "Credit Reform," below.
68. Cited in Thorner, *Agricultural Cooperatives in India*, p. 17.
69. Cited ibid., p. 19.
70. *Evaluation Report on the Procedures...Orissa*, p. 14.
71. The productivity argument is complex. Without extensive documentation or argumentation, the case seems to follow from the following propositions:
1. Because of more intensive land utilization the marginal productivity of capital assets on small holdings is greater than on large holdings. Likewise, credit needs are greater per acre because of intensive use and low net income.
2. Small holdings are more likely than large holdings to be operated by tenants; tenants are even more seriously disadvantaged in (if not altogether excluded from) credit institutions than smallholders.
3. Underfinancing of smallholders leads to the diverting of scarce credit. Likewise, overfinancing of large farmers is common, often diverting credit to consumption or usury.
4. A major reason for low rates of adoption of yield-increasing technology by small farmers in the Intensive Districts was lack of credit for the new costly inputs.
A more careful treatment of this question is needed.
72. *Report of the Committee on Takavi Loans and Cooperative Credit* (Delhi, 1962), p. 4.
73. The Allahabad High Court has recognized what numbers of anthropologists have reported—that access to village land records is part of the societal web which obfuscates state efforts to deal rationally with land relations. In one case, the Court noted that a claimant of sirdari land rights had relatives who controlled the *lekhpal* in the village and "hence it was not at all difficult for the defendents to obtain any sort of revenue entries made in the favor." Singh and Verma, *Cases*, p. 533.
74. Henry Hart, "The Village and Development Administration," in J. Heaphey ed., *Spatial Dimensions of Development Administration* (Duke University Press, 1971).
75. This theme runs throughout Myron Weiner's *Party Building in a New Nation* (Chicago, 1971).
76. Reserve Bank of India, *Studies in Agricultural Credit*, Study no. 3 (Delhi, 1970), p. 204. It should be noted that corruption, too, has positive feedback effects. The study by M.L. Bhat, "Diversion of Long-Term Agricultural Finance," notes that poor farmers sometimes are forced to borrow from moneylenders to pay the bribes necessary to borrow from the government.
77. Ladejinsky, "Green Revolution in Bihar".
78. *Studies in Agricultural Credit*, p. 205.
79. Ghosal, *Agricultural Financing in India*, p. 34.
80. *Report of the Committee on Takavi Loans*, p. 14.
81. Ibid.
82. *Credit Requirements for Agriculture* p. 24 and Table 35.
83. *Rural Credit Follow-Up Survey 1956–57*, p. 49; *Rural Credit Follow-Up Survey, 1958–59*, p. 24.
84. *Report of the Committee on the Working of Cooperative Societies*.
85. Ibid.
86. *Rural Credit Follow-Up Survey, 1956–57*, p. 393.
87. *RCCC*, p. 90.
88. *All-India Rural Credit Survey*, 2:106.
89. The failure of land reforms to provide security of tenure for large numbers of tenants, tending instead to increase their insecurity, is well established by now. See, e.g., Ladejinsky, "Land Ceiling and Land Reform," and "Green Revolution in Bihar"; and the study by the Ministry of Home Affairs cited in Joshi, "A Review Article."
90. For an excellent summary see H.B. Shivamaggi, "Transferability of Rights in Land and Farm Finance," *EPW*, Special Number, July 1968, esp. p. 1052.
91 The Report of the Expert Committee on Assessment and Evaluation of the Intensive Agricultural District Programme (IADP), in the second volume (*Modernizing Indian Agriculture*, Delhi, 1969) notes levels of mechanization in the intensive districts

and reports both an accelerated pace of and increased demand for mechanization.

92. *Report of the Agricultural Finance Sub-Committee* (Delhi, 1945).

93. V.K. Singh, "Long Term Finance to Small Farmers," *Maharashtra Cooperative Quarterly*, October 1970; also N.A. Kalyani, "Problems of Long Term Credit for Agriculture Through Land Development Banks," ibid., January 1971; and C.H.H. Rao, "Farm Size and Credit Policy," *EPW*, 26 Dec., 1970. See also N.S. Jodha, "Land-Based Credit Policies and Investment Prospects for Small Farmers."

94. Ghosal, *Agricultural Financing in India*, p. 88.

95. Jodha, "Land-Based Credit Policies and Investment Prospects for Small Farmers."

96. Singh, "Long Term Finance to Small Farmers."

97. Jodha, "Land Based Credit Policies and Investment Prospects for Small Farmers."

98. Ibid.

99. Singh, "Long Term Finance to Small Farmers." Also Deepak Lal, "Agricultural Development in Maharashtra," *EPW*, 12 Jan. 1969.

100. By "myth-paradigm" I am proposing a loose marriage of a very free interpretation of Murrary Edelman's notion of "myth" and "metaphor" (cf. *Politics as Symbolic Action,* Chicago, 1971 and *Symbolic Uses of Politics,* Urbana, 1962) and Thomas Kuhn's "paradigm" (*The Structure of Scientific Revolutions,* Chicago, 1965). By myth I mean a simplified and simplifying set of inter-related organizing principles, implicit or explicit, which aid all of us in making sense of the blooming, buzzing confusion of the phenomenal world by screening out certain kinds of information and accentuating others. A paradigm is a more "scientific" myth, and serves the same cognitive-epistemological functions— setting rules for what counts as an answer, what counts as evidence, what evidence is important, and so on. In both myth and paradigm, assumptions are typically not tested; as Kuhn argues, to constantly test assumptions would make it impossible to go on with the tasks of information collection, organization, and hypothesis-testing. For myth, it is even more difficult to test assumptions, for the assumptions are (a) socially sanctioned and (b) less consciously held. Both myths and paradigms break down, paradigms probably faster because those who use them self-consciously question at least some aspects of the paradigm in their daily work. When either myth or paradigm is contradicted by so much experience that it becomes dysfuntional to retain it, there is change (slowed in both cases by the screening effect which prevents rapid accumulation of dissonant meanings and by the enormous social-psychological investment of people in their myths and paradigms).

101. Singh, "Long-Term Finance to Small Farmers."

102. This supposition is supported by Deepak Lal, "Agricultural Development in Maharashtra."

103. *Manual for Cooperative Societies in Madhya Pradesh*, vol. 3, *Land Mortgage Banks* (Indore, 1963), p. 137.

104. See K.S. Gupte, *The Gujerat Cooperative Societies Act, 1961, with Rules, 1965* (Poona, 1965), p. 568.

105. *Manual...Madhya Pradesh,* Section IV, p. 4(a).

106. See *Sociological Theory and Modern Society*.

107. Frankel, *India's Green Revolution,* offers some thoughts on how these ties are dissolving in India.

108. Maharashtra seems the ideal-typical case. See Mary Carras, "The Economic Determinants of Political Factionalism," *Economic Development and Cultural Changes*, (Oct. 1972): 118.

109. One of the best treatments is Weiner's *Party Building in a New Nation*.

110. A theme of the concluding chapter of Barrington Moore's *Social Origins of Dictatorship and Democracy* (Boston, 1969).

111. See note 100 supra.

112. Cf. R. Rath and N.C. Sircar, "The Cognitive Background of Six Hindu Castes Regarding the Low Caste Untouchables," and "The Mental Pictures of Six Hindu Castes About Each Other as Reflected in Verbal Stereotypes," in the *Journal of Social Psychology*, 51 (1960): 277–93, 295–306.

113. Cf. Frank Parkin, *Class Inequality and Political Order* (London, 1971), and Erik Erikson, *Childhood and Society* (New York, 1963).

114. Frankel, *India's Green Revolution*.

115. *Studies in Agricultural Credit*.

116. Ibid.

117. Frankel, *India's Green Revolution*, p. 97.

118. *Modernizing Indian Agriculture*, 2:166.

119. Ibid., p. 25.

120. Ibid.

121. Ibid., p. 170.

122. Daniel and Alice Thorner, *Land and Labor in India*, p. 149.

123. Rangan, "Land Disputes Thwarting Green Revolution in India".

124. See P.R. Dubhashi, *Rural Development Administration in India* (Bombay, 1970), p. 215–36.

125. There is evidence that the importance of agricultural credit allocation has been recognized in high political circles. See, for example, *Economic Times* (Bombay), 13 Nov. 1974.

PART THREE
Dimensions of Development and/or Reform

Anthropology and Programs of Village Development: A South Indian Case Study

PAUL G. HIEBERT

WHAT can anthropology contribute to the sophisticated models of economists and others already working in the field of international development? The answer can only be given in the context of the theoretical streams which lead to the present convergence of interest in international development.

I. THEORETICAL BACKGROUNDS

Early theories of economic development, which were constructed largely from quantifiable data gathered in relatively advanced Western nations, focused largely on the contents rather than on the processes of economic change, and on such impersonal sectors as capital formation and foreign trade, rather than on such personal factors as felt needs and motivations. The close relationship of theories like those of Adam Smith, David Ricardo, and Karl Marx to formulations of national policies provided, on the one hand, a laboratory for testing the validity of the theories and, on the other, a widespread acceptance of their value as guidelines for the modern national state. Development and progress were seen as inherently good and were defined in terms of long-range economic processes.

After seventy years of silence, during which theories of development faded into the background, interest in economic growth was revived. The depression of the 1930s killed laissez faire and demonstrated the need for governmental intervention into the private market economy to assure growth and full employment. Keynes defined and analyzed the short-range fluctuations of the aggregate national income, Harrod looked at its long-range growth, and Schumpeter stressed the importance of entrepreneurs in development. Macroeconomic theories based on data from modern nations were well advanced by the time economics turned its attention to assist the developing third world at the end of the colonial era.

There were sidestreams to this broad current of theory of economic development. Veblen and Galbraith stressed the social implications of economic change. Myrdal, Hagen, and Adelman and Morris looked at socioeconomic development at the local community level.[1] Finally, the agricultural economists in more recent times have turned their attention to rural development in non-Western societies.[2]

The roots of economic and applied anthropology lie elsewhere. Early British and American anthropologists, such as Tyler, Frazer, and Morgan, were interested in describing the broad evolutionary development of total cultures. The processes of development were explained largely in terms of the biological evolution—in terms of "primitive mentality" versus the "rational mind." Although the idea of a fundamental biological difference between mentalities of different populations was rejected in anthropology by the 1930s as a form of ethnocentrism, memories of this theory continue to haunt us in some current definitions of "traditional" and "modern" and in discussions of the "peasant mind."

Today anthropologists do recognize fundamental differences in the cognitive systems of different cultures, and possible psychological similarities between peasants in different agrarian societies, but attribute these to cultural rather than biological factors. Consequently, development is analyzed and planned in accord with the principles of culture change.

Reacting to the speculative nature of the early theories, anthropologists of the 1930s and 1940s turned their attention to detailed field studies of tribal cultures. As they began to understand these cultures from within, anthropologists often idealized their strengths and overlooked their weaknesses. The resulting descriptions portrayed static cultures which historians would have looked upon as moribund. This romanticism rejected change introduced from without as inherently destructive.

Despite their weaknesses, the structural-functional theories of this period contributed significantly to our understanding of people and cultures. They drew attention to the relationships which exist between the various cultural systems and to the world view of the people. They also made us aware of the multidimensional needs, resources, and pressures which individuals must play off against each other to achieve their goals. The result has been a growing rejection of the concept of the Asian as a "Religious Man," in contrast to the Western "Economic Man." This idea, begun by the Orientalists and introduced into the social sciences by Max Weber,[3] has widely influenced social thought. The core of the argument was that eastern man was motivated primarily by religious incentives and rejected as materialistic the economic incentives which have given rise to development in the West. Therefore development can take place only after there is a fundamental change in the religious world view of the Asian people. Recent studies, however, show that Asian villagers are responsive to economic incentives.[4]

Only within the last two decades have anthropologists turned their attention to peasant communities and broader civilizations, and to theories of change and development. In the field of economic anthropology some scholars, following Karl Polanyi, contend that current economic theories cannot be applied directly to preindustrial societies and that new models must be formulated to describe their operations.[5] Others have applied conventional economic concepts, methods, and theories to the analysis of peasant and tribal societies.[6] A few have concentrated on the impact of colonialization on economic development.[7] Besides these interested in economic anthropology, there have been some concerned with the application of anthropological insights to the design of development programs.[8]

Today, the interests of a number of disciplines have converged on development programs in the third world. Most of them are concerned with development from above, with impersonal factors and changes introduced largely through governmental policies and programs. Anthropology's contribution lies elsewhere, in its focus on the viewpoint of the people and on development as a cooperative venture of people and planners. To illustrate this approach we can turn to a specific case study in South India and seek to apply anthropological insights to development planning.

II. LAND AND ECONOMIC NETWORKS IN KONDURU

Konduru is the largest of eight villages and a score of hamlets scattered along a small valley on the northernmost plateau of the Nallamalai Hills of Andhra Pradesh, South India. The deciduous forest has been cleared for a

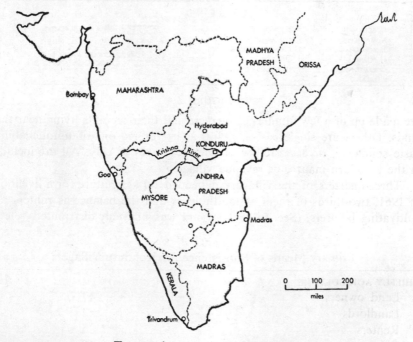

FIGURE 1 : MAP OF SOUTH INDIA

stretch of ten miles on either side of the small stream that wanders down the valley, and a gravel road winds down the hills to the villages on the plains below, connecting the valley to the larger market centers of the region.

Thirteen small hamlets surround Konduru, depending on its markets for trade and its specialized castes for essential services. Some of these hamlets

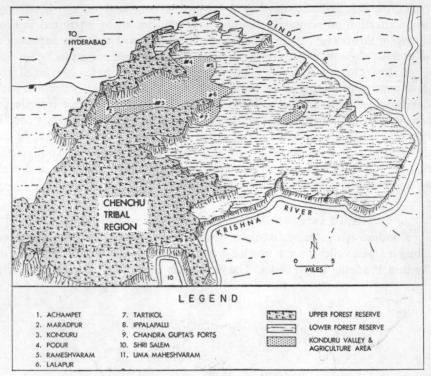

FIGURE 2

are made up of a few families of farmers and their servants living near their
lands. Others are single castes, living apart for reasons of untouchability,
caste solidarity, or accessibility of such resources as clay. All are included
in the Konduru mauza, or revenue village.

Three-quarters of the villagers depended on agriculture for a livelihood
in 1961, two-thirds of them as landholders and the balance as renters and
cultivating laborers. (See Table 1.) Land was unevenly distributed—eleven

TABLE 1
Primary Means of Subsistence for Konduru Villagers

CHIEFLY AGRICULTURE		74%
Land owners	49%	
Landlords	2	
Renters	5	
Laborers	18	
CHIEFLY NONAGRICULTURE		26
Commerce & Traders	7	
Nonagricultural production	6	
Miscellaneous	13	
	100%	100%

TABLE 2

Land Distribution in Konduru Mauza Village

Caste	Number of Land Holders	Percent of Land Owners in Each Caste According to Size of Land Holdings in Acres					Average Size of Holding in Acres	Total Land Holdings by Castes	
		0 to 5.0	5.1 to 10.0	10.1 to 20.0	20.1 to 50.0	50.1 Plus		Acres	%
Brahman	13	30.7	0	0	38.6	30.7	38.3	498	4.7
Merchant	18	16.8	22.2	27.7	33.3	0	16.2	293	2.8
Reddi farmer	29	20.8	6.9	24.1	37.9	10.3	24.0	696	6.6
Munnur farmer & Maden farmer	109	24.8	22.0	24.8	27.5	.9	14.0	1528	14.5
Artisan	11	27.2	36.5	27.3	9.0	0	11.4	126	1.2
Herdsman	40	27.5	30.0	25.0	17.5	0	11.4	459	4.4
Kuruva	31	51.6	29.0	12.9	6.5	0	6.7	205	2.0
Gatherer	45	33.3	28.9	28.9	8.9	0	9.3	421	4.0
Winetapper	29	58.7	17.2	13.8	10.3	0	6.8	197	1.9
Potter	49	42.8	24.5	24.5	8.2	0	8.9	440	4.2
Chenchu	21	38.2	28.6	33.2	0	0	7.2	111	1.0
Gypsy	11	27.3	27.3	9.0	36.4	0	14.0	154	1.5
Washerman	25	36.0	44.0	12.0	4.0	4.0	10.4	260	2.5
Barber	12	8.3	50.0	33.4	8.3	0	10.1	121	1.2
Misc. Shudras	15	13.3	33.3	40.1	13.3	0	12.8	191	1.8
Muslim	108	43.5	24.0	17.6	13.0	1.9	10.8	1169	11.1
Weaver	381	35.5	34.1	23.8	6.6	0	8.5	3260	31.0
Leatherworker	78	64.1	23.1	12.8	0	0	4.9	379	3.6
Total	1025							10,508	
Percentage of total land area		9.8	21.2	29.3	31.6	8.1			

SOURCE: Paul G. Hiebert, *Konduru: Structure and Integration in a South Indian Village* (Minneapolis, 1971).

farmers had holdings of over fifty acres and cultivated 8 percent of the
land, while at the other extreme, 378 farmers owned less than five acres.
In general the higher castes had larger holdings (Brahmans averaged 38.6 acres
and Reddi farmers 24, versus untouchable Sweepers, 8.5, and Leather workers,
4.9) but there were rich and poor farmers at all caste levels. Moreover,
although untouchable holdings were smaller on the average, the untouchables
were more numerous and controlled 34 percent of the total farmland. This
gave them considerable economic and political power. Unlike many of
the plains villages, no single landowning caste dominated the area.

There are nearly 90,000 acres in the Konduru mauza, but more than
75,000 of these are part of the government forest reserve which stretches
south to the Krishna River. The village domain includes 13,000 acres, of
which 10,500 are privately owned agricultural lands. The actual land seeded

TABLE 3

General Statistics on Konduru

1. *Population:*

	1921	1931	1951	1961
Population:	4084	4526	4987	6251
Households:	792	1018	1193	1613

2. *Land and its Uses:*
   A. Total Mauza area: 88,162 acres
      Forest 75,000
      Surveyed 13,162
   B. Usage:

	1958–1959	1959–1960	1960–1961
Single cropped	7108 acres	8679	7372
Double cropped	91	91	13
Fallow	2377	1363	2570
Culturable waste	338	338	438
Unculturable	724	724	724
Permanent pasture	1950	1392	1392

   C. Crops:

	1958–1959	1959–1960	1960–1961
Rice (autumn or *abi*)	49	303	96
(winter or *tabi*)	150	205	42
Jowar (*kharif* or fall)	3231	4184	4001
(*rabi* or spring)	0	0	0
Bajra	977	1452	1151
Ragi	1359	1095	801
Other cereals	332	842	171
Total cereals (dry land)	5889	7573	6124
(irrigation)	199	508	139
Pulses (*gram, tur,* etc)	372	205	210

Vegetables	25	22	20
Fruit	8	0	0
Oils (groundnut, castor, sesamum)	905	964	1026
Total all crops (dry land)	7200	8772	7386
(irrigation)	199	508	139

3. *Animals:*

	Male 3+	Fem. 3+ wet	Fem. 3+ dry	Young stock	Total
Cattle:	1631	421	1687	1332	5071
Buffaloes:	106	167	391	381	945

Sheep:	3602	Goats:	1360
Horses:	21	Poultry:	2034

4. *Miscellaneous:*

Plows: wood	846	Carts:	201
Oil motor pump sets:	2	Wells:	117
Tanks	2 (61 acres)	Houses:	7 *pukka* (permanent),
Area irrigated	43 acres		12 semipukka (semipermanent),
			1590 *kacha* (temporary).

varied over a three-year period (1958–1961) from 69 to 83 percent of the tillable land, depending on the rainfall. Less than 1 percent was double cropped and irrigation varied from 1 to 5 percent, according to the availability of water stored behind the small earthen dams along the stream. Surpluses of such primary crops as *jowar* (sorghum), *bajra* (pearl millet), *ragi* (finger millet), and oil seed were exported to the plains, but rice was imported as a status food.

The supply and distribution of land in Konduru are not typical of the surrounding plains villages. The explanation is historical. In the late eighteenth and early nineteenth centuries, the valley was ruled by three zamindars. When they were killed in a battle with neighboring zamindars, the Nizam granted the region as a military jagir to an Arab. In 1880, the village was taken by the Nizam's government and the ryotwari system introduced. Until 1919 land was available to those who cleared the forest and migrants, including untouchables, came to the valley from areas of overpopulation. In that year, the Nizam instituted a land survey and record system similar to that used in British India. He also declared the forest a state reserve and closed it to agricultural development. Only in the past two decades has Konduru felt the pressures for land characteristic of the plains villages.

A. *The Current Land Situation*

Several factors stand out in the overall agricultural picture of Konduru.

1. *Population pressure and land shortage:* Agricultural acreage was frozen with the establishment of the forest reserve in 1919. The village population, however, grew 53 percent between 1921 and 1961. Migration to larger towns and the city of Hyderabad has been small except among the younger educated sons of the high castes. A few low caste men have government jobs on the plains and send money home, but many of them would like to return to Konduru if land or secure jobs were available.

2. *Fragmentation of the land:* Farms are small; two-thirds of them less than ten acres and 37 percent less than five. Many of them have been fragmented into widely scattered plots, in part by the custom that each male heir should receive not only a portion of each field, but also of each irrigated and nonirrigated section of the field.

3. *Seasonal nature of production:* Agricultural work falls mostly into the wet season of the year (June to January) with a peak during the seeding time. A second peak comes at harvest, although not all crops mature at the same time. There is work for all able-bodied workers during the peak periods and little unemployment throughout the agricultural season. Wealthy farmers reinforce hereditary ties with their field hands by giving them loans and aid in order to assure themselves of an adequate supply of labor when it is needed most.

From January to May there is little work in the sun-baked fields except on the few acres of *tabi* (autumn) rice irrigated by the two small tanks near the village. One enterprising young farmer raised tomatoes and *brinjals* (eggplants) after 1962 by drawing water from his well with oxen for four hours a day in the dry season. He turned a small profit for three years by selling the vegetables in the local market. In 1965, however, another farmer began to raise vegetables, flooding the local market. Lacking methods to preserve and store the crop, and transportation facilities to export it to other markets, both faced the prospect of low returns for their investments of labor and cattle.

Construction and labor in the forest, such as felling bamboo and timber for government contractors, provide some work during the hot season. Farmers leisurely prepare their tools for seedtime and repair their houses. For all this is the social season of the year: the time for weddings, festivals, and visiting relatives.

Food prices and interest rates also fluctuate sharply with the season. Grain prices often drop 30 to 40 percent following the harvest. Fodder pledged and sold at planting time commands only half the price of fodder delivered during the dry season. Poor farmers who borrow their seed must repay interest of 50 percent in grain at harvest, and often a bonus to acquire the loan.

4. *Annual fluctuations*: The variations of rainfall from year to year create a serious problem, particularly since the peasants are dependent on the rains

for dryland farming. Some indications of the fluctuations in production can be seen from the acreage under cultivation. Over a three-year period, this varied from 7,200 to 8,722 acres, a difference of over 22 percent.

Irrigation tanks provide water for a few rice fields, but they do not even out the fluctuation. There are eleven small dams thrown across the stream in the valley, most of which impound less than 200 acres and cannot store water from one year to the next. In a good year they make a second crop possible; in a bad one they barely bring in the first. If the rains are exeptionally heavy, there is the danger of the dams washing out because they lack adequate spillways. This happened in 1964 when one dam broke and the flood took out three dams downstream. It usually takes two or three years before the dams are restored.

5. *Relatively slow rate of change:* Finally,technological changes have been relatively slow in coming despite extensive government programs for agricultural development. Wooden plows, harrows, seeders, iron and leather irrigation buckets, and oxen continued to be the agricultural mainstays. Manure was used for fertilizer but increasing demands were being made on dried dung for use in cooking. Few farmers went the six miles to the government storehouse for chemical fertilizers which were often in short supply. Some attempts at composting were made at the urging of the government village level worker (V.L.W.) but, after the district inspectors left, the farmers generally reverted to their old ways. The V.L.W., thankful that they had complied for the inspection, stopped pressuring them.

Some agricultural changes were apparent. A modified form of the Japanese rice planting method had been adopted by about one-third of the farmers by 1965. Two of the larger farmers had installed diesel irrigation pumps and the village leaders were hoping to bring electricity to the village.

The lack of change in agriculture contrasted sharply with changes which were taking place in other areas of the village economy and social structure. Cycles, watches, buses, trucks, and even radios were common sights. Local merchants stocked flashlights, soaps, gas lamps, galvanized buckets, and kerosene. Aluminum pots and pans were rapidly replacing the traditional potters' wares. Factory-woven cloth had taken over much of the market from the local weaver caste which had organized a union to market its products. Sewing machines were common in the small tailor shops and men's ready-made clothes in western style were appearing in the weekly market.

B. *Place of Land in the Village*

In order to understand the relatively slow pace of agricultural innovation, we must understand the role of land in the total village economy and the ways in which villagers perceive it.

1. *Subsistence and cash economies:* Villagers differentiated sharply between subsistence and cash economies. In general, subsistence labor related directly to agricultural production while cash covered the balance of eco-

nomic transactions. Payments for essential agricultural labor, even that
performed by nonhereditary workers (i.e., those who have no jajmani rights)
was made in grain. Laborers hoped, after paying their debts, to store up
enough grain during the agricultural season to provide food for the coming
year. After harvest, the small huts were often crowded with stacked pots
and baskets of grain, and the ever-present rats which raided them. To sell
grain to merchants for central storage and later to buy it back at twice the
price made no sense to the villager. Only big farmers sold their surplus
crops on the market—and then only after all the laborers had been paid in
grain and sufficient store had been laid aside.

Not all goods and services are linked to the subsistence economy. Contractual exchanges, to use Henry Maine's term, played a major role in
Konduru. Merchants bought and sold an astonishing variety of basic com-
modities in their small narrow shops. Tea stalls and a new restaurant catered
to visitors. On market days, salesmen on the market circuit set up their
wares. Door-to-door salesmen from transient castes made the rounds of
the villages, often selling goods on credit. Cattle sellers from the coastal
regions of Andhra brought in herds of the prized large white hump-backed
zebu oxen which they sold to wealthy farmers for two or three times the
price of the local breeds. They required one-third of the payment in cash,
and one-third on each of the two successive years. They also had a guarantee:
if an ox died of illness during the interval, the debt was cancelled. The
large cattle market at Achampet, ten miles away, was a popular place for
farmers of the valley.

Villagers distinguished between four types of hired labor, each of which
has its own prestige value. The lowest was indentured service in which loans
were repaid by working for a creditor, or a child from a poor family was
given into the service of a wealthy home in exchange for food and clothes.
Above this was *coolie,* or day labor. The units of time used in calculations
were not hours and parts of hours but full and half days. Salaried labor
(*jetham*) was more respectable because it provided greater security and,
over time, often led to patron-client type relationships resembling those of
the agricultural *jajmani* networks. Job contracts (*gutha*) were the most
respected type of labor because they implied a measure of independence
and equality on the part of the contractor. Prices were agreed upon after
lengthy bargaining and an advance was generally paid before the job was
begun.

Village laborers depended on cash incomes for the purchasing of clothes,
utensils, household equipment, and repairs, and for financing weddings and
other displays of status. In times of drought and hardship, these are dis-
pensable. So long as people have grain, they can tide themselves over until
better times.

This sharp dichotomy between subsistence and cash economies appears
frequently in the local proverbs and aphorisms. For example:

"One who gives food in times of shortage [spring when food is scarce],

One who gives money in times of plenty [fall when food is plentiful
    but money is scarce],
One who is brave in times of battle,
One who cheerfully pays off his debts,
To these four, I will bow," says Krishna.

The farmer seems to use different criteria for making his decisions in each of these sectors. In the area of cash economies he is aware of marginal production and profit maximization. In the subsistence sector, however, it is extremely difficult for the farmer to know the marginal product of labor. It is easier and more reliable to calculate the average product per laborer. Payment at the threshing floors is not calculated on the quantity of work performed, but on the fact that all the necessary work has been performed, no matter how much there is. The amount of work varies markedly from year to year, but the traditional fixed payments remain the same.

Moreover, calculations in the subsistence sector are based more on minimization of hardship rather than maximization of profits. Epstein has pointed out that under the traditional system, in bad years farmers and laborers alike have only subsistence portions.[9] There is no surplus. Larger farmers, however, profit greatly in good years when they have large surpluses with little additional outlay. These they use to stage elaborate weddings, build better houses, buy bullocks, or sponsor village entertainment in order to gain status. Good harvests enable the farmers to carry on their struggle for prestige.

Laborers, on the other hand, gain through the security offered by the subsistence economy. In good years there is much work and little added income, but in bad ones when there is little work there is an assured subsistence wage. In 1962 the Konduru Washermen began to charge fees for their weekly services rather than accept their annual portion of the harvest. In 1965, following floods and poor crops, the farmers cut back on the Washermen's services. Soon the Washermen were trying to return to the old subsistence pattern. As Sayanna, the Washerman Headman, said, "We make more money in good years when we charge fees, but in good years no one suffers anyway. It is in the bad years that we must have someone who will take care of us." As will be seen later, this attitude fits into the patron-client relationships which characterize many types of village interaction.

The payment of traditional fixed shares of the harvest for subsistence services rendered does not mean that there is no relationship between work, payments, and production. There is a general adjustment of hereditary payments according to the work involved. For example, the carpenter and the ironsmith receive a "Contract Share" at harvest time for each plow they maintain throughout the year. A farmer with five plows must pay five shares. He must pay an additional "Irrigation Share" for each plow if the crop is rice because there is more wear on the plow. There are similar adjustments for the Barber, Washerman, Potter, Leatherworker, and others in the traditional farm system.

There is also a relationship between pay and production. In addition to the fixed shares, most of the workers receive a bonus portion. This is often given for some insignificant task such as measuring the harvest and the compensation is far greater than the work involved. In practice, the size of this portion fluctuates greatly with the productivity of the harvest. In good years these bonus shares are generous; in bad years they are small or forgotten. Any worker who has done an exceptional amount of work during the year receives a proportionately larger share. On the other hand, workers do not show up at the threshing floor to claim these bonus shares from poor farmers who can barely afford their services.

Land lies at the core of the subsistence economy, which stresses a basic economic security at the expense of larger gains and their attendant risks.

2. *Land and limited good:* Foster suggests in a cogent article[10] that peasants in a traditional society have the notion that all desirables in life including land and wealth exist in a finite, limited quantity which cannot be increased by means within the peasants' power. If any man through effort gains a larger share of this total good than he inherits, he does so at the expense of others. Consequently, the villagers will oppose any man who rises above his original station. An exception is when the increase in good can be clearly shown to have come from outside the system.

While Foster's model fits much of the village economic behavior, there is one significant exception. Land is a limited good, but it also produces goods in the form of crops. Unlike wealth acquired by trade and loans which is gained within the system at the expense of others and is therefore somewhat tainted, crops increase the total supply of goods and ultimately benefit all.

There is, however, a public ethic that such gains should be used to benefit the whole village. This is reflected in local proverbs such as:

> Rivers don't drink their own water,
>   Trees don't eat their own food,
> Clouds don't consume the crops they water,
>   So good men's harvests are used for others.

On the other hand, misers and those who exploit others are roundly condemned:

> Coveting, man grabs everything to his own stomach,
>   Who is there who scatters to others?
> The covetous are numerous and found everywhere,
>   In this world, O Kodanda Rama of Konduru.

And:

> The masters eat the harvest of the laborers these days
> Like those who eat the oxen with the crop.

A respected farmer of means shares a substantial amount of goods in the form of fringe benefits to his clients without any accounting. They build houses on his land and cultivate small gardens rent free. At times of religious festivity he gives them clothing and grain for a feast. He supplies them with fodder to tide their cattle over a dry summer without expecting repayment. He pays passing bards and local drama troupes to provide free entertainment for the villagers and receives in return the praise of his fellowmen.

The increases in goods produced in the agricultural sector are expected to contribute in part to the good of all. The distribution of the crop is not strictly calculated according to the work involved. Other major factors which enter into the distribution are the "mercy" (*daya*) of the landowner and the needs of the particular workers. As old Ironsmith Narayana, well-to-do farmer, said one dry summer day after doling out several cupfuls of grain to his hereditary village beggars who were making their daily rounds, "Some politicians come and say we should be communists. When the harvest comes, the birds, the rats, the wild pigs, the Carpenter, the Washerman and the Barber, the Potter, the field workers, the gods and priests, the government officials, the beggars and bards, and our own relatives all come for a share. What is this, if not communism?"

3. *Land and social networks:* Some have followed Parsons and Smelzer in defining modernization and development in terms of increased structural differentiation—"the evolution from a multi-functional role structure to several more specialized structures."[11] This does not fit the Indian village, which in its traditional form manifests a high degree of role specialization in the form of the caste system. In fact, this very specialization has given rise, in part, to the hereditary social networks which many charge with retarding modernization.

Land exploitation is the center of the jajmani system which links farmers to craft and service castemen in hereditary systems of mutual dependence with the farmer as patron and his workers as clients. The nature of the relationship varies with the rank and wealth of the *jajman*. Between untouchable jajmans and clean caste workers the relations are purely economic, but between high caste jajmans and their workers there are numerous social and ritual bonds as well. The model for the wealthy landlord was that of the petty village kingdom ruled by a local raja or zamindar.

Jajmani assumes two polar forms: the introverted and the extended. In the first a powerful landlord or a small number of related landlords form a separate hamlet with their workers, who are completely within their service. In such cases power lies with the landlords and economic transactions take place primarily in the subsistence sector.

In the extended form of jajmani, which is often found in larger villages, clients serve many farmers. One Konduru Barber, for example, had work rights over more than a hundred homes, and five others served more than fifty. Where clients are not completely dependent on a single powerful farmer, they command a measure of independence. In some cases they form union-like caste associations which preserve their occupational monopolies. Thus, when the peasants of one of the small hamlets fired their Washerman

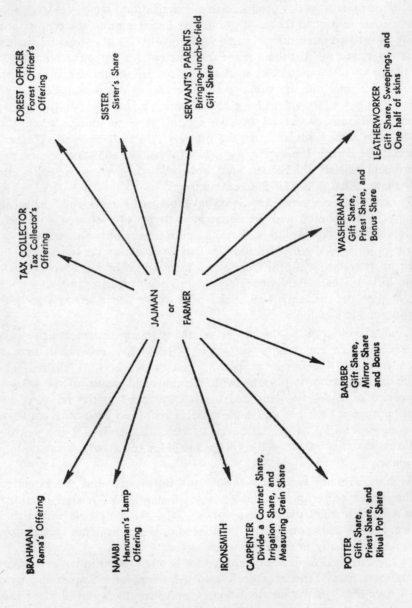

FIGURE 3 :   DISTRIBUTION OF THE HARVEST UNDER THE JAJMANI SYSTEM

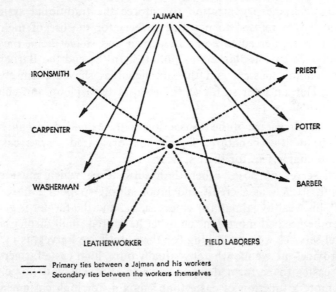

JAJMAN

IRONSMITH   PRIEST

CARPENTER   POTTER

WASHERMAN   BARBER

LEATHERWORKER   FIELD LABORERS

———— Primary ties between a Jajman and his workers
- - - - Secondary ties between the workers themselves

FIGURE 4 :   MODEL OF AN INTROVERTED JAJMANI NETWORK

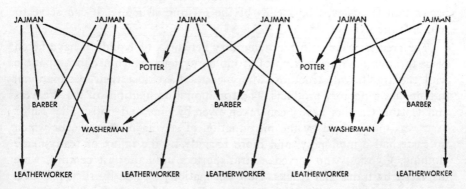

JAJMAN   JAJMAN   JAJMAN   JAJMAN   JAJMAN   JAJMAN

POTTER   POTTER

BARBER   BARBER   BARBER

WASHERMAN   WASHERMAN

LEATHERWORKER   LEATHERWORKER   LEATHERWORKER   LEATHERWORKER   LEATHERWORKER

FIGURE 5 :   MODEL OF AN EXTENDED JAJMANI NETWORK

and hired an outsider, the local Washerman caste *panchayat* drove away the intruder and forced the farmers to come to terms. In other cases castes and villages lack the organization to enforce the traditional system. The local untouchables refused to pay the Barbers for the use of their knives. When the Barbers agreed to come in person and shave them, the wealthy Brahmans boycotted the Barbers as polluted. In the end the Barbers stayed with their wealthy masters and the untouchables shaved themselves. One enterprising Harijan went so far as to set up a barbershop and charge fees for his services.

A growing percentage of the transactions in the extended jajmani structure appear to be of a cash nature. Several well-organized service castes were beginning to charge fees for their services.

Jajmani serves purposes other than subsistence which must be taken into account. It acts as a credit and labor supply. A poor laborer can get loans from his wealthy jajman for emergencies, and the farmer is guaranteed labor when he needs it most. On the other hand, the small farmer is assured of essential services without paying for them until the harvest is in. Finally, jajmani provides an avenue whereby ritually pure, high caste farmers employ less pure castes to perform defiling tasks in the field and home. This is, however, more a function of caste than jajmani, for high castemen outside jajmani networks depend upon the same castes to perform similar tasks.

Epstein differentiates between the growth of economic production, and change within the economic structure. She has demonstrated, in a study of the effects of irrigation on a South Indian village, that economic development does not necessarily produce structural change. In fact, when increased production is achieved by means of the existing structure, it can serve to reinforce the structure.[12]

The greatest change in the hereditary networks of Konduru have taken place through the introduction of economic systems which are incompatible with the traditional structure. Many castes have lost their occupational monopolies to factory products. The traditional occupations of the Weavers and Cotton Carders have been taken over by gins and mills. The Tailor caste was undermined by the introduction of sewing machines over which no caste had a monopoly, and more recently by the influx of ready-made clothing. Gypsies, who served as transporters until the last century, were displaced by trains and trucks. New occupations created by such products as sewing machines, bicycles, trucks, radios, and modern medicines are found in the cash sector. This monetization of the economy is particularly evident in the larger villages and towns where subsistence activities are rapidly breaking down due to technological change. In general, however, it appears that hereditary relations remain so long as both parties see them to be of advantage to themselves, so long as neither is aware of better alternatives, or so long as one has the power to control the other by means of debts or other claims.

4. *Land and the village:* Land is closely identified with the self image of

the village. Villagers pride themselves on their unity and compete with other villages for regional dominance.

The village god, the navel stone (*bord ravi*—the ritual site established at the founding of a village) and the boundaries around the traditional village lands are important village symbols. When disease, famine, or drought plagues the people, crisis rites are instituted at the navel stone in the center of the village to supplicate other deities who are bringing disaster to the village. Unlike Hindu ceremonies, these rites include all villagers irrespective of their caste and religion. Village strength can be generated by sacrificing a water buffalo and performing rituals at the village boundaries. Village borders are sealed when hostilities break out between neighboring villages. When, for example, the men of Mandodi beat the temple buffalo of Danvada, the Danvada men rose in arms and kept Mandodi men from cultivating fields they owned or rented in Danvada territory.

Disputes and internal administration in Konduru were handled largely by the elders and headman of the village. The newly elected Naya Panchayat handled minor affairs like cleaning the roads, and regulating the markets. Caste panchayats settled most matters relating to marriage and caste customs. Land disputes, however, were dealt with primarily by the powerful traditional village panchayat made up of elders from different castes and the village headman. The patwari, or village land accountant, kept official record of all land boundaries and transactions, and used this power to pressure villagers to accept the decisions of the leaders. He could deny that land transactions had taken place, or support the claims of others that the rocks marking the boundaries of the fields were in the wrong place, and order them moved, reducing significantly the size of the small plots.

Those who took their complaints to higher government officials and courts and won often could not consolidate their gains when faced with the opposition of the village leaders. One example can illustrate the processes involved. When Kama Kottayya moved to Konduru in 1962, he purchased a small field near the village. In 1964 he incurred the anger of the local patwari and the village leaders for gathering some disgruntled villagers around himself and agitating for a change in the village government. The original owner of the land suddenly claimed that he had only rented the lands and wanted them returned. The patwari backed this claim in his official records. Kottayya and his friends took the case to the District Collector and charged the patwari with mishandling of funds. After an investigation, the Collector suspended the patwari and gave his office to another villager. Kottayya's gains were short lived, however. The newly appointed patwari kept the records in the house of the old patwari and carried out his orders. Kottayya gained rights over the land, but in the face of the hostility of the local leaders it was impossible for him to continue to live in the village so he moved on.

Land development programs that are opposed by the local leaders often have little chance for success. For example, the untouchable Weavers of Danvada own a fair amount of land and decided as a caste to upgrade their agriculture by taking government loans for fertilizer, good seed, and irrigation facilities. The high caste village leaders were critical of the rising aspirations of the untouchables and ordered them to go back to their old ways. When they refused, the elders banned them from the village well, forcing their women to walk one-half mile to the nearest stream for water.

5. *Land and religious beliefs:* A brief word should be said about the numerous religious connotations associated with land and agriculture. Some of these, such as the Ugadi or Telugu New Year's Day celebrations are associated with Hindu rites. On this day craftsmen worship their tools, Barbers their knives, and Washermen their firepots and washing stones. On this day field work begins for the new crops. Farmers go to their fields with baskets of manure and their tools and cut a few weeds to mark the beginning of another agricultural year.

There are local fertility rites in which blood sacrifices are offered to the many goddesses and demons residing in the fields. Successful harvests are celebrated with Holi ceremonies and prolonged droughts call for elaborate rituals at the village boundaries.

The directions south and west are considered sacred, for they are the dwelling place of the gods. Farmers believe they should enter their fields from these directions for good fortune. Higher level ground has more status than low level ground and older brothers receive the upper portion of each plot of land. High castes use the upper portions of the nearby stream while the lower castes and untouchables divide the lower stream according to status. Untouchables often found it hard to get a regular supply of irrigation water for their fields, which are usually at the end of the canal and the first to be cut off when there is a shortage of water.

III. Concluding Remarks

While anthropological contributions to development are generally tailored to fit specific communities and cultures, a few fundamental principles can be pointed out.

A. Cognitive Maps as Determinants in Strategies for Behavior

Anthropological studies have pointed out the marked cultural differences between people, differences not only at the level of language and behavior, but also in the cognitive maps by which people perceive their world. It is becoming increasingly apparent that people act in their own self interest as they see it, and more or less rationally within the alternatives open to them. To the extent they appear not to do so, we must assume that we have not understood them. As Firth notes, the lack of development is not due to a failure in aspirations, but in the lack of opportunities defined in terms of the peoples' world view.[13] Kusum Nair's poignant description of Indian villagers points out not so much their lack of aspirations, but their realistic assessment of the alternatives which they saw open to themselves.[14]

People have many felt needs and desires, and must arrange priorities and trade-offs between them. Traditional farmers can increase their productivity within their existing technology by more careful planting of seed, more intensive weeding, and more painstaking harvesting of the crops. But the farmer cannot justify the additional labor in view of the diminishing returns and the other needs which he must satisfy. Peasant agriculture is a stable, rational, and relatively successful system of farming, given the level of technology and resources available to the people, and farmers will respond to incentives in which they see real possibilities of an overall net gain.

An example of this was the willingness of the Washermen to shift in the early 1960s from a patron-client relationship to a cash basis for their traditional labor in hopes of increasing their income. The dangers involved were evident in the mid-1960s when crop shortages plagued the area and the Washermen found they could no longer turn to the jajmani system for subsistence when their cash income dropped.

The implications of ecological and cultural differences for development are obvious but difficult to implement. Incentives must be defined in terms of people's perceptions of their world, and caution must be taken that the innovations will indeed work. Failure undoubtedly make villagers wary of future change. As Dalton points out, "It is almost certainly so nowadays that development projects fail more frequently because of faulty ecological, economic and technological analysis than because of cultural resistance...."[15]

B. *The Interlocking Nature of Cultural Systems*

Anthropological studies have pointed out the interlocking nature of cultural systems. Changes in one area of life cannot be made without affecting the others. New technologies such as cloth mills, sewing machines, aluminium and plastic wares, trucks and cycles have undermined the traditional occupations of such castes as the Cotton Carders, Tailors, Potters, and Gypsies, while creating new jobs for laborers and entrepreneurs.

But technological changes frequently have social consequences which are difficult to predict. For example, when Kottayya, a prosperous farmer, moved to Konduru and began to use new farming methods, he soon became a political threat to the established village leaders. He filed a law suit after his crops were cut to the ground one night, but the local land records had no record of the land purchases he claimed to have made. In the end he left, and the methods he used were rejected because they were identified with him.

Programs must deal with the total cultural matrix within which change is planned. They cannot be content to deal with a single factor such as the shortage of capital or land reform as if these existed apart from the rest of the culture. On the other hand, changes in one area often make other changes more possible. Modernization, ultimately is not the introduction of any

specific set of changes, but the gearing of a society to continuous development by linking it to systematic programs of research and innovation.

C. Levels of Innovation

There are different approaches to innovation. Changes in the environment can generally be introduced by means of legislation or intervention
without the participation of the people involved. Roads and dams are built,
swamps are drained, insects are sprayed and electric lines are constructed.
Beside the immediate benefits of these projects there are often significant
secondary gains as people become aware of new opportunities and begin
to accept change as a way of life. In a study of 108 Indian villages, Fliegel,
Roy, Sen, and Kivlin found that electrification and avenues of communication were major factors in explaining differences among villages in the
general adoption of new agricultural practices.

Most programs, however, are concerned with changing practices and
beliefs which require the cooperation of the community. Even where environmental factors are changed, it has been found that people who participate
in the work are more likely to take advantage of the changes. Development
should involve the community not only in the implementation of a program,
but also in the planning and decision-making stages so that goals and
procedures have value and meaning for community members and planners
alike.

On the surface, these principles appear obvious, even trite. In their
application, however, they demand a fundamental change in our concept and
implementation of development programs.

NOTES

1. Gunnar Myrdal, *Rich Lands and Poor* (New York, 1957); Everett E. Hagen, *On the Theory of Social Change: How Economic Growth Begins* (Homewood, Ill., 1962); Irma Adelman and Cynthia Taft Morris, *Society, Politics and Economic Development* (Baltimore, 1967).

2. William O. Jones, "Food and Agricultural Economies of Tropical Africa: A Summary View," *Food Research Institute Studies* 2 (1961):3-20; Marvin P. Miracle, "African Markets and Trade in the Copper Belt," in P. Bohannon and G. Dalton, eds., *Markets in Africa* (Evanston, Ill., 1962); T.W. Schultz, *Transforming Traditional Agri-culture* (New Haven, 1964); W. Allan, *The African Husbandman* (London, 1965); John W. Mellor et al., *Developing Rural India* (Ithaca, N.Y., 1968); John C. deWilde et al., *Agricultural Development in Tropical Africa* (Baltimore, 1967); and Clifford R. Wharton et al., *Subsistence Agriculture and Economic Development* (Chicago, 1969).

3. Max Weber, *The Religion of India,* Hans Gerth and C.W. Mills, trans. (New York, 1960); see also Amer K. Singh, "Hindu Culture and Economic Development in India," *Conspectus* 1 (1967): 9–32, for a good review of Weber's influence in this regard.

4. See, for example, Frederick C. Fliegel et al., *Innovation in India: The Success or Failure of Agricultural Development Programs in 108 Indian Villages* (Hyderabad, 1967).

5. See, for example, C. Arensberg, et al., *Research in Industrial Human Relations: Critical Appraisal* (New York, 1957); Paul Bohannon and Laura Bohannon, *Tiv Economy* (Evanston, Ill., 1968); Marshall D. Sahlins, "On the Sociology of Primitive Exchange," in M. Banton, ed., *The Relevance of Models for Social Anthropology* (London, 1965) and Sahlins, *Tribesmen* (Englewood, N.J., 1968); G. Dalton, "Economic Surplus, Once Again," *American Anthropologist* 65 (1967):389, and Dalton, *Economic Development and Social Change: The Modernization of Village Communities* (Garden City, N.Y., 1971).

6. Raymond Firth, *Malay Fishermen: Their Peasant Economy* (2nd ed., Hamden, Conn., 1966), and Firth, *Themes in Economic Anthropology,* A.S.A. Monograph no. 6 (1967);

Edward E. LeClair, "Economic Theory and Economic Anthropology," *American Anthropologist* 64 (1962): 1179–1203; Richard F. Salisbury, *From Store to Steel* (London, 1962); Polly Hill, *Migrant Cocoa Farmers of South Ghana: Study in Rural Capitalism* (London, 1963), and Hill, *Studies in Rural Capitalism in West Africa* (London, 1970).

7. See Clifford Geertz, *Agricultural Involution* (Berkeley, 1963); Eric R. Wolf, *Sons of the Shaking Earth* (Chicago, 1959); and Hagen, *On the Theory of Social Change.*

8. See, for example, H.G. Barnett, *Innovation: The Basis of Cultural Change* (New York, 1953); Margaret Mead, ed., *Cultural Patterns and Technical Change* (Paris, 1954); Charles J. Erasmus, *Man Takes Control: Cultural Development and American Aid* (Indianapolis, Ind., 1961); Ward Hunt Goodenough, *Cooperation in Change* (New York, 1963); Conrad M. Arensberg and Arthur H. Niehoff, *Introducing Social Change* (Chicago, 1964).

9. S. Epstein, *Comparative Analysis of Economic Development and Social Change in South India and New Guinea Villages* (Mysore, 1971). See also Epstein, *South India: Yesterday, Today and Tomorrow: Mysore Village Revisited* (London, 1973).

10. G.M. Foster, "Peasant Society and the Image of the Limited Good," *American Anthropologist* 67 (1965):293–315.

11. Neil J. Smelzer, "Mechanisms of Change and Adjustment to Change," in B.F. Hoselitz and E. Moore, eds., *Industrialization and Society* (New York, 1963), p. 35.

12. T. Scarlett Epstein, *Economic Development and Social Change in South India* (Manchester, Eng., 1962).

13. Raymond Firth, "Social Structure and Peasant Economy: The Influence of Social Structure upon Peasant Economies," in C.R. Wharton, ed., *Subsistence Agriculture and Economic Development.*

14. Kusum Nair, *Blossoms in the Dust* (London, 1961).

15. Dalton, *Economic Development and Social Change*, p. 11.

All figures in this chapter are reproduced by permission from Paul G. Hiebert, *Konduru: Structure and Integration in a South Indian Village* (Minneapolis: University of Minnesota Press, 1971).

Agricultural Mechanization in the Punjab: Some Comparative Observations from India and Pakistan

CARL H. GOTSCH

INTRODUCTION

IT is evident from even a cursory acquaintance with the empirical material on mechanization, that the specific characteristics of the technology and the institutional setting in which it is used are intensely interacting.[1] Among the most obvious examples of this process have been the effects of such highly indivisible machines as tractors, combines, cotton pickers, etc., in explaining the large increases in holding size that occurred in many developed countries. However, it should not be overlooked that there have also been important cases in which adjustments have consisted primarily of designing a technology that was consistent with an institutional situation in which land agglomeration was exceedingly difficult. For example, in Japan and Taiwan, small mechanical tillers, threshers, and motors have been the basis for a sophisticated mechanization of even very small holdings.

The dynamic patterns that emerge from attempts by farmers to resolve the contradiction between farm size and machines have been used to describe several development "models." Perhaps the most prominent of these is the attempt to distinguish between the so called "Mexican" and "Japanese" development strategies, two paths that are characterized, among other things, by differences in initial holding size and by subsequent choices of mechanical technology.[2]

As they have been used, these notions make concrete certain ideas about development strategies; however, there are too many violations of the "other things equal" assumption to be able to draw many comparative conclusions about specific mechanization processes. While it is certainly true that one would expect the size of holdings and the pattern of income distribution to influence the development of technology and vice versa, a number of other matters—including factor and product pricing, the extent of an indigenous industry capable of adapting machines to the specific needs of the farming community, a culture that has had some experience with mechanical technology in the past, etc.—are also likely to be important. Even when they do not alter the direction of change they will surely affect the speed with which the contradiction is resolved.

Two areas that suffer less from the "other things equal" problem than the aforementioned examples are the Indian and Pakistan portions of what was, under British rule, the State of Punjab. In this paper, I have tried to set down some preliminary observations on the somewhat different patterns of mechanization that are appearing in these two areas. As the tentative character of the comments indicates, there are a number of unresolved issues that will require substantial further investigation. However, even in this preliminary form, the evidence underlines the potential for altering the long-run distributive effects of growth by the systematic application of modern engineering skills to redesign and adapt mechanical technology to small farm sizes. In so doing, it simultaneously undermines the frequently heard argument that only with the retention of large holdings can agriculture become a highly modernized sector.

SIMILARITIES AND DISSIMILARITIES

While East Punjab (India) and the West Punjab (Pakistan) have greater environmental and cultural similarities than most areas for which comparative studies are made, there are also differences which bear on the rate and type of mechanization.[3] With respect to the similarities, both are a part of the great Indus Basin that stretches across the northern part of the Indian sub-continent. The flat plains and alluvial soils in both regions are ideal for mechanizing a variety of tillage and harvesting operations. Moreover, the arid climate and the presence of substantial surface irrigation supplemented by a large body of groundwater permits double cropping, a possibility that places a premium on the availability of timely sources of power.

A good deal of cultural similarity also prevails across the area. Important religious and caste differences do exist, but language and a variety of other cultural characteristics are rooted in centuries of more or less communal living. As a result of the great irrigation works of the late nineteenth and early twentieth centuries, substantial internal migration took place from the areas that are now East Punjab to what were then the arid lands to the west. Colonization itself was a selective process requiring a positive attitude toward change and a willingness to leave behind that which was familiar to face that which was new and uncertain. Millions of Punjabis were again uprooted in the violent days following the creation of Pakistan and the partition of the State of Punjab in 1947. Hordes of refugees crossed the border in both directions as they sought either to avoid or to become part of the newly created Muslim state.

The effects of such drastic changes on the world view of those involved is, of course, difficult to ascertain. However, one gets the impression in conversations with a cross-section of the populace on both sides of the border that the refugees, in each case seeking to preserve the status to which they were accustomed, have consistently been among the most rapid innovators and the most progressive farmers in both areas.

There are, however, important differences in the agrarian structure of the two areas. Among the most important of these are the tenure system and the distribution of land. In East Punjab, data from the mid-1960s suggest that owner-operators make up 80–85 percent of the cultivator population. The figure given for West Punjab in the early 1960s is 50 percent. Moreover, as Table 1 shows, considerably more land in West Punjab was operated in

TABLE 1

Size Distribution of Cultivated Land

Holding Size	Indian Punjab[a] (percent cultivators)	(percent land)	Pakistan Punjab[b] (percent cultivators)	(percent land)
Below 25 acres	89	70	93	64
25–50 acres	10	23	6	21
Over 50 acres	1	7	1	15
	100	100	100	100

a Government of Punjab, "Size and Distribution of Holdings in Punjab, 1964/65," Statistician, Department of Agriculture, 1967.
b Government of Pakistan, *Pakistan Census of Agriculture, 1960*, Vol. II (West Pakistan Report), Agricultural Census Organization, Ministry of Agriculture (Karachi, 1963).

holdings over 50 acres in size. Unfortunately, in neither area do reliable data on the important variable, i.e., on the distribution of land ownership, exist. However, one would expect that since tenants usually lease land from owners larger than themselves, the area with the greatest degree of tenancy would also be the area in which land was most concentrated in the larger size groups. Indeed, Alavi has estimated that in Pakistan. nearly 70 percent of the land is in holdings larger than 25 acres.[4]

The higher percentage of large landlords in West Punjab stems from several sources. First, at Partition those cultivators who returned to India and were settled on lands in East Punjab were more numerous than those who moved to Pakistan. Consequently, the man/land ratio declined in India as a result of Partition and the settlement efforts helped to produce a more equitable distribution of land and a strong owner-cultivator class. Secondly, at least some measure of a land reform in subsequent periods was carried out in East Punjab. In Pakistan, on the other hand, only the most nominal changes were brought about. This is reflected in the fact that until recently the acreage ceiling was 500 acres. The comparable figure in East Punjab is 30 acres. The latter limit has been frequently violated, of course, but there is considerable evidence to indicate that large holdings of the sort which are fairly common in West Punjab are now nonexistent in the East. Lastly, the holding sizes in East Punjab were historically smaller than those of the West. When portions of the western Punjab were colonized in the early 1900s, the minimum holding size granted was 25 acres. At that time, the mean holding size in the older districts from which the settlers came was on the order of 6–8 acres. Thus, a major input to the current situation is the land bonuses that were granted as an incentive to the early settlers of the Canal Colonies.

With respect to economic performance, until the last few years the differences between the two areas have been marginal. Both have been among the major beneficiaries of the improved seeds-fertilizer-water "package" that has been the basis for one of the most spectacular success stories of the green revolution. As Figure 1 indicates, the gross value of crop production in the two regimes was almost identical in 1952/53. There was some divergence during the late 1950s and early 1960s as East Punjab grew more rapidly than West Punjab. By the mid-1960s, however, this advantage had been wiped out and the two areas grew at similar rates during the 1965–1969 period.

The year 1969/70 marks a turning point in which a divergence between the two Punjabs reappears. Although it was a good year in both areas, increase in the gross value of crop output in East Punjab was an incredible 20 percent over the previous year. West Punjab on the other hand, added only 8 percent. Furthermore in 1970/71, when West Punjab experienced a significant downturn in the gross value of crop output, East Punjab went on to set new production records. This latter gap was only slightly lessened in 1971/72 when some recovery was experienced in West Punjab, although the aggregate figures did not return to their 1969/70 peak. East Punjab in that same year set still another output record to more than double the gross value of crop output between 1956/57 and 1971/72.

It is beyond the scope of this paper to provide a detailed analysis of the sources of growth in the two areas. During the most recent period, i.e., when the most significant divergences occur, the picture is muddied considerably by the war between Pakistan and India. In addition to over a hundred thousand acres on the Pakistani side where crops were not harvested, the general dislocation and uncertainty caused by the trauma itself must have had some effect on overall output. On the other hand, no visitor to East Punjab can help but suspect that the gap that has been opened up in the last few years may have its origin in the difference between the broad-based pattern of mechanization of the East as opposed to the limited diffusion of tractors and tubewells that one observes in the West. It is to this differential process of mechanization in the two areas that the following paragraphs are devoted.

CHARACTERISTICS OF MECHANIZATION

Table 2 points out one of the most dramatic features of the mechanization patterns by relating the holding size distribution shown earlier to the

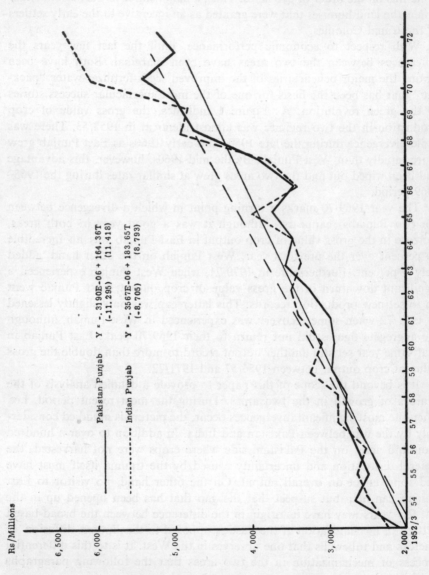

FIGURE 1 : GROSS VALUE OF CROP PRODUCTION (1959/60 PAKISTAN PRICES)

Pakistan Punjab   Y = -.3190E-06 + 164.36T
                      (-11.295)   (11.418)

Indian Punjab   Y = -.3567E-06 + 183.65T
                      (-8.705)   (8.793)

Rs/Millions

6,500
6,000
5,000
4,000
3,000
2,000

1952/3 54 55 56 57 58 59 60 61 62 63 64 65 66 67 68 69 70 71 72

TABLE 2

Distribution of Tractors by Holding Size of Owner

Holding Size	Average Holding Size of Tractor Owners		Distribution of Holdings		Distribution of Tractors	
	Indian Punjab[a]	Pakistan Punjab[b]	Indian Punjab[a]	Pakistan Punjab[b]	Indian Punjab[a]	Pakistan Punjab[b]
	(acres)	(acres)	(percent)	(percent)	(percent)	(percent)
Under 25	15	15	48	13	57	12
25–50	35	43	40	16	40	14
Over 50	58	474	2	71	3	74
Total and Avg.[c]	22.6	345.4	100	100	100	100

[a] "Studies in the Economics of Farm Management in Ferozpur District, 1969/70," Department of Agricultural Economics and Rural Sociology, Punjab Agricultural University, 1970. Ferozpur District passes larger than average holding sizes and hence these figures represent an overstatement when extrapolated to the entire Punjab.
[b] Government of Pakistan, *Farm Mechanization in Pakistan,* Report of the Farm Mechanization Committee, Ministry of Agriculture, 1968.
[c] Weighted average holding size.

characteristics of the technology. The average holding owned by a tractor owner is 35 acres in the East and 267 in the West. Table 3 makes a similar

TABLE 3

Distribution of Horsepower Among Various Tractor Sizes, 1967

Horse-power Size	Number		Percent		Total Horsepower[d]	
	Indian Punjab[a]	Pakistan Punjab[b]	Indian Punjab[c]	Pakistan Punjab[b]	Indian Punjab	Pakistan Punjab
Below 25	4,785	129	29	1	95,700	2,580
25–35	10,065	1,931	61	15	301,950	57,930
35–50	1,650	9,400	10	73	70,125	399,500
Above 50	—	1,417	—	11	—	85,020
Total	16,500	12,877	100	100	467,775	545,030

[a] Government of Haryana, *Statistical Abstract of Haryana,* Planning Department, 71/72. and Government of Punjab, *Statistical Abstract of Punjab,* Planning Department 1971/72.
[b] Government of Pakistan, *Farm Mechanization in Pakistan,* Report of the Farm Mechanization Committee, Ministry of Agriculture, 1970.
[c] Survey of 203 farms done by the Punjab Agricultural University. An even larger percentage of tractors fell below 35 h.p. in the IADP's complete enumeration in Ludhiana District.
[d] Total horse power have been calculated using the mean of the range. For tractors below 25 h.p., 20 h.p. was used. For those above 50 h.p., numbers were multiplied by 60 h.p.

point by showing that nearly all of the tractors in East Punjab are under 35 h.p., while nearly all the machines in the West are over that size. Big farms beget big tractors and vice versa.

Survey data suggest that East Punjab now possesses almost twice as many tubewells and pump sets as does West Punjab.[5] However, and this is a key point, there is reason to believe that the installed capacity in the two areas may not be terribly different, for field observations confirm that the majority of the sets in East Punjab are fractional in size. Where shallow wells exist that formerly used to provide water via a Persian wheel, one now finds a small centrifugal pump of, say, 1/2 cusec. attached to a 5 h.p. electric or 7 h.p. high-speed diesel engine. Alternatively, bores have been sunk at the field's edge and a small pump set installed there. In many, if not most cases, no elaborate housing has been provided and the motor is not permanently attached to the pump-bore assembly. It is simply moved from place to place as the need arises.

In West Punjab, the number of tubewells is also large but the majority are in the 1 cusec. range and powered by 15–20 h.p. stationary, slow-speed diesel engines. These engines are extremely cumbersome, weighing up to 2000 pounds, and once installed are rarely if ever moved. Most of the wells are housed in relatively permanent installations and a reasonably well constructed distribution system links the tubewell to the fields that are to be irrigated.

Curiously, even in the older parts of the West Punjab, such as the districts of Sialkot and Gujranwala which are perhaps most like the major portion of East Punjab, almost no shallow-well pump sets are to be found. At one time, Persian wheels existed by the thousands but, unlike in India, these were replaced by relatively large private tubewells rather than by small pump sets.

Perhaps the most obvious difference between the two areas, however, lies in the mechanical threshing of wheat. Although no formal estimates on the amount of wheat actually threshed by machines exist, figures of 95 percent in East Punjab and 5 percent in West Punjab have been suggested by knoweldgable agriculturalists. The casual observer has little difficulty in noticing the differences, since threshers are to be seen on virtually every farm in East Punjab; in West Punjab, they are still a rarity.[6]

The threshers one sees in East Punjab are largely the small machines that were originally extensions of fodder choppers, a piece of equipment that has been a part of Punjab agriculture for decades. A housing was put around the chopper blades, then a fan introduced, etc., to produce the current machines that are capable of handling several quintals of grain per hour. Touring the two or three workshops in West Punjab which produce threshers, one is struck again by the absence of the small machines and the availability of only the larger types.

Equally striking in the East Punjab are the number of small commercial rigs that do custom threshing and maize shelling. To provide maximum mobility in farmer's fields, large numbers of small entrepreneurs have extended the deck of the traditional bullock cart and mounted a small thresher or sheller on the back. With the increased distance from front to rear provided by the extension, it is possible to mount a 7–10 h.p. high-speed diesel on the front of the cart. The result is a completely self-contained custom unit. Discussions with owners of such rigs indicate that farmers much prefer to have the rig come to them in the fields rather than be forced to transport the newly harvested grain to a larger stationary unit in the vicinity. (Older U.S. readers will appreciate the similarity between this sort of rig and the methods of crew threshing which prevailed in the United States until World War II.)

SOURCES OF DIFFERENT MECHANIZATION PATTERNS

The basis for some important differences in the pattern of tractor mechanization had already been laid when it was established that the tenure systems in the two areas were substantially different. However, it must be remembered that in neither area is the supply and demand for number and types of tractors directly linked through market mechanisms. For the most part, the government is an intermediary and determines the size and make of models that are to be imported or produced.[7] Hence there is the question of how the "modern" farmer who is expected to purchase the tractor is perceived by those in charge of determining the appropriate sizes.

Conversations with government officials in West Punjab reveal that their image of the "tractor farmer" revolves almost entirely around those whose holdings are 50 acres and above. They concede that smaller farmers may still want tractors because of the custom hire opportunities presented by the demand for short-haul transportation facilities, but they argue that the difficulties in recovering costs on farms of smaller sizes mitigate against the introduction of smaller machines. The data in Table 2 reflect this view. Most of the tractors in West Punjab are found on large farms. But then, as indicated earlier, they are mostly large tractors.[8]

In East Punjab, sheer numbers have dictated that the "progressive" farmer be seen as one having 20–25 acres. Otherwise, the constituency of the groups charged with administering programs related to the farming community would be miniscule. The result is that the smaller machines shown in Table 2 were imported or produced.

The importance of this comparison is that in both cases, *government* decisions were involved. This was particularly important in West Punjab where, as Table 1 shows, there are large numbers of farmers in the same size categories as those that make up the dominant classes in East Punjab. However, without a mechanism by which this potential demand could be translated into the kind of machines imported, farms of the same size in the two areas are at significantly different stages in the structural transformation process.

Perhaps equally important in explaining the differences observed are the economics of mechanization. With respect to tractors, there seems to be little difference in the degree of government subsidy. The evidence suggests, for example, that, in terms of wheat, the price for a comparable imported machine did not differ much between India and Pakistan; in both cases tractors were heavily subsidized and reflect the undervaluation of capital that has been typical of both economies. Moreover, when converted into a rough parity with U.S. and U.K. costs by again utilizing a commodity numeraire, farmers in both regions were paying considerably less for their machines than farmers in the developed countries. This despite the obvious fact that the relative scarcities of capital and labor differ drastically between the Indian sub-continent and the advanced countries.[9]

Though the incentives to introduce tractors do not appear to differ much, the same cannot be said of such intermediate technology as small engines, tubewells, pump sets, threshers, etc. Further research is required to understand exactly why this is so, but Table 4 makes clear that the difference is substantial. Not only is the price of wheat higher in India, but the price of machines is lower. Indeed, a West Punjabi farmer owning, say, 15 acres would have to pay nearly twice as much in real terms as did his East Punjabi counterpart for a fractional 1/3–1/2 cusec. tubewell.

Part of the difference in real cost undoubtedly has to do with the price of raw materials. India produces its own iron and steel and some effort has been made to make supplies available to small-scale industry at favorable rates. In Pakistan, not only does the Beco engine contain approximately 40 percent imported parts, but these are brought in under a "spare parts" license rather than a "components" license. The effect of this is to raise the duty by 25 percent and thus to raise the cost of the engine by some 10 percent.

The comparison in Table 4 does not yet, however, reflect fully the economies of intermediate technology in East Punjab. For in fact, both the

TABLE 4

Economics of Pump Sets for Tubewells and Open Wells

	India (Kirolosker)	Pakistan (Beco)
1. 5 h.p. air-cooled diesel engine	Rs. 2,800	Rs. 4,000
2. Pump, 4 × 3, delivery with 50 feet of head @1/3 to 1/2 cusec. (Includes 20 feet of delivery pipe.)	450	600
	Rs. 3,250	Rs. 4,600
3. Price per maund of wheat* at the farm gate	28	20
4. Maunds of wheat required to purchase a pump set	116	230

A maund=82.3 lbs.

Kirolosker and Beco are advanced *air-cooled* engines which local artisans in neither of the two areas can produce. They have been chosen for comparison only because the work horse of East Punjabi mechanization, the 5–10 h.p. high-speed *water-cooled* diesel, does not appear to exist in any numbers in West Punjab! In fact, the price actually paid by small farmers for the most popular engine in East Punjab is some 25 percent less than the air-cooled model—on the order of Rs. 2,500 or 90 maunds (1 maund=82.3 lbs.) of wheat. These engines are locally made and repaired, frequently being bought as kits by the farmer and assembled for him by a local mechanic who puts an engine together and adjusts it until it is running properly.

The difference in the economics of intermediate technology in the two areas goes a long way in explaining why mechanization has spread so rapidly among a size group of farms that have been minimally affected across the border. However, a mystery remains, for *even at double the cost* the small units would yield substantial rates of return in many areas of West Punjab. Why then have they not been introduced there?

The answer remains obscure. Tours of the machine shops in both areas and discussions with local proprietors suggest that there is a considerable skill differential between the making of small high-speed diesels of East Punjab and the large slow-speed diesels that power most of the tubewells, rice mills, and threshers of West Punjab. About all one can say is that it appears, under the pressure of a different demand structure, the local artisans of the eastern regions have mastered the ability to produce a key component of the mechanization process that is not now within the grasp of the same group in the West.

But the lack of skills opens up another area of speculation. Within the Sikh community (East Punjab), there has always been a high premium on mechanical skills. (Sikhs do not dominate India's transportation systems because they are great drivers!). Although this is an area demanding further detailed sociological investigation, the Ramgarhi or artisan class seems historically to have occupied a more prestigious position within the Sikh community than that occupied by their counterparts in the Muslim community. A hypothesis worth examining would be that the advantageous position occupied by this group, both economically and socially, has contributed to the extraordinary vigor and innovation that characterizes the small-scale implement industry in East Punjab.

This aptitude and, indeed, affinity for things mechanical, extends to the cultivator population. Conversations with farmers throughout both Punjabs left the impression that the level of understanding concerning the internal workings of their equipment was highest among the middle-size Sikh farmers. The retention of a mechanic or "driver," a common practice in West Punjab, was unheard of and farmers claimed that 75 percent of the repairs on locally produced machines were carried out on the farm.

One can only speculate about the effects of cultural attitudes on the characteristics of technical change. That it might be significant between culturally diverse groups, i.e., between northern and southern Indians, seems likely. That it exists between groups much more similar in origin, i.e., between Hindu, Muslim, and Sikh Punjabis would seem to be more problematical. Yet there is something unique about the ability and obvious delight of a young Sikh farmer in taking apart the machine he has purchased and showing his visitor the modifications he has made, which suggests that this facet of the whole process ought not to be overlooked.[10]

Conclusions

The observations made in the foregoing paragraphs deserve additional investigation and hopefully will be further clarified in the context of on-going work on rural development in the two areas. However, certain conclusions, sufficient for policy guidance, can already be drawn.

(1) The combination of economic policy *and* a technology that is primarily of interest only to small farmers is one of a limited number of programs that (a) have a positive distributive effect, and (b) can be implemented. Virtually every other program that aims at this class as a target group will, in situations where disparity in holding sizes and power at the local level is substantial, be captured and diverted by the elites of the community. The Indian government's decision, for example, to subsidize the diffusion of 5 h.p. water-cooled diesel engines would, in the Pakistan context, provide a means of reaching a class that is virtually impossible to reach through such traditional small farmer activities as credit, extension, and cooperation.

(2) The fact that the know-how required to produce the engines seems to be lacking in Pakistan suggests the importance of a technical assistance program in intermediate technology. Without question, there is a significant relationship between the acquisition of the necessary skills in the manufacturing sector and the demand for the object to be produced. However, it appears that while local artisans in Pakistan possess a great ability to copy, they lack the engineering skills to design. Hence the need, in the short run, to disseminate prototypes that are relatively simple to produce and easy to maintain.

(3) The experience in East Punjab also undermines the argument in Pakistan, and in similar environments in Latin America and Africa, that small farming units cannot participate fully in a highly sophisticated mechanization process, i.e., that land reform would preclude a "modern" agricultural sector. Instead, land reform and the development of a broad-based, small-scale industrial sector capable of providing an appropriate type of intermediate technology should be seen as intimately linked parts of a comprehensive approach to rural development.

NOTES

1. S. Ishikawa has captured the iterative or dynamic character of this adjustment process by referring to "stable" and "unstable" technology and agrarian structures. The former can be roughly equated with the degree of divisibility of the technology, the latter with the degree of disparity in holding sizes. Since the two interact, "stability" requires not only

that the technology is suited to the holding size, but that the distribution of farm sizes is such that no substantial surpluses are generated by one group relative to another. Where such surpluses do exist, they can be expected to lead to further land agglomeration, even in the presence of a divisible technology. For an alternative formulation of the same idea, see my "Technical Change and the Distribution of Income in Rural Areas," *American Journal of Agricultural Economics* 54 (May 1972).

2. These examples have been further developed within a theoretical framework by B.F. Johnston and Peter Kilby. See their *Agricultural Strategies, Rural-Urban Interactions and the Expansion of Income Opportunities* (Paris, 1972).

3. "East Punjab" or "Indian Punjab" refers to the combined area of the present states of Punjab and Haryana.

4. Hamza Alavi, "Elite Farmer Strategy and Regional Disparities in the Agricultural Development of West Pakistan," in R.D. Stevens, et al., eds., *Rural Development in Pakistan* (East Lansing, Mich., 1971).

5. Figures given in the statistical abstracts of the two areas list approximately 90,000 for West Punjab and approximately 190,000 for East Punjab.

6. Figures for 1969 place the number of threshers in East Punjab at 80,000. No recent estimate exists for West Pakistan; the only available figure is for 1966, when the Farm Mechanization Survey showed a total of 3,000 for West Pakistan.

7. Only India has the capacity to manufacture part of its needs domestically. Here again, however, the sizes that are to be produced are determined by government officials.

8. At this writing the sizes to be produced by the proposed Massey-Ferguson plant have not been disclosed. One can only hope that some sensitivity to the implications of large machines will be displayed in the decision.

9. Nural Islam, "Agricultural Growth in Pakistan: Problems and Policies," Center Paper no. 17, Japan Economic Research Center (May 1972.)

10. Several Indian colleagues have called my attention to similar developments in Coimbatore and elsewhere which certainly undermines any simplistic cultural interpretation.

Rural Landed Rights and Becoming "Twice-Born": Some Interrelations Between India's Sacred and Secular Hierarchies

JOSEPH W. ELDER

SCHOLARS have frequently distinguished two different hierarchies in India. They have referred to the first as the "sacred," "ritual," or "pollution" hierarchy[1]—or simply the "hierarchy"[2]—with Brahmans at the top, scheduled castes or "untouchables" at the bottom, and intermediate groups ranked according to certain pan-Hindu principles of purity (e.g., vegetarianism, avoidance of alcohol, prohibition of widow-remarriage, abandonment of defiling occupations, etc.). In most of Hindu India there is agreement that such a sacred hierarchy exists, even though the relative rank of particular castes may be disputed in different areas. The sacred hierarchy is often described by its participants in terms of which group receives what services from Brahmans, or which groups say they are willing to accept or reject what kinds of food from which other groups.[3]

Scholars have referred to the second hierarchy as the "secular," "social," "pragmatic," or "politico-economic" hierarchy, with the most powerful political and economic groups (e.g., rulers, large landowners, etc.) at the top and the least powerful political and economic groups (e.g., landless laborers, servants, etc.) at the bottom. Whereas the boundaries of the units in the sacred hierarchy are typically endogamous castes (or *jatis*), the boundaries of the units in the secular hierarchy may be castes, but may also be caste segments or even individual families. This secular hierarchy is frequently described by its participants in terms of who is "big" and who is "little"— with "bigness" typically referring to the ability of individuals or families to have their own way even in the face of opposition, and "littleness" referring to the inability of individuals or families to do anything other than accommodate themselves to, or yield to, the demands of others.

Despite their general agreement that analytically separate sacred and secular hierarchies exist in India, scholars disagree regarding how these two hierarchies relate to each other.

Both H.N.C. Stevenson and Louis Dumont argue for minimum overlap of the two hierarchies. Thus, Stevenson states:

In contradistinction to secular status, the ritual status...between individuals and groups and between groups of different categories rests wholly upon behaviour-patterns linked with mystical beliefs in general, and mainly upon behaviour linked with a particular corpus of beliefs concerning purity and pollution. . . .[4]

And Louis Dumont agrees when he says:

it is necessary to distinguish between two very different things: the scale of statuses (called 'religious') which I name hierarchy and which is absolutely distinct from the fact of power; and the distribution of power, economic and political, which is very important in practice but is distinct from, and subordinate to, hierarchy.[5]

Unlike Stevenson and Dumont, K. Gough Aberle and F.G. Bailey argue for high overlap of the two hierarchies. Thus Aberle, in her discussion of caste ranking in South India, maintains that wealth and power are both important in determining the relative ranking of different castes.[6] And F.G. Bailey, on the basis of research in Orissa, refers to: "a high degree of coincidence between politico-economic rank and the ritual ranking of caste. This is a reflection of the general rule that those who achieve wealth and political power tend to rise in the ritual scheme of ranking."[7]

McKim Marriott and Ronald Inden present a third position. Identifying two systems of categorization that Westerners have applied to South Asia (a "natural" one based on genetic substances, and a "moral" or "legal" one based on actions and exchange patterns), they argue that, unlike Westerners, South Asians do not insist on drawing a line between the two systems. From a South Asian perspective, a person can act "morally" or "legally" in such a way (e.g., eating correct foods, marrying into a right family, undergoing certain ceremonies) that his "natural" body substance is improved, which in turn improves his "moral" or "legal" qualities and exchange relationships. From this South Asian perspective, the sacrifice of the "Code Man" Purusa (described many centuries ago in the Vedas) outlined the basic ranked relationships between the four original *varnas* (social genera) according to the higher or lower parts of Purusa's body from which the varnas emerged (with the Brahman varna emerging from the top, followed by the Kshatriya and Vaishya varnas, with the Shudra varna emerging from the bottom). The "natural" qualities of the varnas' origins carried with them "moral" or "legal" obligations in terms of exchange patterns. Subsequent changes in the caste system have occurred through the transformation of coded substances within an established and accepted cognitive framework of nondual units, relationships, and processes. In short, Marriott and Inden argue for discarding the Western conception of two separate hierarchies in India and replacing it with the South Asian view of a single, interpenetrated, interpenetrating, simultaneously "natural" *and* "moral/legal" hierarchy.[8]

With the increasing body of data available on social mobility in India, it would seem possible to begin resolving the differences between the three positions on the basis of evidence. However, the acquisition of relevant evidence poses certain problems. First, there is the problem of the temporal span. Ethnographic reports frequently place their findings in an atemporal frame of reference. Within such a frame, they may describe some cases of

individual mobility. However, the processes we wish to examine are cases
of group mobility. And group mobility is notoriously slow, often requiring
several generations before a change of rank is finally confirmed. Hence,
despite the increasing body of available data, well-documented cases of group
mobility are still in short supply.

Second, there is the problem of separating the indices of the two hierarchies. Despite clear analytic and definitional differences, when one begins
dealing with data, the differences begin to blur. For example, suppose that
several centuries ago particular families of Nayakas in Tamilnadu or Kshatriyas in Bengal engaged in costly temple-building, thereby enhancing their
status in the eyes of their less-affluent relatives and enabling them to refuse
to accept brides from such relatives.[9] Would their ability to restrict their
acceptance of brides be considered another manifestation of their change in
secular status? Or would it be seen as a change in both their secular and their
sacred status? Or would one want to subdivide the concept of sacred status
into, perhaps, "marrying status" and "ritual status," and say that these
particular Nayakas or Kshatriyas retained their former "ritual status" while
enhancing their "marrying status?"

Or suppose, as Sanyal suggests,[10] that some Telis in Bengal were able to
move up from the ranks of Ajalchal to the ranks of Navasakhas primarily
through temple-building. Would this be seen as an improvement in their
sacred status through enhancement of their secular status, even if they continued to marry other Telis, and hence had not changed their "marrying"
status?

Or suppose that certain Nadars in the northern districts of Tamilnadu
were successful in using their newly acquired wealth to gain admission into
Shaivite temples, while their equally wealthy relatives in the southern districts of Tamilnadu were unsuccessful.[11] To the extent the northern and
southern branches continued to intermarry, did the northern Nadars improve
both their secular and their sacred status, while the southern Nadars improved
only their secular status? Or did the southern Nadars indirectly improve
their sacred status also, since they could at least marry into Nadar families
which were admitted into Shaivite temples?

In order to distinguish as clearly as possible between sacred and secular
status, in this paper I have chosen as my illustration of a change in sacred
status a caste's transition from the "once-born" to the "twice-born" category.
Within the four-varna scheme, the Shudras are once-born; the Vaishyas,
Kshatriyas, and Brahmans are twice-born. Symbolic of the distinction is the
fact that only members of the twice-born varnas are entitled to wear the
sacred thread (usually composed of not less than three cotton strands and
worn over the left shoulder, diagonally across the chest, and around the
right hip). Traditionally this thread is bestowed upon boys during their
upanayana (initiation into second birth) ceremony. This paper will examine
instances where formerly once-born jatis attempted to enforce their claim
that they were now legitimately twice-born and hence entitled to wear the

sacred thread. And it will try to identify any preconditions that consistently separate the successful from the unsuccessful efforts of those jatis.

EXAMPLES OF CLAIMS TO TWICE-BORN STATUS

One of the most notably recorded elevations to the status of twice-born was that of Shivaji, the Maratha ruler. Irawati Karve describes a 1697 account in which a Brahman found a suitable genealogy to justify Shivaji's being defined a Kshatriya; whereupon Shivaji "had the thread ceremony performed on him and was made a pure Kshatriya and then crowned king in the year 1674."[12]

Another example of castes' successful efforts to raise their sacred status to twice-born are the Sagar Rajputs of Poona district. Previously they were considered to be Dhangars—shepherds by occupation and Shudras by traditional varna. However, when their economic strength increased and they began to acquire land, they found a genealogist to trace their ancestry back to a leading officer in Shivaji's army, changed their names from Dhangars to Sagar Rajputs, and donned the sacred thread. They have subsequently made their claim stick by punishing any open skeptics of their Kshatriya ritual status.[13]

Another example of a successful move to the ranks of the twice-born is that of the Boad distillers (Sundhi) in Orissa. In the late nineteenth century they were placed among the "Low Hindus," just above the untouchables. However, a forty-year monopoly of liquor manufacture in the area enabled the Boad distillers to acquire unusual wealth, purchase land, and become dominant landowners. They dropped their distilling, gave up such demeaning practices as drinking liquor and keeping chickens, donned the sacred thread, and by mid-twentieth century they were ranked near the top of the "High Hindus," just below the warriors.[14]

The Yogi weavers of Bengal provide an example of a group trying to elevate themselves to twice-born status with somewhat inconclusive results. Before the census of 1911 an author, Radhagovinda Nath, presented a book entitled *The Yogi Caste of Bengal* to the census commissioner, and the Yogi caste journal, *Yogi Sakha,* began publishing articles on Yogi history. By 1921 the priestly branches of the Yogis claimed to be Brahmans. By 1931 *all* Yogis claimed to be Brahmans, and at an annual conference the delegates passed a resolution that all Yogis should wear the sacred thread. Articles entitled "The Ritual of Wearing the Sacred Thread" and "Popularity of the Sacred Thread" appeared in the *Yogi Sakha.* One article recommended that the Yogi priests should begin educating themselves properly in order to deserve their title of Brahman. Perhaps the shifting nature of the Yogis' claims has contributed to the lack of credibility of their claims. At any rate, in Bengal they are still regarded as a weaving caste with aspirations to Brahmanhood.[15]

An effort similar to that of the Yogis was that of the Panchala artisans of South India, normally regarded as Shudras. The Panchalas include the jatis of carpenters, blacksmiths, stonecutters, brass and copper workers, and goldsmiths. Their assertions of their Brahman status rested on their claimed descent from Vishvakarman, the divine architect-builder of the heavens. Like the Yogis, the Panchalas avoided the established Brahman priests, preferring to use their own Panchala priests. Like the Yogis, they donned the sacred thread. And, like the Yogis, their claims to Brahmanhood were not recognized by their neighbors. In fact, in parts of South India even untouchables would not take food and water from certain Panchalas, perhaps precisely *because* of their lofty ambitions.[16]

An equally unsuccessful effort to achieve the status of twice-born occurred among the Ahir cattle-tenders of North India. Over the years, various Ahir families had begun to prosper, largely through trade and government contracting. These families initiated a campaign to change their name from Ahir to Yadav and to be identified as Kshatriyas rather than Shudras. One of their caste members, V.K. Khedkar, brought out a volume entitled *The Divine Heritage of the Yadavas* presenting the case for Ahirs being descended from Lord Krishna through a series of royal families. In 1924 representatives of various regional Ahir organizations met in Allahabad and founded an All India Yadav Mahasabha, which subsequently published a journal and urged fellow Ahirs to adopt a life style appropriate to Yadav Kshatriyas. All of this met little resistance from higher castes. It was not until certain Ahirs in Bihar actually began wearing the sacred thread that the higher caste Bhumihars and Rajputs organized vigorous, and sometimes bloody, opposition to the twice-born aspirations of the Ahirs. It was one thing for the Ahirs to try to upgrade their own lives; it was quite another for them to insert themselves among the established twice-born.[17]

In addition to these cases, where specific mention is made of donning the sacred thread, there are other descriptions of castes expressing their aspirations to be twice-born, even though the accounts do not specifically mention the sacred thread. Thus, Srinivas reports that the Coorgs in the hills between Mysore and Kerala successfully elevated themselves to Kshatriya status.[18] Shah and Shroff report that the presumably extribal Kolis of Gujarat have established their claims to Kshatriyahood sufficiently firmly to have Brahman priests perform their sacred ceremonies.[19] Pocock reports that the erstwhile Kunbis who became Patidar tax-collectors in Gujarat in the eighteenth century eventually established their claims to the rank of the Kshatriyas through trading and arranging hypergamous marriages.[20] Nicholas and Mukhopadhyay report that in Midnapore, West Bengal, the economic and numerical superiority of the cultivator Mahisyas has enabled them to place themselves just below the Brahmans in the caste hierarchy, and to have their cooked food accepted by all castes except the Brahmans.[21] Beteille describes less successful efforts at becoming twice-born on the part of the Shudra Padayachis of Tamilnadu. They produced a book justifying their rank of Kshatriya and formally appealed to the census officials for such a rank. But the census officials denied their request, and they continued to be regarded as Shudras by the other castes.[22] Similarly, Bose reports the unsuccessful efforts of the Bengali Namashudra farmers and boatmen to be recognized as Brahmans. As early as 1908 their journal carried assertions that they were "descended from the ancient sages and *Rishis,* i.e., from pure Brahmins." And they published a book showing that their lineage supported their claims. However, their claims received little recognition from other castes, and even their appeal for protection by, and continuation of, British rule failed to improve their position.[23]

These examples of claims to twice-born status imply that over time there have been hundreds of others about which nothing is known because they went unrecorded by historians or social scientists. Thus, in trying to develop generalizations about the process of becoming twice-born, we are at best working with a small, happenstance sample. Furthermore, the sample that we do have contains a number of instances which are so briefly described that often a caste's efforts to become twice-born are covered in a few paragraphs—or even a few sentences.[24]

Fortunately, there do exist two relatively detailed narratives of castes' efforts to become twice-born: Wiliam Rowe's description of the Senapur Noniya salt manufacturers' efforts to become Kshatriya Cauhan Rajputs, and D.P. Sinha's description of the Gohanakalan Pasi toddy-tappers' efforts to become Kshatriya Rajpasis.[25] Both cases occurred in Uttar Pradesh during approximately the same time period (from the 1920s through the 1940s). One effort succeeded; the other failed. A close comparison of these two cases may throw considerable light on what castes have had to do to become successfully twice-born.

Successful Efforts of the Senapur Noniyas to Become Twice-Born

During the second half of the nineteenth century, an increasing number of Noniya (salt manufacturers) in Uttar Pradesh became wealthy through contracting for brick-making, earth work, and other traditional caste occupations for the British. The ritual uplift of the Noniyas began in 1898, when one of their members, Lalla Mathura Prasad Singh, having amassed a fortune in the princely state of Patiala, returned to Uttar Pradesh and became a landowner. Joining with other professionals and newly wealthy Noniyas nearby, he founded a Cauhan Rajput Organization, the purposes of which were to improve the lot of their caste and to make a claim on the status of Kshatriya. Over the next decades, the Cauhan organization spread across the state, "making gains wherever a group of Noniyas existed whose wealth enabled them to attempt social emulation of the Rajput style of life. The movement seems to have followed economic advancement rather than having preceded it."[26]

During the 1920s and 1930s this organization produced a body of literature supporting the Noniyas' claims to be rightfully Kshatriyas. This literature argued that the present-day Noniyas were relatives of the twelfth-century Hindu King, Prithviraj Cauhan. After Prithviraj was killed by treachery, the

Cauhans had fled from slaughter by the Muslims in western India and had removed their sacred threads and even accepted defiling food in order to save their line. Eventually they had assumed the occupation of makers and sellers of salt, whence came the name "Noniya" ("non" meaning "salt"). Various versions of this genealogy gained increasing acceptance among the Noniyas over the following decades.

In 1924 the organization called a meeting at Sanghaipur, in Jaunpur district, at which leaders of various Noniya communities donned the sacred thread, thereby publicly announcing the restoration of their erstwhile Kshatriya status.

In 1936 another Noniya meeting was called, this one in the town of Kerakat. After hearing speeches by educated Cauhans and various leaders from Jaunpur city, Noniya leaders from the surrounding areas received the sacred thread from a Brahman priest. Each leader was then urged to arrange for all Noniya males in his area to don the sacred thread.

Following the Kerakat meeting, the Noniyas of Senapur returned to their village wearing their sacred threads. When they began arrangements for all local Noniya men to adopt the sacred thread, the resident Kshatriyas intervened, tore off the Noniyas' sacred threads, and slapped a fine on them for their affrontery. Only some years later, quietly, and on an individual basis, did the Noniyas of Senapur begin to wear the sacred thread again, this time unopposed.

Brahmans placed the sacred threads around the Noniyas' necks in the Kerakat meeting. And Brahmans continued to officiate at their weddings, life-cycle rituals, and religious recitations. However, the two Brahmans who most frequently served the Noniyas were "men of dubious background and from another village" who tended to serve a low-caste clientele. Nevertheless, by the 1950s the Noniya Cauhans stood among the top two or three castes in Senapur's twenty-four caste hierarchy. For all practical purposes, their efforts at becoming twice-born had succeeded.

UNSUCCESSFUL EFFORTS OF THE GOHANAKALAN PASIS TO BECOME TWICE-BORN

In certain ways, the toddy-tapper Pasis of Gohanakalan followed the same steps as Senapur's Noniyas in their efforts to become Kshatriyas. They formed a Pasi caste association and, in the 1930s, published literature urging Pasi self-improvement through prohibiting meat and liquor and supporting childrens' education. However, the Pasis lacked the strong economic base on which the Noniyas had built their movement.

Finally, in 1949, after India was independent, the Pasis made their bid for Kshatriya status. On October 2 (Mahatma Gandhi's birthday) in Itaunja, a town 14 miles from Lucknow, Pasis from different parts of Uttar Pradesh convened to discuss ways to improve their caste's status. Along with repeating such slogans as "All Pasis, unite!," "Help your caste-men," and "We are Rajpasis (descendants of Kshatriyas)," the Pasi delegates decided their caste should wear the sacred thread as a mark of their respectability.

On October 5, a local implementation meeting was held at Nawabganj, six miles from Lucknow, at which teams of Pasi volunteers agreed to visit neighboring villages on appointed days, accompanied by a few Brahmans, to invest all Pasis with the sacred thread. On October 18, a team accompanied by Brahmans came to Gohanakalan. There, at the home of Cheda Pasi, a leader of the movement, the Brahmans recited hymns and invested nearly one hundred Pasis with sacred threads.

Within a week, Gohanakalan's panchayat, under the leadership of angry Kshatriyas, declared a boycott against the offending Pasis. Pasis would be deprived of their village watchmanship and would lose all farmlands sublet to them. Brahmans would not serve them; blacksmiths and carpenters would not repair their tools; barbers would not shave them; washermen would not wash their clothes; midwives would not help with their deliveries. They were barred from drawing water from any private wells in the village, nor could they graze their cattle on the village grazing ground.

Within 48 hours most of Gohanakalan's Pasis had been brought to their knees. In the presence of the village panchayat they surrendered their sacred threads and vowed not to repeat their error. In return, the village lifted the boycott.

However, a minority of Gohanakalan's Pasis resisted the surrender and sought help from the greater Pasi panchayat at Itaunja (where the Gandhi birthday meeting had been held). The greater Pasi panchayat agreed to help them. On November 19 about four hundred Pasis went to Gohanakalan, where they condemned the pressures of the village panchayat and reinvested the Pasis with the sacred thread. Whether or not Brahmans were present at this second ceremony is not clear from the account.

The next day, after the four hundred Pasis had left, the village reimposed the anti-Pasi boycott. For nearly three weeks the local Pasis resisted the boycott. Finally, realizing that sustained help could not come from outside the village, they requested a panchayat meeting, surrendered their sacred threads a second time, and apologized to the village for their arrogance. The village panchayat agreed to lift the boycott and recommended that the Pasis pay for a public reading of the scriptures to restore their ritual purity and to ward off the sins caused by their "irreligious activities."

DIFFERENCES BETWEEN THE TWO EFFORTS

Turning to an analysis of the main differences between the successful twice-born efforts of the Noniya Cauhans and the unsuccessful twice-born efforts of the Gohanakalan Pasis (as well as successful and unsuccessful twice-born efforts of other castes), a number of tentative generalizations seem possible. Their tentativeness is underscored by the fact that a few more careful case studies might readily shatter any or all of them.

1. Rural landed rights were a necessary condition for a caste's elevation to twice-born status. The Noniya Cauhans held extensive landed rights before they began their twice-born efforts; the Pasis did not, and they were obviously

vulnerable to their opponents' boycott. The briefer case studies seem to support this generalization. Thus, Shivaji's successful effort at becoming twice-born, as well as the successful efforts of the Sagar Rajputs, the Boad distillers, and the Coorgs might be linked to their prior acquisition of rural landed rights. Similarly, among those castes that attempted—yet failed—to achieve twice-born status, the Yogi weavers, the Panchala artisans, and the Yadav cattle-keepers support the generalization that without rural landed rights it is difficult, if not impossible, to cross the twice-born barrier.

Further evidence for the importance of rural landed rights can be seen in the fact that in our case studies different branches of a caste struggling to establish itself as twice-born had to win their victories in their own localities on the basis of their own landed rights. Thus, it was possible at the same time for stronger branches of the caste to be considered twice-born while the weaker branches of the caste were considered once-born. This observation, incidentally, is at variance with those descriptions of caste that state all members of a caste share the same sacred rank. However, at the point where the sacred and secular hierarchies intersect, such irregularities seem not only plausible but also predictable. Thus, the Noniya Cauhans in Sanghaipur were able to don their sacred threads in 1924. The Noniya Cauhans in Kerakat were able to don their sacred threads twelve years later in 1936. But when the Noniya Cauhans returned to Senapur in 1936 wearing their sacred threads, they were beaten and fined by Senapur's Kshatriya landlords. Not until some years later, when their position was a little more secure, did the Senapur Cauhans wear their sacred threads unopposed. Similarly, the Pasis in Gohanakalan found themselves unable to defend their twice-born aspirations, even though the Pasis in neighboring Itaunja encouraged them to do so, providing at one point a 400-Pasi show of strength. In the end, the Gohanakalan Pasis had to apologize to the rest of the village for their brazenness and surrender their sacred threads, regardless of what Pasis elsewhere in Uttar Pradesh were doing.

The fact that the agricultural Namashudras have considerable rural landed rights and yet have failed in their attempts to achieve twice-born status suggests that even if landed rights may be a necessary condition for becoming twice-born, they may not be a sufficient condition. Other processes apparently also play a necessary part.

2. A plausible genealogy helped legitimate a caste's claim to being twice-born and therefore its right to have its members wear the sacred thread. In 1925 the Noniya Cauhans published *Bans Prabodhni,* an elaborate history of the Cauhans from the start of human times through the death of Prithviraj Cauhan in the twelfth century to the scattering of the Cauhans throughout Uttar Pradesh and Bihar. The genealogy was sufficiently detailed that contemporary Noniya Cauhans could find genealogical links to some Cauhan subgroup that had migrated to their locality centuries earlier. The Noniya Cauhans were eventually able to wear the sacred thread and have themselves accepted as Kshatriyas.

The Pasis, on the other hand, developed no such genealogy. Aside from asserting they really *were* "Rajpasis" (descendents of Rajput Kshatriyas), and making an ideological appeal for fairer treatment for themselves (e.g., by choosing Mahatma Gandhi's birthday for publicizing their claim), they apparently traced no lineages—detailed or otherwise—substantiating their claim to Rajput descent. Their neighbors remained profoundly skeptical, asserting that placing "Raj" in front of "Pasi" was not enough to establish a hereditary link with Kshatriyas.

Most people realize that with a little imagination one or more authors can readily compose a "caste history."[27] But such genealogies can cast some doubt on the flawless accuracy of any given caste hierarchy. After all, who knows for certain that some published genealogy might not—at least in some respects—be correct? Salt traders *might* be descended from Cauhan warriors; who has sufficient hard evidence to dismiss the suggestion out-of-hand?

The presence of a genealogy is not invariably associated with either success or failure in being recognized as twice-born. The Dhangars of Poona district evolved a genealogy and also succeeded in being recognized as twice-born Sagar Rajputs. The Yogis and Namashudras of Bengal, the Ahirs of North India, and the Padayachis of Tamilnadu, among others,[28] developed genealogies yet failed in their aspirations to be recognized as twice-born. Furthermore, certain caste groups have made substantial gains in sacred status without evidence of a legitimizing genealogy (note, for example, the Boad distillers of Orissa and the Mahisyas of Bengal, both of whom achieved Kshatriya status without any apparent reworking of their genealogies). However, I have found no instance of a caste undergoing a successful twice-born ceremony under the supervision of Brahmans without that caste also producing a legitimizing genealogy.

3. Sponsorship by Brahmans was a necessary, though not sufficient, condition for a caste's successful elevation to twice-born status. Brahmans officiated at the sacred-thread ceremonies of both the successful Noniya Cauhans and the unsuccessful Pasis (although one wishes both accounts gave fuller descriptions of where those Brahmans came from and—in the case of the Pasis—where they went back to after their investiture was declared invalid by the other castes in the area). So the Noniyas and Pasis provide only partial evidence for this generalization. However, two castes aspiring to twice-born status, the Yogis of Bengal and the Panchalas of South India, donned the sacred thread, claiming high-caste descent, and had their claims authenticated, but only by priests from their own castes. In neither case was this authentication accepted as valid by other castes in that locality, and both efforts to be recognized as twice-born failed.

It is a truism that in most localities in India there are Brahmans and other Brahmans. The Maratha ruler Shivaji, when he was claiming Kshatriya-hood, went to elaborate efforts to have his claim authenticated by the most prestigious Brahmans not only in Maharashtra but also in Banaras.[29] Other groups seeking twice-born status have lacked Shivaji's political and economic resources. Thus, the Brahmans most frequently serving Senapur's Noniya Cauhans are regarded as slightly dubious by other groups in the area. One might hazard the generalization that the more impeccable the credentials of a caste's Brahman sponsors, the greater the likelihood of success for that caste's claims to twice-born status.

In this regard, an interesting historical hypothesis suggests itself. Is it not possible that some of the geographical mobility associated with Brahman castes is related to a symbiotic relationship between priestly castes seeking legitimacy as Brahmans and newly empowered castes aspiring to twice-born (or at least a higher) status? One could envision an up-and-coming caste trying unsuccessfully to obtain sponsorship from local, respected Brahmans—Brahmans in the service of already established castes that resent the aspirations of the "upstart" caste. Failing in their search for local Brahman sponsorship, the ambitious caste might see what priests were available within a wider geographical area. Eventually finding priests (however dubious) willing to serve as sponsors, the caste and the priests could develop a reciprocal relationship. The priests would authenticate the caste's higher status, while the caste would build a temple for, or give hereditary lands to, the cooperating priests, thereby enabling the priests to move with financial security to the locality of their new patron, and bolstering their own claim to be legitimate Brahmans.

Establishing a sequence such as the hypothetical one above would require a chain of well-documented facts. To the best of my knowledge, no such chain exists in the literature. However, when one sees the number of Brahmans in Uttar Pradesh villages who have been brought in from "near Almorah" or "close to Rishikesh," or when one notes such phenomena as the presence of twelve different Brahman jatis in the same village in South India, who have come to the village from Kannada-, Telugu-, and Tamil-speaking areas, and who can agree on no rank order among themselves,[30] the symbiotic hypothesis appears plausible by way of historical explanation.

If evidence yet to be gathered supports this symbiotic hypothesis, the three generalizations above about becoming twice-born might need modification. For example, the three generalizations might have to be limited to achieving twice-born *nonpriestly* rank. The path for achieving twice-born priestly Brahman rank may be considerably more complex, involving a group's performance of sacred ceremonies, economic and political protection by other groups capable of defending the legitimacy of ceremonies so performed, and, possibly, a sponsorship to twice-born status for the protecting group by the aspiring Brahman group. It seems likely that this process, or something like it, has occurred in the past. It seems equally likely that castes which have participated in this process will not be eager to reveal to outsiders its details.

DISCUSSION

Of the three variables associated with successful claims to being twice-born (non-Brahmans), the possession of rural landed rights appears to be the most fundamental. Especially revealing, it seems, is the way in which branches of the same caste may have different ritual status in various localities, based on their local control of land.

Why might rural land control be so important in improving one's ritual status? One reason may be that in an agricultural setting, land is the major commodity for establishing relationships of continuing dependency. Thus, the family which controls land controls, in part anyway, the lives of those who ultimately depend for their survival on that land—agricultural laborers, artisans such as blacksmiths, carpenters, and washermen, and any who trade their services for grain. Furthermore, in an agricultural setting, resident dependents have few alternatives. They either work for the local landlords, or they don't work—at least in that locality. With land in fixed supply, the power of one landowner expands at the expense of the power of other land-owners. Eventually an expanding landowner can reach a point where he is relatively unassailable. He has enough local residents dependent on him so that he can be impervious to criticisms from other landowners, knowing he can count on his dependents to side with him, or at least not to show sympathies for his opponents.

A hierarchy, whether sacred or secular, implies some collective acceptance of a rank order. At this point dependents may become crucial. They are in the weakest position to argue against whatever new ranking order their landowner espouses. Therefore, they are most likely to become part of that collectivity which accepts the new ranking order. Their acceptance of it helps, in turn, to legitimize it.

If, as a particular type of dependent, a landowner is able to obtain the sponsorship of Brahmans who will confirm a genealogy and publicly award the sacred thread, the new hierarchy comes even closer to being "legitimate." Once again land may be a key commodity in acquiring such sponsorship, for land (or its benefits) may be the price the landowner pays to the Brahman to secure his sponsorship.

A second possible reason for the importance of rural land control in caste mobility has to do with the more general nature of hierarchies and sponsorship. Sponsorship has little meaning unless there is general acceptance that certain statuses exist into which it is desirable to be admitted—and only certain legitimate sponsors who can facilitate candidates' admission into those statuses. In most parts of the world, such well-accepted hierarchies are more likely to exist in rural than in urban areas, and India appears to be no exception. The caste hierarchy is typically better-defined in the countryside than in the cities, with their nonfitting minority groups, administrative hierarchies, foreigners, and transients. Hence, with rural regions the areas of clearest articulation of the caste hierarchy, and with land the predominant means to power in rural areas, it is not surprising that rural land control appears to play such a prominent part in the successful efforts of castes to become twice-born.

It is possible that, with the shifting of the basis of family wealth in India from landed agriculture to more urban financial manipulations, rural land control will become less important as a condition for caste mobility. Damle's brief account of the Panchkalshi caste's recent rise to equality with Brahmans in Bombay through acquiring Western education rather than landed wealth suggests such changes may already be underway.[31] However, an additional result of Western education appears to be a declining interest in competing for rank in the sacred or ritual arena and an increasing interest in competing for benefits in the economic and political arenas. Ironically, the same changing economic circumstances that might reduce the importance of rural landed rights in caste ritual mobility might, at the same time, bring to an end efforts toward such ritual mobility.[32]

In conclusion, it may be useful to return to the three currently competing perceptions regarding how India's sacred and secular hierarchies interrelate to see how the data above support or challenge those perceptions. The first generalization, regarding the importance of rural landed rights, challenges the Stevenson-Dumont argument for minimum overlap between the sacred and secular hierarchies. The second generalization, regarding the usefulness of a twice-born genealogy, and the third generalization, regarding sponsorship by Brahmans, supplement—rather than challenge—the Gough-Bailey perception of high overlap between the sacred and secular hierarchies. And this paper's focus on efforts to manipulate the sacred hierarchy through secular processes suggests that, at least for analytic purposes, it may be useful to distinguish between the two hierarchies, whether or not the Marriott-Inden position is correct that South Asians perceive only a nondual, unified "natural" *and* "moral/legal" hierarchy.

Clearly much work remains to be done on the topic of caste mobility and becoming twice-born. More careful case studies, family histories, and personal biographies are needed to illuminate a process that has played an important, if little understood, part in the social history of India. And from such additional data may emerge a clearer view of the relationships between India's sacred and secular hierarchies.

NOTES

1. See, for example, H.N.C. Stevenson, "Status Evaluation in the Hindu Caste System," *Journal of the Royal Anthropological Society of Great Britain and Ireland* 84 (1954): 45–65; also E.B. Harper, "Ritual Pollution as an Integrator of Caste and Religion," in E.B. Harper, ed., *Religion in South Asia* (Seattle, 1964).

2. Louis Dumont, *Homo Hierarchicus: The Caste System and Its Implications* (Chicago, 1970), p. 251.

3. See for example,McKim Marriott, "Interactional and Attributional Theories of Caste Ranking," *Man in India* 39 (1959): 92–107; also McKim Marriott, "Caste Ranking and Food Transactions: A Matrix Analysis," in M. Singer and B. Cohn, eds., *Structure and Change in Indian Society* (Chicago, 1968), pp. 133–71; also Pauline Kolenda, "A Multiple Scaling Technique for Caste Ranking," *Man in India* 39 (1959): 127–47; also Pauline Kolenda, "A Ritual Pollution Scale for Ranking Hindu Castes," *Sociometry* 23 (1960): 292–306.

4. Stevenson, "Status Evaluation in the Hindu Caste System," p. 45.

5. Dumont, *Homo Hierarchicus,* p. 251.

6. K. Gough Aberle, "Criteria of Caste Ranking in South India," *Man in India* 39 (1959): 115–26.

7. F.G. Bailey, *Caste and the Economic Frontier* (Manchester, 1957), p. 266.

8. McKim Marriott, and Ronald B. Inden, "An Ethnosociology of South Asian Caste Systems," Unpub. Manuscript (University of Chicago, 1973); also Ronald B. Inden, "Exchange, Sacrifice and Hierarchy in Early India," Mimeo. (University of Chicago, 1969) For further discussions of this basic position, see Susan Wadley, "Power in the Conceptual Structure of Karimpur Religion" (Ph.D., diss. Univ. of Chicago, 1973); also Brenda E.F. Beck, *Peasant Society in Konku* (Vancouver, 1973).

9. For illustrations of the importance of temple-building to caste status enhancement, see Burton Stein, "The Economic Function of a Medieval South Indian Temple," *Journal of Asian Studies* 19 (February 1960): 163–73; also Hiteshranjan Sanyal, "Social Aspects of Temple Building in Bengal: 1600 to 1900 A.D.," *Man in India* 48 (1968): 201–19.

10. Ibid., pp. 215–17.

11. For a description of this particular case, see Robert L. Hardgrave, *The Nadars of Tamil Nad* (Berkeley, 1969).

12. Irawati Karve, *Hindu Society: An Interpretation* (Poona, 1961), pp. 43–44.

13. Henry Orenstein, *Gaon: Conflict and Cohesion in an Indian Village* (Princeton, 1965), pp. 145, 159; also Henry Orenstein, "Caste and the Concept of 'Maratha' in Maharashtra," *The Eastern Anthropologist* 16 (1963): 6–7.

14. Bailey, *Caste and the Economic Frontier*, pp. 186–98.

15. Nirmal Kumar Bose, "Some Aspects of Caste in Bengai," *Man in India* 38 (1958): 86–87.

16. M.N. Srinivas, "The Social System of a Mysore Village," in McKim Marriott, ed., *Village India* (Chicago, 1955), pp. 1–35; also T. Scarlett Epstein, *Economic Development and Social Change in South India* (Manchester, 1962), pp. 162, 294.

17. M.S.A. Rao, "Caste and the Indian Army," *Economic Weekly* 16 (1964): 1439–43; also David G. Mandelbaum, *Society in India*, vol. 2, *Change and Continuity* (Berkeley, 1970), pp. 442–45.

18. M.N. Srinivas, *Religion and Society Among the Coorgs of South India* (Oxford, 1952), p. 33.

19. A.M. Shah, and R.G. Shroff, "The Vahāvānca Bārots of Gujarat: A Caste of Genealogists and Mythographers," *Journal of American Folklore* 71 (1958): 264–68.

20. David F. Pocock, "The Hypergamy of the Patidars," in K.M. Kapadia, ed., *Professor Ghurye Felicitation Volume* (Bombay, 1954), pp. 195–204.

21. Ralph W. Nicholas, and Tarashish Mukhopadhyay, "Politics and Law in Two West Bengal Villages," *Bulletin of the Anthropological Survey of India* 11 (1962): 19.

22. Andre Beteille, *Caste, Class and Power* (Berkeley, 1965), pp. 87ff.

23. Bose, "Some Aspects of Caste in Bengal," pp. 87–88.

24. See, for example, Srinivas' description of the Coorgs, or Nicholas' and Mukhopadhyay's description of the Mahisyas.

25. See William L. Rowe, "The New Cauhāns: A Caste Mobility Movement in North India," in James Silverberg, ed., *Social Mobility in the Caste System in India: An Interdisciplinary Symposium* (The Hague, 1968), pp. 66–77; and D.P. Sinha, "Caste Dynamics: A Case from Uttar Pradesh," *Man in India* 40 (1960): 19–29. The following discussion is based entirely on these two accounts.

26. Rowe, "The New Cauhāns," p. 71.

27. See ibid., *n.* 15, p. 73.

28. One hundred and twenty pounds of caste petitions were received by one census official in 1911 (ibid., p. 67); 128 claims to twice-born status came from four census regions in the 1931 census (M.N. Srinivas, *Social Change in Modern India* [Berkeley, 1966], p. 99); and William Rowe saw a shelf of "caste histories" in the 1950s (Rowe, "The New Cauhāns," *n.* 15, p. 73).

29. Karve, *Hindu Society*, pp. 43–44.

30. Beteille, *Caste, Class and Power*, pp. 72–79.

31. Y.B. Damle, "Reference Group Theory with Regard to Mobility in Caste," in Silverberg, ed., *Social Mobility in the Caste System in India*, p. 99.

32. For related discussions, see Rowe, "The New Cauhāns," p. 77; also McKim Marriott, "Multiple Reference in Indian Caste Systems," in Silverberg, ed., *Social Mobility in the Caste System*, pp. 103–114; also Mandelbaum, *Change and Continuity*, pp. 480–82.

An Account of the Failure of Agrarian Reforms and the Growth of Agrarian Tensions in Bihar: 1949-1970*

F. TOMASSON JANNUZI

THE COMMITMENT TO AGRARIAN REFORMS

AMONG the goals enunciated by the Congress movement in India prior to the achievement of independence from the United Kingdom was that of comprehensive agrarian reforms.[1] It was easier then, as now, for the various interest groups within the Congress coalition to reach apparent consensus on the need for such reforms than it was for them to make explicit the meaning of "agrarian reforms." It was not until 1936 that the Congress party as a whole produced an election Manifesto which included a statement advocating "a reform of the system of land tenure and revenue and rent, and an equitable adjustment of the burden on agricultural land, giving immediate relief to the smaller peasantry by a substantial reduction of agricultural rent and revenue now paid by them and exempting uneconomic holdings from payment of rent and revenue."[2] Subsequently, following the 1937 elections, when the Congress established its first ministries, the party encouraged the introduction of agrarian reform legislation.

Yet, power within the Congress, especially in a state such as Bihar, remained in the hands of landholders who were not prepared to commit themselves to farreaching agrarian reforms. In Bihar, proponents of radical reforms were resisted within the Congress until the content of proposed reform legislation was diluted. In a fashion that was to become typical of the Congress, a means was found to preserve the fragile unity of the party by permitting the language of radical economic and social change to be incorporated into its policy resolutions, while assuring that no action would be taken which would unduly upset conservative landed and industrial interests within the party. Even after independence was achieved, radical language on land policy, followed by conservative action, became standard practice within the Congress throughout India, and especially in Bihar.

Successive documents of government have referred to agrarian reforms as necessary to assure favorable conditions for increases in agricultural production within an environment of social justice. Successive leaders of the ruling Congress party have employed the language of agrarian reform in

*Some of the material in this chapter has also appeared in the author's *Agrarian Crisis in India: The Case of Bihar* (Austin, Tex., 1974).

parliamentary debates and when confronting appropriate sections of the electorate. There have been periodic directives from New Delhi to the states both to legislate and implement reforms consistent with the "Directive Principles of State Policy" within *The Constitution of India*. The states have been advised repeatedly to assure "that the ownership and control of the material resources of the community are so distributed as best to subserve the common good..." and "that the operation of the economic system does not result in the concentration of wealth and means of production to the common detriment."[3] However, the Central Government has found itself lacking in effective power to make certain that legislated reforms were consistent with such "Directive Principles of State Policy" and, if so, could be implemented within the political context in which decision-making takes place in the Indian states. Thus, a gulf exists in the 1970s between reforms that have been verbalized and those that have been implemented in the constituent states of the Republic.

In this essay I shall explore the post-independence history of agrarian reforms in the state of Bihar. Bihar (with one-tenth of the people of India within her borders) assumes special significance because it was the first state to initiate agrarian reforms through the enactment of legislation to abolish the zamindari system, and possibly the least successful of all in implementing that and other agrarian reforms. Nowhere in contemporary India is the gulf between articulated ideals with respect to agrarian reforms and solid accomplishment more conspicuous than in Bihar.

In retrospect, it is not surprising that agrarian reforms have been so unsuccessful in Bihar. What is surprising in the Bihar context is that any agrarian reforms were even legislated. The obstacles to the enactment and implementation of such reforms were formidable from the beginning. First, such reforms could not be forced by the Central Government, even if New Delhi had been at all times fully committed to the swift implementation of meaningful agrarian reforms. Under the Constitution, the Government of Bihar, rather than the Central Government, has had the primary authority and responsibility for enacting and implementing agrarian reforms. Second, the Government of Bihar has been either comprised of or strongly influenced by shifting political coalitions of landholding castes (notably Brahmans, Bhumihars, and Rajputs) who have had little incentive to pursue reforms that might have the effect of limiting their own rights and prerogatives. Third, Bihar's civil servants, whether committed in principle to agrarian reforms or not, were faced with the difficult task of having to deal with theoretical or actual questions of agrarian reforms without sufficient up-to-date records concerning rights in land. Without such land records, it is doubtful whether agrarian reforms in Bihar could have been implemented expeditiously and fairly, even had they been framed by a state legislature committed absolutely to the transformation of Bihar's agrarian structure. Fourth, despite some history of peasant movements in Bihar, there was no rural constituency in post-independence Bihar pressing for specific agrarian reforms. Indeed, it is reasonable to suggest that the majority of Bihar's peasants, particularly the landless laborers and sharecroppers, were in no position to conceptualize agrarian reforms, let alone to agitate for them.

That any agrarian reforms were enacted, if not fully implemented, was probably the result of a peculiar combination of factors, among them the following. (1) It was fashionable during the first years of independence to confuse radical sounding words (e.g., "zamindari abolition") enacted into law with revolutionary deeds. In such a climate, even opponents of agrarian reforms could sometimes support the language of reform, while inserting sufficient loopholes in such legislation as was enacted to minimize change in the traditional agrarian structure. (2) Some agrarian reforms had been legislated during the British period in Bihar. Those reforms had not effectively restrained the powers of landholders. In the post-independence period, many powerful landholders in Bihar could acquiesce to agrarian reforms so long as they were assured that the reforms would be conservative accretions to British legal precedent. In this fashion there could be compliance with the Central Government's articulated concern for agrarian reforms within a framework of law under which the rights and prerogatives of the landed elites had traditionally been preserved. (3) It is also possible, though highly speculative, that a substantial number of Congress party members were prepared to legislate some agrarian reforms in the anticipation that, under a system of universal adult franchise, rural voters would someday matter. (4) Finally, the enactment of agrarian reforms in Bihar owes much to the political astuteness of one man, K.B. Sahay, the former Revenue Minister and Chief Minister of the Government of Bihar. His influence was critical to the enactment of post-independence legislation for agrarian reforms in Bihar.

Whatever the record of opposition and support for agrarian reforms, some reforms were enacted into law. However, for a variety of reasons they failed to transform the pre-reform agrarian structure of Bihar. Generally, the rights of Bihar's traditional landholders have been preserved or enhanced at the expense of the peasantry. The reforms have not: led to redistribution of land resources in a manner favoring the cultivating peasantry; provided more secure rights in land to the actual cultivators in rural Bihar; reduced the number of landless agricultural laborers in Bihar; enhanced the prospects of an agricultural production revolution in contemporary Bihar. Nor have the reforms contributed to a lessening of tensions between the landholding elites and the peasants.

Nowhere in India is there a greater gulf separating the landholding elites and the masses of the peasantry than in Bihar. Yet, official reports which detail progress in the implementation of agrarian reforms[4] tell us little about existing relationships of men to land or between various land-holding classes and the tillers of the soil. Such reports give little indication of the degree to which existing laws governing the relationship of men to the land have been bent and abused in calculated attempts by Bihar's land-holding elites to retain control over the land and to deny new rights in land to those below them in the rural hierarchy. Finally, such reports give little documentation to the growing tension in rural areas between haves and have-nots: tension which has resulted in part from the permeation of the countryside with the promises of agrarian reforms followed by the nonfulfillment of those promises, and which has led in recent years, particularly in 1970, to sometimes violent confrontations between organized groups of peasants attempting to seize land and landholders.

In succeeding pages I shall:

1) examine the legislative content of selected post-independence agrarian reforms enacted in Bihar;

2) provide some indication of the degree to which official protestations of commitment to agrarian reforms in Bihar have not been translated into meaningful reforms; and

3) provide insight into the traditional and changing relationships between the landholding elites of Bihar and the peasantry who have been so long subservient to them.

LEGISLATIVE ATTEMPTS TO ABOLISH INTERMEDIARY INTERESTS IN BIHAR
History

My analysis of the evolution of Bihar's land system through successive periods of Indian history from the ancient to the modern suggests certain persistent themes, among them the following: (a) that through successive kingdoms and empires, the ruling authority exercised its power to extract a share of the produce of the soil;[5] (b) that the claim to a share of the produce was frequently and progressively separated from direct performance of agricultural labor; and (c) that layers of "intermediary" claims (to land and a share of the produce) were established over the centuries between the actual tiller and the ruling authority.

While these themes can be said to apply in some respects to India as a whole, they are particularly relevant to the situation prevailing in Permanent Settlement regions, such as Bihar. The Permanent Settlement, established by the British in 1793, was made applicable to parts of Bengal, Bihar, Orissa, and North Madras. The Settlement was the East India Company's attempt to assume the "ultimate landlord's" claim to a share of the produce from the land, while conferring, formally, certain subordinate claims to zamindars of the period. These zamindars were in no sense "owners" of land, but had been receiving a share of the produce from a defined land area while collecting revenue due to Mughal authorities in the pre-British period. The Permanent Settlement gave these zamindars authority in perpetuity to collect "rent" from lands considered to be under their control with the understanding that a fixed amount in cash would be transferred by them to the Company and, later, to the British Government of India. The zamindars were given complete authority to make their own terms with their "tenants," the actual cultivators, the rights to land of such cultivators being entirely ignored by the Settlement.

In this fashion, the British perpetuated and further institutionalized a system of land tenure having many negative consequences. In regions such as Bihar, the actual cultivators were compelled to continue to share their produce with an essentially parasitic class of noncultivating intermediaries. Under British rule, little was accomplished (particularly in areas in which the Permanent Settlement applied) to prevent zamindars from demanding increasingly higher shares of the produce from their tenants or share-croppers; also little was accomplished to prevent the eviction from the land of tenants who displeased the zamindar for one reason or another. Yet, the abuses of the system were increasingly recognized by the British and repeated attempts were made (largely through the enactment of virtually unenforcable legislation during the latter part of the nineteenth century) to provide some security of tenure for certain classes of cultivators and to prevent the progressive transfer of claims to and/or rights in land to non-cultivating classes. These legislative attempts to protect the cultivator were of limited value. They addressed some obvious problems, but did not deal with the question of modifying the prevailing land system. As Vera Anstey once observed, the British Government of India "has invariably and neces-sarily aimed at maintaining and interpreting justly the traditional land systems, radical reforms being politically impossible."[6]

I would argue:

Whether radical reforms were politically impossible during the British period is open to question. From one perspective, it would not have been an act of political wisdom for the British to restructure Indian land systems in a fashion that would alienate the zamindari classes. To have done so in the regions covered by the Permanent Settlement would have been to break a commitment to rent collecting intermediaries and to jeopardize the collection of the state's land revenue. And land revenue was for the British Raj (as it had been in the past for others who held the ultimate right to land) a chief source of income for many years. Given such a perspective, an explanation of the absence of radical reforms in Indian land systems during the British period would not rest with the impossibility of such reforms, but instead would suggest greater British concern for the reliable collection of land revenue than for improvement of the well-being of the cultivating peasantry.[7]

In any event, the agrarian structure in Bihar at the time of Indian inde-pendence was an intricately stratified system of relationships of people to land. In the Permanent Settlement areas of the state especially, there were numerous kinds of landholdings. At the apex of the hierarchy was the state. Below the state were the zamindars, "tenure-holders," and "under-tenure-holders" (i.e., those who had rent-collecting powers). At the base were the peasants with very limited rights, privileges, or authority in relation to land and the landless laborers, wage laborers with no rights, privileges or authority in land.[8] The hierarchy of interests in land existing in rural Bihar when India achieved independence is shown in Figure 1. The figure is represen-

tative only of the stratification of interests in land; there were many unusual relationships which existed according to local custom. Moreover,
many with interests in land combined roles, functioning simultaneously, for
example, as tenure-holder (i.e., rent collector) over a portion of a holding
and as a ryot (i.e., rent payer) over another portion. In practice the distinction between a tenure-holder and a ryot was often hard to draw. Some
clarification was provided by a provision in the Bihar Tenancy Act of 1885
that local custom would be a determinant in defining the nature of a
tenancy.[9] There was the stipulation, also, that where a ryot held more than
one hundred bigahs (62.5 acres), he would be presumed to be a tenure-
holder until the contrary had been shown.[10]

FIGURE 1
HIERARCHY OF INTERESTS IN LAND IN BIHAR IN 1950

The
State of Bihar
(the "super-landlord")

The Zamindar (legally, a "proprietor," but act- ing as an intermediary of the state in the collection of rent from tenants)	The Tenure-holder[a] (acting as an intermediary of the state in the collection of rent from tenants)
The Occupancy Ryot[b] (a rent-paying holder of land having the right of occupancy on the land held by him)	The Nonoccupancy Ryot (a rent-paying holder of land not having the right of occu- pancy on land temporarily in his possession)

The Under-Ryot
(a rent-paying holder of land having temporary possession of a holding
under a ryot)

The Muzdur
(a wage laborer having no rights in land)

a"Tenure-holder" means "primarily a person who has acquired from a proprietor or
from another tenure holder a right to hold land for the purpose of collecting rents or
bringing it under cultivation by establishing tenants on it, and includes also the successors-
in-interest of person who have acquired such a right." Bihar Tenancy Act of 1885 as
reprinted in Government of India, Ministry of Food and Agriculture, *Agricultural Legislation in India,* vol. 6, *Land Reforms* (Delhi, 1955), p. 34.
bRyot is legally defined as "primarily a person who has acquired from a proprietor
or from another tenure-holder a right to hold land for the purpose of cultivating it by
himself, or by members of his family or by hired servants or with the aid of partners, and
includes also the successors-in-interest of persons who have acquired such a right." Ibid.

Bihar Land Reforms Act, 1950

Whatever the motivations of those who failed to promote radical reforms during the British period, many Indian nationalists placed agrarian reforms high on the post-independence agenda. And, among such reforms, none seemed more important in Bihar and Bengal than the abrogation of the British-instituted Permanent Settlement. It was customary to argue that the Permanent Settlement had helped to create a class of noncultivating, absentee landlords (intermediaries between the cultivators and the state) and had contributed to the impoverishment of the actual tillers of the soil. If one accepted this view, then it followed that the whole system of intermediary interests would have to be abolished so as to provide an end to the exploitation of the peasantry by various kinds of intermediaries, among them the zamindars. Thus, "zamindari abolition" became an enunciated goal of the Congress, and in Bihar the terms "zamindari abolition" and "agrarian reforms" were used interchangeably to allude to the need to transform the traditional agrarian structure.

Much debate and controversy preceded the enactment of what was proclaimed by some as the first "land reform"[11] legislation in Bihar. Bihar's zamindars and tenure-holders[12] used every means at their disposal to prevent the enactment of any legislation which threatened to alter the traditional system of rights in land. They successfully challenged certain provisions in the first bill—Bihar Abolition of Zamindari Bill of 1947—to abolish the zamindari system of land tenure and to replace it with a ryotwari system.[13] They maneuvered in the courts to achieve an injunction restraining the state government from implementing the first Act to abolish the zamindari system—Bihar Abolition of Zamindari Act of 1948—and they lobbied in the state legislature to assure the repeal of that legislation. They returned to the courts to argue that new legislation, the Bihar Land Reforms Act of 1950, contravened a provision of the Constitution of India guaranteeing all people equal protection of the laws. They fought against the passage by the legislature of the Central Government of the First Amendment to the Indian Constitution, an amendment which would validate the Bihar Land Reforms Act of 1950. They even challenged the constitutionality of that amendment in a suit brought before the Supreme Court. However, the Supreme Court upheld the constitutionality of the First Amendment and, in 1952, the Court ruled that the Bihar Land Reforms Act of 1950 was valid under the Constitution as amended. Five years had elapsed since legislation had first been introduced in Bihar to abolish the zamindari system of land tenure. This fact alone was possibly more significant than the legal vindication of those who had promoted the original zamindari abolition bill. The record would later confirm that the zamindars and other intermediaries had used their time effectively, not only to delay implementation of any legislation which might alter the state's land system, but also to minimize the eventual impact of such legislation by exploiting in advance loopholes in the law.

The 1952 action of the Supreme Court finally made operative the main provisions of the Bihar Land Reforms Act of 1950. That Act legally abolished the interests[14] of zamindars and tenure-holders and vested these interests in the state. In so doing, the Act abrogated the Permanent Settlement of 1793 as well as such settlements of temporary duration as had existed in Bihar. By vesting the intermediaries' interests in the state, the Act provided for what is, substantially, a ryotwari system. That is to say, by vesting the intermediaries' interests in the state, the Act re-established the state's position not only as "ultimate landlord," but also as the direct, revenue-collecting agent.[15] By means of the 1950 Act, even as later amended, the State of Bihar holds exclusive proprietary interest in land, notwithstanding provisions permitting former intermediaries to retain certain "revenue-free" lands.

By placing the state in a direct relationship with its ryots and assuring the state an exclusive right to revenue derived from lands vested in it, the Act of 1950 provided for an eventual increase in state income from the land (following the replacement of the intermediary system of revenue collectors by an expanded administrative service to collect revenue and fix the revenue demand on holdings for which no records, or only out-of-date records, existed).[16]

Because the Act seemed to curtail the extractive powers of the intermediary classes, it was hoped by some that the new legislation would provide agricultural production incentives for certain classifications of ryots whose initiatives previously were thought to have been curtailed by intermediaries. Yet, there is little indication that Bihar's legislators gave serious consideration to any agricultural production implications of the Act of 1950; nor did they take steps through supplemental legislation to provide agricultural extension services to ryots in order to induce them to modify traditional agricultural practices and to assume the risks of innovation. The Act of 1950 was not associated with an explicit or implicit strategy for agricultural development. Indeed, responsibility for its implementation was assigned to the Revenue Department, rather than to the Department of Agriculture or any other division of government interested in the transformation of agricultural practices in Bihar.

If one studies the legislation itself, quite apart from questions of implementation, the inescapable conclusion is that the Land Reforms Act of 1950 mainly reflects the long struggle and many compromises which were necessary to assure its enactment. The Act is filled with escape clauses and loopholes sufficient to assure the nominal acquiescence of the intermediaries to its implementation. It is an Act which supports minimum change in the agrarian structure of Bihar—a structure dominated both before and after the Act of 1950 by those landholding elites who have traditionally enjoyed superior rights in land.

Whatever the strengths and weaknesses of the provisions of the Bihar Land Reforms Act of 1950, by May of 1952 the Government of Bihar still lacked data essential to the Act's implementation. The latest records of rights in land were thirty years old, and the most obsolete were over fifty years old. Revisional Survey and Settlement operations (which involve cadastral surveys and the checking of village records by Revenue officers) would take time,[17] as would the development of administrative machinery within the Revenue Department capable of coping with added responsibilities—the collection of revenue without the aid of intermediaries, as well as the creation of up-to-date land records. Moreover, the problems of implementation of the Act of 1950 were made even more complex by the failure of intermediaries to provide the government with copies of their personal "estate records."[18]

Given these circumstances, the first phase of the abolition of intermediary interests in Bihar (May through September 1952) affected only 155 zamindars,[19] intermediaries whose gross annual incomes from their estates had been in excess of Rs. 50,000.

Bihar Land Reforms Act, 1950—Amendment

Implementation of the Bihar Land Reforms Act of 1950 continued to proceed slowly until 1954 when the Bihar Land Reforms (Amendment) Bill of 1953 (Bihar Act XX of 1954) removed some of the procedural impediments to more expeditious implementation of the 1950 Act. Whereas the original Act provided for individual notification of "proprietors" or "tenureholders" that their estates had been vested in the state, the 1954 amendment Act made possible the general notification of all intermediaries.[20] Instead of proceeding to "abolish" several hundred thousand intermediary interests in laborious fashion through individual notification, the state was now empowered to publish a proclamation signaling its intention to take over within a specified time all intermediary interests located in any region of the state, or indeed all such interests in the state as a whole.[21]

In an attempt to assure that the intermediaries relinquished documents relating to their estates to the appropriate officials of the government, the amendment Act provided for penalties to be imposed on those failing to do so. The District Collector, for example, was empowered to levy fines—up to Rs. 500—on intermediaries who, following the general notification regarding the vesting of their estates, did not submit the necessary information regarding their holdings.[22]

The amendment Act also tightened provisions governing the intermediaries right to transfer and lease lands held by them prior to zamindari abolition legislation. Where, after the 1st day of January 1946, zamindars were considered to have taken anticipatory action to circumvent the provisions of the Bihar Land Reforms Act of 1950 by transferring or fragmenting their interests for the purpose of defeating any provision of the Act or causing loss to the state, the transactions could be annulled by the District Collector (after suitable investigation).[23]

Similarly, the Collector was empowered to inquire into cases in which zamindars reduced or remitted rents on their holdings with a view toward denying the state of Bihar its full share of land revenue. And, if the Collector found that reductions or remissions of rent had been made to limit the effectiveness of subsequent legislation, he could cancel these and order restoration of the rents at their original rates.[24]

With the authority of the 1954 amendment Act, some sections of the Bihar Land Reforms Act of 1950 were soon implemented, though it would be difficult for anyone other than a zamindar to suggest that the government moved precipitately at any stage during the long process leading to what is commonly—if somewhat incorrectly—referred to as the abolition of zamindari interests. In any event, the amendment Act of 1954 made possible the general notification by which the remaining intermediary interests in Bihar were taken over, legally, on the 1st of January 1956. Yet, much remained to be done in the face of inadequate land records, rent rolls, etc., to assure meaningful administration of the Bihar Land Reforms Act of 1950 as amended. There continued to be strong opposition from the zamindars to all measures of agrarian reform in Bihar and steps continued to be taken by them to impede implementation of the enacted legislation.

Bihar Land Reforms Act, 1950—Amendment

Within a few years another amendment Act, Bihar Act XVI of 1959, was passed and received the assent of the President of India. This amendment Act made further attempts to clarify the meaning of the original Act and, belatedly, to eliminate loopholes which were impeding implementation of the 1950 Act. The 1959 amendment Act was another episode in the continuing struggle between the state, acting as the super-landlord to protect its interests, and the erstwhile landlords or intermediaries, whose interests had been assumed by the state. As such, the amendment Act of 1959 continued to focus on the primary interests (land revenue and compensation) of the principal antagonists, rather than on the interests of the peasantry having a direct cultivating interest in the land. Nowhere in any of this "land reform" legislation were the interests of the landless laborers or bataidars (share-croppers) considered. Such was never the intent of the Act of 1950, or of the amending Acts of 1954 and 1959.

Intermediaries' Interests as Affected by the Amended Act of 1950

It is sometimes suggested that (through the vesting of all intermediary interests in the state) the zamindars and tenure-holders of Bihar lost all rights in land. Such is not the case. Though the state assumed the right to collect rent directly from its tenants, rather than indirectly through intermediaries, and also took over the interests of intermediaries in trees, forests, fisheries, minerals, mines, bazaars, etc., and any buildings of an estate used, primarily, for rent collection purposes,[25] Sections 5, 6, and 7 of the Bihar Land Reforms Act of 1950 specifically provided for the retention by intermediaries of certain interests. These sections have not been altered in substance in the amendment Acts of 1954 and 1959. The following are excerpts from these important sections of the Act as amended.

Section 5. (1) With effect from the date of vesting, all homesteads[26] comprised in an estate or tenure and being in possession of an intermediary on the date of such vesting shall be deemed to be settled by the State with such intermediary and he shall be entitled to retain possession of the land comprised in such homesteads and to hold it as a tenant under the State free of rent: Provided that such homesteads as are used by the intermediary for purposes of letting out on rent shall be subject to the payment of such fair and equitable ground-rent as may be determined by the Collector in the prescribed manner. (2) If the claim of an intermediary as to his possession over such homesteads or as to the extent of such homesteads is disputed by any person within three months from the date of such vesting, the Collector shall, on application, make such inquiry into the matter as he deems fit and pass such order as may appear to him to be just and proper.

Section 6. (1) On and from the date of vesting, all lands used for agricultural or horticultural purposes, which were in *khas*[27] possession of an intermediary on the date of such vesting, shall be deemed to be settled by the State with such intermediary and he shall be entitled to retain possession thereof and hold them as a *raiyat* under the State having occupancy rights in respect of such lands subject to the payment of such fair and equitable rent as may be determined by the Collector in the prescribed manner: Provided that nothing contained in this sub-section shall entitle an intermediary to retain possession of any land in respect of which occupancy right has already accrued to a *raiyat* before the date of vesting. (2) If the claim of an intermediary as to his *khas* possession over lands referred to in sub-section (1) or as to the extent of such lands is disputed by any person prior to the determination of rent of such lands under the said sub-section, the Collector shall, on application, make such inquiry into the matter as he deems fit and pass such order as may appear to him to be just and proper.

Section 7. (1) Such buildings or structures together with the lands on which they stand, other than any buildings used primarily as offices [for the collection of rent][28] as were in the possession of an intermediary at the commencement of this Act and used as golas,[29] factories or mills, for the purpose of trade, manufacture or commerce or used for storing grains or keeping cattle or implements for the purpose of agriculture and constructed or established and used for the aforesaid purposes before the 1st of January, 1946, shall, notwithstanding anything contained in this Act, be deemed to be settled by the State with such intermediary and he shall be entitled to retain possession of such buildings or structures together with the lands on which they stand as a tenant under the State subject to the payment of such fair and equitable ground-rent as may be determined by the Collector in the prescribed manner. (2) If the claim of such intermediary as to the possession over such buildings or structures, or lands on which they stand or as to the extent of such buildings, structures or lands is disputed by any person within three months from the date of vesting, the Collector shall make such order as may appear to him to be just and proper. (3) Where a building or structure, constructed by an intermediary in his estate or tenure after the first day of January, 1946, is used for the purposes mentioned in sub-section (1), the intermediary shall be entitled to retain the possession of such building or structure together with the land on which it stands as a tenant under the State subject to the payment of the rent if and only if the State Government is satisfied that such building or structure was not constructed or used for the aforesaid purposes with the object of defeating any provisions of this Act.

The key words in these "saving" sections of the Land Reforms Act of 1950 were "khas possession" and "homestead." Note that the term "khas possession" was made applicable not only to lands cultivated personally by the intermediary, but also to lands cultivated by his servants, or hired labor with their stock. This broad definition of possession allowed the former intermediary to claim rights in land which he had not previously cultivated—even when that land had remained continuously in the cultivating possession of a ryot, so long as the ryot did not possess the means (monetary or documentary) of establishing his right of occupancy. The former intermediaries were adroit in exploiting the khas possession provision of the Act. They not only used this provision to evict, legally, their former tenants from lands traditionally cultivated by those tenants, but also attempted to modify the meaning of khas possession so that the phrase might serve to justify adding acreage to the sizeable landholdings that the former intermediaries hoped to maintain, within the law, following zamindari abolition.

The intermediaries' attempt to enlarge the definition of khas possession received support, initially, from the Patna High Court. That court ruled that the phrase khas possession was broad enough to include what was referred to as "constructive possession" of land. This interpretation would have further expanded the right of the intermediary to recover possession of lands which had been in the actual possession of a ryot on the date when the intermediary's estate had been vested in the state. Eventually, however, the Supreme Court overruled the "constructive possession" interpretation of the Patna High Court.[30] This fact notwithstanding, the original khas possession provision has continued to make possible the legal eviction of uncounted thousands of ryots in Bihar who cannot prove that they possess an occupancy right to the lands they have customarily tilled.

In general, the peasants have been in no position to justify their claims to land by entering into litigation with the former intermediaries. Who would support the claims of former tenants in a legal confrontation with the traditional, landholding elites? Which records could be cited to confirm a tenant's rights in land? Who would finance necessary litigation? Unorganized politically, subservient to those above them in the rural hierarchy, lacking in support from any source, the peasants have tended to avoid unequal competition with former intermediaries in civil courts.[31] As a result, former intermediaries have been free to contend publicly that their former tenants had enjoyed no rights in land and had previously performed agricultural functions only as "personal servants" or as "hired laborers."

In this fashion, the landholding elites continued to maintain their superior priveleges in land and the prerogatives of power derived in part from control of the land. Former tenants often continued to till the same lands they had worked prior to 1950, but with their claims to land becoming even more tenuous with the passage of time as they accepted their de facto positions as personal servants or hired laborers performing agricultural operations on lands in the khas possession of former intermediaries.

In much the same fashion, the "homestead" provision of the Act has served the interests of the former intermediaries. Note that homesteads could be retained rent free by former intermediaries if the homesteads and the lands integral to them were used as private residences. And, in the event that a former intermediary decided not to occupy his homestead, he could rent it to someone else within the terms of the law—so long as he remembered to pay "fair and equitable ground-rent" himself to the state.[32] What constituted "fair and equitable ground-rent" was, in practice, a matter to be "negotiated" between the former intermediary and the District Collector. Not infrequently, the Collector could be persuaded to set the ground-rent at a level considered reasonable by the former intermediary.

To summarize, the saving provisions of the Act (a) allowed the former intermediary to retain certain portions of his original estate as an occupancy ryot (i.e., as a tenant of the state with occupancy rights), subject to the payment of rent to the state and (b) permitted the former intermediary to retain another portion of his estate rent free. The loose definitions of the terms "khas possession" and "homestead" have been fully utilized by the former intermediaries, permitting some of them to retain all of the lands they held prior to abolition, excepting only those lands for which an occupancy ryot had incontrovertible, documentary evidence in support of his claim. Consequently, it was possible, as recently as August of 1970, to find former intermediaries in possession of estates comprised of 5,000 acres or more. Some were held loosely within the terms and conditions of the Bihar Land Reforms Act of 1950, as amended, and in the absence of effective implementation of later laws limiting the size of holdings. Others were evidence of the capacity of some of the more powerful zamindars to circumvent the legislation.[33]

LEGISLATION TO LIMIT THE SIZE OF AGRICULTURAL HOLDINGS IN BIHAR

The principle that there should be an absolute limit to the amount of land which an individual might hold in India was commended in the First Five-Year Plan,[34] endorsed by official committees of government,[35] and made national policy. The Second Five-Year Plan not only proposed the introduction of ceilings on existing agricultural holdings, but also recommended ceilings on future acquisitions of land.

It remained for the various constituent units of the Republic in the 1950s and 1960s to respond to the Central Government initiative by framing and implementing ceiling legislation. With the states exercising final authority over the nature, extent, and timing of such legislation, the pattern of response varied enormously. There was no national consensus regarding the purposes of legislation to limit the size of agricultural holdings. Each state established its own definition of a maximum holding and its own regulations affecting the implementation of ceiling legislation. Some state governments proceeded, with a minimum of debate, to enact their laws. Others, such as the Government of Bihar, employed various means—procedural and legislative, as well as overtly political—to delay the enactment and implementation of any legislation which might alter the long-established agrarian structure of the state by eroding the power of the landed elite.

Provisions of the Bihar Land Reforms (Fixation of Ceiling Area and Acquisition of Surplus Land) *Act of 1961*

A ceiling bill was eventually framed in Bihar in 1955, referred to a select committee for modification, and then tabled. It was not until 1961 that a revised version of this bill was enacted into law. This new land reform legislation, known popularly as the ceilings Act of 1961, contained sufficient loopholes to satisfy the most militant opponent of the earlier draft legislation.

Bihar's ceilings Act of 1961 established a variable ceiling on landholdings to be based in each instance on an assessment of the quality of land in the possession of a landholder. Within the terms of reference of the Act, the agricultural lands of Bihar were considered to be of five classes, the finest lands being Class I and the worst Class V. Having thus classified the lands of the state, the Act of 1961 stipulated that a "person" would be permitted to retain possession of no more than (a) 20 acres of Class I land; (b) 30 acres of Class II land; (c) 40 acres of Class III land; (d) 50 acres of Class IV land; or (e) 60 acres of Class V land.

However, there were numerous supplementary provisions in the Act which were designed to permit a landholder to retain lands in excess of the ceilings stipulated above. For example, a landholder could retain, in addition to his ceiling area, lands forming part of his "homestead" not exceeding 10 acres in area. He could retain all established structures together with the lands on which they stood, and such other lands as might be considered by the appropriate local authority (in this instance the Collector) necessary for the use and enjoyment of his homestead lands. He could retain any land in consolidated blocks (not exceeding 15 acres in area) used for growing fodder at the time of the Act's commencement, and destined to be used for that purpose in future. Moreover, a landholder with more than four dependents could retain lands in excess of his ceiling area provided that the aggregate of lands held by him would in no case exceed two times his specified ceiling area.

Other provisions of the Act permitted a landholder to transfer (within one year following the commencement of the Act) any lands held by him as a ryot to any person or persons who might have inherited the land or have been entitled to a share of it at his death. In other words, either prior to the commencement of the Act or subsequent to it within a period of twelve months, a landholder with lands in excess of the ceiling could transfer his excess lands to sons, daughters, children of his sons or daughters, or others within the terms and conditions of the Act of 1961—the only limitation being that the aggregate of lands held by the recipients not exceed, in each instance, the ceiling specified by the Act. Within the framework of this provision, the Act permitted a landholder to retain within his "extended" family lands greatly in excess of his own ceiling area.

The Act of 1961 also contained provisions which permitted landholders to resume for "personal cultivation"[36] lands within their ceiling areas being cultivated at the commencement of the Act by tenants or under-ryots who were unable to establish that they were entitled to permanent occupancy of the lands they tilled. That is to say, any landholder who was himself an occupancy-ryot within the terms and conditions of the Bihar Tenancy Act of 1885 could legally eject any of his tenants who were nonoccupancy-ryots (as defined by the Bihar Tenancy Act of 1885) and therefore not entitled to permanent security of tenure. Moreover, having ejected his former tenants, he could satisfy the "personal cultivation" criterion fixed by law simply by having the same under-ryots continue to till the lands as hired laborers on fixed wages, rather than as tenants.

In addition to those provisions which permitted a landholder to resume lands for "personal cultivation," broadly defined to permit the use of hired laborers, the ceilings Act of 1961 permitted the landholder, under specified conditions, to sub-let any land within his ceiling area for a period not to exceed seven years on any occasion. It was made clear that no sub-lessee (or tenant) who tilled the lands of a ryot (whose lands were no more than those permitted by the ceilings legislation) could ever hope to acquire an occupancy right to such lands, irrespective of the duration of his tenancy. Furthermore, the Act made explicit provision for the ejectment of the sub-lessee by a landholder (a) for failure to pay an arrear of rent; (b) for using the land in a manner which rendered it unfit for the purposes of the tenancy; or (c) on the ground that the term of a lease had expired.

There were other provisions in the Act which were based on the assumption that substantial amounts of "surplus land" would accrue to the state when ceilings on the size of landholdings were fixed and implemented. Accordingly, procedures were set forth to facilitate the vesting of such surplus lands in the state of Bihar, it being implicit in the Act that these lands might someday be distributed among peasants having no rights in land.

The Act stipulated that such surplus lands as were occupied by under-ryots, when those lands were legally vested in the state, might be settled permanently with the under-ryots *if* they made formal application to achieve occupancy-ryot status and paid a prescribed amount to the state.

Methods of retaining control of lands in excess of the ceiling area were sometimes suggested by certain provisions of the Act of 1961. A landholder could claim that he had promised acreage to the *Bhoodan* (land gift) movement which should not be considered in fixing his ceiling—even if that acreage were nominally in his possession and the lands comprising it had not yet been distributed by Bhoodan authorities or formally registered in accordance with state law as Bhoodan land. If the landholder had a licensed sugarcane farm, he could apply for exemption from the ceiling provisions of the law. And, in the absence of up-to-date survey and settlement records in the state, each landholder, either by withholding information from authorities or influencing them when he had the power and wealth to do so, could delay the implementation of the ceilings legislation and limit its impact on him.

Assessment of the Bihar Land Reforms (Fixation of Ceiling Area and Acquisition of Surplus Land) Act of 1961

By establishing variable ceilings and allowing the landholder to resume lands from his tenants for "personal cultivation," the Act permitted the eviction of under-ryots or tenants from lands they had tilled for many years, sometimes for generations, without being accorded occupancy-ryot status. The landholder could select from his best quality lands the area he wished to retain within his ceiling; he could evict the tenants on those lands, reducing them in the process to the status of landless agricultural laborers; and he could, if necessary, give up poor quality lands in excess of the ceiling. Legal and extra-legal evictions of under-ryots were therefore an inevitable byproduct of the Act of 1961. Such evictions continued to be commonplace in Bihar throughout the 1960s, despite the fact that the Government of Bihar made no sustained effort to implement the ceilings Act.

Government's nonimplementation of the Act of 1961 was noteworthy throughout the 1960s. The Act came into force on the 19th of April 1962. By 1964 the state had taken only preliminary action to implement the law.[37] A small staff had been collected, consisting of one upper-division clerk for each district headquarters and one lower-division clerk for each sub-divisional headquarters, but no higher staff had been appointed. Sometime later the state began printing notices (required by the Act) asking each landholder in the state to submit returns relating to lands in his possession, but there is no evidence to suggest that these notices were actually issued until the summer of 1970 when roving bands of peasants, organized by various political parties, were seizing the lands of former intermediaries and other occupancy-ryots and posing a threat to the political stability of Bihar. Only then did government begin to take visible steps to implement its ceilings legislation, promising as it did so that hundreds of thousands of surpius acres would be quickly distributed to appease the land hunger among the peasants. Even so, the Act of 1961 is unlikely to be implemented fully for many years. The absence of up-to-date survey and settlement records alone limits the speed with which government can act to implement ceilings.

Meanwhile, in 1970, a situation persisted in Bihar in which: (1) thousands of landholders retained holdings in excess of the ceiling area, few steps having been taken to determine the size of their holdings; (2) tenants and under-ryots had either been evicted from their holdings or continued to till them in fear of imminent eviction; (3) no one in government knew how much surplus land would vest in the state and be available for distribution to landless agricultural laborers;[38] (4) no surplus lands had been made available for distribution as a direct result of ceilings legislation; and (5) no under-ryots had been recorded as ryots having a permanent occupancy right, as would have been possible had the Act been implemented.

It is an inescapable conclusion that the ceilings Act has served no constructive purpose thus far. Indeed, its enactment without implementation has permitted those who wish to circumvent the Act's provisions to do so, and with time to spare. Its enactment without implementation has helped to engender a climate of apprehension in the countryside among those under-ryots who fear eviction. Its enactment without implementation has raised expectations among the landless who, on the advice of representatives of political parties and others, anticipate receiving surplus lands which may prove eventually to be almost nonexistent.

In sum, the ceilings Act of 1961 has neither contributed to a more equitable distribution of existing land resources nor provided changes in the agrarian structure which can be considered conducive to increasing agricultural output. Enacted, but not implemented, the Bihar ceilings Act has nonetheless contributed to the sense of insecurity in rural Bihar as the haves and have-nots maneuver for control of rights in land.

We have now completed our survey of some of the highlights of agrarian reform legislation enacted in Bihar since 1947. This is by no means a comprehensive survey. We have chosen not to discuss the following legislation: (1) the Bihar Consolidation of Holdings and Prevention of Fragmentation Act, 1965; (2) the Bihar Tenancy (Amendment) Act, 1970; (3) the Bihar Public Land Encroachment (Amendment) Ordinance, 1970; (4) the Bihar Tenancy (Amendment) Bill, 1970; (5) the Bihar Land Reforms Amendment Bill, 1970; (6) the Bihar Consolidation of Holdings and Prevention of Fragmentation (Amendment) Bill, 1970; and (7) the Bihar Privileged Persons Homestead Tenancy (Amendment) Bill, 1970. However, none of this legislation, as enacted or proposed, has transformed the agrarian structure of Bihar or solved the problems which we have discussed at length in the context of the Bihar Land Reforms Act, 1950, as amended, and the ceilings Act of 1961.

THE GROWTH OF AGRARIAN TENSIONS IN BIHAR

Rural "Apathy" in the 1950s

In Bihar in the 1950s the force of tradition still governed relationships among unequals. Those who held land enjoyed the prerogatives of power and status that have accompanied control of that most primary of resources in agrarian societies. Those without land, those with tenuous rights in land, and those with holdings lacking in quality or size enjoyed few prerogatives—except in relationships with others of even lower social (caste) or economic (class) status. The structure of power in Bihar seemed to be immutable. The traditional society of the village had only begun to be disrupted and the pattern of life (while in many respects unacceptable to the alien observer) had been so regularized that the Bihar peasant seemed to accept as datum his position in the social and economic hierarchy. He was in no position to conceptualize a world in which change could occur in his social and economic condition. Lacking a basis for comparative judgment, he was prepared to accept his world as it was and as it seemed likely to remain for some time.

A sense of frustration among some peasants concerning the nature and quality of their existence was, no doubt, incipient, but barely discernible by scrutiny of peasant behavior. The peasant's condition was one of apparent apathy, as if he were devoid of feelings concerning the forces acting upon him.

Gradual Awakening of the Bihar Peasant

The years since the early 1950s have been ones in which there has been unprecedented penetration of Bihar's rural areas by outsiders acting in behalf of various institutions, both governmental and nongovernmental. Among governmental penetrations, there were the following.

(a) A rural community development program was established in 1952 when 16 development blocks were initiated.[39] This program was rapidly expanded during the following 12 years until a network of 587 blocks encompassed, at least nominally, all of Bihar's 67,665 villages.[40]

(b) An attempt was made to develop a viable set of cooperative institutions and, by 1965–66, the government claimed to have extended the coverage of primary cooperative credit societies to 85 percent of the villages and to 23 percent of the rural families in the state.[41]

(c) An effort was made to decentralize administration and decision-making associated with various developmental programs through the introduction of village self-government (panchayati raj) institutions in three Districts of the state, Ranchi, Bhagalpur, and Dhanbad. A State Directorate of panchayati raj was established, training centers for panchayat functionaries initiated, and legislation enacted in anticipation of the spread of panchayati raj institutions to all regions of the state.

(d) The decisions of the state to pass legislation designed to abolish the right of intermediaries to collect land revenue in behalf of government and to establish the state's own rent collection machinery meant that, from 1956–57 on, thousands of new employees were recruited and incorporated in state service. Many of those were placed in direct relationship with the peasantry.

(e) Finally, all instrumentalities of government having responsibility for any facet of rural development (for example, major and minor irrigation, power, flood control, rural electrification) greatly expanded their numbers of employees and posted many of them in the countryside.

Less sustained and comprehensive penetration of Bihar's rural areas was effected by various nongovernmental institutions, such as Bhoodan, and, particularly in 1966–67, by famine relief agencies, both Indian and foreign.

Added to these penetrations were those of the politicians, mainly at five-year intervals preceding general elections, and the mass media, especially radio with the advent of the transistor.

Whatever the successes or failures of such government programs as community development and panchayati raj, and whatever the penetrative significance of the work of political parties, the mass media, and non-governmental institutions, their cumulative effects have ended the historical isolation of Bihar's rural areas. This is not to suggest that the villages of Bihar, uniformly and without exception, have experienced change produced by the penetration of outsiders. As of 1970, thousands of villages no doubt remain relatively untouched by the programs and policies of external institutions, governmental and private. Tangible or physical change, the result of externally influenced social, political, or economic programs, may not be discernible in such villages. Nevertheless, substantial numbers of people in these villages have experienced the kind of contact with outsiders which contributes to awakening. That is to say, new expectations have been generated among the people, even by programs classified as failures when evaluated in conventional terms. Above all, perhaps, the effects of these programs have been to intrude into the villager's consciousness the concept of the legitimacy and possibility of change in the traditional mode of life. This concept has been endorsed and nurtured by the politician soliciting votes, by the second son who migrates to the city and returns to his village with new perspectives on the world outside, and by government servants charged with implementing development programs.

The source of the idea that change is both legitimate and possible is less important, of course, than its existence and persistent growth in recent years among rural Biharis. This profound attitudinal change has been set in motion in Bihar among people whose subservience to authority and malleability under pressure had been assumed to be constants by the ruling elite. The irony in this rural transformation is that the ruling elite (unwittingly in most instances) imposed the programs and transmitted the ideas which have contributed to the great awakening.

The general elections of 1967 provided striking evidence of the awakening of the peasantry of Bihar. The election results helped to confirm that the rural masses were no longer docile and lacking in capacity to think and act independently of their superiors in the rural and urban hierarchies. The shattering of Congress party dominance in that election showed the power of previously subordinated groups—often in direct confrontation with Bihar's traditional, high caste and landed elites. Symbolic of that breaking of the monopoly of power of the traditional elites has been the emergence of Chief Ministers in successive Bihar governments (in the period 1967–70) who have invariably been drawn from backward or scheduled castes, rather than from the landholding, high caste elites.

In the late 1960s the inarticulate were becoming articulate. Many villagers, landless and landholders alike, who earlier had referred to the immutability of their condition were prepared, in 1967, to cry out in protest against the circumstances which denied them the ability to provide the barest necessities for their children. Their expressions of frustration and anger were diffuse. Their ability either to assess blame or to identify as a scapegoat any individual, faction, or group was limited. Yet, they were in the process of repudiating a traditional life-style and it seemed only a matter of time before leadership would emerge to give focus to the newly articulated feelings.

In the period immediately before and after the general elections of 1967, incidents of agrarian unrest associated with what the Home Ministry called "the persistence of serious social and economic inequalities. . . ."[42] began to be reported with some frequency not only in Bihar but also in Assam, Andhra Pradesh, Gujarat, Kerala, Manipur, Orissa, Punjab, Rajasthan, Tamil Nadu (formerly Madras), Tripura, Uttar Pradesh, and West Bengal.[43] Among the cases of unrest reported in this period were many involving peasants in land occupation activities. In Bihar, in the period June through December 1967, roving bands of peasants had forcibly harvested standing crops in separate incidents in Purnea, Bhagalpur, Santhal Parganas, and Darbhanga districts. During January–February of 1968 in Champaran District, Bihar, 200 persons had attempted to encroach upon government lands. Also in 1968, there had been repeated demonstrations[44] in which landless peasants were said to have demanded land from officials of government.

Bihar Government's Reaction to Rural Unrest

In 1969, in response to Central Government pressures and the threat of continuing tension in rural areas, unprecedented attempts were made by Bihar state officials (and Central Government officials during a period of President's Rule) to implement existing agrarian reform legislation and to introduce new legislation conforming in broad outline to various recommendations made by the ruling faction of the Congress led by Indira Gandhi.

During the last months of 1969 and the first months of 1970, perhaps the most conspicuous activity in Bihar in the broad field of agrarian reforms occurred in the state legislature where numerous measures were introduced. That there should have been a flurry of attempts to introduce new land reform legislation in Bihar in 1969–70, following years of plodding implementation of existing legislation, cannot be interpreted simply as that state's almost immediate response to a new round of exhortation from New Delhi. Central Government exhortation had been tried frequently in the past and had been mainly ineffective in producing results at the state level. A more credible, if not complete, explanation for the timing of the introduction of new legislation is that Bihar's ruling "minority" (comprised generally, irrespective of party affiliation, of landed, urban-based and high caste communities) was responding symbolically to its instincts for self-preservation as it contemplated the gradual mobilization and politicization of a rural-based majority of economically depressed, backward, and scheduled castes. Fearing that the emerging majority would be led by dissident politicians prepared to exploit land hunger and other parochial issues for diverse purposes (including possibly the destruction of existing institutions and the men who had so long dominated them) the ruling elite acted swiftly to preempt the programs of the dissidents and to demonstrate their own "radical" and "socialist" credentials. From this perspective, the new legislative proposals can be seen as a rather desperate attempt to anticipate peasant demands by demonstrating that lawful changes in the agrarian structure might be effected by a genuinely responsive government before unlawful changes became a prevalent and accepted mode of addressing agrarian problems in Bihar.

Agrarian Tensions in Bihar in the Context of Government's Failure to Implement Agrarian Reforms

Neither the spate of agrarian reform legislation introduced in 1969–70 nor the government's promises that existing legislation would be implemented was effective in preventing land grab activity in July and August of 1970. The promises of government (together with its police power) did provide the basis for short-term political adjustments between the political elite and the organizers of land grab. However, the short-term truce is in large measure dependent on government's carrying out its program of reforms, and it is unlikely that these reforms can be implemented in the near future. The old obstacles to the implementation of agrarian reforms persist: (1) up-to-date land records are available for only a fraction of Bihar's territory and new records are being produced with something less than deliberate speed; (2) there is a dearth of trained personnel to execute the reforms, particularly at lower levels of the administrative hierarchy; (3) the administrative procedures which determine the manner in which the reforms can be implemented are archaic, fitted to conditions of the nineteenth century but not to those of the twentieth—even when manipulated by able and dedicated administrators; (4) those who oppose any change in Bihar's agrarian structure remain adept at exploiting existing loopholes in the law and at circumventing its provisions; (5) There is no consensus within government regarding the place and significance of agrarian reform measures in Bihar's general program for agricultural development. Indicative of this lack of consensus is the continuing administrative separation of agricultural production issues from agrarian reform issues in the Central Secretariat of Bihar. Dichotomous thinking on rural development is thus endorsed and nurtured. Agrarian reform, as an issue, stands divorced from agricultural development, however defined. In current government policy, agrarian reform is related vaguely to the reduction of agrarian tensions because it is supposed to address peasant demands, or at least the demands of certain political parties; agricultural development means simply the application of new technology (essentially "miracle" seeds, fertilizer, and water) in rural areas in a fashion thought to assure increases in production. The goal is to achieve increases in aggregate output. Who produces on what holdings and who benefits from any increases in output are questions to be set aside—or referred by those concerned with agricultural development to the Revenue Department, the unit primarily responsible for effecting agrarian reforms. (6) Finally, political consensus leading to the implementation of new agrarian reform measures is difficult to achieve, or maintain, among the diverse political parties which comprise the Government of Bihar. This was so in the era of Congress dominance prior to 1967 when factions vied for power under the "umbrella" of that party and it was so in 1970 at a time of eight-party coalition government in Bihar. Whereas caste and other factional struggles used to be carried on within the boundaries of the old Congress coalition, they are now carried on more obviously among the parties which support or buffet the Congress (R). In this atmosphere, it is difficult to discern much commitment to the implementation of the new (or old) reforms, except when one faction seeks political advantage over others by escalating its rhetorical commitment to radical agrarian reforms in the belief that such reforms are an increasingly significant (peasant mobilizing) issue in rural areas.

The immediate prospect in Bihar in the 1970s is for increasingly radical talk about the need for agrarian reforms, and little action in the field of implementation. Meanwhile, agrarian tensions will continue to build—and not only for reasons associated with the failure of government to implement its promised and legislated reforms.

Agrarian Tensions in Bihar in the Context of Social Change

In considering the growth of agrarian tensions in Bihar and discussing the failure of government to implement various measures of agrarian reform it is not our purpose to obscure other factors that have been instrumental in producing a climate of tension in rural areas.

For example, contemporary agrarian tensions are associated not only with the land hunger of the poor and the failure of agrarian reforms in Bihar to meet newly articulated peasant demands, but also with a less conspicuous struggle for power among competing elites and newly emerging groups. Given the structure of power that has so long prevailed in Bihar—a structure which has both perpetuated traditional inequalities in the social and economic system and fostered new inequities—it is easy to predict that issues such as distributive justice and land to the tiller will again become fashionable in the days ahead as the old elites and those who oppose them wrestle for effective control over the peasantry. The results of this competition cannot be anticipated at present, but of one thing we can be certain: the competition will further the process already in motion by which the masses are being politicized. The next decade may determine whether the peasantry of Bihar will be stabilized or destabilized as a political force. I am convinced that the peasantry are the critical group in Bihar as in all India today. Whoever controls the peasantry will control the future of India. Whether or not this is already obvious to those currently in power or seeking power in Bihar can be questioned. However, efforts on the part of leaders in the Central Government of India to identify their regime more closely with the plight of the peasantry are evident. The resurgent rhetoric of

Mrs. Gandhi's dominant faction of the Congress—including new promises to implement existing land reform laws and to check the rich, uplift the poor, and make the country more self-sufficient—can be seen as part of an effort both to identify with peasant interests and to respond to peasant demands.

NOTES

1. The phrase "agrarian reforms" is used in this paper to refer to a constellation of programs designed to effect structural changes in the agricultural sector. Thus used, "agrarian reforms" is a comprehensive term applying to "zamindari abolition," "ceilings" on landholdings, the "consolidation" of holdings, and any other programs introduced to modify rights in land in the agricultural sector. The term may have extended meaning, implying the removal of basic inequalities between landholders and weaker sections of the peasantry.

2. Jawaharlal Nehru, as quoted by W. Norman Brown, *The United States and India and Pakistan* (Cambridge, Mass., 1958), p. 228.

3. Government of India, *Constitution of India* (as modified up to October 1969), Article 39 (Delhi, 1970).

4. See, for example Government of India, Planning Commission, *Implementation of Land Reforms, A Review by the Land Reforms Implementation Committee of the National Development Council* (New Delhi, August 1966), p. 283.

5. The historical record regarding Indian land systems is variously interpreted. Some writers have contended that the ruler's claim to a share of the produce meant that he "owned" the land and the peasantry were his "tenants," paying a share of the produce in the form of "tax." Still others have argued that the juristic concept of "ownership" never existed in Indian history until the advent of British rule. The weight of evidence appears to rest with those who suggest (with Daniel Thorner) that no system of absolute ownership of land has existed in India. From this perspective, not even the British introduced private property in land. "To no holder was granted the exclusive right to occupy, enjoy and dispose of land which in practice, is the hallmark of Western private ownership" (Daniel Thorner, *The Agrarian Prospect in India* [Delhi, 1956], p. 7). While the British did introduce rights normally associated with "ownership" of private property (e.g., right of transfer, mortgageability and heritability), these were always subordinate to the rights of the state, acting as a "super-landlord" claiming a rent-share of produce from the actual cultivators of the soil, many of whom claimed a traditional right of occupancy to the lands they tilled. To this day, it can be argued that private property in agricultural land does not exist in India. This is the de facto situation in Bihar where "ultimate ownership" of land rests with the state following the enactment of various land reform measures.

6. Vera Anstey, *The Economic Development of India*, 4th ed. (London, 1957), p. 103.

7. F. Tomasson Jannuzi, "Land Reform in Bihar, India, The Agrarian Structure in Bihar," Agency for International Development, Spring Review on Land Reform, Country Paper 22 (Washington, D.C. 1970), pp. 8–11.

8. The numerous and complex relationships of people to land in rural Bihar are best enumerated in the tenancy acts which are applicable to the state: Bihar Tenancy Act of 1885, Santal Parganas Tenancy Acts of 1872, 1886, and 1949, and Chota Nagpur Tenancy Act of 1908. See Government of India, Ministry of Food and Agriculture, *Agricultural Legislation in India*, vol. 6, *Land Reforms* (Delhi, 1955), pp. 31–174.

9. Bihar Tenancy Act of 1885, ibid., p. 40.

10. Ibid.

11. "Land reform" is a phrase used to suggest changes in the distribution of landholdings. It is used narrowly in this paper to refer to changes in the agrarian structure which redistribute control of land resources.

12. "Zamindars and tenure-holders" comprise those classes holding intermediary interests between the state, which is the holder of the superior proprietary right, and the peasant.

13. A "ryotwari system" is one in which the state deals directly with the ryot, rather than through an intermediary. The ryot possesses a claim to his holding subject to the payment of land revenue to the government.

14. "Interests" refers to interests in land, including interests in trees, forests, fisheries, bazaars, mines, and minerals, etc. See Bihar Land Reforms Act, 1950 (Bihar Act XXX of 1950), "Introduction," in *The Bihar Local Acts* (Allahabad, 1964) vol. 3.

15. Prior to the Bihar Land Reforms Act of 1950, in the areas of the state affected by the Permanent Settlement, a distinction could be made between the terms "rent" and "land revenue": "rent" was paid by the peasants to intermediaries; the intermediaries, in turn, paid a fixed sum to the state as "land revenue" (revenue received by the state from its interests in land).

Following the enactment of the 1950 Act, the distinction between "rent" and "land revenue" became somewhat blurred because the state now holds an exclusive proprietary right to "all rents, cesses and royalties accruing in respect of lands" not specifically excluded from the terms and provisions of the legislation. Thus "rent" collections become "revenue" collections now made by the state.

It should be noted that there is nothing in the Act of 1950, even as subsequently amended, to prevent former intermediaries and other classifications of ryots from subletting lands still in their possession, and deriving what could be called a rent-share of the produce from those lands.

To avoid confusion in this paper, I shall use the phrase "land revenue" to refer to payments made to the state; the term "rent" will be used to designate payments (in cash or in kind) made by one private party to another for the use of the land.

16. Problems associated with determining revenue demand from lands and of collecting revenue will be alluded to elsewhere in this paper, but not discussed in detail. It should be noted, however, that revenue collections have lagged from the beginning and costs associated with implementing the Act of 1950 have mounted. Bihar's potential revenue from the land has been estimated to be approximately Rs. 85,850,000 rupees or, possibly, as much as Rs. 100,000,000, considering potential revenue from agricultural lands and forest lands and royalties from mines and other miscellaneous sources.

17. The Survey and Settlement procedures are painstaking and time-consuming in the best of circumstances. Yet the delays associated with completing revisional Survey and Settlement operations in Bihar in the period following the enactment of the Bihar Land Reforms Act of 1950 seem to be extraordinary. By August of 1970, twenty years after the validation of the 1950 Act, revisional Survey and Settlement operations had not been completed for the state as a whole. Repeated exhortations by various officials of government to speed procedures seemed to be ineffective.

18. Within the frame of reference of the Permanent Settlement, "estate records" were documents pertaining to the intermediaries' rights in land.

19. In 1957, the Revenue Department of the Government of Bihar estimated that, when the Bihar Land Reforms Act of 1950 was passed, there were at least 205,977 revenue-paying, permanently settled estates in Bihar. Later, the Land Reforms Implementation Committee of the Central Government suggested that there were as many as 474,000 intermediaries affected by the Act. The Land Reforms Implementation Committee's figure may be inflated by the addition of thousands of "petty zamindars" and tenure-holders not included in the Bihar Revenue Department's 1957 estimate. The larger figure may also reflect imperfections in the state's records and the subdivision of estates by intermediaries in an attempt to retain larger land holdings than otherwise would have been permitted within certain provisions of the Bihar Land Reforms Act of 1950, as subsequently amended.

20. Bihar Land Reforms Act, 1950 (as amended by Bihar Act XX of 1954) Section 3A, in *The Bihar Local Acts,* vol. 3.

21. Ibid., Section 3B.

22. Ibid.

23. Ibid., Section 4, Clause (h).

24. Ibid., Clause (hh).

25. Bihar Land Reforms Act, 1950 (as amended by Bihar Act XX of 1954 and Bihar Act XVI of 1959), Section 4, Clause (a), ibid.,vol. 3

26. "Homestead" means a "dwelling house used by the intermediary for the purposes of his own residence or for the purpose of letting out on rent together with any courtyard compound and includes any out-buildings used for purposes connected with agriculture or horticulture and any tank, library, and place of worship appertaining to such dwelling house." Ibid., Section 2, Clause (j).

27. "Khas possession" refers to land cultivated personally by an intermediary or by his own stock or servants or by hired labor or with hired stock." Ibid., Clause (k).

28. This bracketed phrase is a paraphrase of the Act's wording.

29. "Golas" are structures used for the storage of grain, implements, etc.

30. See the Indian Supreme Court's decision in Ramranvijoy Prasad Singh et. al. *v.* Bihari Singh, C.A. 195 of 1961, decided on April 25, 1963.

31. This generalization holds for much of Bihar; however, there are some districts, notably Purnea, in which legal confrontations (as well as physical confrontations) between former tenants and former intermediaries have been common.

32. Bihar Land Reforms Act, 1950 (as amended by Bihar Act XX of 1954 and Bihar Act XVI of 1959), Section 5, Clause (1), in *The Bihar Local Acts,* vol. 3.

33. When queried on this subject by the author on December 7, 1967, the former Chief Minister and Revenue Minister, K.B. Sahay, confirmed the existence of such estates and admitted tersely that: "The largest zamindars have managed to circumvent the legislation."

34. Government of India, Planning Commission, *Second Five-Year Plan* (New Delhi, 1956), pp. 193–94.

35. See, for example, "Report of the Committee on Size of Holdings," January 1956, in Government of India, Planning Commission, *Reports of the Committees of the Panel on Land Reforms* (Delhi, 1959), pp. 95–110.

36. Personal cultivation means "cultivation by a raiyat himself or by members of his family or by servants or hired laborers on fixed wages payable in cash or kind but not in cropshare under his personal supervision or the supervision of any member of his family...." See Bihar Land Reforms (Fixation of Ceiling Area and Acquisition of Surplus Land) Act. 1961, Section 2, Paragraph (i), in *The Bihar Local Acts,* vol. 3.

37. See Government of India, Planning Commission, *Implementation of Land Reforms, A Review by the Land Reforms Implementation Committee of the National Development Council.* p. 47.

38. There have been various estimates of the amount of surplus which would be generated if the Act of 1961 were strictly enforced. The Planning Commission reported in 1964 that between 100,000 and 150,000 acres would become available as "surplus" land when the ceiling was enforced in the state as a whole. The original proponent of ceilings legislation, K.B. Sahay, said in a 1968 interview that no surplus land would become available, even if the Act were strictly enforced.

39. The block is the primary administrative unit for the Community Development program. An "ideal" block should consist of 100 villages and 60,000–70,000 people. A Bihar block has, on the average, 116 villages and a total population of nearly 78,000.

40. For data showing where (by district) and when (by year) the various blocks were initiated, see Government of Bihar, Directorate of Economics and Statistics, *Bihar Statistical Hand Book, 1966* (Patna, 1970), p. 378.

41. If one were discussing the quality of the cooperative movement in Bihar, a number of rather critical comments would need to be made. However, the purpose in this instance is merely to show the extent of coverage claimed by government for the cooperative credit dimension of the program.

42. Government of India, Home Ministry, Research and Policy Division, "The Causes and Nature of Current Agrarian Tensions" (unpublished report, 1969), p. 4.

43. Ibid., Annexure I.

44. Such "demonstrations" occurred in the districts of Bhagalpur, Monghyr, Gaya, and Chapra.

Political Conditions of Land Reform: Kerala and Maharashtra

HENRY C. HART and RONALD J. HERRING

IF we accept Doreen Warriner's definition of land reform—"the redistribution of property or rights in land for the benefit of small farmers and agricultural laborers"[1]—we can readily imagine that it is both developmental and revolutionary. It is developmental in the sense that many other steps toward long-term political goals—changes in farming technology and productivity, linking of the whole rural population to the cities, participation in elections and in local self-government, popular control of administration, even rural education—may require it as a prerequisite.[2] But the definition also suggests that land reform is not easily accomplished. In the characteristically wry language of John Kenneth Galbraith:

> Unfortunately some of our current discussion of land reform in the underdeveloped countries proceeds as though this reform were something that a government proclaims on any fine morning—that it gives land to the tenants as it might give pensions to old soldiers or as it might reform the administration of justice. In fact land reform is a revolutionary step.[3]

It always overturns power in the villages, and often it calls for a new source of support for the government.

THEORIES OF DEVELOPMENT AND THEORIES OF POLICY

It is not surprising, therefore, that ideas about the political conditions of land reform come from two very different intellectual perspectives. One looks toward revolution, the other toward policy. "If we can solve the land problem universally and completely we shall have obtained the most fundamental condition for the defeat of all our enemies."[4] Mao Tse-tung reached this point because for the twenty preceding years he had entrusted the revolution to peasants[5] motivated by their demands for land and their rejection of dependence on the landlords. In the Sinification of Marxism he had tapped a new energy for world revolution, energy which would, according to the Chinese reformulation of Marxist ideology, lead on to "the encirclement of cities by the rural areas."[6]

Social scientists have not remained insensitive to historic breakthroughs in China and North Vietnam. Barrington Moore, Jr., Eric Wolf, and James C. Scott, each contributing explanations of revolutionary change in land tenure from a somewhat different macrotheory of political development, share the assumption that change comes in response to what Moore calls "the challenge of commercial agriculture"; Wolf, the "world spread of the special capitalist institutions and attitudes toward the land"; Scott, the "erosion of patron-client bonds" under the joint impact of the "commercialization of subsistence agriculture" and "colonial administration."[7] If we are to deduce from this literature propositions which might explain the success or failure of land reform, we can focus upon the linkages between the peasant village and the large society, the state and the economy.

In Moore's formulation, as long as the landlord and priest remain incorporated in the village social fabric, and conserve that fabric even under the onslaughts of nature and war, the system continues. But then modernization, meaning the strong state and the market economy, intervene, not necessarily in phase. If peasant society remains untransformed, but now saddled with new burdens of the modernizing state, then fascist repression to maintain landlord power or peasant revolution to shatter it are the alternatives. Revolutionary change of peasant tenures is really the only kind Moore envisions, for along his commercializing route peasants diminish to insignificant numbers.[8]

Wolf specifies what Moore assumes: an objective threshold below which peasants' shares of the crop cannot long be driven without triggering revolt. It is the calories he needs to feed his family until the next harvest after he has saved his seed and nourished his livestock.[9]

Agreeing, Scott goes further to explain changes in the legitimacy of patron-client relations in terms of changes in the balance of exchanges between them—exchanges largely material.[10]

We might call these systemic theories. Their time perspective is long: decades reaching to centuries. While they are sensitive to preconditions of tenurial changes, their purpose is to use such changes to explain alterations in political systems. They do not seek to explain changes in economic systems, for these they assume.

In all these respects the other body of thinking about land reforms, the policy literature, differs. It seeks to specify what can be done straightaway. It conceives changes in tenure as effects of changes in political institutions. It is very much concerned with consequences for economic productivity and distribution.

Currently there are signs of partial convergence. The land reform policy littérature no longer expresses much confidence in discovering just the right wording for legislation or even the appropriate reorganization of administrative agencies and judicial procedures to effect land reform.[11] An authoritative U.N. committee, addressing itself to the "widening gap between the declared objectives of land reform and their actual realization," asserts:

> The experience of many countries, including India and Pakistan, has shown that even where a large centralized and efficient bureaucratic system has accomplished certain types of changes at the national level, it has been unable to bring about or supervise any substantial changes

in tenurial relationships at the local level, [especially any] which involve a continuous and comprehensive surveillance of the multi-
faceted landlord-tenant relationship.[12]

Institutionalization and differentiation, often posited as characteristics of the
developed political system, do not help. Even a bureaucracy modern enough
to recruit by examination tends to take in the sons of landlords or of the
urban professional class who could afford education.[13] The "organization
memory" of even the most rational field administration perpetuates routines
designed to maintain order and get the landed to pay their moderate taxes.[14]
The watchdogs of bias and the guarantors of impartial enforcement, the
independent judiciary, cannot help giving unequal access to wealth and
status.[15] Government is thus recognized as institutionalized against land
reform.[16]

A comparative analysis of means by which twenty-five countries achieved
more or less of the expected objectives of land reforms concludes that the
single most determinative factor was "a new posture of administrative and
political resources deployed to encourage local popular initiatives."[17] For
Latin America, mobilizing the political power of peasant beneficiaries is
now taken to be a necessary means of implementation.[18] Some contemporary
policy literature takes revolution to be one end of a continuum of available
means.[19]

Some policy prescriptions now question the equity and deny the economic
utility of compensating dispossessed landlords.[20] The legal guarantee of
property was a pillar of the liberal democratic state.

If we are to map the suggested area of convergence of reform policy with
revolutionary theory, India seems a likely case in point. This is because
India has been taken as the troublesome limiting case by both schools of
thought. India presents a limiting case to Barrington Moore, not because
India has a full set of working democratic institutions without having followed the English route of landlords turning entrepreneurs and merging with the
bourgeois liberal elite; for he remains uncertain at this point in Indian
history, whether democracy is permanently installed. He recognizes the more
basic challenge the Indian case poses to his theory: if the readiness of
peasants to revolt has an objective basis in their poverty and loss of traditional services from landlords and priests, why is there no spreading peasant
revolt in India? (Such a revolt is, in his theory, an additional prerequisite of
democratic modernization.) It is more than coincidental that while class
conflicts triggered by changes in production are the dynamic factors in his
general comparative theory (they are amenable to policy choice only to "a
very limited degree,"), his commendably searching analysis of the failure of
commercialization of agriculture in India and the resulting "democratic
stagnation" fixes the blame on the "makers of government policy in Delhi,"
specifically on Nehru. But now it is too late; India frustrates his ad hoc
policy solutions as well as his general sociological theory: "Under Indian
conditions for a long time to come, no political leadership—no matter how

intelligent, dedicated and ruthless—could, it seems to me, put through a revolutionary agrarian policy."[21]

Approaching the Indian case from the opposite direction, taking the macrotheories of system-formation to be ideological chaff irrelevant to the pragmatic solution of policy problems, and the Chinese commune model to be "out of this world,"[22] Doreen Warriner ends, nonetheless, with the same conclusion. India does not fit world-wide generalizations as to the conditions of land reform policy. Why could the Indian state, whose leaders genuinely wanted to reform tenure, not do it, when the much less complex political systems of Iran and Iraq could?

> The explanation is, no dobt, that India *was* politically so much more advanced. When it became independent, it inherited from the past an immense administrative machine, a federal political system with a division of functions between central and provincial governments, and a land system with an intricate network of rights in land, recognized in law with land records at least in some states. All these things should have facilitated the enforcement of reform laws, and yet they have proved to be impediments.[23]

Reform theory thus takes us to the same point already reached by the candid observers of actual reforms. The political *will* to redistribute power is the missing ingredient. Reform comes readily if imposed from without, whether by MacArthur's occupation or the Kuomintang in Taiwan. It can be done by certain, perhaps exceptional, kings or colonels. But each of these is a *deus ex machina,* neither available to those who are trying to plan development strategy, nor institutionalized into the political system so as to assure long-term outcomes. Is there any long-term development scenario which will generate a will to reform intrinsic to an open political system based upon popular consent corresponding to the intrinsic will to redistribute rural property generated by the Maoist model of cadre-directed revolution?

The theoretical problems are very specifically exhibited in Samuel Huntington's *Political Order in Changing Societies.* From a wide-ranging comparative perspective he identifies the prerequisites of a political will to reform. The central institutional requirement is *concentrated political power.* If the political system be elective, that concentration implies a dominant party. Unless such a party is firmly in control, a "basic incompatibility exists between parliaments and land reforms."[24] There is also a demographic determinant of political will. Those who govern must have a support base autonomous of the rural landed. Like Warriner, he sees this support base in the new urban classes, commercial, industrial, intellectual.[25] But there is something of a dilemma here for political will, since the rise of such classes also reduces the political salience of land reform.

Of course, those in whom power is institutionally concentrated must be committed to reform. What gives them such a commitment, particularly if, as is only reasonable to assume, landlords are not entirely out of the political picture? Huntington observes one answer—fear of the alternative. "The willingness of landowners to lose their property through land reform short of revolution varies directly with the extent to which the only alternative appears to be to lose it through revolution."[26] Huntington sees two ways of countervailing landed power. One is by the politicization of future peasant beneficiaries as a preparation to reform. The other is to bring small holders, tenants, and laborers into the implementation of the reforms at the local level. This will offset the administrative bias toward "substantial farmers" and the status quo.[27]

There is an apparent inconsistency, however, in this set of specifications. If power is concentrated, how can the rural have-nots mount a threat of revolutionary take over? If power is centralized, how can committees of small people in the villages countervail the administration?

It is a signal merit of Huntington's book, for our purposes, that he takes the long-term, system-development view along with the views of policy decision and political strategy. Perhaps in his theory of the development of political alignments of elites with peasants we can find a resolution of the inconsistency.

Even more for the new nations, overwhelmingly rural, than for the early European nations, politicization of the countryside is the formative phase of long-term system development. Huntington calls it the Green Uprising. Modernization, starting in the cities, opens new gaps between their middle classes and tradition rural power.

> In a colonial society, the Green Uprising may occur under the auspices of the nationalist intellectuals who, as in India and Tunisia, mobilize peasant groups into politics within the framework of the nationalist movement . . . . Once independence is achieved, however, the problem for the nationalist leaders is to organize and sustain this rural participation and support. If the nationalist party fails to do this, some other group of urban leaders opposed to it or opposed to the political system . . . may move to win the support of the peasants.[28]

The double reason Huntington gives for India's negotiating the Green Uprising with prospects of political stability is that colonial bureaucratic and other institutions which could carry the load were conserved, while the anti-colonial movement adapted itself to peasant participation.[29]

This perspective explains why India has a firmly rooted political system. It does not tell us whether the system can concentrate power. Still less does it tell us that an enlistment of the peasants in the nationalist period will permit concentration of power not dependent on landlords. Indeed, we have two reasons for thinking the opposite, even aside from empirical observations of contemporary India. One is that the Indian nationalist movement, even more than others, tried to disregard incipient class conflicts and to build a united front against colonial power. Second, at this early stage of politicization in the countryside, it was the educated, hence wealthy, agriculturalists who had ties to the cities and thus made up a disproportionate share of the political participants.

Huntington's picture of the Green Uprising in India, therefore, leaves us with only his second alternative—a counterelite mobilizing disaffected peasants against the nationalist leadership—as a promising explanation of a political base committed to redistribution. But aside from his empirical judgment that the Indian system is too firmly institutionalized for such a movement to be a threat, this alternative connects theoretically to his revolutionary, not his reform, scenario. It can lead to concentrated power only via revolutionary triumph, setting aside the problem how to reform. The theoretical dilemma is only hardened by this developmental conceptualization.

We have been considering institutional conditions of a political will to reform. Our long-term developmental perspective ought also to be directed at the socio-economic base of power as it may be affected by tenure policies. As to this question, too, Huntington's specifications of the conditions for reform seem, *prima facie*, self-contradicting. Clearly thinking of political support as based partly upon numbers of people (an assumption relevant to the elective politics of India), Huntington sees extreme inequality as easier to upset than moderate inequality: "the ability of government to carry out land reforms may well vary directly with the degree of concentration of ownership."[30]

Such extreme concentrations of land as Huntington has in view may be diluted by the growth of urban economic sectors, though the Latin American pattern illustrates Huntington's specification. But there is another difficulty. The specification assumes that the ultimate redistribution must be accomplished at a stroke. For once a numerous class of prosperous land owners— Huntington uses the term "kulaks"—are given security, taking further land away from them or regulating their relations with tenants or laborers becomes politically much more difficult.[31] The outline of Huntington's book suggests a paradigm which seems indispensable in explaining revolutionary reform: a spiral of causation, in which the outcomes of earlier decisions are seen as building the demands and supports for further system changes. But if we apply it to his specifications, each increment of redistribution heightens the difficulty of the next.

Such a political dead end is, in fact, attributed to the first major nationwide land reform of independent India by Huntington, Moore, and Warriner.[32] That reform was the abolition of zamindari or the vesting of revenue, and in practice law and order, authority in landlords. The zamindars were vulnerable—many had sided with the British empire—but their numerous kulak successors, some of whom had been active nationalists, were too strong to displace. This diagnosis is not one that gives much hope that India may meet the political conditions of land reform now. It is, however, one fitting Huntington's characterization of the Indian nationalist elite as forging very early links to the then-active strata of the peasantry.

A quick review of comparative theory has made clear what questions we must ask if we are to specify the conditions of land reform at the system level of comprehensiveness. If we are to demystify the concept of "political will" increasingly invoked by the policy analysts, though, we will have to hunt for our own answers. The questions are:

1. How can peasants be politicized so that their effective power will be thrown toward redistribution, even after the early rounds of reform? Huntington has alerted us to the lasting impact of the enlistment of peasants in the nationalist movement—his "Green Uprising." And we are concerned with open, elective channels of politicization; the path to redistribution via a revolutionary, cadre-directed politicization is already well marked.

2. What tenurial changes will generate more support for than resistance to further redistribution?

ECONOMIC COMPARISON

We will use our comparison of two Indian states to answer the second question first. Before that, however, we should explain our choice of states to compare.

By the end of the 1950s (it may surprise some readers to note), India stood above three-fourths of the world's nations as to equality of ownership of agricultural land. But it also exceeded three-fourths of all nations as to the percent of work force engaged in agriculture.[33] According to the comparative theory we have examined, then, as well as the direct evidence of manifest difficulties, India should have had an unusually hard time reforming further: there was not yet a very large potential base of support in the urban sector, but there was already a fairly broad interest in the status quo established among the peasantry. If we could hit upon any case in India where reforms had proceeded to redistribute land and power beyond the initial post-Independence thrust, we would have crucial evidence to answer our questions.

There are, in fact, in India two such cases: Kashmir and Kerala.[34] Kashmir is, for our purposes, doubly exotic.[35] Landlords were mostly Hindu absentees exploiting a much more numerous Muslim tenantry. Secondly, decision makers were not regularly dependent upon local political support. Kashmir's case, like, e.g., Taiwan's, could not assure us an answer to our questions. Kerala on the other hand, has shifted to the rural poor power rights in land which belonged to well-established elites, i.e., it has redistributed some of the landed power of groups thoroughly able to fight back politically. It is our obvious Indian case of at least some success under generally adverse conditions.

In comparison we could examine any state where land reform has been on the political agenda without actually producing results beyond the commitments of the anti-colonial struggle, but where commercialization of farming has gone far enough to provide occasion for the disruption of traditional agrarian relations according to the criteria of Moore, Wolf, and Scott. Punjab, Hariana, Western Uttar Pradesh, and perhaps Gujarat might have served. However, we have chosen Maharashtra because of the salience of land reform to its politics and because its political system offers, within the parameters of elective politics, a thoroughgoing contrast to Kerala's.

Ecological and Tenurial Contexts

There is a wide and obvious difference in the natural settings of agriculture in Kerala and Maharashtra. Kerala is a high rainfall, densely populated agricultural economy based on rice, tapioca, coconuts, and plantation crops. Except for scattered irrigation of sugar cane, Maharashtra produces coarse grains and cotton under sparse rainfall.[36] These are ecological differences quite possibly, fundamental enough, to account for some of the differences in political economies: perhaps even some of the differences in caste distributions are responses to intensive farming under assured rainfall as against extensive, higher risk agriculture. Differences so profound would vitiate our comparison, were we trying to test hypotheses. Since we are merely trying to suggest them, we can try to keep alert to the risk of incomparability while considering the contextual differences that can be reduced to observable dimensions.

Inequalities of access to land, according to theories we noted, increase the potential demand for land reform. According to this generalized criterion, Kerala's need was marginally greater in 1960–61. But the two states were not far apart. The Lorenz curves of Figs. 1 and 2 plot cumulative percentages of rural families against cumulative percentages of acreage farmed (Fig. 1) and acreage owned (Fig. 2) in the two states.[37] Percentages along the horizontal axis are of all rural households; those not deriving income from agriculture, or working as laborers on the farms of others are counted as farming zero acres. Figure 1 shows the inequality of distribution of operational holdings to be great, and quite similar in the two states. Figure 2 illustrates one of the major theses of this essay: inequality of land ownership is quite dramatic in Kerala compared to Maharashtra. For the poorest 40 percent of the rural population the share of landed wealth is similar (and minimal) in the two states. But whereas the Kerala curve illustrates extreme concentration of ownership at the top of the land tenure hierarchy, Maharashtra illustrates the case of a large middle-sized farming class which owns a major portion of the land in the State.

The curves are, however, of percentages. A different conclusion as to land reform potential appears when we look at the absolute size of agricultural holdings in the two states. We can start with averages: Maharashtra farms average 11.5 acres, Kerala's only 1.85, the smallest of any Indian state.[38] To be sure, Kerala acres are more intensively cultivated and more productive. If we consider staple food crops only (adding tapioca to the Kerala total at one-third its weight, since it provides only one-third the calories of grains, pound for pound),[39] the greater yield of each Kerala acre approximately offsets the much smaller size of a Kerala farm. Multiple cropping is managed both by growing food crops under coconut trees and by harvesting a second crop on almost 30 percent of the cultivated area

FIGURE 1 : DISTRIBUTION OF LAND AMONG FARM OPERATORS IN MAHARASHTRA
AND KERALA.

(Cumulative percentages of rural households and of total acreage farmed
by them in 1960-61)

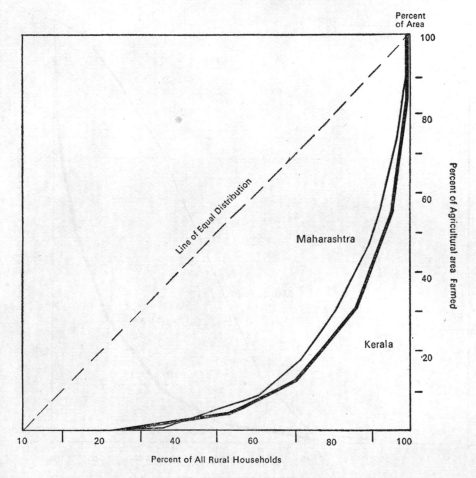

SOURCE: India, Cabinet Secretariat, National Sample Survey, Number 144, Tables
with Notes on Some Aspects of Landholdings in Rural Areas, 17th Round (Delhi:
Manager of Publications, 1968) pp. 155, 157, 161 (corrected per corrigendum slip.)

FIGURE 2 : DISTRIBUTION OF LAND AMONG FARM OWNERS IN MAHARASHTRA
            AND KERALA.

(Cumulative percentages of rural households and of total area owned
by them in 1960-61)

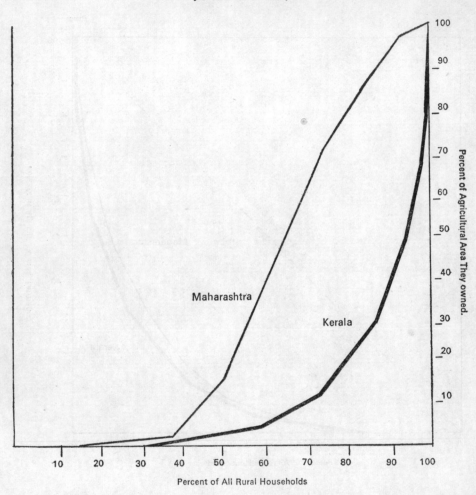

(compared to less than 1 percent in Maharashtra). The most telling sign of intensive farming is the rapid spread of tapioca cultivation. More than compensating for its lower caloric content, tapioca produces ten times more pounds per acre than rice.[40]

Against this background must be examined the arithmetic of any possible redistribution of holdings to the Kerala landless. The perspective changes when we switch from percentages to actual acres. Precisely because the need is so great, there is simply not enough land to satisfy it. Dandekar and Rath have made the calculations. Bare subsistence, they estimate, requires in Kerala a one-acre minimum farm. But even with a ceiling set at 7.5 acres, the amount of land available for redistribution (assuming no slippage in enforcement) would be a mere half million acres. Redistributing that amount would raise all those now farming less than half an acre to ownership of half an acre. This would include both owners of still tinier farms and all tenants owning no land or less than half an acre.[41] It would do nothing at all for farm laborers. And it would leave the enlarged set of minifarm owners still only halfway to subsistence. By Eric Wolf's criterion this would hardly lower the revolutionary potential. And there would be more direct obstacles to the feasibility of such a redistribution. First, how could an elected government discriminate among the land-hungry farmers? Second, would not their competition for the inadequate supply of allotments weaken their solidarity and hence their bargaining power, economic and political?[42]

From the perspective of the arithmetic of possible redistribution, then, Kerala presents an intractable case compared to Maharashtra. Indeed, the involuted agriculture of Kerala presents one of the most intractable cases confronting land reformers anywhere.

The arithmetic of acreage operated can give but a superficial view of the balance of support and opposition to any contemplated land redistribution. We must certainly add the dimension of tenure classes: differences in what a man can do with his farm under the law, in what power and prestige it brings him in rural society, and in the government and market privileges to which it entitles him. We might think of any contemplated land reform as entering a field of vectors exerting pressure for or against it: above-ceiling owners would obviously be against; eligible tenants and minifarm owners for it. Below-ceiling owners might ally with larger owners on the principle of sanctity of private property, though this would be less likely if their holdings were below subsistence size. Large tenants would be pressing for protection of their operating unit by suitable revision of the bill. We would begin by weighting each vector by the numbers in each tenurial class, but we would certainly wish to multiply that weight by the quite different degrees of political influence per capita among classes.

Without proceeding far enough in such analysis to compare the vector sums, it becomes plain that Maharashtra had, on the eve of the 1971 demand for land reform, vastly more powerful forces opposed, and Kerala had more powerful forces favoring, the kind of redistributive reforms urged from Delhi.

Consider first, among farming households, the distribution of owners versus tenants in the two states. Setting aside mixed holdings, upon which the effects of redistribution are difficult to infer, pure owners outnumbered

TABLE 1

Tenure of Farming Households, Kerala and Maharashtra, 1961

State	Farm Wholly Owned		Farm Wholly Unowned		Part Owned, Part Rented		Total Farming Households	
	No. (000s)	%	No. (000s)	%	No. (000s)	%	No. (000s)	%
Kerala	559	55.3	326	32.2	126	12.5	1,011	100.0
Maharashtra	2,948	78.8	272	7.2	522	14.0	3,742	100.0

SOURCE: Census of India, 1961, Vol. 1, *India*, Part III (i) *Household Economic Tables*. Census figures, which were of a 20 percent sample, have been multiplied by 5.

tenants in the 1961 census in Kerala 3 to 2, in Maharashtra 11 to 1. Table 1 shows the distributions of households. The difference is even greater in terms of acres farmed: wholly rented area was 34.7 percent of cultivated area in Kerala, 3.8 percent in Maharashtra.[43] Later noncensus surveys, though not precisely comparable, show that neither land reforms in the early 1960s nor the mix of owned versus rented land in mixed holdings changed the comparison. In 1966, 42 percent of all agricultural land in Kerala was rented by the cultivator;[44] a careful field study of tenures in two *high tenancy* districts of Maharashtra in 1964–65 disclosed tenancy rates of 5 to 10 percent of cultivated area.[45] Either on the assumption that small landowners might be drawn by economic ties or symbolic attachment to side with those having above-ceiling holdings, or on the assumption that tenants think of themselves as beneficiaries, one could infer a more favorable context in Kerala.

The conclusion is reinforced when we add agricultural laborers to the picture. The addition is warranted if we assume them to be conscious beneficiaries of redistribution, or claimants (as political slogans, e.g., "land to the tiller," would make them). Table 2 shows that between 1961 and 1971 laborers rose from one-third to almost half the agricultural work force in Maharashtra; in Kerala they rose from less than half to almost two-thirds. The rate of increase probably has an importance even apart from the proportion of the labor force. It is reasonable to assume that the economic vulnerability of agricultural laborers has increased in the last decade, along

TABLE 2

Cultivators (Owners plus Tenants) and Laborers in the Agricultural Work Force, Kerala and Maharashtra, 1961 and 1971

State	Numbers in the Agricultural Work Force		Percent of the Agricultural Work Force Made up of Owners & Tenants Laborers			
	1961	1971	1961	1971	1961	1971
Maharashtra	13,247,077	12,002,078	66	55	34	45
Kerala	2,156,499	2,992,199	55	37	45	63

SOURCE: For 1961: India, Census of India, 1961, Vol. 1, *India*, Part II-A(ii), p. lviii. For 1971: India, Census of India, 1971, Series 9, *Kerala;* Series 11, *Maharashtra:* Paper 1 of 1971—Supplement XX, *Provisional Population Totals.*

with their numbers pressing upon a limited supply of employment, though whether that vulnerability was translated into economic dependence or a political demand for protection is another matter. Table 3 shows that the

TABLE 3

Number of Agricultural Laborers in Thousands, Kerala and Maharashtra, 1951–1971

State	1951	1961	1971
Kerala	1,115	978	1,888
Gujarat & Maharashtra	5,752	5,762	
Maharashtra		4,510	5,430

SOURCE: For 1961: India, Department of Labour and Employment, *Agricultural Labour in India, A Compendium of Basic Facts* (Delhi, 1969), pp. 9, 22. For 1971: India, Census of India, 1971, Series 9, *Kerala;* Series 11, *Maharashtra:* Paper 1 of 1971—Supplement XX, *Provisional Population Totals.*

number of farm laborers, which was static or declining in both states before 1961 turned up sharply thereafter. But while the increase was a bit over 20 percent in Maharashtra since 1961, it was a doubling in Kerala. (An indeterminable portion of the increase was the result of a change in the operative census definition, but the same change occurred in both States.)

The best measure of the resistance vector, short of weightage for relative influence per capita, is the proportion of the rural population from which land would be taken in any redistribution significant enough to be considered. Here again, we can turn to Dandekar and Rath to specify what might be reasonable assumptions for ceilings in ecologically and demographically different states.[46] They reason from a tough 7.5 acre ceiling in Kerala and a generous 30 acre ceiling in Maharashtra; this is a wider spread than Indira Gandhi's guidelines envisioned. Even so, only 2.6 percent of all owning households would be above ceiling in Kerala, and 5.28 percent, twice as great a proportion, in Maharashtra.[47] The condition which gives rise to this difference can most readily be pictured by a second pair of Lorenz curves (see Fig. 2) plotting acreage *owned* against rural households, again, of course, in terms of cumulative percentages. Seen in these terms, the tenurial distribution of the two states is dramatically different. There is as much inequality among owners in Kerala as we saw there was among farm operators, tenants included. But in Maharashtra, once we leave aside the landless tenants and laborers, who make up almost 38 percent of the rural households, land distribution is astonishingly even. Indeed the Maharashtra curve shows at its top reaches a remarkable phenomenon: as one follows the curve above the 25-acre line (the size classes likely to be affected by ceilings) each increment subsumes a larger percentage of households than of acreage under the curve. Whether the increased frequency of multi-household holdings in the largest size brackets is due to the evasion of previous ceilings by the sharing of ownership on paper we can only guess. The fact remains that proportionately several times more families will be upset by any ceiling within the bounds of policy in Maharashtra than in Kerala. The difference in percent of families must, realistically, be multiplied by some factors accounting for the inequalities of wealth, control of jobs and credit, and influence on political representation and administrative implementation as between big landholders and small. Even a very mild ceiling must upset more rural power in Maharashtra than a rigorous redistribution in Kerala. Comparison of the resistance vectors does not counteract but rather strongly reinforces our comparison of the support vectors.

Recent Tenurial Change: Outcomes as Inputs

Although we have, to use the available data, looked at the tenurial systems of Maharashtra and Kerala in slightly different years, our concepts so far have been static ones, balances of present forces. This is a flatland view. The present balance of forces is itself the product, at least in part, of recent government intervention. Governments justify what they have done, in the process attaching favorable symbols to beneficiaries. The clients of one government reform use the access thus gained to press their advantage. And governments direct development programs other than land reforms at the classes established by reforms, sometimes with reinforcing effects. The dynamics as well as the statics of tenurial reform must be considered in the field of forces favoring or obstructing further reform. We will not present a full account of tenure policies in the two states from the abolition of zamindari to the new round of reforms beginning in 1969. But we will illustrate the impact of recent reforms on the context of the latest reforms.

1. Maharashtra enlarged and established, or gave security and recognition to, the already large class of owner operators.[48] The 1948 reform, aimed primarily at security and improving the rental terms of tenants, failed. It was drastically amended so that on "Tillers' Day" in 1956, all tenants "were deemed to have purchased the land held by them in tenancy." In fact about half the former tenants (more than 800,000 according to one estimate) thereby became owners—typically the half whose landlords were absentees. The other half, induced by landlords to give up their purchase rights, lost government protection of their tenure.[49] Maharashtra redistributed more land (even relative to its acreage) taken by ceilings in the 1960s than did Kerala.[50] The greatest expansion of owner cultivation in the state, however, came by a politically costless means unavailable to crowded Kerala. This was the distribution of just over a million acres of cultivable wastelands.[51]

To suppose, however, that Maharashtra had been remaking its tenurial system in the 1950s and 1960s while Kerala waited until 1969 would be a mistake. Kerala's tenures changed in that period, but in a different direction. While Maharashtra was establishing owner cultivators, Kerala was securing tenants on the fields they rented[52] and giving legal recognition to two classes at the very bottom of the tenurial ladder: the *kudiyirippu,* or renters of tiny hut sites plus garden plots, and the *kudikidappukars,* holding even tinier plots without rental arrangements with a landlord. In 1966 there were close to a million households in these two classes taken together.[53] Too marginal in agriculture even to be counted in the agricultural work force by the Census,[54] they nevertheless operated (though they did not own) enough of the farmland in Kerala in 1961 to account for Kerala's slightly more equal distribution at the very bottom of the Lorenz curves in Figure 1. Contrariwise, it is partly the effect of Maharashtra's recent reforms that gave that state so nearly equal a distribution among owners in our second set of Lorenz curves.

2. Equally important with the substantive thrust of recent reforms was their legislative and administrative strategy. The Communist government in Kerala from 1957 to 1959 attempted thoroughgoing redistribution of ownership at a stroke. After raising a genuine conflict of rural classes it was ousted through central intervention.[55] Its enactments were subject to extraordinary attrition in the courts.[56] Maharashtra approached redistribution piecemeal. Loopholes in the laws permitted purely formal deeding of over-ceiling holdings to relatives; there was time enough to make necessary arrangements with the local record-keepers and revenue officers. High rates of compensation for the small amounts of land taken as surplus allowed landowners to invest in capital improvements or in agro-industries.[57]

Before 1969, Kerala's reform measures had put owners on notice without settling their status and brought the landless into some relation to the state. Maharashtra had not only greatly enlarged the owner class, but had brought it into close relation to government.

3. The consequences of these differences spread farther into the general development strategies of the two governments. There are two processes at work. In economic terms, planners wish to allot public investment to sectors promising returns in the form of productivity. In more telling political terms, those who have numbers combined with the security of property and access to local government are in a position to win further political allocations. S.K. Rao has presented evidence to argue that regions of India with concentrations of wealthy farmers experience the highest growth rates, not because of higher rates of investment by these farmers, but because their political power enables them to induce high levels of public investment. Also, rich farmer regions are generally more industrialized, providing expanding markets and ready capital, and industrial development has favored the previously industrialized regions.[58] Maharashtra ranks considerably higher on percentage of farmers with assets in excess of Rs. 10,000, and the influence of these farmers in the Congress government of the State has been weighty. In terms of total public investment per family between 1951 and 1965, Maharashtra ranked first nationally by a wide margin at Rs. 4493; Kerala ranked near the bottom at Rs. 743.[59]

An expanding economy, spurred by public investment and making possible higher levels of public investment, may build supports for, and decrease dissatisfaction with, the political elite in a number of ways; for the rural population, among the more important means may be direct distribution of boons and provision of employment opportunities and upward mobility channels. Of critical importance to agriculturalists is the fact that Maharashtra had developed probably the most vigorous cooperative system in India, dispensing credit for production and capital formation and providing processing and marketing facilities. Government involvement in the cooperative movement is pervasive and the Congress party takes over where the official bureaucracy leaves off. In 1952 average borrowing from government and cooperatives per cultivating household per year was only Rs. 22 in Maharashtra, but only Rs. 8 in Kerala. By 1961–62, Maharashtra's figure was an all-India high of Rs. 103, compared to Rs. 27 in Kerala.[60] In 1967, about 50 percent of total agricultural borrowing in Maharashtra came from government and cooperatives; in Kerala the total was less than 10 percent.[61]

Almost as critical for cultivators as credit is a solid extension service. A study by the Programme Evaluation Committee of the Planning Commission in 1968 estimated the percentage of cultivators benefited by State governments' agricultural extension programs. In Kerala that percentage ranged around one-third of all cultivators, but was less than half that figure for scheduled castes and tribes; in Maharashtra the percentage benefited stabilized across the various measures at more than three-fourths of all cultivators.[62] Although these efforts, like credit, tend to be most beneficial to the agrarian elite, Maharashtra has also used its public surpluses to provide jobs for the landless, as in the massive bunding projects. As a manifestation of this capacity, we may note that disastrous harvests recently in Maharashtra have resulted in scarcity relief projects which over 1970 and 1971 distributed job opportunities to the poor at a cost of Rs. 500,000,000.[63]

4. The spiral of consequences which become causes makes still another round. As operators of viable farms are established on the land and extended both public investments and support for self-help, economic growth is generated. The compound growth rate of crop output in Maharashtra was 2.45 percent per year between 1952 and 1965. In Kerala it was 0.96 percent. A parallel, though mostly independent, factor also enters the picture—industrial expansion. There is, of course, nothing in Kerala comparable to the industrial complex centered on Bombay city, reaching now almost continuously as far inland as Poona. The increase in value added in industry per capita from 1955 to 1965 was Rs. 17.45 in Kerala and Rs. 67.86 in Maharashtra. The difference in nonagricultural growth is likely to continue. Investment from agencies of the central government such as the Industrial Development Bank of India favor developed regions such as Maharashtra. We do not argue that jobs in mills, and in the tertiary sector that develops around them, constitute a direct alternative to the politics of class conflict in the countryside. Political factors intervene. But the provision of non-agricultural employment for the economically surplus children of overcrowded villages certainly lessens the pressure for legislative and administrative redress for rural have-nots. Indian unemployment figures afford only a pale reflection of this difference, since they neglect those without hope of employment. But they do show some difference. The latest sample survey data available put rural unemployment at 5.5 percent of the labor force in Kerala, 2.9 per cent in Maharashtra.[64] More telling is the contrast presented in Table 1 above. In the decade 1961–71 Maharashtra's work force in agriculture declined almost 10 percent; Kerala's grew more than a third. And the astonishing addition of almost a million to the agricultural laborer population revealed by the 1971 census (Table 3 above) drives home the point.

One way to quantify the human misery of the poor classes in an agrarian system is to determine how many of them, proportionately, do not have enough to eat. This is the test Eric Wolf proposes to determine the potential for peasant revolt. One extensive study found that Kerala was the only state in India to register consistently some percentage of the population at the "starvation" level (i.e., 75 percent or more deficiency in caloric intake), ranging from 10 to 19 percent between 1960 and 1965. Kerala had by far the highest percentage of "undernourished" people in India, three times the Maharashtra proportion.[65]

Alternatively, misery may be conceived as deprivation of one's accustomed condition of life. We do not have data directly measuring real living standards, statewise, through the decade of the 1960s. We do have two National Sample Surveys, one taken in 1960–61, the latest in 1964–65, of the value of per capita consumption among rural people. The simplest indicator we can draw from them is a statewise index, based upon the all-India consumer expenditures as 100. They show nonfood expenditures rising in both Maharashta and Kerala during the four years by about 10 percent, relative to the all-India figure. But food consumption (including the value of food produced ·by cultivator families and consumed in the family) rose in Maharashtra four points on the national index, while it dropped three points in Kerala. Putting the two kinds of consumption together, Kerala made no progress, remaining at 84 per cent of national per capita consumption, while Maharashtra climbed from 89 per cent to 95.[66]

If we turn from observations of the whole rural population over a period of time to focus on the poorest strata, we begin to get somewhat different signals. Hard data take us only to 1965. They show Kerala continuing to have a much larger percent of rural population below the poverty line than either Maharashtra or India as a whole. But Kerala did not in the early 1960s either gain or lose its relative standing in this respect.[67] One projection from this data to 1969, based upon changes in total state income, estimates that Kerala has undergone some remarkable equalizing upward of income shares.[68] A narrower set of statistics upon the money wages paid to farm laborers, discounted for changes in costs of living, shows that Kerala's real wages have gone up by 51 percent, more than any state except U.P., 1956 to 1971. But Kerala's farm laborers averaged more days of unemployment per year than any state's in 1956, and this poor showing continued in 1971.[69] We are left in some doubt whether Kerala's poor have dropped still lower in living standards during the 1960s or have made relative gains over the period. One point is clear. A relatively steep increase in real wages for the bottom agricultural class could nôt coincide with an unmatched unemployment level unless political forces in Kerala were countervailing economic ones.

POLITICAL COMPARISON

Contemporary Political Systems

The two states we have chosen to compare have contrasting political systems. Maharashtra's is, in the word of the political scientist who has studied it most scientifically, hegemonic.[70] Kerala is peculiarly unstable, intensely competitive, and apparently riven by class conflict. The area that became Maharashtra in 1960 has been governed by Congress party ministries without interruption since the British admitted elective rule. In 26 years since Independence there have been five chief ministers, but each has been chosen under the firm control of an established Congress leadership. The party's control has been not only continuous but overwhelming.

Congress won from 52 to 81 percent of the seats in the state legislature in the five elections since Independence. While its popular votes have been merely 45 to 51 per cent of the total, the strongest among the opposition parties has not, save for the 1957 election at the height of the struggle for a linguistic state, polled more than 10 percent. A survey of the political systems of Indian states would locate Maharashtra at one extreme, securely controlled by an undivided party of both state and national dominance, and Kerala at the other, divided, volatile, approaching ungovernability.[71]

Kerala, now under a coalition of the less radical of the two Communist parties (the CPI), the Muslim League, the Congress, along with the tiny Revolutionary Socialist, and Praja-Socialist parties under a CPI chief minister, differs in every respect. The Congress popular vote has fluctuated between 19 and 41 percent and the party has often (as at this writing) lacked a majority of seats in the legislature.[72] In six of the eight state elections, the leading Communist party (CPM) has been within 5 percentage points of the leading Congress party, indeed outpolling it in the latest (1970) election. The reason is not political underdevelopment. Myron Weiner has shown that of all the Indian states, Kerala shows the highest percent of voter turnout (84 percent in the 1960 election) and the lowest percent of candidates polling so few votes that they must forfeit their deposits.[73] The mobilization of the adult population in elective competition has been extraordinary by any standards.

But even under tightening competition both parties have split, in fact have split twice. For the Congress, the most serious continuing split-off is the Kerala Congress, a Nair-Christian coalition powerful in Kottayam district. The opposition CPM of E.M.S. Namboodiripad is stronger in Kerala elections and mass organizations than the CPI of the current ruling coalition. Most Muslim votes continue to go to the Muslim League,[74] a unique situation we will explore. There are, in addition, three small but durable Marxist splinter parties.

An intensely and evenly competitive party contest, complicated by fragmented parties, has yielded extreme instability of party control. The five years of Achutha Menon's chief ministership sets an endurance record for Kerala, which has had 11 chief ministers in 26 years, interrupted by four periods of administration from Delhi.[75]

Rural people have been widely politicized in both states, but by quite different institutions and appeals.[76] Maharashtra has, more than any Indian state, opened control of development programs to elective rural bodies. Zilla parishads there are directly, not indirectly, elected, and they make the crucial allocations of the development budget in the countryside. Professor V.M. Sirsikar has published a perceptive study of this system at work in three districts of Maharashtra.[77] The system certainly locates at the district level some decision power which elsewhere resides in the state capital. It has also entrenched in district power the Congress party; Sirsikar found the Congress holding 85 percent of elective district offices. Administrative power, further, is fused with electoral in the district council offices and committees, and in making the development budget. Votes are exchanged for roads, wells, jobs, and subsidized agricultural inputs. Quite apart from questions of corruption, we recognize in this a variant of the "machine" politics which characterized American cities in the late nineteenth and early twentieth centuries. Such a system draws peasants into politics in search of highly particularized rewards, not improved general conditions, e.g., of tenure. Since all the rewards to politicians flow through the ruling party, such a system also starves potential opposition parties, and thus inhibits the kind of independent prodding and criticizing of the local administrative apparatus which would be necessary to wean it away from its relationship with larger owners.

Competition is not wanting in rural Maharashtra's politics. It is not between parties, but between factions within the Congress. Operating mainly up to the district level, such personalized factions, led by presidents of district cooperative banks or sugar mills, would not be expected to struggle over the kind of ideologically identifiable issues which are articulated by urban intellectuals or party workers, and which are necessary to energize land reform. In recent research, to be sure, Mary Carras found an ideological basis in the district factional struggles: to the benefit of what economic stratum would government power be used?[78] This interpretation however, was immediately challenged by another researcher on Maharashtra, Don Rosenthal: "It is on the basis of a shared vision of a relatively costless expansionary rural economy that their political game can be conducted with factional fluidity in relation to which questions of ideology are largely irrelevant."[79] Whatever the outcome of this scholarly controversy (Rosenthal's view fits our own generalizations better), district leaders of the Congress in Maharashtra acted without significant disagreement, as we shall presently note, in opposing the recent land reform measure sought to be imposed on their state from above.

It is a curious fact that Kerala, for all the politicization of its rural population, lags behind almost all other Indian states in implementing the national panchayati raj blueprint. Legislation to create taluq and district elective bodies was introduced only in 1968 (ten years after the first such legislation in Rajasthan), and has since languished in the state assembly.[80] Why? We guess there may have been three reasons. Panchayati raj, first, entrenches in power whichever party holds the upper hand in the countryside, and no regime has had the strength or stability, or perhaps courage, to decentralize in the highly politicized and competitive conditions. Second, rural elective bodies threaten the rural legislator's monopoly of his political power base. He does not like it; neither does his party central committee, trying to discipline him to support legislation which may be locally unpopular. Third, Kerala parties already had organizations to link up their rural followers: the Communist cadres, or the Catholic church and other communal organizations in some districts.

We suspect there is an important political implication in the difference we have already noted in the development program emphases of the states. Consider rural cooperative societies as they are fostered by the governments. In Maharashtra they enhance the economic power of land-owning farmers; they also cement the interdependence of these farmers with the dominant party. In Kerala, the expansion of cooperatives during the late 1950s and early 1960s was of toddy-tappers' organizations. They tied poor Ezhava workers to the local Communist party cell. The same formal institution which, according to Sirsikar, creates a single web of power in rural Maharashtra—linking district Congress, panchayati raj office, and credit or marketing institution—in Kerala keeps alive the sparks of class conflict.[81]

Kerala makes up in educational development what it lacks in programs furthering agricultural enterprise. The National Sample Survey shows that in 1963–64 Kerala, with less than one-third of Maharashtra's rural population, had 776,000 rural school teachers compared to 813,000 in Maharashtra. Half of Kerala's villages had libraries, one-sixth of Maharashtra's.[82] If these narrow differences are clues to a broad difference in development priorities, Maharashtra stressing productivity, Kerala enlightenment, we could use the Gurr-Davies theory to deduce that Kerala's program mix would generate the greater revolutionary potential, since enlightenment without productivity would increase "relative deprivation."[83]

It is evident that different political institutions and policies dovetail with different rural economies in the two states. An expanding economy in Maharashtra, spurred by public investment and supporting still higher levels of public investment, may build support for, and decrease dissatisfaction with, the political elite. Contrariwise, a congested agriculture whose population burden grows faster than its productivity—Clifford Geertz's "involution" is apposite in some ways—might in Kerala provide a high potential for opposition politics, which might in turn inhibit the development of a single network of growth producing representative-administrative institutions in the countryside. This institutional view is a necessary corrective of a simple class analysis using the Gini index as point of departure.

The institutional view we have taken so far is still aggregate and almost static. It does not meet all the relevant conditions. There were and are large numbers of destitute farm laborers, tenants, and smallholders in Maharashtra. Probably only a comparative minority of the agricultural populace benefits directly from either the economic or the political boons and opportunities which we have said characterize the state. In the Travancore region of Kerala there were at one time commercially successful landowning cultivators; they may have operated more than half the acreage of that region.[84] Why were not the grievances of the Maharashtrian have-nots articulated into a powerful opposition, the satisfactions of the Tranvancore haves into a self-sustaining support base? The questions require a longer time perspective than we have yet taken. But we are not digging into the past in search of some prime mover, either political or economic. We assume that each major economic shift had political consequences, and that for several centuries, at least, government policies have reallocated economic opportunities. What we want to find out is why one political system has been more sensitive to a particular kind of claim, responding even when the claim was weak, and thus in turn strengthening the claimant group for the next round of policy struggles.

Anti-Colonial Enlistment of the Peasants: Maharashtra

Hunting for prime causes of differences so fundamental to the political system of the two states could turn into an infinite regress. Our development theories, however, point attention toward the impact of capitalist institutions on peasant farming, and toward the shaping of the anticolonial movement. These developments put latent social forces under enough stress in both states to make them manifest in agrarian outbreaks.

In Maharashtra these were the Deccan Riots of 1875, with their soft echo in 1896–97. The first striking fact about the Deccan Riots is that for all their prominence in all-India histories of peasant unrest, they were neither bloody nor extensive. A recent historian could find no record of anyone being killed; thirty villages were affected in two districts; 951 people were arrested and 501 convicted.[85] The causes fit nicely the Moore-Wolf-Scott thesis. Maharashtrian peasants had, within a half-century of British control, felt the effects of commercial agriculture and the law of contracts enforced in British courts. Population grew, poorer soil had to be plowed. Cotton yielded more income per acre, but also drew the peasant into a price system responsive to Manchester and the American South. Whether the Deccan peasant lost his farm to the Marwari moneylender because British mortgages replaced village trusteeship of the land,[86] or because the new scarcity combined with the new mobility to create a market for land, the significant point for us is that an old security was shattered. Peasants perceived the change as the words of an 1840 petition express it. "Under the present Government, by the sale of our immovable property we are reduced to a starving condition in the same manner, as a tree when its roots are pulled out, dies."[87]

The Bombay government reacted belatedly; some of its policy responses had untoward consequences. Concurrence of a new, higher revenue assessment with the collapse of cotton prices following the end of the American Civil War, for instance, created the tension released in the 1875 riots. And the precipitating factor was an intended government concession that backfired: by deferring forfeiture of land for nonpayment of the new tax levies the government merely assured moneylenders that land they might foreclose would not be sold for taxes. Peasant violence came. Even the violence, however, was part of a muddling, episodic, but nevertheless patient and ultimately responsive dialogue between a basically pragmatic government and a basically self-confident peasantry. Contrary impulses were rejected. The peasants used force to do only one thing—to get possession of the moneylender's mortgage records—burning his house only if he resisted. Observing that limited offense, the government rejected the punitive law-and-order response proposed by the Collector of Poona District. Instead, it constrained foreclosures through the Deccan Agriculturalists' Relief Act of 1879.[88]

The cycle was repeated more than once. The new legal context and the new market opportunities were exploited by the more urbanized moneyed classes. Then the government responded to new peasant unrest by further adjustments of policy to protect peasant proprietorship.[89] When the nationalist movement galvanized many of the Maharashtrian villages in 1930 and again in 1942, they were still villages of land-owning cultivators.

Peasant confidence was bolstered by the size and unity of the principal cultivating caste-cluster. The Marathas grew in the twentieth century from 30 percent to perhaps 45 percent of the Marathi-speaking population through the common processes of horizontal aggregation and vertical fusion.[90] Their leaders became educated. The British cultivated them as a reliable support-base, counterpoised against the Marathi-speaking intellectual caste, established in governing roles in Sivaji's empire, and highly responsive to modernization.[91] Leaders of this Chitpavan caste, centered in Poona, made desultory attempts to recruit Maratha peasant support for their own nationalist demands. Tilak tried it through the manipulation of symbols (Ganesh, Shivaji). There were powerful anti-Brahman responses from the Maratha counterelite.[92] Most Marathi-speaking nationalists drew together only in the 1930s and 1940s in response to Gandhi's leadership. With the decompression following Independence, the cleavage of peasant Maratha from intellectual Chitpavan politicization reopened. Two of the most prominent Maratha leaders quit the Congress to form the Shetkari Kamkari Paksh (Peasants' and Workers' Party) in 1948.[93] But they never really integrated their Marxist slogans with their appeal to caste grievances; more basically, one suspects, their class appeal to Maratha tenants would split their Maratha caste constituency, some of whom were landlords.[94] Key Maratha leaders returned to the Congress in 1954·

Meanwhile Nehru's leadership of the Congress had incensed the language-identity feeling of virtually all politically active Maharashtrians, and the Congress lost the 1957 election in the Marathi-speaking constituencies of Bombay state. Significantly, though the P.W.P. and all other opposition parties vigorously championed the language state issue from 1953 to 1960 (when it triumphed in the creation of Maharashtra), the main effect on the Congress was to force it to displace its Brahman by its Maratha leadership in the state. Y.B. Chavan, Maratha, and Bombay chief minister from the 1957 elections, personified the change.[95]

Clearly, between 1875 and 1957 the Maharashtra peasants, or at least their caste leaders, moved from protest to participation in rule. The move was powerfully facilitated because they were mainly of one caste-cluster, and because most of them owned their fields. Even so, their access to power was not foreordained. Again and again the government in Bombay, or in Delhi, or the nationalist movement, adopted policies which might well have arrested their climb to proportionate power. Rival leaders then protested on behalf of the aggrieved peasantry and the grievances were substantially redressed. One has to conclude that the Green Uprising in Maharashtra was negotiated under nationalist leadership, and remains entrenched under elective government, as much because those who held power always believed they needed the peasants as because the peasants had the resources and commitment to take it. The British saw the cultivating peasants as their reliable support base; the anti-British patriots saw them as symbolically or actively essential; when elections made numbers count they had the necessary numbers. As three systems of politics succeeded one another, Sivaji's, British, independent Indian, overlapping a good deal, the Maratha farming community rose toward power *within* each one.

Anti-Colonial Enlistment of the Peasants: Kerala

In Malabar, that northern part of the present state of Kerala which was directly ruled by the British, nineteenth-century peasant uprisings were far more extensive and much bloodier than the Deccan Riots. The Malabar outbreaks began in 1836, peaked in 1841, were never wholly quiet for the remainder of the century, and flared up again dramatically in 1921. The rioting tenants were Muslim Moplahs, their landlords (jenmis) were Hindus, and the initial British diagnosis was "religious fanaticism."[96] Later, a more careful British investigation concluded "that the Mapilla outrages were designed to counteract the overwhelming influence, when backed by the British courts, of the *jenmis* in the exercise of their novel powers of ouster and of rent raising."[97]

The formal tenure and revenue policy of the Madras government was similar to that of Bombay—ryotwari—and the economic and legal contexts were not very different. But British influences operated upon a tenurial situation unlike that of the Deccan. The rural class established by British policy as fee-simple owners in Malabar were 24,714 landlords, Brahmans or Nairs, "most of whom," Logan reported, "do not know where much of their property lies, *having never even seen it.*"[98] Their million tenants or subtenants were half Muslims, half outcaste Hindus (mostly Tiyas, corresponding in status to Ezhavas further south).[99]

The nineteenth-century "Moplah Outrages" met a very different response (as the name the British gave them suggests) than the Deccan Riots. After much controversy between on-the-spot administrators (including Logan) and the courts and higher officials, legislation to constrain evictions was finally dropped.[100] Simultaneously, the Malabar Special Police were established, a heavily armed all-Hindu force under British officers, and collective fines authorized upon Moplah communities in which violence occurred. Why so different a British response here? Malabar was no doubt peripheral to the British center of power in Madras; a harsh policy risked less. But there was a more fundamental reason. The British took Malabar in 1792 by defeating the Mysore Sultans. During their rule, the Sultans had based their dominion on their fellow-Muslim tenants, had indeed made them de facto ryots for the same reasons that the British patronized the Maratha peasants of the Deccan. That left the Hindu landlords, absentee or not, as the trust-worthy support base for the incoming British. Sir Thomas Munro, however staunch an advocate of ryotwari settlement, had no use for the Muslim ryots here. In his words the Moplahs were "the worst race in Malabar and the most hostile to our dominions."[101]

Against this background we can see why the first surge of anti-colonial popular action, 1920–1922, was held within Gandhian discipline in Maha-rashtra, but burst out in a bloody cycle of killing and repression in Malabar. Named the "Moplah Rebellion" in all-India history, this is even now characterized by the District Gazetteer as "a gigantic popular upheaval the like of which has not been seen in Kerala before or since."[102] It has been conceived as an agrarian revolt since many of the rebels were tenants: they burned land records, killed jenmis and looted their granaries.[103] It has been conceived as a religious outburst since it was a tragic distortion of the original Khilafat cause championed by Gandhi, and since some Hindus were made Muslims *wille nille* by circumcision and forced eating of beef.[104] K.P. Kesava Menon, the first newspaper editor of the district, subordinates these factors to a simpler explanation: "It was born out of police repression ... the excessive violence used by the authorities to suppress the Khilafat movement."[105] Certainly when the British regained control of the Moplah towns and villages in August 1921, their repression was ruthless. In Novem-ber 61 prisoners died of suffocation inside the box car in which they were being shipped to Coimbatore.[106]

A rereading of Gandhi's contemporaneous comments on what must have been to him a bitter product of the Khilafat movement he helped launch in Malabar does him credit. He understood peasant violence as a response to police provocation. He even respected the Muslims who con-verted Hindus the wrong way more than Hindus who foresook their faith to save their lives. But he did not detect the old agrarian roots of Moplah disaffection, and neither he nor any Gandhian workers could keep control of the situation in August 1921, nor moderate the British repression.[107] Malabar Muslims, whose grievances as tenants might have been met, had now been abandoned not only by the colonial administration, but also, as it seemed to them, by the nationalist movement as well.[108]

The Muslim League became the vehicle of Moplah nationalism, not upon the appeal of any external Muslim elite, much less interest in Pakistan, but as the unintended consequence of larger strategies, colonial and anti-colonial, which left a tenant grievance to fester. The Muslim League did not, then or now, champion that grievance. It did bar the enlistment of Malabar Muslims in the Congress movement before independence and since. The economic grievances of the Moplahs awaited another champion.

Communal Basis

In Malabar the British cultivated an absentee landlord class, tenant rebellion ensued and turned communal. But in Travancore a succession of strong maharajas had established de facto ryotwari tenure upon 75 percent of the land,[109] creating a tenurial situation more like Maharashtra's than Malabar's. That political development did not follow the Maharashtra course might be explained in two ways: a different communal configuration and insulation from anti-colonial politics.

The 1931 census reported that the 5 million people of Travancore consisted of one-third Christians, another one-third evenly divided between Nairs and Ezhavas, and the remaining third a miscellany of small Hindu castes plus 350,000 Muslims.[110] Had Nairs and Ezhavas been one caste-cluster, Travancore might have had its counterpart to the powerful land-owning caste of Maharashtra; but Malayalam myth ascribed utterly different origins to the two, and Hindu *dharma* required the Ezhavas to keep a distance of 24 feet from Nairs lest they pollute them.[111]

A large, upwardly mobile Christian community, open to Ezhavas by conversion, undermined the legitimacy of traditional caste discriminations. Ezhavas in the 1890s petitioned the Maharaja for the same right to enroll in government schools and compete for the public service that their caste-fellows possessed after conversion to Christianity. In 1903 a great Ezhava religious teacher, Sri Narayana Guru, joined forces with the campaign for civil rights to form the Sri Narayana Dharma Paripalana Yogam. Still powerful today, particularly through its control of a statewide network of schools, the S.N.D.P. Yogam has raised the Ezhavas to a position of political power roughly equal to their numbers.[112]

In 1914 the Nairs also organized a caste association. Its first campaigns were for breaching subcaste barriers and dispensing with the costly ceremonials at which Brahmans officiated; the Nair Service Society later came to operate the largest number of schools in Kerala, next to the Catholic Church. An indication of the unity and stability of caste associations in Kerala, compared to political parties other than the Communist, is that Mannath Padmanabhan, founder of the N.S.S., was still its charismatic leader when in 1959 it spearheaded the popular agitation against Communist rule.

Travancore politics of the twentieth century was a succession of struggles by coalitions of excluded communal groups, each group solidly organized, to gain equal treatment from the Maharaja's government. First it was the Christians, Ezhavas, and Muslims against the favored Brahmans and Nairs. In the 1931 legislative assembly of 23 seats, the Nairs, with a sixth of the population, had 15 seats, Ezhavas with an equal population had none, Muslims none, Christians with double the Nair population had 4 seats. The Christian-Ezhava-Muslim coalition agitated throughout Travancore by boycotting the next election. They won some quotas of seats and civil service positions. But in 1936 the Maharaja appointed an authoritarian dewan (a Tamil Brahman); the dewan's highhandedness moved many Nairs to join the opposition movement.[113] Travancore State Congress was thus formed in 1937, a coalition of communal groups joined in a struggle for civil rights and responsible government.[114] Such incorporation of Travancore peasants in politics as occurred came primarily through the communal organizations.

Statewide political causes occasionally mobilized peasant participation, however. The 1938 demand for responsible government did. Initiated by the new Congress, it was supported by mass *satyagraha*, by a strike of the several thousand *coir* professors in Alleppey, by *kisans* in some villages, and by a long march across the state led by A.K. Gopalan. At this juncture, Gandhi's policy of avoiding attacks upon Indian maharajas did indeed quench a popular agitation. He asked the Congress to withdraw its memorandum detailing the misdeeds of the dewan. The movement subsided, but the Youth League, defying the national Congress, read the memorandum to crowds across the state.[115]

Exploiting hindsight, one can see that the main processes of Congress social mobilization were set at least thirty years ago, and in the princely state of Travancore, not in the British-Indian portion of Kerala. The Congress has been a shifting coalition of communal groups and interests. Its durable core has been not a dominant peasant caste-cluster but an educated Catholic community, not without land, but not identified by its tenurial status either. Its militant wing has been its students and youth, more numerous and more political in Kerala than anywhere else in India. When the Congress did reach out for peasant support after its decisive defeat by the Communist party in 1957, it did so by appealing to the Ezhavas as a community; it took R. Shankar, general secretary of the S.N.D.P., as its state president and shortly thereafter as its chief minister.[116]

Hindsight does not show either the communal-coalition or the class-conflict basis for party competition to have been inevitable in Kerala. The former shaped Travancore's party alignments, the latter Malabar's;[117] Cochin reflected a mix. Certainly it was in part the political art of E.M.S. Namboodiripad, himself a pioneer in the reform of Namboodiri Brahman social practices, to draw many of the young organizers of communal reform into the orbit of the Communist party, and thus to gain leadership of the Congress Socialist party in the 1930s, long before class-conflict politics was dominant among Malayalam-speakers. A separate and more enduring factor has been the gradual acceptance by virtually all political activists in Kerala of the ideas of class conflict.

Ideology of Class Conflict and Redistribution

The Marxist ideas which make up a prominent strand in contemporary Indian thought comprise in Kerala the overwhelmingly dominant one. We can see it in contemporary literature. In Malayalam it is the outstanding novelist, Thakazhi Sivasankara Pillai, and the best-known poet, Sankara

Kurup, who developed their art within the canons of "socialist realism."[118] Vallathol, who occupied about the same place in Malayali culture that Tagore did in Bengal, won the Lenin Peace Prize. We are glimpsing here a pervasive orientation of thought that did not occur all at once, or by the exertions of a political party. Once more, we find the pattern was hammered out in the anti-colonial forge.

Among Kerala nationalists, an ideological competition between Gandhi and Marx was joined in 1920. It was formally decided, against Gandhi, in 1934. In 1920 the Congress, then organized only in British Malabar, split along class lines. Landlords and professional men led by Annie Besant walked out when they were outvoted by a new group of "extremists" who backed not only Gandhi's noncooperation, but also tenancy reform. Fourteen years later the same cleavage had extended throughout what is now Kerala. Again the leftists carried a vote in the Congress, this time with a resolution expressing "lack of confidence in the efficacy of the Gandhian principles of truth and nonviolence as weapons in the fight for Swaraj."[119] Against the all-India background, this was a remarkable development. Both the intellectual creativity of individual nationalists, and the hard lessons of the strength and direction of social forces unleashed in the anti-British struggle must be taken into account to explain it.

At the individual level we can trace the competition in the mind of E.M.S. Namboodiripad. "The first signs of political consciousness came to me," he later wrote, "through the personality of Mahatma Gandhi and the nationwide movement that he initiated and led in 1920-21."[120] Namboodiripad, aged 12, could hardly have concluded then that Gandhi's handling of the Moplah Upising was what he later called it, a "disgraceful betrayal" of an aroused tenant class by a bourgeois movement.[121] He tried to organize the Congress among the Muslim tenants in the late 1920s and he must have sensed their disaffection. In any event, when Gandhi next appealed for mass action India-wide in 1930, then called it off, Namboodiripad was ready to offer his Kerala followers independent mass struggles. The "extremists" were finding their own political line, one of class conflict in the countryside. A jail sentence, 1932-33, put Namboodiripad into contact with theoreticians of all-India prominence, both Gandhian and Marxist.[122] With Nehru heading up the Congress Socialist party, it was not yet necessary to make a choice.

Namboodiripad was clear, however, as to the political action he intended for the Congress in Kerala. He had found his cause and his organizational medium. Parliamentary efforts of older Congressmen in Malabar had won the Malabar Tenancy Act of 1930.[123] It gave security to the upper strata, mostly Nairs. To the vulnerable elements of Muslim and Ezhava (Tiya) subtenants, the Marxist Congress intellectuals brought the message of economic as well as legislative action. The district-wide corps of village primary school teachers, themselves aggrieved economically and of peasant families, became the organizational network.[124] "[I]t was the combination in one

Political Conditions of Land Reform: Kerala and Maharashtra   261

and the same person of the office-bearer of the Village Congress Committee, the leader of the Teachers' Union and the organizer of the Kisan
Sangham that made the anti-Imperialist movement strike deep roots in the
countryside."[125]

Through this network Namboodiripad and Gopalan organized tenant
protests against lease renewal fees ("feudal levies") in the late 1930s, culmi-
nating in an effective rent strike in North Malabar, 1938–39.[126] It was at
this point that they, as leaders of the Kerala nationalist movement, founded
the Communist party in Kerala. In 1940 Namboodiripad was able to take
virtually the whole of the Congress Socialist leadership into it.[127] He had
found for his Marxist line in Kerala the vindication Gandhi had demonstrated for Gandhian ideology nationwide—the trust of such peasants as
were politicized.

As Communist leader of the major fraction of the nationalist movement,
Namboodiripad now confronted a more troublesome ideological problem.
The world Communist line collided with the nationalist interest when the
Comintern switched its strategy toward World War II with Hitler's attack
upon Russia. Ten years later, Namboodiripad published *The National
Question* in Kerala, his own Marxist accommodation to Kerala nationalism.
The revolutionary struggle would unfold differently in Kerala, he reasoned,
because unlike other parts of India, or other Asian nations, Kerala had
reached its anti-colonial stage via feudalism and not the centralized despotism Marx called "Oriental society." Bureaucratic despotism had not
developed because Kerala agriculture did not require irrigation.[128] Whatever its merits as materialist interpretation of history, this rationale could be
used to justify an autonomous line for the Kerala party. Namboodiripad
used that autonomy to campaign for the 1957 elections on a nonrevolu-
tionary platform, and won.[129]

We do not contend that Namboodiripad's Marxism has become the
ideology of Kerala. On the contrary, the failure of his parliamentary Communism to solve the obdurate economic problems of the state confronts
his party with fresh ideological problems.[130] We do find Kerala's anti-
colonial energies to have been distinctive in India, certainly different from
Maharashtra's. There was an aggrieved and suppressed agrarian underclass
centered in one part of the state, plural elites, and a large, mobile lower
caste competing for the benefits of modernization in another. No established
set of intellectual castes championed a Hindu version of nationalism.[131]
What the India-wide movements extended into this peripheral region were
strategies responsive to other needs. So did revolutionary Marxism as an
all-India movement. But the politician who assumed the largest burden
of justifying both the break from empire and the creation of the Malayali
state undertook to adapt Marxism to the task. His adaptation had, among
its essential concepts, an economy perceived as zero-sum, and within this
economy a distributive struggle between the relatively rich and the des-
parately poor. These concepts we believe to be the common currency of

Kerala politics among both Marxists and non-Marxists to whom ideology is salient.

Politicization of Educated Youth

"The student union building," Huntington remarked, "is the symbol of revolt."[132] Where, one would ask, would students be more revolutionary than in contemporary Kerala. Between 1967 and 1969 the Kerala Students' Union did gain control of 70 percent of the college unions in the state. But it was an organization of radical Congress youth, battling the left Communists.[133] The Union first championed with notable success the demands of its own constituents, including free tuition, and abolition of the statewide secondary school-leaving examination. It systematically organized unemployed graduates. The split in the national Congress precipitated by Indira Gandhi in 1969 posed a contest of good against evil for the K.S.U. youth. Through their Kerala Youth Congress they helped the Indira Gandhi faction nationally, and won it overwhelming support in Kerala.[134]

The Youth Congress steadily drove the Congress party in Kerala to the left. It frustrated an alliance with the Catholic-Nair splinter Kerala Congress, pressed for radical changes in the Congress platform, and then favored its joining the Achutha Menon ministry.[135] In 1972 the Youth Congress won planks in the state Congress platform for lower ceilings on landholdings, inclusion under the ceilings of religious trusts, and nationalization of plantations.[136] A.K. Antony, the leader of the Youth Congress in these battles, became secretary of the parent state Congress.

The tactics of the Youth Congress were partly electoral. In the special election of 1970, it got four of its own leaders, including A.K. Antony, on the legislative ticket. All four won. In the present CPI–Muslim League–Socialist coalition, Mr. Antony is the convener of the Liaison Committee whose monthly meetings lay the policy guidelines for the coalition.

The Youth Congress has been ready, meanwhile, to supplement electoral with agitational tactics whenever necessary. It proposed (1971), for example, to take over cultivation of the rich rice fields in the Kuttanad tract when the owners of the land threatened to suspend cultivation rather than pay increased agricultural wages. The militant tactic worked then, and remains a continuing counterpressure to the normal conservatism of bureaucracy, courts, and ministry.[137]

Both Lipset and Huntington explain the revolutionary stance of politicized students partly in terms of their personal alienation.[138] The economic frustration of educated youth in Kerala is extreme, even for India. A recent Indian Institute of Public opinion sample survey of literate young Indians aged 18 to 24 showed 25 percent unemployed. In Kerala it was 44 percent. (Note the much higher levels of these data compared to the National Sample Survey of general unemployment already cited.) Those whose unemployment had extended at least two years were 8 percent of the national sample, 20 percent in Kerala.[139] In the face of this, student-led youth politics in

Kerala is not the anarchy or quixotic violence of alienation. Unused man-power is committed instead to the cause of moving the political system, with redistribution of rights in land among the first priorities.

System Differences

Differences in the developmental experiences left the two states at the end of the 1960s with different political structures connected differently to the economic and cultural contexts of politics. The comparisons which have been detailed can now be drawn together in summary form. Sources are cited only where they have not already been adduced. The summary will, we are convinced, show that we are dealing with differences of an entire pattern, differences at the system level.

SUMMARY OF RELEVANT DIFFERENCES

MAHARASHTRA	KERALA
Social Structures	
Rural population outnumbers urban.	Urban majority.
Dominant and large owner-cultivator caste.	Cultivating population fragmented by religion and highly stratified by caste.
Rural organizations for economic enterprise: credit, production, marketing.[140]	Organizations to press claims upon the system: unions.[141]
Economy	
Urban economy generates surplus for investment and off-farm jobs.	Urban economy less productive, stagnant relative to population growth.
Modern sector penetrates subsistence agriculture via credit, processing, and marketing.	Modern agricultural sector isolated in plantations. Exception: Kuttanad.
Rural economic growth.	Agricultural involution.
Tenure Structure	
Owner-operators a majority, owner-ship *relatively* equally distributed among them.	Owner-operators a minority, land relatively unequally held.
Tenant class small, disestablished by law.	Tenant class large, protected.
Laborers mostly nonowning, insecure.	Majority of laborers settled, wages regulated.

MAHARASHTRA (*cont'd*)   KERALA (*cont'd*)

Political Culture

Ideology not salient.

Society perceived as an expanding-sum game.

Politics highly ideological.

Zero-sum assumptions; justice perceived in distributive terms.

Political Inputs

One party dominant system.

Competition and turnover of two main parties. Splinter parties require coalition governments.

Dominant party is plural. Its active workers are election-oriented.

One party is plural, election-oriented. Other is disciplined, ideological, organized by cadre hierarchy.

Demands channeled through factional competition; factions personal and centered at district level.[142]

Demands channeled through interparty struggles directed at state level.[143]

Strong elective representation at district level.

Elective representation weak at levels between state and village.

Public influence exerted by votes.

Influence exerted by votes, but also by agitation, legal and illegal.

Political Outputs

Development programs emphasize facilitating enterprise.

Emphasis on education and welfare.

Development budget and staff controlled largely by elected district councils.[144]

Ministers and departments control development budget from state level.[145]

"Fused" government rural staff, party leadership, and cooperative leadership.

Party control of rural government staff contested. Parallel organizations of bureaucracy, parties and in some areas churches or caste associations.

LAND REFORM OUTCOMES

Indian society as a whole, certainly including Maharashtra and Kerala, was at the end of the decade of the 1960s drawn into a field of forces demanding, and resisting, agrarian transformation. We can think of these forces as providing a common stimulus to both our states, and of the responses of the states as evidencing the differing system potentials we have just summarized.

Pressure from the Center

In accordance with Indira Gandhi's commitment to "abolish poverty," as well as continuing economic, demographic, and political pressures, the ruling Congress established in September of 1970 the Central Land Reforms Committee (CLRC) to draft recommendations for a national land policy structured around increased productivity and enhanced economic equality. That Committee, in its *Report* of May 1972,[146] explained the urgency of agrarian reform in terms of the dramatic increase in landlessness, as well as the increased tensions in rural areas exacerbated by a new technology which accentuates income differentials.

But it would be wrong to view the central government as an unqualified force for agrarian reform. The Ministry of Agriculture and the National Commission on Agriculture, which influenced the guidelines, as well as the CLRC itself, are sensitive to the demands of large "progressive farmers."[147] The first recommendations of the CLRC, submitted to Parliament in August 1971, sought a lowering of the land ceiling to "10–18 acres of perennially irrigated land or land capable of growing two crops" and a change in the unit of ceiling from the individual to the family. The vast surplus thus obtained was to be distributed to the landless. A later report of recommendations by the Agriculture Ministry changed this provision to a "range of 10–18 acres of perennially irrigated land or land under assured irrigation from government sources capable of growing two crops a year."[148]

The latter formulation is considerably weaker; very little land is perenially irrigated, as this is not necessary for optimal irrigation, and even less land could be classified as having "assured irrigation from government sources." The net irrigated area in India in 1969 was about 22 percent of the total. The percentage of land sown more than once was only 17.6 percent of net sown area. Government canals accounted for only 37 percent of the net *irrigated* area (and how many canals could be classified as providing "assured" irrigation?); a majority of tube wells are privately owned, primarily by the largest farmers.[149] Nor does the ceiling look radical when placed in Indian perspective; as of the last National Sample Survey, 75.22 percent of all agriculturalists owned less than five acres of land and in aggregate only 19.9 percent of the area. Holdings above 15 acres accounted for only 6.83 percent of the agricultural households, but 45.5 percent of the area.[150] The final CLRC guidelines would allow up to double the ceiling for large families, with an absolute ceiling of 54 acres per family.

In this context, it is important to consider why V.P. Naik, the Chief Minister of Maharashtra and a member of the CLRC, was a leader of the opposition to lowering the ceiling,[151] and why Kerala enacted a land reform far more radical than the CLRC recommendations long before pressure from the Center began. Why has there been intense, persistent, and increasingly effective pressure within the Kerala political system for renovating the agrarian structure and virtually none in Maharashtra?

Watered down though the CLRC's final guidelines are, effective implementation could constitute an agrarian revolution. If the ceiling were 15 acres across the country, 70 million acres of land would have to change hands.[152] To date, after several decades of agrarian reform, less than 2 million acres have been redistributed.[153] Yet even Indira Gandhi, the primary force at the Center for fundamental land reforms, has told the Chief Ministers that there is "no point in competing in proposing radical measures," for "where is the organizational structure and administrative set-up to implement a more radical policy?"[154] The *Economic and Political Weekly* is more direct.

> Yet none of the circumstances which have thwarted the implementa-
> tion of existing laws have really changed. There is also no reason to
> believe that the balance of economic and political power in the rural
> community has undergone any change and so the administrative
> machinery may be expected to continue to collude with the landlord
> class.[155]

This all-India picture is but a sharply focused version of the worldwide picture (apart from Communist revolutionary regimes and a handful of reforming autocracies): a resistible force meeting an immovable object. That makes the difference in outcomes which we shall find between our two states worth studying.

Response: Maharashtra

There was genuine shock in political circles when the Chief Minister of Maharashtra, V.P. Naik, announced in October of 1971 that the State government would "shortly" promulgate an ordinance lowering the land ceiling and making the family the unit for assessment of holding size, in accordance with the Center's recommendations.[156] Naik was well known as a critic of new land reforms and had spoken publicly of the economic, political, and administrative arguments for retaining the existing ceilings.[157] The ordinance was to take effect in a matter of months, before the coming elections, though Naik stated that "the question might be discussed with leaders of the MPCC" (state Congress Committee).[158] Hints of serious opposition within the party came a month later when Vasantrao Patil, President of the MPCC, called a meeting of party leaders to "discuss the ceiling issue."[159] The meeting was to include not only MPCC members but also members of Parliament, the Legislative Assembly, zilla parishads (district councils), district Congress committees, and officials of cooperative sugar factories. At this stage, the reform was no longer an established governmental policy, but a question to be discussed by the lower echelons of the party.

Significant opposition to the reform emerged from the well-organized farmer lobby and from lower levels of the Congress party; the groups over-lap considerably. A well-publicized and typical incident in what the *Times of India* termed an "open revolt" was a meeting at Malishiras attended by wealthy cultivators of canal-irrigated sugarcane and presided over by

Shankarrao Mohite-Patil, a Congress member of the legislative assembly. Warning that the land reform would lead to Congress' being "wiped out" in Maharashtra, he argued in a classically populist vein that urban industrialists who were escaping socialist redistribution were the villains and would be fattened while farmers were impoverished.[160] An indication of the kind of opposition emerging is that other speakers included the vice-chairman of a cooperative sugar factory and the brother of the Minister of State for Cooperation. Mohite-Patil himself is chairman of a sugar cooperative and a district cooperative bank. He threatened that if the state party leadership proceeded with the ordinance, the interests represented at the meeting would refuse to give campaign contributions and work against party candidates in the election. There was also a threat to mobilize "even small-holders against the new ceiling under the slogan that the proposed ordinance would ruin the state's farming community and social fabric."[161]

Similar meetings were held throughout the state in the following month. At one meeting attended by Congress party workers a no-tax campaign was threatened. In Akola district, the pattern of pressure for reform from above and resistance from below was illustrated as the Congress Member of Parliament from the area spoke for lowered ceilings and opposition came from district-level elected officials and party leaders.[162] Opposition throughout the state was concentrated among overlapping groups of large farmers, local government units, Congress party workers, and people involved in cooperatives.

In late November, the *Times of India* described the "frantic efforts" of the top Congress leadership to "pacify the lower rungs of the party" on the ceiling issue. It was explained that "they should have 'no unfounded misgivings or fears' about the proposed lowered ceiling." Vasantrao Patil reassuringly stated that "the economic needs of the family will be considered." After meeting with Mohite-Patil, he said that the views of the dissidents would have to be taken into account.[163]

At the January meeting of the MPCC, Y.B. Chavan, the Center's Finance Minister and once undisputed leader of the state Congress, urged acceptance of the proposed reform. But the party overwhelmingly repudiated the idea of lowering the land ceiling by ordinance. Most speakers endorsed Mohite-Patil's position of opposing reduction of land ceilings until simultaneous action on a national urban land ceiling was taken.[164] The decision was to delay reform until a bill could be introduced in the first Assembly session after the elections. A left pressure group, the Congress Forum for Socialist Action, demanded that a reduced land ceiling be included in the election manifesto. The MPCC general meeting agreed, and endorsed the Central Land Reform Committee's recommendations, but urged more strongly an all-India ceiling on urban property.[165]

The opposition of wealthy agriculturists outside and within the Congress continued; later in the year the Shetkari Sanghatna was founded by Mohite-Patil to mobilize farmers' opinion against reform.[166] Another avenue of resistance was a familiar one; the *Times of India* reported that:

> Ever since the Chief Minister announced the decision to promulgate an
> ordinance revising ceilings, reports reaching Bombay from the districts
> stated that there had been a stampede of bagaitdars to register
> partitions, gift deeds, and transfers of land holdings. . . .

One Socialist party leader noted a marked increase in the sale of stamp
papers in rural areas.[167] Other farmers even found divorce a solution to the
family unit provision of the law.[168]

Naik's early announcement of the ordinance was bitterly denounced by
spokesmen for the Congress Forum for Socialist Action as "most irregular"
and "improper." The history of land reforms in India suggests that announcement of an ordinance, and failure to promulgate the ordinance,
while giving Naik claim to the Center's support in his factional fight to
retain the Chief Ministership, clearly served the function of alerting the
landed elite and producing the evasive actions described above, vitiating
systemic capacity to restructure the agrarian system.

In the pre-election period, important factional cleavages were articulated.
Indeed, it is possible to argue that the necessity of removing the Center as
a potential ally for an opposing faction forced Naik to proclaim reform
principles he had long opposed.[169] Thus competition within the dominant
party, and the resulting search by each faction for allies at the Center, particularly Indira Gandhi, allowed ratification of a reform position for which
neither powerful faction showed great enthusiasm. As both factions were
based in an elite rooted in the existing agrarian system, there was little
chance for effective pressure for radical reform of that system, although the
Congress Forum for Socialist Action and some members of the Bombay
Congress Committee pushed in that direction. And certainly there was no
organized pressure for radical reform from militant groups in the countryside possessed of the political resources of violence or threats thereof, and
electoral strength, as was the case in Kerala.

Congress swept the elections; we have no detailed analysis of the new
cabinet and legislature in terms of support for reforms but there is no reason
to believe that the "kulak" lobby and its allies are significantly less well
represented.[170] The bill which the government introduced does not provide
for a fundamental change of the agrarian system. The ceiling on perennially
irrigated land was not changed; wealthy canal-irrigated farmers had spearheaded the opposition to lowered ceilings. Thus the ceiling on the most
valuable land was unchanged at 18 acres. The unit of holding was to be the
family but a large family would be allowed legally to own up to twice the
ceiling. Ceilings on the other classes of irrigated land were reduced and the
maximum for dry land was set at 54 acres, subject in both cases to enhancement by family size up to twice the ceiling.

The assessment of Y.B. Chavan that very few farmers in the state would
be affected by the new law seems corroborated by a report in the *Economic
Times* of Bombay that the farmers' lobby had ceased vigorous opposition

to the bill after the CLRC's recommendations were diluted with the private irrigation clause and a liberal definition of "family."[171] The maximum possible redistributive effect may be judged by estimates of surplus available for redistribution to the landless. The *Economic and Political Weekly* on June 17, 1972, said this figure "had been reliably estimated" to be 2,500,000 acres. The Government's slightly later estimate was 1,500,000 acres. The estimate in the Preamble of the bill in August 1972, was 375,000 acres.[172] This last figure represents well under 1 percent of sown area and certainly less than 1 percent of net land wealth since the best land will presumably be least affected. Estimating the actual redistributive impact is impossible, but it is almost certain to be less than the target; under the 1961 Ceiling Act, only 62,000 acres were redistributed of an estimated 2,718,000 acres declared surplus.[173]

The redistributive impact was further blunted by a rate of compensation set above that of the 1961 Act, a change which several legislators feared would strengthen rural elites. Since the Indian Constitution has been amended to allow confiscation of surplus land without compensation, this provision struck some opposition legislators as imposing an unnecessary burden on the State and on the landless who would receive the land. Other legislators worried that little land would become surplus because of the absence of land records and official collusion with landowners at the local level. As a response, the opposition urged inclusion of a provision for popular committees, but with assurances from the Revenue Minister that "advisory committees" would be provided for in the working rules, the motion failed.[174] The *Times of India* reports of the legislative debates give reason to believe these committees, if instituted, would only advise on distribution of surplus land and there is no mention of representation of political parties on the committees.[175]

The difficulty in implementing a ceiling law is less in distributing the surplus than in obtaining something to distribute—obtaining correct information on land ownership and applying pressure at the local level to prevent fraudulent transfers and evasions. Yet the Maharashtra bill offers no new solution to these problems. The same machinery—the Revenue Department and the Collectors—which failed to implement the 1961 Ceiling Act is to be employed. The penalty for suppression of landholding information is the same nominal Rs. 25 fine of the 1961 Act, acknowledged by the Government to have failed in preventing previous evasions.[176] And the bill itself seems to abound in potential for new evasions—inclusion of bogus family members, claiming majority status for minors, backdated partitions, registration of irrigated land as dry, etc.

Though the opposition argued that very little would be changed by the bill,[177] there was no real pressure to alter it or to mobilize support for a change. This absence of pressure probably represents, on the part of both dissident Congressmen and opposition leaders, an accurate appraisal of the configuration of political forces in the state, as we have illustrated.

Response: Kerala

We have presented the tenurial, demographic, and economic situation of Kerala as one characterized by acute deprivation for rural have-nots under conditions which have prevented significant distribution by the government of boons and benefits to a large percentage of the rural population. The insecurity and deprivation engendered by the distribution of resources and power in the agrarian system, aggravated by a low level of aggregate development and largely unrelieved by channels of upward mobility, found expression in a highly politicized and competitive electoral system in which the rural underclass can no longer be mobilized by traditional rural elites. Contrary to some propositions of comparative theory, this configuration of conditions produces a political capability for restructuring the agrarian system which is unique in India.

The latest reform was enacted under the CPM-led United Front ministry in late 1969 and became effective on January 1, 1970, under the Achutha Menon CPI-led ministry. Technically an amendment to the 1964 Act, the law represents in itself a thorough-going response to the defects in earlier legislation. The failure of the earlier act has been implied; Kerala after its enactment was found in an official all-India comparison to have the highest percentage of intermediaries, the highest percentage of tenants, and the lowest percentage of owner-cultivators in India.[178]

Recognizing the previous failures in tenancy reform, indeed the near impossibility of regulating the terms of tenancy, the 1969 act abolished tenancy completely.[179] Maharashtra attempted the same thing in 1957, as have other states, but the sensitivity of the Kerala response to earlier failures is reflected in the concept of "deemed tenant." Whether because of intimidation by landlords, complicated bureaucratic procedures, or landlord control of local land records, less than 1,000 of Kerala's 1.5 million tenants successfully applied for ownership rights under the 1964 Act. The 1969 amendment specifies that numerous categories of tenants as well as any cultivator "honestly believing himself to be a tenant" become owners on the enacted date, and must subsequently pay the State 16 times the "fair rent" (one-half the contract rent) in yearly installments.[180] The burden of landlord compensation is assumed by the State. Unpaid installments do not affect the tenants' ownership rights but become recoverable as arrears of land revenue.

Not only does the "deemed tenant" concept potentially weaken one elite advantage—superior access to record-keepers—but theoretically could eliminate many of the crippling delays caused by litigation over discrepancies in land records, litigation which clearly advantages elites because of the cost involved, the sympathies of the courts to established property rights, and the frequent unwillingness of dependents to challenge patrons, especially in the unfamiliar legal arena. Previous evictions of tenants are declared void. Right of resumption, which has caused waves of tenant evictions, e.g., in Maharashtra, was severely constrained and ended absolutely six months after the effective date of the act.[181]

Recognizing the vulnerability of tenants economically vis-à-vis money-lenders and former landlords, the law reduces significantly the amount of arrears of rent that can be claimed. And in July 1970, the Agriculturists' Debt Relief Act brought a six-month moratorium on collection proceedings in the courts.[182]

Besides abolition of the tenant-landlord mode of production, the law seeks to correct the neglect in earlier legislation of the totally landless who are dependent on owners even for housesites and often live with the constant fear of eviction. The law allows these "kudikidappukars," mostly agricultural laborers, to purchase their housesites at nominal prices, assisted by the State. They are then protected by law from eviction, sanctioned by a stiff penal provision. Although the plots are to be small (.03 acres to .1 acres), the provision of a garden plot, a few coconut trees, and freedom from dependence on an owner should increase the security and independence of these people. This independence may eventually allow more effective mobilization of have-nots for further agrarian reforms.[183]

Compared to the "land to the tiller" provisions, the Act's reduction in the legal ceiling, already the lowest in India, was less significant. It was also enormously difficult both to define a surplus and to specify classes of beneficiaries. The new ceiling ranges from six to twenty acres varying by family size. Owners with tenants are further constrained in the amount of land they may keep.

In contrast to the Maharashtra case, opposition to the reform did not emerge openly. Political parties clearly sensitive to landed interests supported the bill.[184] Opposition instead came in the enforcement stage, mainly through delays, noncooperation, illegal transfers, and the challenging of key sections of the law in the courts. This pattern is familiar in Indian land reforms, but in Kerala this opposition was countered by mobilization of political forces to pressure the system toward innovative responses to landowner resistance.

As an early response to delays and litigation, an amendment in 1971 empowered the Land Board to take over and before full investigative and survey work was done and gave the Board sole authority to review its own decisions, removing such questions from the conservative and tedious court system.[185]

Surplus taken for redistribution is still to be paid for, but the 1971 amendment facilitated the compensation process and reduced the burden on the State. It lowered the rate of compensation and significantly fixed it at a statutory sum per acre, depending on the class of land.[186] A major source of litigation was thus eliminated. An absolute ceiling was set on the amount of compensation any individual could receive.[187]

Despite the clear intent of the legislators, implementation was tedious and slow, as all parties admitted. Partially this was a result of the magnitude of the task: in contrast to the Maharashtra law, which would affect at the most 1 percent of sown area, the Kerala reform aimed at a renovation of the entire agrarian system and would affect tenures on about half the sown

acreage. The principal obstacles to such drastic change in Kerala, as elsewhere in the world, were the courts, the administrative apparatus, and the
landlords and large landowners. The courts issued stay orders to landowners
obviating the obligation to release surplus land. Key provisions of the 1969
law and the 1971 amendment were ruled unconstitutional by the High Court
and the Supreme Court.[188] As a response, under pressure from the CPM,
the ruling coalition took steps to have the 1969 legislation and its amendments included in the Ninth Schedule of the Constitution of India, which
exempts listed land reform laws of the States from judicial review.[189] A
constitutional amendment had to be enacted in Delhi; with the support
of the Indira Gandhi majority, this was accomplished (29th Amendment)
on May 31, 1972.[190]

Progress of implementation of the reform in Kozhikode District by
May 1973 provides a view of both the initial delays and the far-reaching
administrative effort to break through them.[191] Under Section 72 the 250,000
tenancies in the district ended on Jan. 1, 1970; rent payments stopped. But
former tenants could obtain title, and former landlords could receive compensation, only upon formal assignment by the government land tribunal.
One must note here that the main burden of delay was shifted by law to the
former landlord, since in the hiatus the tenant paid neither rent nor taxes,
yet enjoyed security. Almost three and one half years after the effective
date, less than half (110,000) of the holdings had been brought before the
21 decentralized tribunals in the district and only 47,000 of these had been
disposed of. Though the administrative staff costs of implementation were
running at Rs. 10,000,000, it might thus take as much as twenty years to finish
the Statewide job. It was found in Kozhikode that the average case had to be
called twelve times instead of the necessary two because of absence of documents or parties. Now the work of the tribunals is being taken right into the
villages. Each village revenue staff is called on to initiate sixty cases per
month, progressing from one end of village lands to the other. The tribunal
hears the cases in the village, issues its proposed assignment of ownership
to the former tenant and compensation to the former landlord on the spot,
and simultaneously notifies the parties of the final hearing. Assignments
are thus completed at four times the former rate, and with better access by
the tribunals to the real state of affairs.

Obstruction by the big landowners took the form of failure to register
legal surpluses. As a response, the CPM has directed recurrent "land grab"
actions in which tenants, laborers, or sometimes landless tribal people
would occupy, harvest, and till land the CPM claims to be above the legal
ceiling. In December 1972, for instance, the CPM had a list of holdings
totalling 175,000 acres earmarked for takeover since the owners had not
declared them surplus, and the government had not seized them. These
actions, while not always accurate in delimiting surplus land, clearly energized both the Revenue administration and political leadership in the State,
thus facilitating effective implementation.[192]

The most stubborn resistance came from highly capitalized rice farm owners in the Kuttanad tract, an area reclaimed from coastal waters by the polder method. Twice in the last three years the landowners, whose holdings before the present reform averaged 150 acres, have defied the law requiring payment of minimum wages to agricultural laborers. On the first occasion in 1971, the Youth Congress proposed to take over cultivation of the fields to break the owners' boycott.[193] Again in 1972, the Achutha Menon government itself took over 1900 acres for direct cultivation when the owners refused to comply with a government wage order.[194] Legal loopholes were closed, too, by a 1972 amendment and sanctions strengthened against land-lord obstructions: land transfers after introduction of the 1969 legislation, except to children, are *retroactively* voided, and the penalty for violation now includes imprisonment.[195]

Neither judicial interference, administrative delay, nor landlord obstruc-tion could have been overcome without continuing agitation, threatened or actual, by the strongest parties in the state and their peasant leagues. The Youth Congress fought off amendments which would have preserved the exemption of land in religious trusts. It was perfectly ready for "an agitational approach" if necessary.[196] The CPI-led peasant association charged in its April 1972 convention that the government headed by a CPI Chief Minister was conniving to thwart implementation of reforms. It propos-ed mass action beginning on May Day, including *dharna* or silent picketing before the houses of guilty landlords.[197] The CPM has continually threatened "land grabs" whenever implementation was obstructed by legal or adminis-trative difficulties, or a reform amendment was bogged in the legislative process. This was the history of the enactment of the 1972 amendment, for example, after agitation from May until August. Mobilizing the strength of the poor by these agitations has been commended by the government in power. The Revenue Minister announced in 1972 that the government would not interfere with agrarian agitations.[198] indeed, Chief Minister Achutha Menon blamed failures in implementation on "administrative mechanisms," and "inadequate mobilization of the people."[199]

To institutionalize this participation of the rural poor, the Chief Minister proposed in the spring of 1972 establishment of taluq-level popular com-mittees, representing all political parties, to assess, take over, and distribute surplus lands. He was supported at once by A.K. Antony, leader of the Youth Congress.[200] Only after four months of agitation was legislation passed to this effect. The popular committees meet a requirement widely stipulated in the worldwide policy literature as necessary to break the crust of rural power structure.[201] Since they are capable of freeing rural have-nots from the domination by landowners of access to information, village records, and the revenue bureaucracy, their consequences may prove to be profound. Evaluation, however, will have to wait for the evidence.

Despite the continuing pursuit of legislative remedies, implementation of tenurial change since January 1970 is a mixed picture. Only about 10,000 cultivated acres have been taken by the government, and only 1,800 acres actually redistributed.[202] The government estimated when the 1969 bill was introduced that it would define 245,000 acres as surplus. On its effective date, the estimate was down to 150,000. Returns from the landlords listed 53,000 acres.[203] Even the highest of these figures, we have observed, would be less than half enough land to bring present tenants and squatters up to the half-acre size of a Kerala subfarm. Perhaps to offset this failure, the government also took over the untilled land of the great Kannan Devan tea estate, estimated to amount to 25,000 acres. Stayed by the courts, the seizure was made good by a new ordinance applying alike to all private forest land in the state, and denying judicial review.[204]

Converting tenants to owners is not halfway to formalization : unpublished figures of the Land Board, Trivandrum, show that as of October 31 1974, of the estimated 1.5 million tenants, 951,742 cases have been registered and 525,267 finally acted upon. But the landlords suffer from the lag, not the erstwhile tenants. For more than three years now, Rs. 170 or 180 million of rent has not been transferred; only when deeds are made over to the tenants will payments resume in the form of compensation in 16 installments. Tenants already have, then, both the economic and the administrative advantage, though these are important exceptions.

Most successful has been the confirmation of homestead and garden plots to kudikidappukars. Half the kudikidappukars in the state applied for plots within two years after the new law took effect, and a quarter of them had already received allotments.[205]

The effects of the reform upon political power in the state have, on the contrary, been consistent and crucial. A characteristic cycle recurs. Injustices to those on the periphery of the system are met with agitation for redress. Under that pressure, reform comes. The agitations and resultant reforms give the deprived political as well as economic status. They make new redistributive demands. The reform was legislated in 1969 under the shadow of threatened and actual terrorism by Naxalite dissidents of the CPM and frequent clashes between landowners and communist-led laborers, particularly in the rice areas.[206] By 1972 the CPM's peasant agitations had so far entered the system that the government leaders met with the state secretary of the CPM. The government spokesmen established that they meant business about amending the law to create "people's committees." The CPM in response suspended "land grabs," to launch them again if progress did not follow.[207] Meanwhile a million tenants are turning owners, in the process becoming taxpayers and dealing directly with the state. Another third of a million laborers are getting homesteads, assisted and subsidized by the State. Thus the conditions for political development of the kind that produces a capacity to restructure the agrarian system are enhanced and extended by the process of restructuring. With the institution of popular committees, further peasant participation and political competition should result in further politicization and exercise of the new powers as producers and citizens. The system is further energized to make future responses for which there is only the feeblest support in the Maharashtra situation.

The recent cycles of reform do not solve the economic problem of Kerala agriculture : too many people trying to make a living from the land. For the state's agricultural involution still more innovative responses will be needed. Here again, the political system has shown itself ready to innovate. The government has launched joint farming on 2,700 acres confiscated from the Kannan Devan estate. Three collective farms are planned on state land; two were opened in 1972.[208]

CONCLUSIONS

We have used an intranational comparison to try out, and hopefully to refine, some current theories of the political conditions of land reform. Our examination of Kerala and Maharashtra has certainly demonstrated that there may exist, at least within the subcontinental nation of India, ample variance across most of the supposed determinants of the success of reform. We have observed that in the late 1960s, when reform was inserted into the policy agenda by the economic consequences of the Green Revolution, the political alarms of the Naxalbari movement, and the insistence of Prime Minister Indira Gandhi, the relevant decision-context differed in the two states along at least these four crucial dimensions :

1. Maharashtra's economy was expanding, Kerala's stagnant, especially in the rural sectors.
2. Maharashtra's land tenure structure contained a relatively undifferentiated owner-operator class, protected and favored by the government, a tiny tenant stratum officially disestablished, and a large minority of unorganized, insecure laborers. Owner-operators were approximately half of the rural population. In Kerala severe inequalities of land holdings and economic bargaining power were counterbalanced in part by prior legislative protections of tenants and laborers, but more importantly by the political strength of sharecroppers and laborers through organized unions and the left political parties.
3. Maharashtra's rural development programs emphasized productivity and economic growth via assistance to individual and cooperative farm enterprise. Kerala led in rural education and welfare.
4. Popular impulses reached government, finally, in very different ways. Demands in Maharashtra were for localized facility and subsidies; they were aggregated at the district level through personal factions and elective councils, and at the state level through the interplay of these rural Congress leaders with administrators attuned to urban interests.[209] Kerala rural demands were for redistribution and regulation, aggregated at the state level by two clusters of parties, one led by the Congress cultivating the constituency of the "haves," the other led by the CPM, championing the "have-nots." Maharashtra's institutions worked to mitigate and diffuse class consciousness, Kerala's to heighten it.

Our explanatory problem is thus not to find contextual differences adequate to explain contrasting reform responses. It is, rather, to identify which of a plethora of differences are essential, which coincidental. Two cases do not suffice to do this in anything approaching a scientific way. We shall be more faithful to our evidence if, instead, we draw our conclusions upon the premise that what we have been examining are different political-economic systems. In each, economic, tenurial, government output, and political input characteristics have evolved together and now powerfully reinforce one another. We shall, accordingly, look for the crucial connection of whole-system characteristics to the theoretical propositions with which we began this essay.

Maharashtra : Hegemony via Expansion

Maharashtra, controlled by one cohesive party, could not seriously attempt agrarian transformation in the 1970s. Kerala's fiercely competing, sometimes dividing parties could. Huntington's theory that concentration of power is necessary for redistribution, and that competition of parties in parliaments precludes reforms[210] is not confirmed by our comparison. From two cases we cannot claim that the theory is disconfirmed. But we can fruitfully ask whether the lack of fit of evidence to theory is incidental or accidental, or whether it is central and relevant, and if the latter, whether the theory can be restated to accommodate such cases as ours.

Perhaps we have simply been looking at Maharashtra several decades too late to catch the reforming impact of concentrated power. After all, British policy rescued the ryots from the moneylenders in the last quarter of the nineteenth century. But if we try more rigorously to characterize Maharashtra's rural political and economic development the concepts of "concentrated power" and "redistributive reforms" seem less and less appropriate to the case. During the very period when incremental tenurial reforms were protecting the owner-cultivator class, their allegiance was in doubt as between rival parties or movements. And the essence of tenurial reform was never redistributing, but rather enlarging, ownership.

If we attempt to identify the necessary conditions for this course of development in terms general enough that they might be looked for in other states or nations, four conditions are unmistakable.

1. The formation of a modern Maharashtrian political elite pre-dated and was part of the formation of an all-Indian nationalist elite. Kerala's political elite formation was, by comparison, more isolated from the nation's.[211]

2. The powerful nationalist orientation of the regional elite is only part of the explanation of their incremental, finally complete, extension of political power to the land-owning peasantry. The other necessary condition was that they had, if they wanted peasant following, to compete for it. They never could take it for granted. The nationalist intelligentsia had to

compete on two fronts. First, they had to outbid the British hold on rural administration to whom, in obvious contrast with the Madras administrators' attitudes toward Malabar ryots, the Deccan cultivators were an indispensable support base. Not only did the British cultivate that base by legislating protection of owner-cultivators against "capitalist" creditors, but they cultivated it by extending local board elections into the countryside, thus fostering a set of village politicians at the district level with whom the Congress nationalists had to come to terms. The nationalist leaders had also, from the very beginning to compete for peasant followings with a militant non-Brahman political leadership working initially through the Satya Shodnak Samaj[212] and the anti-Brahman politics of the Maharaja of Kolhapur,[213] then at the very time of Independence, through the Peasants and Workers party. In one sense the non-Brahman movement was backlash to the quick preemption by the Chitpavans of modern roles opened by the British : the more traditional Namboodiris evoked no such backlash in Kerala politics. But also it was the working in the minds of non-Brahman leaders and in virtually all Maratha caste members, as they became literate, of the same memories of a nation in arms under Shivaji, and of the Western ideas of equality which attracted the intelligentsia.

The history of nationalism in Maharashtra up to the death of Gokhale (1915) and Tilak (1920) has often been presented as a struggle for power between two towering Chitpavan leaders projecting onto the all-India stage rival strategies of nationalism, "moderate" and "extremist." From a later perspective, one can see a wider and deeper struggle temporarily cut across by this factional competition. That is the struggle of the whole of the Congress nationalist leadership to win the confidence and participation of the Maratha peasantry from the non-Brahman leadership to whom the British were opening district elective roles. A 1936 document, the *Report of the Peasant Enquiry Committee* of the Maharashtra Provincial Congress Committee, makes this competition manifest :

> we did not take long to see the crux of the non-Brahmin movement. In thousands of villages spread over all the districts, the agents of the peasant's exploitation are the upper castes .... Thus it was an easy way to appeal to the peasantry that such rights and privileges as the 'Mai Bap' Sarkar deigns to confer on the people of India must be secured for the non-Brahmins of the Province. Thus the class-antagonism inherent in the existing economic situation viewed superficially appeared to be in reality caste-antagonism, an old and continued tension with a history going back to the feudal times of the Maratha Empire.[214]

Two points about this self-diagnosis are of comparative interest. First, the Congress organization is here alerted to the usually latent class conflict in the countryside, manifesting itself as caste demands, a perception which such then Congress leaders as E.M.S. Namboodiripad tried in vain to bring home to the Kerala provincial Congress in that same year. Second, while Namboodiripad was failing and A.K. Gopalan was leading a Malabar rent strike in opposition to the provincial Congress government, in 1938-39, the Maharashtra Congress used its newly won provincial power to pass the Bombay Tenancy Act of 1939. The act was not enforced until 1946, since the Congress quit power in protest to British war policy. But it drew a legislative line between landowners who intended to operate land by family or hired labor, and those who intended mainly to get rent, and it sought to permit the former to resume occupancy from the latter.[215] The comparative conclusion is that the nationalist movement in Maharashtra had to win a peasant following partly in competition with a rival movement which championed peasant grievances, first on a caste basis, but later in 1948-54 upon economic grounds.

Along with Chitpavan Congress leaders, the committee which drew up the 1936 report included Keshavarao M. Jedhe, the outstanding political figure of the Maratha caste, and a man who would have been quick to sense the exploitation of the peasants by the Brahman landlords and revenue officials. The continuing tension upon the Maharashtra Congress from such sources is indicated by Jedhe's later role in taking his followers out of the Congress to form the Peasants and Workers party in 1948. In 1954, after much deliberation and negotiation, he led them back in.[216] The 1956 land tenure reform followed this reorientation of the party just as the 1939 act followed upon the need of the Congress to regain peasant followers preparatory to an election (1937) in a depression year.

The political situation from 1875 to 1954 was not, then, one of concentrated but of insecure power. The nationalist leaders conceived of themselves as leaders of a peasant nation, to be sure, but they had to win the peasants not by symbolic appeals, but by laws protecting and expanding their economic class, and by extending them political power. In 1954, they opened the Congress to peasant control. Only then was power concentrated.

3.   A broad stratum of rural population was relatively undifferentiated by caste in Maharashtra. Marriage barriers did exist. But there were not, among the vast majority of the families who operated farms those deep divisions of clean—unclean sanctioned by religious culture which separated tenurial classes in Kerala. From this point of view, Maharashtra, like, for example, the Jat districts of Western U.P., escapes from the handicap of traditional fragmentation of the peasantry which Barrington Moore advanced as explanation for the lack of peasant revolt in India.[217] We attach the same importance to this condition as he does. But we note that, at least among traditionally clean castes, adult suffrage and tenurial policy operating in an expanding economy can, over decades, have the effect of amalgamating castes for political and economic purposes. Moreover, we see the effects of relatively undifferentiated caste structures as working toward peasant power in all its forms, not peasant revolt alone.

4.   An expanding, indeed, from 1880 to 1930 a mushrooming, urban economic center—Bombay—is a condition for the Maharashtrian course of development. We believe urban economic growth underwrites "the shared

vision of a relatively costless expansionary rural economy" which, as Don Rosenthal has put it, characterizes the rural-political game in Maharashtra.

One impact of an expanding urban-industrial growth upon rural politics is straightforward. The general State budget pays for more than nine-tenths of the development expenditures of the panchayati raj elective institutions in the State. Urban taxes thus fuel the rural patronage process which maintains Congress hegemony. It is, to be sure, a two-stage distribution. Bigger landholders are able to take unequal advantage of government development expenditures.[218] But they in turn draw their followings to them by further distribution of "amenities" under control of panchayat and cooperative institutions.

Penetrating further, we find the relation of metropolitan to rural wealth and power complex, even paradoxical. Linked though they were by Maharashtrian national leaders, e.g., Gokhale, Bombay city politics was not part of a single provincial system. That is well shown by the decision of the Congress in 1920 to leave the city organization separate from the Maharashtra Pradesh Congress Committee—the notable exception to the regional reorganization of the Congress upon linguistic lines throughout India.[219] Nor was the investment of capital accumulated in Bombay during the nineteenth century, public or private, invested in rural infrastructure as a base for growth of an entire urban-rural economy; the railways, for example, were directed across the Deccan toward more distant commercial and strategic centers. In fact, a case could be made that Maharashtra developed a political economy responsive to the demands of a peasant majority *because* there nationalists enlisted nonelites in a linguistic region quite apart from, and finally as a challenge to, the political forces of the cosmopolitan metropolis. The three decades beginning with the salt *satyagraha* and ending with the absorption of the multilingual Bombay in a state of Marathi speakers in 1960 demarcate this development. Poona, not Bombay, was the cultural center; Maratha domination of the Congress was the specific power stake; and language was the mobilizing issue. The outcome was that the State, governed by a peasant-dominated party, took control of the city.

There is a further nonobvious connection between urban development and rural. Bombay State, and now Maharashtra, could deploy to the solution of rural problems the strong hierarchical structures and the superb administrative and professional talents which urban centers develop. The Reserve Bank, for instance, was watching over the development of rural credit cooperatives in the State from its headquarters in the city. The 1936 Congress Peasant Enquiry Committee acknowledged the close advice of D.R. Gadgil of the Gokhale Institute of Economics and Politics.[220] The Maharashtra model of powerful elective control of rural development is the product of confident, creative administrative leadership as well as of rural political institutions and leadership capable of bearing the responsibilities.[221]

The overall result is a linkage between city and countryside in which shared assumptions accompany autonomous spheres of control. "Instead of being antagonistic to the interests of urban businessmen, many of the leading politicians in the Maharashtrian countryside have become rural entrepreneurs ... linking the countryside to the city," writes Don Rosenthal "some even *think* like businessmen."[222] But the institutional bases of their power—the great processing cooperatives, district cooperative banks, district councils—have their roots in the countryside. The influence accumulated by their rural leaders, drawn together by the district Congress faction heads, is seen by Mary Carras as countervailing the pressures on the State government of concentrated urban economic interests.[223] Big peasants who share the urban assumption of *expanding* opportunities while they have their own modern, growing sources of patronage to distribute, are prepared to expand political participation. Redistribution is not a serious threat.

It is intriguing to speculate on the fit of the Maharashtra developmental path to large-scale comparative theories of system development. Curiously, the parallel which seems most attractive is England's. Barrington Moore's interpretation of it sees the eighteenth-century Parliament as an "instrument of a commercially minded, landed, upper class." But it was "an arena into which new social elements could be drawn as their demands arose and an institutional mechanism for settling peacefully conflicts of interests among these groups."[224] This is a reasonably appropriate characterization of the party and legislative—the political input—system of Maharashtra. J.H. Plumb's more detailed description of the stratum of the politically powerful in England of that time fits too: "men of property ... whose tap-root was in the land, but whose side roots reached out to commerce, industry and finance."[225] In England, the system consequences of the accession of these commercialized rural landholders to power was the construction of Walpole's machine, an eighteenth-century roll-back of political competition.[226] That, too, fits.

Since Moore sees in the English experience a pathway from agrarian to urban-industrial society ending in an open democratic state, it would be possible to see Maharashtra as a counterpart, perhaps as pioneering the English pathway for the whole Indian nation. But there are two principal conditions for the English model which are evidently missing in Maharashtra's case. The English commercializing landlords established their secure, yet open control of nineteenth-century politics while government policy (enclosure law) was eliminating tenants from the countryside, and subsidizing jobs for them in commerce and manufactures. Maharashtra, by contrast, remains overwhelmingly agrarian, and her tenants have been eliminated (though not her farm laborers) by a different kind of policy intervention, i.e., converting some of them to owners. Secondly, Moore sees the sixteenth-century revolution in England as a key prerequisite, England represents to him "the contribution of violence to gradualism."[227] Maharashtra's rural transition we have seen to have been relatively non-violent, and the Deccan Riots largely symbolic. Is revolutionary violence a symptom rather than a root cause of the prerequisite condition we have found in Maharashtra: the centrality of the peasantry to the ruling classes as commercialism and nationalism upset village structures? Is the early vigor of nationalism in England rather than the Cromwellian revolution the essential condition of a commercialization in which landowners can participate, not be displaced, and in which a parliament intervenes to adapt rural society incrementally to change? If so, we could by altering a basic proposition in Moore's theory, find the solidarity of the rulers and the intellectuals with the peasantry, peculiar in all India to Maharashtra and Sikh Punjab, fits our case to his theory revised.

Kerala: Harnessing Class Conflict

As we understand it, Kerala poses an anomaly for the current theory of the politics of agrarian reform; systematically divided and competing power, not concentrated power, effect redistribution of rights in land.

Is this reformist expression of class conflict an ephemeral outcome? It is hard to gauge revolutionary potential. On the one hand, the raw materials of revolution accumulate in Kerala: more high school and college graduates unemployed longer, and more minifarm owners and laborers unable to make a living from their holdings than anywhere else in the country. On the other hand, remarkably, disaffection from the political process has thus far been lower here than in some Indian states possessing far less of the supposed potential for revolution. A competing, elective, reforming system seems to maintain legitimacy here; if one judges by the tenure in office of a single coalition, it seems to have gained in legitimacy over previous periods of lower potential for disaffection. Our tentative verdict, then, is that Kerala demonstrates a route of system development in which class conflict is enlisted to energize redistribution while contained within rules of largely parliamentary competition.

How has it come about? Extending our interpretation to general terms, we can identify these conditions:

1. Acute tenurial grievances, in the district where they occurred, were perceived as peripheral both by colonial rulers and all-India nationalists.

2. A Marxist counter-leadership responded to these grievances, but not within the constraints of external models. Communist strategy for Kerala was created, it is important to observe, at variance with the western Marxist-Leninist model of dependence on the industrial proletariat, but stopping short of the Maoist model of creating dual power in rural revolutionary enclaves.

The point will become clearer if we contrast the opposite tendency of the Communist movement in Maharashtra. Gail Omvedt's recent studies find the early Communist leaders in Bombay to have been constrained either by a cosmopolitan or a Brahman orientation. To the cosmopolitans, the mill workers of Bombay, however tiny a proportion of the State's work force, fit too neatly the premises of world revolutionary ideology to warrant rethinking the possible revolutionary role of poor peasant. Most Bombay

Communist leaders were Brahman intellectuals, moreover, who could hardly
intuit the almost completely inarticulate demands of the Maratha tenants.
Omvedt discovered one exception, Dinkarrao Javalkar, a Maratha Communist who designed a flag for the party bearing the plow as its symbol, but
he died in 1932.[228] So the non-Brahman mill workers and the non-Brahman
tenants were never drawn into a single movement for economic redress;
in the end, as we saw, the latter were absorbed into the Congress.

3. Equally deviant, at least from the Westminster model, has been
Kerala's version of parliamentary democracy. We may fairly conclude that
extra-constitutional agitation, both within and outside the law, has become
a convention of Kerala democracy. Certainly the resistances which powerful
conservative administration, courts, national government oversight, and the
routines of land record-keeping pose to redistribution of property rights could
not be overcome, even partly without the present threat of land seizures, agitation, and violence organized by parties out of power, and sometimes even in
power.

4. The structural differentiation of the Indian political system, which so
discouraged Doreen Warriner, may here exert a positive influence for reform.
The government in Delhi has not been even-handed. It has, however, given
assurance to the fiercely competing parties in Kerala that the next elections
would take place. It is difficult to conceive of the Kerala system—sincerely
revolutionary parties competing against parties which sincerely believe them
subversive of the constitutional rules—without an outside power, even a
less than neutral outside power, holding the ring.

5. Along this route, the educational system produced a nonagricultural
majority, regardless of the failure of the economic system to employ them.
At the very least, this urbanized population comprises a political support
base outside landlord control; at most, its economic frustration and accessibility to the ideology of redistributive justice brings it into political
struggles on the side of land reform.

Kerala appears thus to be a stable polity capable of maintaining the
conditions of contained conflict which we found supportive of an ongoing
land reform program. But whether Kerala can generate the economic productivity her politicized people will demand in the longer run is another
matter. One of us (Ron Herring) is, after visiting Kerala late in 1974, impressed by the polarization of political life. Ironically, the very polarization
and politicization which produced innovative reform measures now threa-
tens to vitiate reform potential. Horizontal class solidarity is broken by
partisan competition, identification, and violence. The major agent of the
rural under-class, the CPM, has, because of electoral tactics in a bid for
parliamentary power, lessened the pressure on the ruling coalition and
bureaucracy for rapid implementation. The popular committees cannot be
formed because the political parties refuse to cooperate, fearing losses in the
electoral game. The economically dubious strategy of creation of ever more

fragmented subsistence holdings is necessary because of the imperatives of electoral politics. Cooperative or collective solutions to longer-range problems of production in the involuted economy would seem to be even more hopeless in this atmosphere of highly charged partisanship. The obverse of the Maharashtra case, Kerala has purchased political options at the price of economic rigidity

The Uses and Limits of Political Will

We have noted that the most popular current explanation of Indian inaction upon the redistribution of land is the lack of political will.[229] "Will" has two connotations: to desire, and to choose. As to the first, subjective, meaning, social scientists can gain no special information; we do not know whether Indira Gandhi, or V.P. Naik, or E.M.S. Namboodiripad inwardly wanted land redistributed. But as to the second meaning our comparison can be clarifying. The range of choice is narrow. To be sure, Indira Gandhi is free to *advocate* any among a wide range of reform options. Those upon which she could choose *action* in 1970 occupy a narrow range close to the status quo. Naik and Namboodiripad, on the contrary, had power to move the levers of action in their states, but their power would dissolve quickly if they embarked upon a line of policy inconsistent with the expectations of their rural followers and the configurations of rural political power. Political power is, as Doreen Warriner complained, compartmentalized in India. Those outside, or above, the State arena cannot act; those in the arena have entered preprogrammed to a particular direction of tenurial policy. There is no *deus ex machina*.

Political will can, therefore, carry little of the weight of explanation at any one point of history. Hopefully, we have demonstrated a supplementary perspective, the view of policy choices as opened by a particular route of political-economic development, and of that path of development itself as a human artifact. We have viewed the political economy of a State as a succession of adjustments made by large numbers of people to problems and changes in other sectors of life inside and outside the State. Sometimes those adjustments are under concerted leadership; in such cases they may be guided by visions of the future in the minds of leaders, visions exogenous to the State, or even to the culture. Herein lies room for will in the sense of choice. To recall two of many examples: the decision to use village school teachers to awaken and organize tenant consciousness in Malabar opened a very unusual political option in India—to build and maintain a modern political party firmly rooted in a following of the agrarian poor[230] which in turn pulled Kerala agrarian policy in the direction of establishing, regulating the wages of, and conferring housesites and garden plots to the laborer class. The decision to invest in modern sugar mills as peasant-owned cooperatives in the irrigated tracts of Maharashtra not only enriched a powerful rural stratum but put extensive patronage in its hands to enlist support from small farmers.

Second, it is evident that system-building options were not evenly distributed through the years, a century in all, that we examined. They were concentrated at certain historical junctures. One such antedated our review —the institutionalization of a system of land revenue by the British Empire. The second we did observe: it was marked by the opening of a large-scale market in crops, and thereafter in farm land. Great change suddenly became possible, for wealth could be accumulated within the village outside traditional norms, and (even more consequential) new wealth, rural and urban, could gain nontraditional control of land. Both Maharashtra and Kerala exhibit the crucial passage identified in the writings of Moore, Wolff, and Scott. We saw two general options for policy response. Government could intervene on behalf of those operating the land, as in Maharashtra and to some extent Travancore, shielding them from market forces. Or, as in Malabar, a government attuned to different interests and concerns could legitimize the dissolution of traditional constraints upon commercial exploitation of inferior tenures.

That choice, taken about a century ago in both states, strongly loaded the alternatives opened in the next system-building episode. This was the initial politicization of the countryside in the anticolonial movement— Huntington's Green Uprising. Rural followings were now available to nationalist intellectuals on different terms. In Maharashtra, Travancore, and even Cochin political participation, access to education, and the further protection of owner-operated farms were effective appeals. The tenant population of Malabar, in contrast, answered appeals to religious millenarianism and to class conflict. The resulting party system penetrating the countryside was not inevitable. Creative leaders developed these potentials, politically insensitive ones neglected them. But the opportunity for choice presented at this historical passage could not be later regained. Our cases strongly reinforce the conclusion of Lipsett and Rokkan upon the party systems of the European democracies; once established in elective politics, or more precisely, in the politicization of a hitherto latent stratum of the population, a party alignment proves extraordinary durable.[231] At the time when nationalist leaders of a future political party make the appeals, and build the institutional links with which to enlist largely latent peasant groups, they have enormous latitude to design the future. The only information they possess beyond personal experience upon the still poorly articulated demands of the peasants comes from the evidence of religious movements, or caste redemption movements, neither very relevant, and the obscure history of episodic risings. For this reason, ideologies are consequential at this stage. But ideologies extrapolate from the experience of very different nations facing very different crises, or at best, from the experience of other regions of a nation whose tenurial contexts are locally diverse. Neither the revolutionary counter-elite nor the nationalist elite, therefore, escaped the penalty of untoward consequences, neither S.A. Dange nor M.K. Gandhi. This is, perhaps, one last vindication of the latitude an open and federalized system provides for the try-out of competing appeals to the peasants of a single tenurial system, and for regional party systems seeking the allegiance of peasants whose tenurial grievances differ regionally. Indira Gandhi did not, of course, in her tenurial program of 1971, make use of this possibility of regional diversity.

Independence opened a period of about twenty years in which the links forged by nationalist leaders with differing strata of the peasants could be elaborated and extended administratively as well as politically. There was opportunity during this period for incremental creativity, for building co-operatives, elective district councils, unions of farm laborers and tenants, tactics of land seizures and other agitations, splinter parties. Looking back, the main thrust of these activities was in the direction set in the Green Uprising: hegemony via expansion in Maharashtra, harnessing of class conflict in Kerala. Tenurial policy differences can be understood in these terms.

The new round was signalled nationally by Indira Gandhi's takeover of the Congress with redistributionist slogans. A more basic condition was the rise of a national consciousness of poverty. Universal sufferage contributed. Alarms were created by a few new strategists of revolution, and by the consciousness among established officials of a vast pool of unemployed educated people who might listen to them.[232] We see Kerala as acting upon this new condition more quickly and decisively than other states for two principal reasons. Her closely balanced, competitive political system was fine-tuned to just such an upswing of demand, and her associations, representatives, and administrators had been working out, and struggling over, specific measures that would channel such demands into action.

Explaining the present in terms of the past, our language has conveyed more of a sense of the inevitability of the present directions of development in the two states than we in fact possess. We have been impressed with the stubborn difference with which Kerala and Maharashtra reacted to the powerful nationwide stimuli introduced in the late 1960s. The systems are different. But whether they can continue their present directions of adjustment to the more powerful stresses we see in India's future is another question. In Maharashtra, to consider but one possibility, will the growing pool of unemployed people in the cities, many of them young and educated, reach out to the farm laborers, mostly of Untouchable caste, who are excluded from the rural power system? Toward what change will the majority of rural households in Kerala who cannot make a living on the land they have now won direct their frustration? Looking back, we have had to remind ourselves that there have been political choices. Looking ahead, that is evident enough.

NOTES

1. Doreen Warriner, *Land Reform in Principle and Practice* (Oxford, 1969), p. xiv. This is the more pointed meaning given to the term "agrarian reform" in contemporary United Nations circles. United Nations, Department of Economic and Social Affairs, International Labour Organization, and Food and Agriculture Organization, *Progress in Land Reform, Fifth Report* (New York, 1970), p. 303 [cited hereafter as U.N., *Fifth Report*.]

2. Peter Dorner, *Land Reform and Economic Development* (Baltimore, 1972).

3. "Conditions for Economic Change in Under-developed Countries," *Journal of Farm Economics*, vol. 33, pp. 695–6, quoted by Dorner, *Land Reform and Economic Development*, p. 29.

4. "The Present Situation and Our Tasks," December 1947, published in *Selected Works of Mao Tse-Tung* (Peking, 1967), 4: 165.

5. "Report on an Investigation of the Peasant Movement in Hunan," March 1927, ibid., 1: 33, 46.

6. "Liu Shao-Ch'i on the Sinification of Marxism by Mao Tse-Tung," 1945, Lin Piao, "Long Live the Victory of the People's War," 1965, both reprinted in Helene d'Encausse and Stuart R. Schram, comps., *Marxism and Asia: an Introduction with Readings* (London, 1969), pp. 260, 364–65.

7. Moore, *Social Origins of Dictatorship and Democracy; Lord and Peasant in the Making of the Modern World* (Boston, 1966), pp. 419 ff.. Wolf, *Peasant Wars of the Twentieth Century* (New York, Harper and Row, 1969), p. 276; Scott, "The Erosion of Patron-Client Bonds and Social Change in Rural Southeast Asia," *Journal of Asian Studies* 32 (Nov. 1972): 6.

8. Moore, *Social Origins of Dictatorship and Democracy*, pp. 469–70. It seems to be the linkage function Moore conceives as explanatory, since he rejects (pp. 454–56) the mere presence of the landlord and priest in the village as decisive. See also pp. 466, 468; p. 430; chs. 8, 9 (specifically pp. 460–67); p. 30 (the case of England); pp. xv and 422, 426 (generalization).

9. Ibid., 471; Wolf, *Peasant Wars*, p. 15. Wolf's proposition runs partly counter to Crane Brinton's that revolutions occur when conditions have begun to improve.

10. Scott, "Erosion of Patron-Client Bonds...," especially p. 10. In "Patron-Client Politics and Political Change in Southeast Asia," *American Political Science Review*, 66 (March 1972): 91–113, Scott puts more stress on political conditions, particularly colonial administration and elections, as affecting the balance of influence.

11. Warriner, *Land Reform*, U.N., *Fifth Report*, U.N. Department of Economic and Social Affairs, F.A.O. and I.L.O., *Progress in Land Reforms, Fourth Report* (New York, 1966); Solon L. Barraclough, *Agricultural Policy and Strategies of Land Reform* (Beverly Hills, Cal, 1969).

12. U.N., *Fifth Report*, p. 202.

13. Ibid., p. 201.

14. Ibid., p. 202; Erich H. Jacoby, *Man and Land, the Fundamental Issue in Development* (London, 1971), p. 86. For documentation of the disability of the Indian administrative system see India, Planning Commission, *Seminar on Land Reform, Proceedings and Papers* (New Delhi, Planning Commission, 1966), pp. 83, 146, 226–28.

15. Ibid.

16. 'Although all persons are supposed to be equal before the law, the traditional judicial process places a heavy advantage on the side of the more educated, and more powerful (usually landed) classes." U.N., *Fifth Report*, p. 220. See also p. 217.

17. John D. Montgomery, "Allocation of Authority in Land Reform Programs: A Comparative Study of Administrative Processes and Outputs," *Administrative Science Quarterly*, 17 (March 1972): 68.

18. U.N., *Fifth Report*, p. 227; Gerrit Huizer, "Peasant Organizations and their Potential for Change in Latin America," in *Land Reform, Land Settlement and Cooperatives* (F.A.O., Rome), no. 2 (1971), pp. 1–8.

19. "To make a sharp distinction between 'evolutionary' and 'revolutionary' land reforms in underdeveloped countries is a mistake . . . ." Jacoby, *Man and Land*, p. 171.

20. Warriner, *Land Reform*, pp. 47, 161.

21. Moore, *Social Origins of Dictatorship and Democracy*: ". . . the extraordinary difficulties that liberal democracy faces there...," p. 431; the Indian case "constitutes both a challenge to and a check upon the theories advanced in this book...," p. 315; on why India's peasants have not revolted, pp. 369, 378–85. See also pp. 413, 506, 406–7, 409.

22. Warriner, *Land Reform*, p. 435.

23. Ibid. pp. 137–38.

24. (New Haven, 1968). See pp. 366, 384 ff., 388.

25. On the need for "some new elite group which is able to displace the landed interests," see ibid., pp. 384–394; Dorner, *Land Reform and Economic Development*, p. 79; Warriner,

Land Reform, p. 114. On the need for an urban frontier see ibid., p. 381; Wolf, *Peasant Wars*, p. 59. On the stimulus and reinforcement to peasant militancy from cities, see Gerrit Huizer, *The Revolutionary Potential of Peasants in Latin America* (Lexington, Mass., 1972), pp. 142–45; James F. Petras and Robert LaPorte, Jr., *Cultivating Revolution, The United States and Agrarian Reform in Latin America* (New York 1971), pp. 187, 239, 241–42.

26. Huntington, *Political Order in Changing Societies*, p. 385. "Divide your lands or face revolution or death,' Prime Minister Amini warned the Iranian elite." Ibid., p. 394.

27. See *n.* 16 Supra.

28. Huntington, *Political Order in Changing Societies*, p. 75. "Green Uprising" seems to us to be a misnomer, for two reasons. It suggests a sharp, sudden process, spontaneous among rural people. We conceive the process as long and drawn out, and as being an interplay of peasant with urban initiatives.

29. Ibid., pp. 75, 84.

30. Ibid., p. 385. This "minimax" strategy of implementation was earlier proposed by V.M. Dandekar at the 1966 seminar on Land Reforms of the Indian Planning Commission: "phase the programme such that at each stage, minimize the number of those who are adversely affected and maximize the number of those who are likely to be benefitted." India, Planning Commission, *Seminar on Land Reform, Proceedings and Papers* (New Delhi, 1966), p. 81.

31. Huntington, *Political Order in Changing Societies*, p. 385.

32. Ibid, p, 391; Moore, *Social Origins of Dictatorship and Democracy*, pp. 390–92; Warriner, *Land Reform*, p. 170.

33. Charles L. Taylor and Michael C. Hudson, *World Handbook of Political and Social Indicators* (2nd ed., New Haven, 1972), Tables 4.14 and 5.9. India ranks 42nd among 54 nations as to inequality of land distribution (the most unequal at the top of the ranking), and 26th among 106 as to percent of the male labor force in agriculture.

34. Only Kerala and Jammu and Kashmir have made "significant progress" in land reform, according to Mohan Daria, national planning minister. *The Hindu* (Madras), 4 May 1973.

35. India, Planning Commission, *Task Force on Agrarian Relations Report* (New Delhi, 1973), pp. 29–31 [Cited hereafter as *Appu Report*]. Jammu and Kashmir had, in 1973, redistributed more land than any other States. Ibid. p. 96. The same was true 10 years earlier. India, Planning Commission, *Progress of Land Reform* (Delhi, 1963) pp. 14–15.

36. The relevant data on Kerala are in India, 1961 Census, Vol. VII, *Kerala*, Pt. 1A(i) *General Report* (Delhi, 1965). Iravati Karve wrote a fascinating interpretation of the ecology of the regions of Maharashtra in Maharashtra, State Gazetteer, *Maharashtra—Land and Its People* (Bombay, 1968), ch. 5.

37. V.M. Dandekar and N. Rath "Poverty in India, Pt. II," *Economic and Political Weekly*, 9 Jan. 1971, pp. 110, 111.

38. India, Cabinet Secretariat, National Sample Survey, Number 144, *Tables with Notes on Some Aspects of Landholding in Rural Areas, Seventeenth Round*, September 1961–July 1962 (Delhi, 1968), p. 175, [Cited hereafter as NSS, No. 144].

39. Dandekar and Rath, "Poverty in India," p. 31.

40. Comparison based on Maharashtra, Bureau of Economics and Statistics, *Statistical Abstract of Maharashtra State, 1965-66* (Bombay, 1969); and Kerala, Bureau of Economics and Statistics, *Statistical Handbook of Kerala, 1968* (Trivandrum, 1969).

41. Dandekar and Rath, "Poverty in India," p. 121.

42. Ibid.

43. These are 1961 Census figures published in C.H. Hanumantha Rao, "Agricultural Growth and Stagnation in India," *Economic Weekly*, vol. 27 (1965), p. 410. He attributes them to P.S. Sharma, "A Study of Structural and Tenurial Aspects of Rural Economy in the Light of the 1961 Census," Mimeo. We have not been able to find them in a Census publication.

44. M.A. Oommen, *Land Reforms and Socio-Economic Change in Kerala: An Introductory Study* (Bangalore, 1971) p. 58. He cites an important source only thus indirectly available to us: Kerala, Bureau of Economics and Statistics, "Land Reforms Survey," Mimeo. (Trivandrum, 1968).

45. M.L. Dantwala and C.H. Shah, *Evaluation of Land Reforms with Special Reference to the Western Region of India* (Bombay, 1971), pp. 46, 186.

46. Dandekar and Rath, "Poverty in India," p. 115.

47. NSS, No. 144, pp. 121, 122.

48. Both Kerala and Maharashtra now consist of areas governed by reform laws passed by other states, before the present boundaries were drawn; no comprehensive treatment of land reform in the two states is feasible in the space available. For a general view, see, "History of Tenancy Relations in the State of Maharashtra," *Artha Vijnana*, March 1970. A detailed, but perhaps unrepresentative study is Dantwala and Shah, "Pre-reform and Post-reform Agrarian Structure in Maharashtra," *Indian Journal of Agricultural Econo-*

mics, July 1971. Most of the observations in this section are drawn from K.R. Nanekar, *Land Reforms in Vidarbha* '(Calcutta, 1968) and Kandekar and Khudanpur, *Working of the Bombay Tenancy Act, 1948* (Poona, 1957). Planning Commission, *Implementation of Land Reforms,* (Delhi, 1966), p. 278.

49. *Appu Report,* p. 96. See also Warriner, *Land Reform,* p. 168.

50. India, Planning Commission, *Implementation of Land Reforms* (New Delhi, 1966), p. 278.

51. India, Planning Commission, *Progress of Land Reforms* (New Delhi, 1966), p. 21; *Appu Report,* p. 96.

52. For reports from Palghat and Allepey, see the relevant chapters of *Modernizing Indian Agriculture,* Report of the Expert Committee on Assessment and Evaluation of the Intensive Agricultural District Programme and Francine Frankel, *India's Green Revolution* (Princeton, 1971). The same impression is relayed by T.C. Varghese, *Agrarian Change and Economic Consequences* (Bombay, 1970).

53. From data published by Oomen, *Land Reforms and Socio-Economic Change in Kerala,* pp. 55–56, calculated by applying the percentages on p. 55 to the total number of agrarian households (2,825 thousand) of which they are taken (p. 56). Note the agreement of the Land Reforms Survey total with the National Sample Survey total, allowing for five years of increase in households between 1961–62 and 1966–67.

54. According to the definition in the 1961 Census, a cultivator must have worked in agriculture at least an hour per day during the crop season. India, Census of 1961, Vol. I, Part XI—A(ii) *Land Tenures in India* (Delhi, 1966), p. ii.

55. For provisions of the Communist legislation, see Jitendra Singh, *Communist Rule in Kerala* (New Delhi, 1959), pp. 28–36. President's Rule was proclaimed upon an agitation over education policy, not agrarian reform. For the political issue of the reform in the subsequent 1960 election see K.P. Bhagat, *The Kerala Mid-Term Election of 1960* (Bombay, 1962), pp. 21–23.

56. Planning Commission, *Implementation of Land Reforms,* p. 66.

57. Nanekar, *Land Reforms in Vidarbha,* p. 219.

58. S.K. Rao "Interregional Variations in Agricultural Growth," *Economic and Political Weekly,* 3 July 1971, p. 1333.

59. Ibid.

60. Ibid.

61. India, Programme Evaluation Organization, *Regional Variations in Social Development and Levels of Living* (Delhi, 1967), Vol. 1, p. 154. The gap between the two states was greater with regard to government loans than in the cooperative sector.

62. Ibid., Vol. II (Delhi, 1968), pp. 45, 46, 48ff.

63. The Editors, "Maharashtra: New Organization Men," *Economic and Political Weekly,* 1970 Annual Number, p. 247. See also V. Nath, "Regional Development in Indian Planning," ibid.

64. National Sample Survey, *Tables with Notes on Employment and Unemployment in Rural and Urban Areas of India,* Nineteenth Round, July 1964–June 1965 (Delhi, 1970), Tables 1.6, 2.6. To arrive at our unemployed percentages we have added those employed but not at work, those unemployed and seeking work, and those unemployed, not seeking work, but available for work. For the rationale, and for urban figures as of 1961–62, see India, Planning Commission, *Report of the Committee of Experts on Unemployment Estimates* (New Delhi, 1970).

65. S.S. Madalgi, "Hunger in Rural India," *Economic and Political Weekly,* 1968 Annual Number, pp. 61–68; also Dandekar and Rath, "Poverty in India," p. 29.

66. India, Cabinet Secretariat, National Sample Survey, No. 138, *Tables with Notes on Consumer Expenditures, Sixteenth Round* (Delhi, 1969) p. 37; Ibid., No. 179, *19th Round* (Delhi, 1972) p. 7, (Cited hereafter as NSS, No. 138, and NSS, No. 179].

67. NSS, No. 138, p. 15; NSS, No. 179, p. 19. In estimating the percentage of population in the poverty stratum, the line has been drawn at Rs. 15.00 per month consumption expenditure in 1960–61, Rs. 19.00 per month in 1964–65 (allowing for rise in consumer prices according to Dandekar and Rath, "Poverty in India," p. 144). The 1964–65 percentage was estimated by interpolation within the Rs. 18 to 21 class.

68. "Strategies for Narrowing the Poverty Gap, 1974–79," *Quarterly Economic Report of the Indian Institute of Public Opinion* 20, no. 1 (Sept.–Oct. 1973), p. 15.

69. A.V. Jose, "Trends in Real Wage Rates for Agricultural Labourers," *Economic and Political Weekly,* Review of Agriculture, March 1974, pp. A25–A30.

70. V.M. Sirsikar, *The Rural Elite in a Developing Society, A Study in Political Sociology* (New Delhi, 1970), p. 7. A generally similar conclusion was reached by Ram Joshi, "Maharashtra," in Myron Weiner, ed., *State Politics in India* (Princeton, 1968).

71. For the overall judgment, see Myron Weiner, "Political Development in the Indian States," Ibid, p. 52: "the most extreme situation [of instability] has been in Kerala . . . ," and p. 54: " . . . one should not conclude that large states must necessarily be unstable, since Maharashtra is not . . . ." For election evidence, see Weiner's tables, pp. 46–47;

plus India, Ministry of Information and Broadcasting, *India: A Reference Annual, 1971–72* (Delhi, 1972).
72. A handy place to read Kerala election figures is Victor M. Fic, *Kerala, Yenan of India, Rise of Communist Power, 1937-69* (Bombay, 1970), Tables beginning p. 487. For 1970 see Bhabani Sen Gupta, *Communism in Indian Politics* (New York, 1972), p. 191.
73. Weiner, "Political Development in the Indian States," pp. 34, 41,
74. Ibid., pp. 194–95. "The League, then was still able to deliver the block votes of the Muslims [in 1970], but the Marxists . . . in many constituencies were able to penetrate deep into the Muslim masses."
75. We use Victor Fic's listing, counting only the cabinet changes involving a new Chief Minister.
76. Compare Sirsikar, *Rural Elite in a Developing Society,* with Donald S. Zagoria "The Grass Roots of Indian Communism: West Bengal and Kerala," Indian Institute of Public Opinion, *Monthly Public Opinion Surveys* 18 (March, 1973): i–xii.
77. Sirsikar, *Rural Elite in a Developing Society,* pp. 7, 74, 187.
78. Mary C. Carras, *The Dynamics of Indian Political Factions: A Study of District Councils in the State of Maharashtra* (Cambridge, Eng., 1972), pp. 9–10.
79. From his review of ibid. in *Economic and Political Weekly,* 19 Aug. 1972, pp. 177.
80. E.H. Valsan, *Community Development Programs and Rural Local Government, Comparative Case Studies of India and the Philippines* (New York, 1970), p. 448; and *India · A Reference Annual, 1971–72,* p. 100.
81. Sirsikar, *Elites in a Developing Society,* p. 11.
82. India, Cabinet Secretariat, National Sample Survey, No. 172, *Tables with Notes on India Villages, Some Important Results* [1963–64] (Delhi, 1970), p. 39.
83. See Hugh Davis Graham and Ted Robert Gurr, eds., *The History of Violence In America* (New York, 1969), chs. 17 (Gurr), and 19 (James C. Davies).
84. T.C. Varghese, *Agrarian Change and Economic Consequences, Land Tenures in Kerala 1850-1960* (Calcutta and New Delhi, 1970), pp. 29–32, 64–69, 85–91. The 75 percent figure comes from the first revenue settlement of Travancore, 1883–1911.
85. I.J. Catanach, "Agrarian Disturbances in Nineteenth Century India," *Indian Economic and Social History Review* 3 (1966): 67.
86. Ravinder Kumar, *Western India in the Nineteenth Century, A Study in the Social History of Maharashtra* (London, 1968), pp. 16, 25.
87. Ibid., p. 154.
88. We have relied on Ravinder Kumar, *Western India in the Nineteenth Century,* ch. 5, and Catanach, "Agrarian Disturbances in Nineteenth Century India."
89. See, for example Richard Cashman, "The Famine Campaign Among the Deccan Peasantry, 1896–97," unpublished paper, 1969–70.
90. For 1901 figures, see Gordon Johnson, "Chitpavan Brahmins and Politics in Western India in the Late Nineteenth and Early Twentieth Centuries," in Edmund Leach and S.N. Mukherjee, eds., *Elites in South Asia* (Cambridge, Eng., 1970), p. 96, n. 3. For the contemporary estimate (usually taken in political commentary on Maharashtra as 45 percent) see Iravati Karve, *Maharashtra—Land and Its People,* p. 76: "Kunbis and Marathas together comprise 50 per cent of the state population [p. 29], 40 per cent of the total in western Maharashtra."
91. Gordon Johnson, "Chitpavan Brahmins and Politics," pp. 100–108.
92. Richard Cashman, "The Political Recruitment of God Ganapati," *Indian Economic and Social History Review* 7 (1970); 347–74; and "The Development of the Shivaji Tradition," unpublished paper, 1969–70.
93. Maureen L.P. Patterson, "Caste and Political Leadership in Maharashtra," *Economic Weekly,* (1954): 1065–67.
94.i V.M. Sirsikar, "Politics in Maharashtra: Problems and Prospects," in Iqba Nara n, ed., *State Politics in India* (Meerut, 1967/68), p. 197.
95 Aloo J. Dastur, "The Pattern of Maharashtra Politics," ibid., pp. 185–88.
96· Kerala, Kerala District Gazetteers, *Kozhikode* by A. Sreedhara Menon (Trivandrum, 1962), pp. 171–75.
97. Excerpts printed in William Logan, *Malabar* (Madras,1887, reprinted 1951), vol.I,p.584.
98. Ibid.
99. T.C. Varghese, *Agrarian Change and Economic Consequences,* pp. 39–40.
100. "[T] hough the cause for tenancy law arose as far in the past as 1880, the whole period up to 1930, that is nearly half a century produced nothing but polemics and reports." T.V.S. Rao, "Land Legislation in Kerala State, 1800-1960," *Artha Vijnana* 12 (1970): 108.
101. In a minute of 1822, quoted in Varghese, *Agrarian Change and Economic Consequences,* p. 35.
102. Gazetteer, *Kozhikode,* p. 182. See also A. Sreedhara Menon, *A Survey of Kerala History* (Kottayam, 1967), pp. 350–51.
103. C. Gopalan Nair, *The Moplah Rebellion, 1921* (Calicut, 1923). This is an official view of the colonial period.

104. E.M.S. Namboodiripad, *Kerala Yesterday, Today and Tomorrow* (Calcutta, 1967), pp. 141–52. Namboodiripad emphasizes the small proportion of Hindus forcibly converted.

105. Gazetteer, *Kozhikode*, p. 182.

106. Ibid., pp. 180–81.

107. Mohandas K. Gandhi, *Collected Works* (Delhi, 1966), Vol. 21, pp. 47–49, 70–72, 112, 120–21, 216–18, 320–22, 355–56, 512-13, 523–44.

108. Gazetteer, *Kozhikode*, p. 184.

109. Varghese, *Agrarian Change and Economic Consequences*, pp. 22, 62. See also *n.* 84 supra.

110. Kerala, Kerala District Gazetteers, *Quilon* (Trivandrum, 1964), p. 151.

111. On the basis of fieldwork in Malabar District, Eric J. Miller gave the "statutory" distance at which Tiyas polluted Nairs as 24 feet. "Village Structure in North Kerala," *Economic Weekly*, vol. 4 (1952), p. 160. C. Achyuta Menon, superintendent of the Cochin Census, gave "24 Malabar feet [about 19 English Feet]" in *Cochin State Manual* (Cochin, 1911), pp. 195–96.

112. T.K. Ravindran, *Asan and Social Revolution in Kerala* (Trivandrum, 1972), pp. iv, lxxiii, lxxxiv; Kerala, Kerala District Gazetteers, *Trivandrum* (Trivandrum, 1962), pp. 233, 277–78. For a glimpse of the S.N.D.P. school system today, see K.P. Bhagat, *The Kerala Midterm Election of 1960* (Bombay, 1962), p. 61.

113. Gazetteer, *Trivandrum*, pp. 235–38.

114. M.J. Koshy, *Constitutionalism in Travancore and Cochin* (Trivandrum, 1972), pp. 102–122.

115. Namboodiripad, *Kerala*, pp. 170–73; Koshy, *Constitutionalism in Travancore and Cochin*, pp. 134–44.

116. Bhagat, *Kerala Midterm Election of 1960*, pp. 37-39.

117. This is the view of the Communist leader, A.K. Gopalan, in his *Kerala, Past and Present* (London, 1959), p. 38.

118. C. Paul Verghese, "Thakazhi Sivasankara Pillai, An Assessment," *Indian Literature* 13 (1970): 119; Narayana Menon, "Thakazhi Sivasankara Pillai," ibid. 5 (1962): 14–20; K.M. George, "G. Sankara Kurup," ibid. 9 (1966): 12–16.

119. Gazetteer, *Kozhikode*, 177, 188–89.

120. E.M.S. Namboodiripad, *The Mahatma and the Ism* (New Delhi, 1959), p. vii.

121. E.M.S. Namboodiripad, *The National Question in Kerala* (New Delhi, 1952), p. 121.

122. Namboodiripad, *The Mahatma*, p. viii, and *The National Question*, p. 132.

123. Varghese, *Agrarian Change and Economic Consequences*, pp. 138, 227–31.

124. There is a more recent parallel—the linkage of rural teachers in Ceylon, 1956.

125. Namboodiripad, *The National Question*, p. 138.

126. Namboodiripad, *Kerala*, p. 167.

127. Fic, *Kerala*, p. 22. Namboodiripad's version of the relation of the Communist party to the earlier Congress Socialist party is published in his polemic, *Let us Work Together, An Open Letter to Delegates to the Convention of the All-India Socialist Party* (Bombay, 1952). He and four others had been members of the Communist party within the Congress since 1937. Fic dates the founding of the Communist party of Kerala from 1940; Namboodiripad records it as 1939. For a critical perspective, see Gene D. Overstreet and Marshall Windmiller, *Communism in India*, (Berkeley, 1959), pp. 160–66.

128. Namboodiripad, *The National Question*, pp. i–ii, 29–30. Namboodiripad's assumption that Kerala agriculture was comparatively unirrigated is highly questionable. In 1958–59, Kerala had 19.2 per cent of its net sown area irrigated; the all-India average was 17.3. The Maharashtra percentage was only 5.6. The data are from the article by Hanumantha Rao cited in n. 43 supra.

129. This interpretation was put forward by R. Ramakrishnan Nair, *How the Communists Came to Power in Kerala* (Trivandrum, 1956). It is concurred in by D.R. Mankekar, *The Red Riddle of Kerala* (Bombay, 1965), and Karl F. Spielman, "Regionalism, Nationalism and Revolution: A Profile of Communist Tactics in Kerala," *Public Policy* 15 (1966): 139–78.

130. Fic, *Kerala*, ch. 13.

131. Some of the reasons and the political consequences are analyzed by Joan Menscher, "Namboodiri Brahmins: An Analysis of a Traditional Elite in Kerala," *Journal of Asian and African Studies*, 1 (1966): 183-96. One consequence was the absence of an anti-Brahman movement in Kerala, since the Namboodiris, in contrast to the Chitpavans, did not take the lion's share of the governmental and legislative positions created by modernization.

132. *Political Order in Changing Societies*, p. 371.

133. *Hindustan Times* (Delhi), 26 September 1970.

134. *The Hindu* (Madras), 17 and 25 November 1969; *Malabar Herald*, 1 May, 1971.

135. *New Age* (weekly) 15 June 1969; *The Hindu* (Madras), 27 October 1969.

136. *Economic and Political Weekly* 6 May 1972; and 1972 Annual Number, p. 1484.
137. Ibid., 18 September 1971, p. 2001; *New Age* (weekly), 30 April 1972, p. 6; *People's Democracy*, 18 July 1971, p. 15.
138. Huntington, *Political Order in Changing Societies*, p. 372.
139. Indian Institute of Public Opinion, *Monthly Public Opinion Survey* (November 1972), vol. 18, pp. 1–viii following p. 14.
140. Warriner, *Land Reform*, p. 199: "The most efficient organizations which I saw in India were the processing and marketing cooperatives in Maharashtra." For data on growth and further references, see Carras, *Dynamics of Indian Political Factions*, pp. 32–39.
141. Some participants in a seminar organized by the Department of Sociology, Kerala University, in 1970 adduced fractious unionism as a hindrance on economic development. P.N. Krishna Pillai, "Industrial Relations in Kerala," in P.K.B. Nayar, ed., *Development of Kerala, Problems and Promises* (Trivandrum, 1972), ch. 19.
142. Carras, *Dynamics of Indian Political Factions*, pp. 9–10.
143. A revealing view from the village perspective was provided by Kathleen Gough, "Village Politics in Kerala," *Economic Weekly*, vol. 17, (1965), pp. 363–72, 413–420.
144. Lawrence L. Shrader and Ram Joshi, "Zilla Parishad Elections in Maharashtra and District Political Elite," *Asian Survey* (March 1963): 143–56.
145. Ibid., pp. 46, 106–7.
146. Published in *Socialist India*, 8 and 15 July 1972.
147. For example, see "Land Ceiling and the New Farm Entrepreneur," *Economic and Political Weekly*, 3 October 1970, p. 1629. Also *Mainstream*, 13 May 1972.
148. *Economic and Political Weekly*, 6 May 1972, pp. 915–16.
149. Ibid.
150. *Mainstream*, 13 May 1972, p. 8.
151. *Economic and Political Weekly*, 3 October 1970, p. 1629.
152. Calculated from NSS, No. 144, p. 13. As of 1960–61, 4,951,000 households owning 144,631,000 acres occupied the 15 acres and over size classes. Allowing each of these households 15 acres would leave 70,366,000 acres surplus.
153. *Economic and Political Weekly*, vol. 7, (1972), p. 736.
154. Quoted in Wolf Ladejinsky, "New Ceiling Round and Implementation Prospects," *Economic and Political Weekly*, Agriculture Supplement, 30 September 1972, p.A-125. This article contains a useful summary of past efforts and obstacles in the light of new proposals.
155. "Land Ceilings," vol. 7, p. 736 (1972).
156. *Economic and Political Weekly*, 6 November 1971, p. 2269; *Times of India* (Bombay), 28 October 1971.
157. *Economic and Political Weekly*, 1972: 17 June, p. 1175; 14 April, p. 1743.
158. *Times of India* (Bombay), 28 October 1972.
159. Ibid., 23 November 1971.
160. Ibid., 21 November 1971.
161. *Economic and Political Weekly*, 27 November 1971, p. 2382.
162. Cf., e.g., *Times of India* (Bombay), 1971: 12, 21, 27, 29 November; 3, 4 December.
163. Ibid., 28 November 1971.
164. *Economic and Political Weekly*, 8 January 1972, p. 56 Opposition to rural land ceilings was frequently linked to a demand for ceilings on urban income and property; this was Naik's original position. We may conceptualize this demand motivationally as an equity consideration, since landed elites see no reason to be deprived of privilege in the name of socialism when other elites escape, but functionally, and perhaps motivationally, in terms of broadening the base of opposition to redistributive policies and especially redistribution of property. And of course linking land ceilings to urban ceilings delays the passage of land legislation and generates additional obstacles to implementation of either.
165. *Times of India* (Bombay) 2 January 1972.
166. Ibid., 5 June 1972; for a summary of the opposition, see "Tactics of a Farmers' Lobby," *Mainstream*, 4 December 1971.
167. *Times of India* (Bombay), 23 November 1971.
168. Ibid., 26 November 1971.
169. This conclusion would emerge from the analysis in the *Economic and Political Weekly*, 1971: 27 November, p. 2382; 1972: 8 January, p. 56; 17 June, p. 1174; 14 August, p. 1743.
170. Cf. *Mainstream*, 1972: 26 February, pp. 11, 41; 1 April, p. 36; *Times of India* (Bombay), 16 March 1972.
171. Ibid., 2 August 1972.
172. *Economic and Political Weekly*, 17 June 1972, p. 1175; *Economic Times* (Bombay), 1972: 2, 18 August.
173. Figures from the Central Land Reform Committee; see *Economic and Political Weekly*, 8 April 1972, p. 736. The Task Force on Agrarian Relations gave the figures as

123,000 acres (50,000 hectares). Planning Commission, "Report of the Task Force on Agrarian Relations," Mimeo. (New Delhi), 1973.
174.   *Economic Times* (Bombay), 17 August 1972.
175.   *Times of India* (Bombay), 17 August 1972.
176.   *Economic Times* (Bombay) 18 August 1972.
177.   *Times of India* (Bombay), 19 August 1972; *Economic Times* (Bombay), 17 August 1972.
178.   Programme Evaluation Organization, *Regional Variations in Social Development and Levels of Living,* vol. 1, p. 45.
179.   Theoretically, a number of states have made this move, but with sufficient loopholes to render the abolition unnforceable or meaningless. Uttar Pradesh, which did effectively grant permanent rights to superior tenants, allows what is called "joint farming," which is in effect sharecropping with a *sajhidar.* The actual impact of the Maharashtra Act of 1956 was often the eviction of tenants; only about half became owners.
180.   See A. Gangadharan, *The Law of Land Reforms in Kerala* (Cochin, 1970) for the 1964 Act and 1969 Amendment. For a commentary by the Revenue Minister, see K.T. Jacob, *Tiller Gets Land in Kerala* (Delhi, 1972).
181.   Ibid.
182.   Jacob, *Tiller Gets Land in Kerala,* p. 9.
183.   Cf. Zagoria, "The Grass Roots of Indian Communism," p. 51, and *n.* 13 supra, for a suggestion that this pattern often applies cross-culturally.
184.   *New Age,* 24 May 1970; *The Hindu* (Madras), 21 August 1969.
185.   *The Hindu,* 15 May 1971.
186.   "Report of the Task Force on Agrarian Relations," p. 34.
187.   *New Age,* 11 July 1971.
188.   Ibid., 4 June 1972; *The Hindu* (Madras), 31 December 1969.
189.   *Economic and Political Weekly,* Special Number, August 1972, p. 1481.
190.   For a brief summary of this rather complex legal situation, see H. M. Jain, "Constitutional Amendments and Property Rights," *Mainstream,* 29 July 1972.
191.   *The Hindu* (Madras), 1 June 1973.
192.   *Economic Times* (Bombay), 1 December 1972; Interviews with Revenue officials, Trivandrum and Cochin, 1974, by Ronald Herring.
193.   *Economic and Political Weekly,* 18 September 1971, p. 2001.
194.   *Economic Times* (Bombay), 1 December 1972.
195.   *The Hindu* (Madras), 27 October 1972.
196.   *New Age,* 30 April 1972.
197.   Ibid., 16 April 1972.
198.   *The Hindu* (Madras), 27 October 1972.
199.   *Mainstream,* 11 June 1971.
200.   *The Hindu* (Madras), 6 May 1972.
201.   See *ns.* 17, 18 supra.
202.   "Report of the Task Force on Agrarian Relations," p. 96.
203.   Oommen, *Land Reform and Socio-Economic Change in Kerala,* p. 89.
204.   *The Hindu* (Madras), 20 February 1973; 12 May 1971.
205.   "Report of the Task Force on Agrarian Relations," p. 33.
206.   For coverage, see *The Hindu* (Madras), 1968: 30 November, 23 December; 1969: 3 March. Frankel, *India's Green Revolution,* pp. 139–50.
207.   *Economic and Political Weekly,* 13 January 1973, p. 55.
208.   *The Hindu* (Madras), 10 October 1972.
209.   Carras, *Dynamics of Indian Political Factions,* pp. 17–19.
210.   See *n.* 24 supra.
211.   Bhabani Sen Gupta, *Communism in Indian Politics* (New York, 1972), p. 174.
212.   For a full, uncritical account, see Dhananjay Keer, *Mahatma Jotirao Phooley, Father of Our Social Revolution* (Bombay, 1964).
213.   Don Rosenthal, "From Reformist Princes to Cooperative Kings," Part I, *Economic and Political Weekly,* 19 May 1973, pp. 909 ff.
214.   (Poona, 1936), p. 91.
215.   V.D. Deshpande, "History of Tenancy Relations in the State of Maharashtra Since 1900," *Artha Vijnana* 12 (1970): 206–211.
216.   Maureen Patterson, "Caste and Political Leadership in Maharashtra," pp. 1065, 1067.
217.   *Social Origins of Dictatorship and Democracy,* pp. 458–59.
218.   Sirsikar, *Rural Elite in a Developing Society,* p.189.
219.   See Article V of the 1920 constitution adopted in Nagpur in M.V. Ramana Rao, *Development of the Congress Constitution* (New Delhi, 1958), p. 35. There were other small departures from unilinguism—the Hindi area was of course divided for organization purposes—but only the Bombay Congress was designated as bilingual.
220.   *Report of the Peasant Enquiry Committee,* p. 3.

221. See the Government of Maharashtra, *Report of the Committee on Democratic Decentralization* (Bombay,1961). V.P. Naik, soon to become Chief Minister, chaired the committee.
222. Rosenthal, review of Carras, *Dynamics of Political Factions,* p. 259.
223. Carras, ibid., 17–33.
224. *Social Origins of Dictatorship and Democracy,* p. 29.
225. *The Origins of Political Stability in England, 1675-1725* (Boston, 1967), p. 69.
226. Keith Grahame Fielding, *The Second Tory Party, 1714–1832* (London, 1938), p. 24.
227. This is the title of his chapter on England which also presents the evidence for elimination of the peasantry by enclosures. *Social Origins of Dictatorship and Democracy,* Ch. 1.
228. Gail Omvedt, "Non-Brahmans and Communists in Bombay," *Economic and Political Weekly*, 28 April 1973, pp. 800 ff.
229. This is the heading of a section of the "Report of the Task Force on Agrarian Relations," p. 7. Wolf Ladejinsky advanced this diagnosis at least as early as 1965. See his appendix to David Hapgood, ed., *Policies for Promoting Agricultural Development: Report of a Conference* (Cambridge, Mass., 1965).
230. Strong confirmation of the stout links of poor Kerala peasants to the CPM is provided by Donald Zagoria, "The Grass Roots of Indian Communism: West Bengal and Kerala," Indian Institute of Public Opinion, *Monthly Public Opinion Surveys,* vol. 18 (March 1973), pp. i-xii.
231. Seymour M. Lipset and Stein Rokkan, eds., *Party Systems and Voter Alignments: Cross-National Perspectives* (New York, 1967), pp. 35, 38, 40, 51.
232. An enlightening record of the national government assessment of rural risings in the "Naxalite" period is available in the unpublished report of the national Ministry of Home Affairs, "The Causes and Nature of the Current Agrarian Tensions," December, 1969. It was summarized and reviewed in *Seminar*, No. 129, "The Rural Base," May 1970, pp. 31–34.

List of References

Ady, Peter, ed. *Private Foreign Investment and the Developing World*. London : Pall Mall, 1974.

Agarwal, G.D. *Agrarian Reform and Agricultural Reconstruction*. Delhi : S. Chand, 1948.

Agarwal, N.C. *Land Utilisation Statistics : Some Suggestions*. All India Congress Committee Economic Review 16. 10 August 1964.

Agarwal, R.R. *Soil Fertility in India*. New York : Asia Publishing House, 1965.

Agarwal, Santosh Kumar. "Bhoodan in Uttar Pradesh." *Eastern Economist* 47 (28 October 1966).

Agarwala, A.N., and Singh, S.P., eds. *The Economics of Underdevelopment*. Oxford, 1958.

Agarwala, Ram Gopal. "Size of Holdings and Productivity : Further Comments." *Economic and Political Weekly* (21 November 1964).

Agarwala, S.N. *The Gandhian Plan of Economic Development for India*. Bombay, 1944.

Ahmad, Rafiq. "Taxations and Tenure of Agricultural Land in the Punjab between 1707 and 1849." *Punjab Journal of Research : Humanities* 1 (July 1966).

Ahmed, Ejaz, and Malik, K.K. *Commentaries on U.P. Consolidation of Holdings Act, 1953, U.P. Act no. V of 1954*. Lucknow : Eastern Book Company, 1968.

Ahmed, Zainul Abidin. *The Agrarian Problem in India*. Allahabad : All India Congress Committee, 1937.

Ahmed, Zainul Abidin. *Ceiling on Agricultural Land*. New Delhi : Communist Party Publication, 1972.

Aiyar, C.S. Subramaniya. "Kerala Agrarian Relations Act." *The Madras Law Journal* (January 1962).

Allen, Zoe. "Land Reforms in a Democratic Framework." *South Asian Review* 3 (October 1969).

Alpert, Paul. *Partnership or Confrontation? Poor Lands and Rich*. Collier-Macmillan.

Amir, Hasan. "Problems of the Land and Agriculture among the Kols of Uttar Pradesh." *Vanyajati* 18 (January 1970).

Anajwala, Chimanlal C. *The Bombay Tenancy and Agricultural Lands Act, with Rules and Notifications*. Bombay : C. Jamnadas, 1969.

Andrews, Ronald L. *India : An Introductory Geography*. Auckland, 1967.

Anstey, Vera. "Land Reform in India." *Journal of Local Administration Overseas* 1 (1962).

Appleby, Paul H. *Public Administration in India*. Delhi, 1953.

Appleby, Paul H. *Public Administration in India : Report of a Survey*. Delhi, 1957.

Appu, P.S. *Ceilings on Agricultural Holdings*. Delhi : Government of India, Ministry of Agriculture, 1972.

Baden-Powell, B.H. *The Indian Village Community*. London, 1896.

Baden-Powell, B.H. *Land Revenue and Tenure in British India*. 2d ed. Oxford : Clarendon Press, 1913.

Baden-Powell, B.H. *The Lands Systems of British India*. Vols. I-III. Oxford : Clarendon Press, 1892.

Barān, Paul A. *The Political Economy of Growth*. New York, 1957.

Bardhan, Kalpana. "Size of Holdings and Productivity : Further Comments." *Economic and Political Weekly* (22 August 1964).

Bardhan, Pranab. "Trends in Land Relations." *Economic and Political Weekly* (5 January 1970).

Beaglehole, T.H. *Thomas Munro and the Development of Administrative Policy in Madras, 1792-1818: The Origins of "The Munro System."* London, 1966.

Beidelman, Thomas O. *A Comparative Analysis of the Jajmini System*. Locust Valley, N.Y., 1959.

Bernstorff, Dagmar. *Wahlkampf in Indien*. Dusseldorf, 1971.

Beteille, Andre. *Caste and Power : Changing Patterns of Stratification in a Tanjore Village*. Berkeley, 1965.

Beteille, Andre. *Castes Old and New : Essays in Social Structure and Social Stratification*. London, 1969.

Beteille, Andre. "Ideas and Interests : Some Conceptual Problems in the Study of Social Stratification in Rural India." *International Social Science Journal* 21 (1969).

Beteille Andre, ed. *Social Inequality : Selected Readings.* Penguin, 1969.
Bhattacharya, D., and B., eds. *Report on the Population Estimates of India, 1820-1830.* Census of India, 1961. Delhi, 1963.
Bhattacharyya, K.C. "Some Observations on the Ceiling of Existing Holdings for Agricultural Land in India." *AICC Economic Review* 17 (March 1966).
Bohannan, Paul. " 'Land,' 'Tenure' and Land-Tenure." In *African Agrarian Systems,* by Daniel Biebuyck. Oxford University Press, 1963.
Bombay, University of. *Evaluation of Land Reforms : With Special Reference to the Western Region of India.* Bombay, 1969.
Bose, Ashish. "Six Decades of Urbanization." *Indian Economic and Social History Review* (1965).
Bose, Devbrata. *The Problems of Indian Society.* New York, 1968.
Bose, Nirmal Kumar. *Peasant Life in India.* Calcutta : An'hropological Survey of India, 1962.
Braibanti, Ralph, ed. *Asian Bureaucratic Systems Emergent from the British Imperial Tradition.* Durham, N.C., 1966.
Brecher, Irving, and Abbas, S.A. *Foreign Aid and Industrial Development in Pakistan.* Cambridge : Cambridge University Press, 1974.
Brown, L. *The Social Impact of the Green Revolution.* Carnegie Endowment for International Peace, 1971.
Buschman, K.H. "Settlements and Habitations in India." *Geographical Review of India* 16 (1954).
Catanach, I.J. *Rural Credit in Western India : Rural Credit and the Cooperative Movement in the Bombay Presidency, 1875-1930.* Berkeley : University of California Press.
Chandras, G.S. "A Review of Land Reform in Non-Arable Lands in India with Special Reference to the Forest Lands." *Artha Vijnana* 12 (March/June 1970) : 237-269.
Chayanov, A.V. *The Theory of Peasant Economy.* Homewood, Ill., 1966.
Cohn, Bernard S. *The Development and Impact of British Administration in India : A Bibliographic Essay.* Delhi, 1961.
Cohn, Bernard. "From Indian Status to British Contract." *Journal of Economic History* (1961).
Cohn, Bernard, and Singer, Milton, eds. *Structure and Change in Indian Society.* Chicago, 1968.
Crane, R.I., ed. *Regions and Regionalism in South Asian Studies : An Exploratory Study.* Durham, N.C., 1967.
Dandekar, M.L. "Economic Theory and Agrarian Reforms." *Oxford Economic Papers* 14 (February 1962).
Dandekar, V.M., and Rath, Nilakantha. "Poverty in India — I: Dimensions and Trends." *Economic and Political Weekly* (2 January 1971).
Dantwala, M.L. "Agrarian Structure and Economic Development." *Indian Journal of Agricultural Economics* 16 (1961).
Dantwala, M.L. "Agricultural Credit in India — The Necessary Link." *Pacific Affairs* 25 (December 1952).
Dantwala, M.L. "Agricultural Taxation and Land Reform in India." *International Seminar on Land Taxation, Land Tenure and Land Reform in Developing Countries.* John Lincoln Institute, University of Hartford, 1967.
Dantwala, M.L. "Land Reforms in India." *International Labour Review* 66 (1952).
Dantwala, M.L. "Prospects and Problems of Land Reform in India." *Economic Development and Cultural Change* 6 (1957).
Datta, Bhupendranath. *Dialectics of Land Economy in India.* Calcutta : Mohendra Publishers, 1952.
Davis, Kingsley. *The Population of India and Pakistan.* Princeton, N.J., 1951.
de Josselin de Jong. *Levi-Strauss' Theory of Kinship and Marriage.* Leiden, 1952.
Derrett, J. Duncan. *Religion, Law, and State in India.* New York, 1968.
Deshpande, V.D. "History of Tenancy Relations in the State of Maharashtra Since 1900." *Artha Vijnana* 12 (March/June 1970).
Dey, Abani Kumar. *Geology of India.* New Delhi, 1967.
Dobb, Maurice. *Studies in the Development of Capitalism.* New York, 1947.
Dorner, Peter. *Land Reform and Economic Development.* Harmondsworth, Middlesex : Penguin, 1972.
Driver, Peshotan Nasserwanji. *Problems of Zamindari and Land Tenure Reconstruction in India.* Bombay : New Book Co., 1949.
Dube, Shyama Charan. *Indian Village.* Ithaca, N.Y. : Cornell University Press, 1955.
Dube, S.C. *India's Changing Villages.* Ithaca, N.Y., 1958.
Dumont, Louis. "Hierarchy and Marriage Alliance in South Indian Kinship." *Occasional Papers, Journal of the Royal Anthropological Institute* (1957).
Dumont, Louis. *Homo Hierarchicus : The Caste System and Its Implications.* London, 1970.

Dumont, Louis. *Religion ,Politics, and History in India: Collected Papers in Indian Sociology*, The Hague, 1971.

Dutta, Narendra Chandra, *Land Problems and Land Reforms in Assam*. Delhi : S. Chand, 1968.

Dutta, N.C. "Land Reform Policy in the Fourth Five Year Plan." *Economic Affairs* 14 (July/August 1969).

East India Company. *The Fifth Report from the Select Committee on the Affairs of the East India Company*. Vol. II, *Madras Presidency*. London, 1812.

Emmanual, Arghiri. *Unequal Exchange : A Study of the Imperialism of Trade*. Translated by Brian Pearce. London : NLB, 1974.

Epstein, T. Scarlett. *Economic Development and Social Change in South India*. Manchester, 1962.

Epstein, T. Scarlett. "Productive Efficiency and Customary Systems of Rewards in South India." In *Themes in Economic Anthropology*, edited by Raymond Firth. London, 1967.

Etienne, Gilbert. "The Green Revolution—Its Economic and Socio-Political Implications." 1972.

Etienne, Gilbert. *Studies in Indian Agriculture : The Art of the Possible*. Berkeley, 1968.

Falcon, W.P., and Papanek, G.F., eds. *Development Policy II : The Pakistan Experience*. Cambridge, Mass. : Harvard University Press, 1971.

Frankel, Francine R. "Agricultural Modernisation and Social Change." *Mainstream* (29 November 1969).

Frankel, Francine R. *India's Green Revolution : Economic Gains and Political Costs*. Princeton, N.J., 1971.

Frankel, Francine R. "India's New Strategy of Agricultural Development : Political Costs of Agrarian Modernization." *Journal of Asian Studies* (August 1969).

Frykenberg, Robert Eric. *Guntur District, 1788-1848 : A History of Local Influence and Central Authority in South India*. Oxford : Clarendon Press, 1965.

Frykenberg, Robert Eric, ed. *Land Control and Social Structure in Indian History*. Madison: University of Wisconsin Press, 1969.

Galanter, Marc. "Changing Legal Conceptions of Caste." In *Structure and Change in Indian Society*, edited by Bernard Cohn and Milton Singer. Chicago, 1968.

Galanter, Marc. "Equality and 'Protective Discrimination' in India." *Rutgers Law Review* 16 (Fall 1961).

Gandhi, M.K. *Economic Thought*. Edited by J.S. Mathur. Allahabad, 1962.

Ganganathan, V.S. *Economic Geography of India*. New Delhi, 1967.

George, P.T. "The Evolution of Land Tenures in India." *Artha Vijnana* 12 (March/June 1970).

George, P.T. "Land Reforms in Andhra Pradesh : Some Problems of Implementation of Tenancy Reforms." *Artha Vijnana* 12 (December 1970).

George, P.T. "Land System and Laws in Mysore State." *Artha Vijnana* 12 (March/June 1970).

George, P.T. "Land System and Legislation in Madras." *Artha Vijnana* 12 (March/June 1970)·

George, P.T. "Land Tenures in India — Results of the 1961 Census." *Asian Economic Review* (May 1969).

Gerschenkron, Alexander. *Economic Backwardness in Historical Perspective*. Cambridge, Mass., 1962.

Ghoshal, U.N. *The Agrarian System in Ancient India*. Calcutta University, 1929.

Ghoshal, U.N. *Contributions to the History of the Hindu Revenue System*. Calcutta University, 1929.

Giri, R. "Changes in Land Use Pattern in Madras State." *Agricultural Situation in India* 22 (March 1968).

Giri, R. "Land Records and Land Use Statistics." *Agricultural Situation in India* 17 (December 1962).

Godwin, C.J. "Land Reforms in Salsette." *Social Action* 20 (October/December 1970).

Goody, Jack, ed. *The Development Cycle in Domestic Groups*. Cambridge, 1962.

Goswami, Prabhas Chandra. "Land Systems and Land Reforms in Assam." *Journal the University of Gauhati* 2 (1960).

Government of Andhra Pradesh. Assembly Secretariat. *The Andhra Pradesh Land Reforms (Ceiling on Agricultural Holdings) Bill, 1972 — Report of the Joint Select Committee*. Hyderabad, 1972.

Government of Andhra Pradesh. Land Revenue Department. *Andhra Pradesh : Report of the Land Revenue Reforms Committee, 1958/9*. Parts I and II. Hyderabad, 1959.

Government of Bihar. *The Bihar Land Reforms : Fixation of Ceiling Area and Acquisition of Surplus Land Act*. Patna : Pahuja Brothers, 1963.

Government of Goa. *Land Reform Commission Report*. Daman, 1964.

Government of India. Cabinet Secretariat. *National Sample Survey*. 8th Round, no. 10. Delhi, 1958.
Government of India. Cabinet Secretariat. *Tables with Notes on Income of Rural Labour Households*. 18th Round, no. 134, Delhi, 1969.
Government of India. Cabinet Secretariat. *Tables with Notes on Some Aspects of Landholdings in Rural Areas (State and All-India Estimates)*. 17th Round, no. 144. New Delhi, 1968.
Government of India. *Census of India, 1961*. Vol. I, Part XI-A (ii), "Land Tenures in India." Delhi, 1968.
Government of India. Department of Economic Affairs. *First Report on Land Holdings, Rural Sector*. Delhi : Manager of Publications, 1958.
Government of India. Famine Enquiry Commission. *Land Tenures in India*. Bombay, 1946.
Government of India. Imperial Record Department. *Index to the Land Revenue Records*. 2 vols. Delhi, 1940-1942.
Government of India. Ministry of Food and Agriculture. Directorate of Economics and Statistics. "Land Reform in India During the First and Second Five Year Plans." *Agricultural Situation in India* 15.
Government of India. Ministry of Labour. *Agricultural Labour*. Delhi : Manager of Publications, 1952.
Government of India. Planning Commission. *Implementation of Land Reforms : A Review by the Land Reforms Implementation Committee of the National Development Council*. New Delhi, 1966.
Government of India. Planning Commission. *Progress of Land Reform*. Delhi, 1963.
Government of India. Planning Commission. *Reports of the Committees of the Panel on Land Reforms*. New Delhi, 1959.
Government of India. Planning Commission. *A Review by the Land Reforms Implementation Committee of the National Development Council*. New Delhi, 1966.
Government of India. Planning Commission. *Seminar on Land Reforms*. New Delhi, 1966.
Government of India. *The Uttar Pradesh Zamindari Abolition and Land Reforms Act, with Rules*, Lucknow : Eastern Book Company, 1968.
Govindan, K. "Ceiling on Land Holdings — A Study of the Problems with Particular Reference to Tanjore District of Madras State." *Indian Journal of Agricultural Economics* (April/June 1960).
Grant, James, *An Inquiry into . . . Zamindari Tenures in the Landed Property of Bengal*. London, 1790.
Gray, H. Peter. *The Economics of Business Investment Abroad*. London : Macmillan, 1974.
Gruchy, Allen G. *Comparative Economic Systems*. Boston, 1966.
Guha, Ranajit. *A Rule of Property for Bengal*. Paris : Moulton and Co., 1963.
Gupte, Shivial. *An Exhaustive Commentary on the Rajasthan Pre-emption Act, 1966*. Jodhpur: India Publishing House, 1969.
Habib, Irfan. *The Agrarian System of Mughal India (1556-1707)*. Bombay : Asia Publishing House, 1963.
Hart, Judith. *Aid and Liberation : A Socialist Study of Aid Policies*. London : Gollanz, 1974.
Hauser, Walter. "The Indian National Congress and Land Policy in the 20th Century." *Indian Economic and Social History Review* 1 (1963).
Hayter, Teresa. *Aid as Imperialism*. Penguin, 1974.
Hensman, C.R. *Rich Against Poor : The Reality of Aid*. London : Allen Lane, 1974.
Hiebert, Paul G. *Konduru, Structure and Integration in a South Indian Village*. University of Minnesota, 1971.
Hill, Polly. "A Plea for Indigenous Economics : The West African Example." *Economic Development and Cultural Change* 15 (October 1966).
Hjejle, Benedicte. *Slavery and Agricultural Bondage in South India in the Nineteenth Century*. Joint Reprint Series no. 1. Copenhagen : The Scandanavian Institute of Asian Studies, 1967.
Hodson, Thomas. *India, Census Ethnography, 1901-1931*. Delhi, 1937.
Hollingberry, R.H. *The Zamindari Settlement of Bengal*. Vols. I and II. Calcutta, 1879.
Hunter, P.E., and Rielly, J.E., eds. *Development Today : A New Look at U.S. Relations with the Poor Countries*. London : Pall Mall, 1974.
Huntington, S. *Political Order in Changing Societies*. New Haven, 1968.
Husain, Imtiaz. *Land Revenue Policy in North India — The Ceded and Conquered Provinces, 1801-1833*. Calcutta : New Age Publishers Pvt. Ltd., 1967.
Indian Journal of Agricultural Economics 22:1 (1966).
Indian National Congress. *Agrarian Reforms Committee Report*. New Delhi : All-India Congress Committee, 1951.
Isaacs, Harold. *India's Ex-Untouchables*. Bombay : Asia Publishing House, 1965.
Iyengar, B. Sundararaja, *Land Tenures in the Madras Presidency*. Madras, 1916.

Iyengar, Kesava S. *Rural Economic Enquiries in the Hyderabad State, 1949-1951*. Hyderabad: Hyderabad Government Press, 1951.

Jain, Netrapal. *Rural Reconstruction in India and China : A Comparative Study*. 1970.

Jana, Prahlad. "Problems of Capital Formation in India." M.S. thesis, University of Wisconsin. 1955.

Jannaki, A.E.K. "Introduction to the Subsistence Economy of India." In *Man's Role in the Changing Face of the Earth,* edited by W.L. Thomas. New York, 1956.

Jannuzi, F. Tomasson. *Agrarian Crisis in India — The Case of Bihar*. Austin : University of Texas Press, 1974.

Jannuzi, F. Tomasson. *Land Reform in Bihar, India : The Agrarian Structure in Bihar*. Washington, D.C. : U.S. Agency for International Development, 1970.

Jathar, G.B., and Beri, S.G. *Indian Economics : A Comprehensive and Critical Survey*. 9th ed. Madras, 1949.

Jha, Aditya Nath. "Agrarian Reform in the State of Uttar Pradesh, India." In *Land Tenure : Proceedings,* Conference on World Land Tenure Problems. Madison : University of Wisconsin Press, 1956.

Jha, Satish Chandra. "Indian Land Reform Research Literature : A Critical Appraisal." Ph.D. dissertation, University of Illinois. 1967.

Jodha, N.S. "Land Pclicies of Rajasthan : Some Neglected Aspects." *Economic and Political Weekly* 5 (27 June 1970).

Joshi, P.C. "Problems and Prospects of Ceilings on Land-holdings in India." *Agricultural Situation in India* 15 (1960).

Kalra, B.R. "Land Reforms Legislation and its Implementation in Different States." *Indian Journal of Agricultural Economics* (January 1962).

Kalra, B.R. "Regional Variations in Policy Regarding Size of Agricultural Holding." *Indian Journal of Agricultural Economics* 20 (April 1965).

Kanel, Don. "Size of Farm and Economic Development." *Indian Journal of Agricultural Economics* 22 (1967).

Karve, D.G. "An Approach to Agrarian Reform." *Indian Journal of Agricultural Economics* 19 (July/December 1964).

Karve, Irawati. *Kinship Organization in India*. Bombay, 1965.

Kaye, John William. *The Administration of the East India Company; A History of Indian Progress*. London, 1853.

Khanna, Gopal Krishna. *A Complete Digest on U.P. Zamindari Abolition and Land Reforms Act, 1951 to 1968 (March)*. Lucknow : Northern Law House, 1968.

Khusro, A.M. *Economic and Social Effects of Jagirdari Abolition and Land Reforms in Hyderabad, 1958*. Hyderabad : Osmania University, 1958.

Khusro, A.M. *The Economics of Land Reform and Farm Size in India*. New Delhi: Institute of Economic Growth.

Khusro, A.M. "Farm Site and Land Tenure in India." *Indian Economic Review* 4 (October 1969).

Khusro, A.M.,and Agarwal, A.N. *The Problem of Co-operative Farming in India*. New York: Asia Publishing House, 1961.

Klein, Ira. "Population and Agriculture in Northern India, 1872-1971." *Modern Asian Studies* 8 (April 1974) : 191-216.

Kohr, Leopold. *Development Without Aid : The Translucent Society*. Llandybie, Carmarthenshire : Christopher Davis, 1974.

Kotdawala, M.R. *A Report on the Working of Co-operative Farming Societies in Gujerat*. Chunilal Gandhi Vidyabhavan, 1958.

Kotovski, G.G. *Agrarian Reforms in India*. Translated by K.J. Lambkin. New Delhi : People's Publishing House, 1964.

Kotovski, G.G. "Indian Agricultural Labourer : A Soviet View." *Economic and Political Weekly* (April 1956).

Krishna, Raj. "Agrarian Reform in India : The Debate on Ceilings." *Economic Development and Cultural Change* 7 (April 1959).

Krishna, Raj. "Some Aspects of Land Reform and Economic Development in India." In *Land Tenure, Industrialisation and Social Stability,* edited by Walter Forelich. Milwaukee : Marquette University Press, 1961.

Krishnamachari, T.S. "Land and its Problems." *Journal of Annamalai University* (1964).

Krishnamachari, T.S. "A Study of the Agricultural Economy of South Arcot." *Journal of the Annamalai University* (1962).

Krishnamurty, J. "Changes in the Composition of the Working Force in Manufacturing 1901-51 : A Theoretical and Empirical Analysis." *Indian Economic and Social History Review* (1967).

Krishnaswami, S.Y. *Rural Problems in Madras*. Madras : Madras Government Press, 1947.

Kuhnen, Frithjof. "The Development of Land Tenure in India." Translated by Anneliese Lamp. *Zal* 4 (1965).

Kumar, Dharma. *Land and Caste in South India*. Cambridge : CUP, 1965.

Kuznets, Simon. "Distribution of Income by Size." *Economic Development and Cultural Change* 11, Part II (January 1963).

Kuznets, Simon. *Modern Economic Growth: Rate, Structure, and Spread.* New Haven, 1966.

Kuznets, Simon, ed. *Economic Growth : Brazil, India, Japan.* Durham, N.C., 1955.

Ladejinsky, Wolf Isaac. *A Study on Tenurial Conditions in Package Districts.* New Delhi : Government of India, Planning Commission, 1963.

Lahiri, R. "Geographical Background of the Soils of India." *Geographical Review of India* 26 (1964).

Lakshman, T.K. "Indian Farming and the Need for its Reorganisation." *Economic Review,* All-India Congress Committee, 1964.

Lal, R.A. "A Case for Lower Ceilings." *Economic Review,* All-India Congress Committee. 1960.

Lambert, Jacques. *Social Structure and Political Institutions.* Berkeley, 1967.

Lasswell, Harold, and Arora, S.K. *Political Communication : The Public Language of Political Elites in India and the U.S.* New York, 1969.

Leach, Edmund R. *Levi-Strauss.* London, 1970.

Leach, Edmund R., ed. *Aspects of Caste in South India, Ceylon, and Northwest Pakistan.* Cambridge, 1960.

Leach, F.R., and Mukherjee, S.N., eds. *Elites in South Asia.* Cambridge, 1970.

Levkovsky, A.I. *Capitalism in India : Basic Trends in its Development.* Bombay, 1966.

Lewis, Oscar. "Aspects of Land Tenure and Economics in a North Indian Village." *Economic Development and Cultural Change* (April 1956).

Lewis, Oscar. *Village Life in Northern India.* Urbana, Ill., 1958.

Lewis, W. Arthur. *The Theory of Economic Growth.* London, 1955.

Lipton, Michael. "The Underdevelopment of Development." *Times Literary Supplement* (1974) : 830-831.

Liversage, V. *Land Tenure in the Colonies.* Cambridge, 1945.

Long, Erven J. "The Economic Basis of Land Reform in Underdeveloped Economies." *Land Economics* 37 (1961).

Low, D.A., ed. *Soundings in Modern South Asian History.* Canberra, 1968.

Lynch, Owen M. "Some Aspects of Rural-Urban Continuum in India." In *Anthropology on the March,* edited by Bala Ratnam. 1963.

Madan, G.R. *Co-operative Movement in the Punjab (India) with Special Reference to its Rehabilitation and Reorganization :* Delhi : S. Chand, 1958.

Madan, G.R. "Land Reforms in U.P." *Economic Review,* All-India Congress Committee, 1965.

Madiman, S.G. *Land Reforms and Institutional Planning for India.* Rome : Food and Agriculture Organisation, 1968.

Madiman, S.G. "Land Tenure in India." In *Papers : Part 4, Handbook of References,* Conference on World Land Tenure Problems. 1951.

Maine, Henry S. *Village Communities in the East and West.* New York, 1876.

Malaviya, H.D. *Implementation of Land Reforms.* Delhi : Socialist Congressman Publication, 1970.

Malaviya, H.D. *Land Reforms in India.* Delhi : All-India Congress Committee, 1954.

Mann, Harold H. "The Agriculture of India." *Annals of the American Academy* (September 1929).

Mann, Harold H. *The Social Framework of Agriculture : India, Middle East, England.* New York, 1967.

Marriott, McKim. *Caste Ranking and Community Structure in Five Regions of India and Pakistan.* Poona, 1960.

Marriott, McKim. "Interactional and Attributional Theories of Caste Ranking." *Man in India* 39.

Marriott, McKim, ed. *Village India.* Chicago, 1955.

Mathur, Man Singh. "Changing Patterns of Tenancy and Leasing Land in Punjab." *Agricultural Situation in India* 22 (September 1967).

Mazumdar, Dipak. "Size of Farm and Productivity : A Problem of Indian Peasant Agriculture." *Economica* 32 (May 1965).

Mellor, John W. *The Economics of Agricultural Development.* Bombay : Vora and Company, 1969.

Mende Tibor. *From Aid to Re-Colonization.* London : Harrap 1974.

Menon, M.S. "Cooperative Farming in India." In *Land Tenure,* edited by K.H. Parsons, et al. Madison, Wis., 1956.

Merillat, H.C.L. *Land and the Constitution in India.* New York : Columbia University Press 1970.

Minhas, B.S. *Rural Poverty, Land Redistribution and Development Strategy : Facts and Policy.* Washington, D.C. : Economic Development Institute, 1970.

Mishra, R.R. *Effects of Land Reforms in Saurashtra.* New Delhi : Research Programmes Committee, Planning Commission.

Misra, B.B. *The Administrative History of India, 1834-1947*. Oxford, 1970.
Misra, S.D. "Natural Regions of the Indian Subcontinent." *Indian Geographic Journal* 43 (1969).
Mookherjee, Debnath. "Urbanization Pattern in India, 1951-1961." *Professional Geographer* 21 (September 1969).
Moreland, William Harrison. *Agrarian System of Moslem India : A Historical Essay with Appendices*. 2d ed. Delhi : Oriental Books Reprint Corp., 1968.
Morris, Morris D. *The Emergence of an Industrial Labor Force in India : A Study of the Bombay Cotton Mills, 1854-1947*. Berkeley, 1965.
Mukerji, Karuna Moy. *The Problems of Land Transfer : A Study of the Problems of Land Alienation in Bengal*. Santiniketan, Birbhum : Santiniketan Press, 1957.
Mukherjee, Nilmani. *The Ryotwari System in Madras, 1792-1827*. Calcutta : Firma K.L. Mukhopadhyay, 1962.
Mukherjee, Radhakamal. *Land Problems of India*. London, 1933.
Mukherjee, R.K., and Dey, H.L., eds. *Economic Problems of Modern India*. London, 1941.
Myint, Hla. *The Economics of Developing Countries*. New York, 1965.
Myrdal, Gunnar. *Asian Drama : An Enquiry into the Poverty of Nations*. New York : Pantheon Publishers, 1968.
Nair, Kusum. *Blossoms in the Dust*. New York : Praeger Publications, 1961.
Nair, Kusum *The Lonely Furrow*. Ann Arbor, Mich., 1969.
Nanavati, Sir Manilal Balabhai, and Anjaria, J.J. *The Indian Rural Problem*. 6th rev. ed. Bombay : Indian Society of Agricultural Economics, 1965.
Nanekar, K.R. *Land Reforms in Vidarbha*. Calcutta : Oxford and I.B.H. Publishing House, 1968.
Narasimham, N.V.A. "Inequalities in the Distribution of Holdings and Income of the Farmers in India in 1961-62." *Agricultural Situation in India* 24 (September 1969).
Narayan, B.K. *Agricultural Development in Hyderabad State, 1900-1956*. Secunderabad : Keshav Prakashan, 1960.
Narayan, Jayaprakash. "The Bhoodan Movement in India." *Asian Review* (October 1958).
Neale, Walter C. "Economic Accounting and Family Farming in India." *Economic Development and Cultural Change* (April 1959).
Neale, Walter C. *Economic Change in Rural India*. Yale Studies in Economics, no. 12. New Haven: Yale University Press, 1962.
Neale, Walter C. "Land Reform in Uttar Pradesh." In *Spring Review of Land Reform*. Washington, D.C. : U.S. Agency for International Development, 1970.
Neale, Walter C. "The Limitations of Indian Village Survey Data." *Journal of Asian Studies* (May 1958).
Neale, Walter C. "Revolutionary Reform' vs. Politics and Social Structure." In *The Carnegie Seminar*. Bloomington : Indiana University, 1967.
Newell, Richard Smith. "Congress Agrarian Reform Policy : A Case Study of Land Redistribution in Northern India." Ph.D. dissertation, University of Pennsylvania. 1966.
Nicholas, Ralph. "Rules, Resources, and Political Activity." In *Local Level Politics*, edited by Marc J. Swartz. Chicago, 1968.
Nicholas, R.W. "Structures of Politics in the Villages of Southern Asia." In *Structure and Change in Indian Society,* edited by Bernard Cohn and Milton Singer. Chicago, 1968.
Oommen, M.A. "The Economics of Cropping Pattern — A Case Study of Kerala." *Indian Journal of Agricultural Economics* (January 1963).
Oommen, T.K. "Non-violent Approach to Land Reforms : The Case of an Agrarian Movement in India." *Zeitschrift für Auslandische Landwirtschaft* 9 (March 1970).
Oommen, T.K. "Problems of Gramdan : A Study in Rajasthan." *Economic and Political Weekly* 26 (June 1965).
Padki, M.B. "Consolidation of Holdings." *Agricultural Situation in India* 20 (August 1965).
Panikar, P.G.K. "The Burden of Debt in Indian Agriculture." *Journal of Farm Economics* 45 (February 1963).
Parekh, Satishchandra Balwantrai. "Problems of Agricultural Credit in India." Thesis, New York University, 1963.
Parthasarathy, G., and Prasada Rao, B. *Implementation of Land Reforms in Andhra Pradesh*. Waltair : Andhra University, 1969.
Patel, Govindlal D. *Agrarian Reforms in Bombay. The Legal and Economic Consequences of the Abolition of Land Tenures*. Bombay : Mogal Lane.
Patel, G.D. *The Indian Land Problem and Legislation*. Anand, India, 1970.
Patel, G.D. *Land Systems of Union Territories of India*. Anand, India, 1970.
Patel, M.S. "Land Tenure Legislation in India." *Agricultural Situation in India* 17 (February 1963).

Patel, S.J. *Agricultural Labourers in India and Pakistan*. Bombay, 1952.

Patil, N.P. "Land Tenure Reforms in Mysore and Ceiling on Holdings." *Indian Journal of Agricultural Economics* 17 (January 1962).

Patil, R.V. "All Land to the Tiller : The Problem of Land Reform in India." *Economic Development and Cultural Change* 3 (July 1955).

Pillai, Velu Pillai Raman. *Land Reclamation in Kerala*. New York : Asia Publishing House, 1965.

Potter, David C. *Government in Rural India : An Introduction to Contemporary District Administration*. London : G. Bell and Sons, 1964.

Quereshi, Anwar Iqbal. *The Economic Development of Hyderabad*. Vol. I, *Rural Economy*. Madras : Orient Longmans Ltd., 1947.

Raghavaaiyangar, S. Srinivasa. *Memorandum on the Progress of the Madras Presidency During the Last Forty Years of British Administration*. Madras : Madras Government Press, 1893.

Raj, Jagdish. *The Mutiny and British Land Policy in North India, 1856-1868*. Bombay, 1965.

Raj, K.N. "Ownership and Distribution of Land." *Indian Economic Review* (April 1970).

Rajagopala Rao, N. *Land Utilisation and Agriculture in North Kanara District*. Kumta : Kanara College Planning Forum, 1965.

Rajmani, A.N. "Land Reforms and Land Policy in Fourth Five Year Plan." *Economic Affairs* (October 1967).

Raju, Sarada A. "Economic Conditions in the Madras Presidency, 1800-1850." Ph.D. dissertation, University of Madras. 1941.

Ram, Moti. *Commentary on the Punjab Security of Land Tenures Act, 1953 (Act no. X of 1953)*, etc. 2d ed., rev. by Shukdev. Chandigarh : Jain Law Agency, 1969.

Ramanadham, V.V. *The Economy of Andhra Pradesh*. New York : Asia Publishing House, 1959.

Ranga, N.G., and Parachuri, P.R. *The Peasant and Co-operative Farming*. New Delhi : Indian Peasants' Institute, 1958.

Rao, C.H. Hanumantha. *Taxation of Agricultural Land in Andhra Pradesh*. Studies in Economic Growth, no. 8. New York : Asia Publishing House, 1966.

Rao, G.A. "Land Tribunals in Land Reform Legislation : Kerala and Bombay." *Economic Weekly* 11 (1959).

Rao, Prasada N. *Progress of Land Reforms : A Critical Review*. New Delhi : New Age Printing Press, 1960.

Rao, Rajagopala N. "Land Utilisation and Agriculture in North Kanara District." In *Symposium on Land Utilisation and Agriculture in North Kanara District*. Kumta: Kanara College Planning Forum, 1965.

Rao, Sarveswara B. *The Economic and Social Effects of Zamindari Abolition in Andhra*. Waltair : Government of India Press, 1963.

Rao, T.V.S. "Land Legislation in Andhra Pradesh (1800-1950)." *Artha Vijnana* (8 September 1966).

Rao, T.V.S. "Land Legislation in Kerala State (1800-1960)." *Artha Vijnana* 12 (March/June 1970) : 75-116.

Rathore, B.S. "Land Tenures and Land Reforms in Rajasthan." *Economic Review*, All-India Congress Committee. 1967.

Ravindran, T.K. "Land Tenures of Malabar." *Journal of the Asiatic Society of Bombay* (1959/60).

Ray, Rajat, and Ratna. "Zamindars and Jotedars : A Study of Rural Politics in Bengal." *Modern Asian Studies* 9 (February 1975) : 81-102.

Ray, S. Chandra. *Land Revenue Administration in India*. Calcutta : Calcutta University, 1915.

Reddi, Rama P. *The Andhra Pradesh Tenancy, Forest, Revenue, Agency, Village Officers and Rice Milling Code*. Hyderabad : Panchayat Publications, 1971.

Ridker, Ronald G. *Land Reform and Rural Poverty in India*. Washington, D.C. : U.S. Agency for International Development, 1970.

Robinson, Austin. "The Economic Development of Malthusia." *Modern Asian Studies* 8 (October 1974) : 521-534.

Robinson, E.A.G., and Kidron, M. *Economic Development in South Asia*. London, 1970.

Rosen, George. *Democracy and Economic Change in India*. Berkeley : University of California Press, 1967.

Rosin, Robert Thomas. "Changing Land Tenure and Village Polity in Rajasthan, India : An Interactional Perspective." Ph.D. dissertation, University of California-Berkeley. 1968.

Ross, Martin H. "Family Organization and the Development of Agrarian Capitalism in a North Indian Village." Thesis, University of Wisconsin. 1968.

Rostow, W.W. *The Economics of Take-Off into Sustained Growth*. New York, 1965.

Rudolph, Lloyd I., and Susanne H. *The Modernity of Tradition : Political Development in India*. Chicago, 1967.
Rudolph, Susanne Hoeber. *Some Aspects of Congress Land Reform Policy*. Cambridge, Mass. : Center for International Studies, Massachusetts Institute of Technology, 1957.
Sanderatne, Nimal, and Zaman, M.A. "The Impact of the Agrarian Structure on the Political Leadership of Undivided Pakistan." LTC Paper no. 94. Madison: Land Tenure Center, University of Wisconsin, 1973.
Sandu, K.S. *Indians in Malaya : Immigration and Settlement, 1786-1957*. Cambridge, 1969.
Sarkar, Prafulla C. *The Planning of Agriculture in India*. Rotterdam, 1966.
Schusky, Ernest L. *Manual for Kinship Analysis*. New York, 1965.
Schwartzberg, Joseph E. 'The Distribution of Selected Castes in the North Indian Plain." *The Geographical Review* 55 (1965).
Schwartzberg, Joseph E. *Occupational Structure and Level of Economic Development in India : A Regional Analysis*. Census of India, 1961, Monograph no. 4. New Delhi, 1969.
Segre, D.V. *The High Road and the Low : A Study of Legitimacy, Authority, and Technical Aid*. London : Allen Lane, 1974.
Sen, Amartya Kumar. "Size of Holdings and Productivity : A Reply." *Economic and Political Weekly* (2 May 1964).
Sen, Bandhudas. "Output on Indian Farms in Relation to Farm Size and Land Value." Thesis, University of Wisconsin. 1966.
Sen, Bhowani. *Evolution of Agrarian Relations in India : Including a Study of the Nature and Consequences of Post-Independence Agrarian Legislation*. New Delhi : People's Publishing House, 1962.
Sen, Bhowani. *Indian Land System and Land Reform*. Delhi : People's Publishing House, 1955.
Sen, Siba Pada, compiler. *Studies in Modern Indian History : A Regional Survey*. Calcutta, 1969.
Sen Gupta, P., and Sdadyuk, Galina. *Economic Regionalization of India : Problems and Approaches*. Census of India, 1961, Monograph no. 8. New Delhi.
Shah, S.H. "Class and Agrarian Change : Some Comments on Peasant Resistance and Revolution in India." Rejoinder by Kathleen Gough. *Pacific Affairs* 42 (Fall 1969).
Sharma, P.S. "Pattern of Land Concentration (1961 Census) and Elasticity per Acre Composite Crop Elasticity." *Agricultural Situation in India* 20 (August 1965).
Sharma, P.S. "A Study of the Structural and Tenurial Aspects of Rural Economy in the Light of 1961 Census." *Indian Journal of Agricultural Economics* (October 1965).
Sharma, P.S. "Tenancy Situation and Agricultural Productivity in India." *Agricultural Situation in India* 23 (August 1968).
Shea, Thomas J., Jr. "Implementing Land Reforms in India." *Far East Survey* 25 (January 1956).
Shukla, B.C. *An Analytical and Exhaustive Commentary on the U.P. Zamindari Abolition and Land Reforms Act, 1950*. Vol. I. Allahabad : Central Law Agency, 1968.
Silverberg, James, ed. *Social Mobility in the Caste System in India : An Interdisciplinary Symposium*. The Hague, 1968.
Singer, Milton. "The Indian Joint Family in Modern Industry." In *Structure and Change in Indian Society*, edited by Bernard Cohn and Singer. Chicago, 1968.
Singh, Baljit. *Next Step in Village India*. Bombay, 1960.
Singh, Baljit, and Misra, Shridhar. *A Study of Land Reforms in Uttar Pradesh*. Honolulu : East-West Center Press, 1965.
Singh, Darshan. "Review of Cropping Patterns and Land Utilisation in Punjab During Plan Periods." *Agricultural Situation in India* 21 (May/June 1966).
Singh, Dool. *Land Reforms in Rajasthan : A Study of Evasion, Implementation, and Socio-Economic Effects of Land Reforms*. Pilani, India : Berla Institute of Technology, 1964.
Singh, R.S. *Encyclopedia of Tenancy Laws*. Allahabad : Hind Publishing House, 1969.
Singh, Ram Sarat, and Prakash, Sant. *Practice and Digest of U.P. Zamindari Abolition and Land Reforms Act*. Allahabad : Hind Publishing House.
Singh, S.N., and Reddy, S.K. "Adoption of Improved Agricultural Practices of Farmers." *Indian Journal of Social Work* 26 (October 1965).
Singh, Sukdev. "Land Reforms and Indian Left." *Mainstream* 10 (July 1972).
Singh, Tarlok. *Poverty and Social Change*. 2d ed. Delhi : Orient Longmans. 1969.
Sinha, Ram Narain. *Bihar Tenantry, 1783-1833*. Bombay : People's Publishing House, 1968.
Sivaswamy, K.G. *The Co-operative Movement in Bihar : A Study in Organization and Technique*. Delhi : University Press, 1956.
Sivaswamy, K.G. *Legislative Protection and Relief of Agriculturist Debtors in India*. Poona : Gokhale Institute of Politics and Economics, 1939.

Smith, Marian W. "Structured and Unstructured Class Societies." *American Anthropologist* 55 (1953).

Sonachalam, K.S. "Land Reforms and Their Implementation." *Indian Journal of Agricultural Economics* (January 1962).

Sonachalam, K.S. *Land Reforms in Tamil Nadu.* New Delhi : Oxford and I.B.H. Publishing Co., 1970.

Spate, O.H.K. *India and Pakistan : A General and Regional Geography.* New York, 1957.

Srinivas, M.N. *Caste in Modern India and Other Essays.* London, 1962.

Srinivas, M.N. "The Dominant Caste of Rampura." *American Anthropologist* 61 (1959).

Srinivas M.N *Social Change in Modern India.* Berkeley, 1968.

Srinivas, M.N., ed. *India's Villages.* 2d ed. Bombay, 1960.

Srinivas, M.N. Damle, Y.B.; Shahani, S.; and Beteille, Andre. "Caste, A Trend Report and Bibliography." *Current Sociology* 8 (1959).

Steward, Julian. *Theory of Culture Change : The Methodology of Multilinear Evolution.* Urbana, Ill., 1955.

Streeten, Paul, ed. *Trade Strategies for Development.* Papers of the Ninth Cambridge Conference on Development Problems. London : Macmillan, 1974.

Sukhadia, Mohanlal. "Land Reforms in Rajasthan." *Economic Review*, All-India Congress Committee. 1965.

Sultan, Mohd. *Size and Distribution of Holdings in Two Villages in the Delhi State 1953-54.* Jamia Institute of Agricultural Economics and Rural Sociology, 1957.

Sultan, Mohd. *Survey of Rural Employment in Two Villages in the Delhi State, 1955-56.* New Delhi : Jamia Institute of Agricultural Economics and Rural Sociology, 1957.

Swaroop, Bhagwat. "Trends in Land Utilisation in Rajasthan, 1951-1962." *Artha Vijnana* 8 (June 1966).

Tagare, R.M. *The Bombay Prevention of Fragmentation and Consolidation of Holdings Act, 1947.* Poona, 1967.

Thorbecke, *et al.* "Unemployment : Challenge to Development." *Ceres* 3 (1970).

Thorner, Daniel. *The Agrarian Prospect for India.* Delhi, 1956.

Thorner, Daniel. "Agricultural Manpower in India : Labourers." *Economic Weekly* 9 (1957).

Thorner, Daniel. "India's Agrarian Revolution by Census Redefinition." *Indian Economic Review* 3 (1956).

Thorner, Daniel, and Alice. *Land and Labour in India.* London, 1962.

Tinker, Hugh. *The Foundations of Local Self-Government in India, Pakistan and Burma,* London, 1954.

Tinker, Hugh. *A New System of Slavery : The Export of Indian Labour Overseas, 1830-1920.* Oxford : OUP, 1974.

Turner, Louis. *Multinational Companies and the Third World.* London : Allen Lane, 1974.

United Nations. *Land Reform — Land Settlement and Co-operatives.* Rome : Food and Agriculture Organisation, 1968-71.

United Nations. *Progress in Land Reform.* 4th Report. New York, 1966.

United Nations. *Progress of Land Reform.* 5th Report. New York, 1970.

Uppal, J.S. "Attitudes of Farm Families Toward Land Reforms in Some Punjab Villages." *Journal of Developing Areas* 4 (October 1969).

Uppal, J.S. "Implementation of Land Reform Legislation in India — A Study of Two Villages in Punjab." *Asian Survey* 9 (May 1969).

Varghese, T.C. *Agrarian Change and Economic Consequences : Land Tenures in Kerala, 1850-1960.* Bombay : Allied Publishers, 1970.

von Furer-Haimendorf, C. "Indian Kinship Systems." *Economic Weekly* 17 (25 September 1965).

Wadhwa, D.C. *Agrarian Legislation in India, 1793-1966.* Vol. I. Poona : Gokhale Institute of Politics and Economics, 1973.

Ward, Barbara; Runnalls, J.D.; and D'Anjou, Leonore, eds. *The Widening Gap : Development in the 1970's.* New York : Columbia University Press, 1974.

Ward Richard J. "Absorbing More Labor in LDC Agriculture." *Economic Development and Cultural Change* (January 1969).

Warriner, Doreen. *Economics of Peasant Farming.* London, 1964.

Warriner, Doreen. *Land Reform in Principle and Practice.* Oxford : Oxford University Press, 1969.

Washbrook, David. "Country Politics : Madras 1880 to 1930." *Modern Asian Studies* 7 (1973) : 475-531.

Whitcomb, Elizabeth. *Agrarian Conditions in Northern India.* Vol. I, *The United Provinces Under British Rule, 1860-1900.* Berkeley : University of California Press, 1972.

Wilson, H.H. *A Glossary of Judicial and Revenue Terms of British India.* Calcutta, 1855. Rev. ed. by A.C. Ganguli and N.D. Basu. Calcutta, 1940.

Wiser, William H. *The Hindu Jajmani System : A Socio-Economic System Interrelating Members of a Hindu Village Community in Services.* Lucknow, 1936.

Wiser, William, and Charlotte. *Behind Mud Walls, 1930-1960*. 2d rev. ed. Berkeley, 1963.
Wunderlich, G.L. "The Bombay Tenancy Act in the Villages of Jaska, Badlapur and Madhbavi, 1953." Mimeo.
Wunderlich, G.L. *Land Reform in Western India : Analysis of Economic Impacts of Tenancy Legislation, 1948-1963*. Washington, D.C. : United States Department of Agriculture, 1964.
Wunderlich, George. *Land Reforms in India*. Washington, D.C. : U.S. Agency for International Development, 1970.
Yule, H., and Burnell, A.C. Hobson-Jobson. *A Glossary of Colloquial Anglo-Indian Words and Phrases*. London, 1886.

Glossary and Index

Aberle, K. Gough, 195, 206
Abwab: cess, tax. 33
Achampet, village, 171
Achutha Menon Ministry, Kerala, 251, 270, 273
Adami: agricultural laborer of Tamil Nadu, bonded to land by debt, 94
Adamson, Sir Harvey, 114
Adelmann, Irma, 161
Adivasi: transitional tenancy in land reform legislation, Uttar Pradesh. 136
Agraharam: Brahman holding in village, free of assessment, by grant (*inam*), 39
Agrarian system, concept, 81
Agricultural credit: and capital, 120; Ahmadnagar Land Development Bank, 147; credit tenure, 122; Land Development Banks (LDBs), 146, 147; rural credit in lower Burma, 111, 115; rural credit, 248, 249
Agricultural Extension Programs, 248
Agricultural work force, 245
Ahir, 198
Ahmadnagar District, 57, 58, 64
Akola District, 267
Alavi, Hamza, 184
Allah, Salim, 24
Altamgha-inam: royal grant conferring rent-free land in perpetuity. 40
Amani: lands or revenue sources directly managed by government, 69
Amaram: revenue grant conditional on service by recipient, 43
Ameen Dustore: land court. 24
America, 192; Civil War, 254
Amil: revenue "farmer" or contractor collecting on behalf of government or zamindar. 20
Amin Duftar: office for *Amin* accounts. 24
Anakala: inam grant to porters and supply carriers, 43
Anderson, 25-26
Andhra Pradesh, 132, 137, 163, 227
Anglo-Burmese War, Second, 106
Anicut: dam, weir, 45
Annamalai, 41
Anstey, Vera, 212
Antony, A.K., 262
Arcot, 71
Arensberg, Conrad M., 163
Arudikarai: land tenure in Tamil village, of fixed boundary. 33, 95
Asami: tenant-cultivator, dependent, criminal, one who is exploitable. 136

Ascoli, F.D., 28
Assam, 137, 145, 227
Athin: guild, family or clan (Burma). 104
Azamgarh District, 63

Bach: revenue assessment apportioned among co-sharing landholders in North Indian villages, 63
Baden-Powell, B.H., 55, 60, 61, 65
Bagaitdar: holder of canal-irrigated land, Maharashtra, 261
Baghayat: well watered garden land; superior arable land, 86
Bailey, F.G., 195, 206
Bairagi (vairagi): wandering religious mendicant. 41
Bajra: pearl millet. 168
Bangla Desh, 133
Bania (baniya): merchant, trader, banker or moneylender. 27
Baramahal, 43, 45, 46, 48, 71, 83, 84, 85, 94; —Records, 94
Bareilly District, 62
Bargadar: insecure sub-tenants, or those paying half rental in produce. 155
Baroda, 132
Bataidar: "holder of a share or part," hence insecure tenure holders. 217
Batta: charge or discount against non-standard coin; extra allowance. 43
Bazi-zamin: revenue-exempt land. 30
Beco engine, 147, 190, 191
Belgaum District, 58
Bellary District, 56, 64
Bengal, 106, 137, 145, 152, 211, 214; Mughal administration of, 20-29
Berar, 146
Besant, Annie, 260
Beteille, Andre, 198
Bhagalpur District, 225, 227
Bhagdar: partner who apportioned crops between co-sharers and government. 59
Bhagirati River, 34
Bhaiachara: common holdings of (Jat) brotherhood. 63
Bhatta-vritti-inam: grant of revenue or lands for maintenance of Brahmans. 40
Bhoodan: land gift movement. 222
Bhumidar: superior landholder. 136
Bigah: unit of land area measurement, about one-third acre. 213
Bihar, 26, 131, 137, 140, 145, 146
Bissoy: Orissan hill chieftain. 42
Bloch, Marc, 101
Boad, 197

ERRATA

Page	Line	For	Read
7	9	Southeast Asia	South Asia
34	10	arears	arrears
45	27	wires	weirs
52	11	capable to of holding	capable of holding
91	14	seen	seem
108	22	and	land
108	23	an	on